Exploring Cognitive Grammar in English

ALSO AVAILABLE FROM BLOOMSBURY

English Lexical Semantics: A Cognitive Linguistics Approach, Zeki Hamawand

Cognitive Grammar in Stylistics: A Practical Guide, Marcello Giovanelli and Chloe Harrison

Morphology in English: Word Formation in Cognitive Grammar, Zeki Hamawand

Exploring Cognitive Grammar in English

ZEKI HAMAWAND

BLOOMSBURY ACADEMIC
LONDON • NEW YORK • OXFORD • NEW DELHI • SYDNEY

BLOOMSBURY ACADEMIC
Bloomsbury Publishing Plc, 50 Bedford Square, London, WC1B 3DP, UK
Bloomsbury Publishing Inc, 1359 Broadway, New York, NY 10018, USA
Bloomsbury Publishing Ireland, 29 Earlsfort Terrace, Dublin 2, D02 AY28, Ireland

BLOOMSBURY, BLOOMSBURY ACADEMIC and the Diana logo are trademarks of Bloomsbury Publishing Plc

First published in Great Britain 2026

Cover design: Jade Barnett
Cover image © Rifqyhsn Design / Getty Images

A catalogue record for this book is available from the British Library.

A catalog record for this book is available from the Library of Congress.

ISBN: HB: 978-1-3505-6708-5
PB: 978-1-3505-6709-2
ePDF: 978-1-3505-6705-4
eBook: 978-1-3505-6706-1

Typeset by Newgen Knowledge Works Pvt. Ltd., Chennai, India
Printed and bound in Great Britain

For product safety related questions contact productsafety@bloomsbury.com.

To find out more about our authors and books visit www.bloomsbury.com and sign up for our newsletters.

CONTENTS

FIGURE

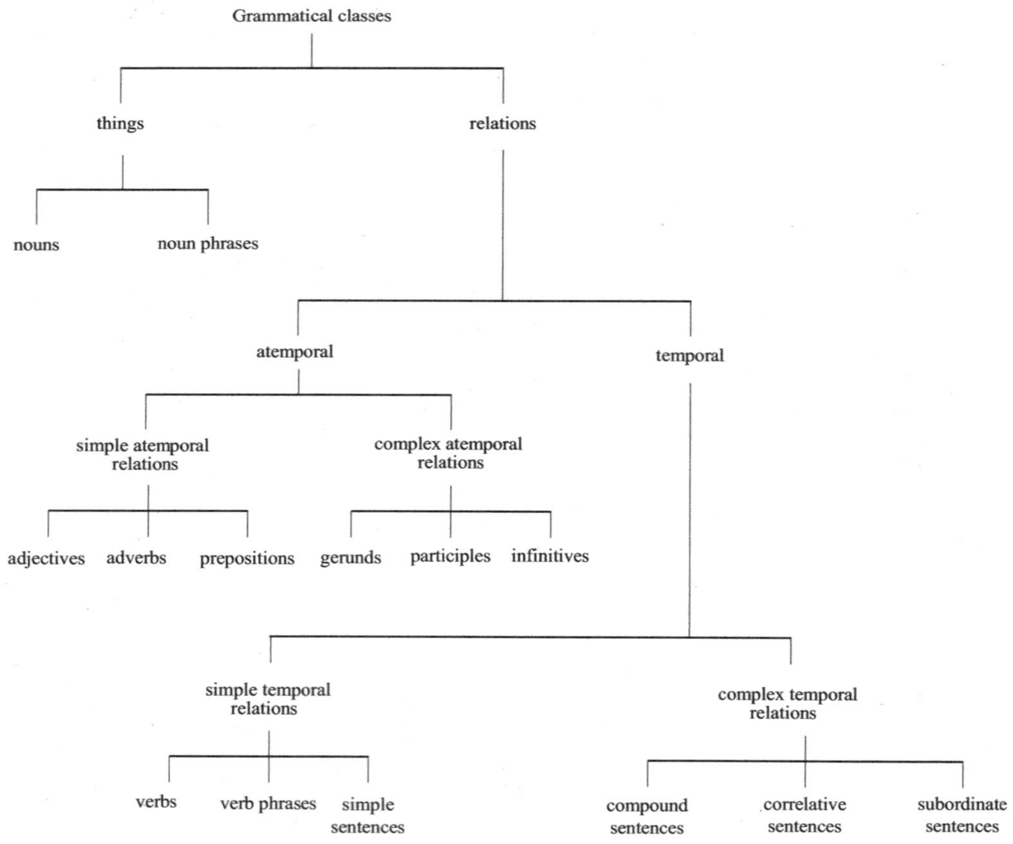

Figure 0.1 *Grammatical Classes in Cognitive Grammar*

PREFACE

This textbook, designed for university students, provides a comprehensive introduction to Cognitive Grammar with a focus on syntax. Cognitive Grammar offers an innovative approach to language study by integrating linguistic structure with human cognition. Unlike traditional grammars that treat language as an isolated system governed by strict rules, Cognitive Grammar views linguistic knowledge as part of broader cognitive processes shaped by mental and sociocultural experiences. Grammar is inherently symbolic, with constructions carrying meaning beyond structure. It highlights the interplay of meaning, form, and function in communication and demonstrates how embodied cognition, our physical experiences, influences the way we conceptualize and express ideas. Through this material, students will discover how grammar functions as a cognitive tool that organizes thought, facilitates social interaction, and shapes perception. Presenting grammar as dynamic and meaningful, the textbook equips learners with analytical tools and practical examples to apply cognitive foundations to real-world linguistic data.

ACKNOWLEDGMENTS

This textbook seamlessly integrates theory with practice. On the theoretical front, it is grounded in Langacker's pioneering ideas, which provides the foundational basis for this work. I am deeply grateful to Langacker for his invaluable contributions, which have greatly influenced the development of this resource. On the practical side, the textbook reflects my extensive research and dedicated efforts. The design and organization are entirely my own creation, with complex ideas carefully simplified and rephrased to ensure accessibility for a wider audience. Every explanation has been meticulously refined to enhance clarity, and the concepts are presented in diverse ways to demonstrate their application across different grammatical structures. What sets this textbook apart is its unique blend of current examples and a broad range of practical applications. These elements, combined with its clear and engaging format, establish it as a distinctive and independent contribution to the study of grammar. My ultimate goal has been to craft a comprehensive, user-friendly companion for learners navigating the intricacies of grammar.

The development of this textbook has been enriched by the valuable research of other cognitive linguists, mentioned in the "references" section, which has greatly strengthened its academic rigor. I am sincerely grateful for their insights, which have helped elevate this work into a valuable learning tool for students. I also wish to acknowledge Microsoft Copilot for its invaluable assistance in drafting and refining challenging sections of the manuscript, significantly enhancing its clarity, coherence, and overall quality. Special thanks are due to Sarah MacDonald, commissioning editor at Bloomsbury, whose outstanding editorial expertise and guidance were instrumental throughout this process. I am equally appreciative of the dedicated Bloomsbury team, whose tireless efforts and commitment were essential in bringing this publication to life. Above all, I extend my deepest gratitude to my family for their unwavering support and encouragement; their confidence in this endeavor was truly the foundation that made it a reality.

PART ONE

Cognitive Grammar

Cognitive Grammar is a groundbreaking linguistic theory that has been evolving since the late 1970s, and it occupies a central place within the broader field of Cognitive Linguistics. It emerged as a response to the limitations of formal linguistic theories, offering a fresh and innovative perspective. Rather than treating grammar as a rigid system detached from meaning and centered solely on sentence rules, Cognitive Grammar adopts a different perspective. It advances a holistic view of language, integrating phonology and semantics and emphasizing their inseparability. Instead of viewing language as a fixed system of abstract rules, Cognitive Grammar sheds a light on the relationship between language and cognition. Rather than functioning merely as a set of formal rules, Cognitive Grammar demonstrates how language mirrors our understanding of the world, underscoring its psychological relevance and affirming that language is deeply embedded in our mental processes. This shift from traditional or formal methods has significantly deepened our insight into how language operates in the human mind.

Ronald Langacker is the founder of Cognitive Grammar. His two-volume work, *Foundations of Cognitive Grammar*, lays out the framework for this innovative system. The first volume, *Theoretical Prerequisites*, provides the philosophical and cognitive underpinnings of the theory, while the second, *Descriptive Application*, showcases practical applications of his ideas. The goal is to offer a comprehensive description of language, presenting a cohesive view that sees semantics, lexicon, and grammar as interconnected rather than isolated elements. It places a strong emphasis on psychological plausibility, highlighting how grammar and language naturally integrate as vital components of cognition. Adopting a usage-based perspective, it underscores the symbolic and communicative roles of language, aligning with the functionalist tradition. Within this framework, grammar is not just a set of rules; it is deeply meaningful and intricately linked to semantics. Every linguistic unit in grammar, no matter how small, carries meaning.

Historical Development

Cognitive Grammar is a significant linguistic theory that originated in the late twentieth century as a response to dominant formalist approaches in linguistics. Rather than adhering to objectivist semantics centered on truth conditions and logical deductions, Cognitive Grammar adopts the framework of **Conceptual Semantics**. In this approach, word meanings exist in the minds of speakers, reflecting how they perceive the world rather than merely pointing to it. Conceptual Semantics acts as a bridge between language and thought, offering new insights into how we create meaning and represent ideas. Langacker, the mastermind behind this theory, proposes that grammar is not merely a collection of abstract rules; it is intricately tied to how we conceptualize things. He believed that grammar, semantics, and vocabulary are all part of a continuum rather than isolated processes, which underscores the close relationship between language and cognition. Grammar gains meaning and merges with semantics, challenging the idea of grammar as purely formal.

Early foundations:

- In the 1970s, Ronald Langacker introduced Cognitive Grammar during a heated debate known as the linguistic wars, which took place in the spring of 1976 between Generative Semantics and Interpretative Semantics. Originally called Space Grammar, this approach aimed to provide a fresh perspective on language by linking it to general cognition, rather than sticking to traditional formal/generative grammar. Langacker's groundbreaking ideas highlighted that grammar is not just a set of rules but a vital part of how we think and understand the world. This viewpoint helped Cognitive Grammar emerge as a key theory in linguistics.
- Moving into the 1980s, Cognitive Grammar gained traction as a significant part of the broader Cognitive Linguistics movement. This theory aimed to see language as a fundamental component of our cognitive processes, stressing the importance of grammar's symbolic and meaningful aspects. It suggested that lexicon, syntax, and semantics are all interconnected, rather than existing as isolated

parts. Language was viewed as a treasure trove of expressions deeply embedded in the minds of speakers. The decade also witnessed the release of several influential publications that played a crucial role in establishing Cognitive Grammar as a leading theoretical framework in linguistics.

- By the 1990s, Langacker's two-volume work, *Foundations of Cognitive Grammar*, had a lasting impact on the field. These volumes provided a thorough and insightful examination of the principles and applications of Cognitive Grammar, becoming essential reading for researchers and students alike. They played a crucial role in solidifying Cognitive Grammar as a framework for understanding language, moving away from traditional rule-based approaches toward a more holistic view that links language to general cognition. This expansion of linguistic inquiry inspired a new generation of linguists to explore Langacker's innovative concepts.

Contemporary advancements:

- 2000s: During this decade, the theory continued to evolve, with researchers exploring its applications across different language elements. This exploration provided us with deeper insights into the interconnectedness of linguistic structures and cognitive processes. The theory was also applied to a wide range of languages, showcasing its flexibility and broad relevance. Additionally, scholars began using Cognitive Grammar to investigate different linguistic phenomena, such as language acquisition, bilingualism, and language disorders, expanding its impact and significance.
- 2010s: The theory made significant progress, with researchers conducting more detailed analyses of language structure, processing, and discourse. They started exploring the connections between Cognitive Grammar and other cognitive functions, such as perception and memory. This decade also saw a growing interest in how culture influences linguistic structures and meanings, enhancing our understanding of Cognitive Grammar. It became evident that language should be viewed not only as a cognitive process but also as a cultural one, emphasizing the diverse ways in which different societies communicate and convey meaning.
- 2020s: The theory became more integrated with cognitive science, psychology, and anthropology, resulting in a more holistic understanding of language as a cognitive process. These interdisciplinary collaborations helped to bridge linguistics with other fields, fostering a more inclusive approach to the study of language. This period also saw the emergence of new methods and tools for analyzing linguistic data through the lens of Cognitive Grammar.

With the aid of technological advancements, researchers were able to conduct more advanced studies, further emphasizing the relevance of Cognitive Grammar in everyday language use.

Cognitive Grammar is a dynamic and evolving field, with researchers continuously refining and expanding the theory to account for the complexity and variability of natural language.

Objectives

Cognitive Grammar provides a holistic view, emphasizing meaning, simplicity, and effective description while addressing fundamental challenges in understanding language. It aims to understand language structure while maintaining a functional perspective and offering an effective framework for describing any language. Cognitive Grammar aims to

- Bridge the gap between conceptual and linguistic elements, connecting meaning with form. For example, consider the sentence *The sun rises*. On the conceptual side, it relates to our mental image of the sun moving up in the sky, while on the linguistic side it is about expressing that idea through words, specifically using the verb *rises*.
- Bring together semantics, lexicon, and grammar into one cohesive framework. This framework views linguistic units, such as morphemes, words, and phrases, as inherently symbolic. For example, in the sentence *She runs every morning*, the verb *runs* not only describes an action (semantics) but also fits neatly into the grammatical structure by following the subject (syntax).
- Simplify and clarify the explanation of language phenomena. Instead of delving into complex rules, it focuses on meaningful patterns and the cognitive processes that help us construct meaning. For example, the distinction between *I am reading* (an ongoing action) and *I read* (a completed action) can be elegantly captured without unnecessary complications.
- Describe linguistic structures in the best possible way by following principles that aim for optimality. This includes examining how different constructs fit into categories. For example, the concept of prototypicality suggests that some members of a category, like *bird*, are more central than others, such as *penguin*, which helps in efficiently describing category membership.
- Address significant issues in linguistic theory by clarifying the structure and relationships of grammatical classes. This involves exploring the continuum between grammar and lexicon, revealing how grammar

rules emerge from cognitive processes, and considering the intricate connections between them. For example, understanding a sentence like *She said that she would come* involves both complementation and subordination.

Architecture

Cognitive Grammar explores two main areas: grammatical and semantic organizations. **Grammatical organization** focuses on the structure and rules that guide how we put together words and phrases in a language, honing in on the structural aspects. On the other hand, **semantic organization** is all about how we build and interpret meaning in language, shedding light on the concepts and ideas that underpin those structures. What is truly fascinating is how closely grammatical and semantic organizations are intertwined, revealing the significance embedded in every grammatical element. They work together to create language that truly resonates. Cognitive Grammar forges a direct link between linguistic form and semantic structure, doing away with the need for a separate system to handle these two elements. It views the connection between language structure and meaning as clear and unified, without requiring additional rules or layers of organization. By merging semantics and grammar, Cognitive Grammar emphasizes their interdependence, providing a fresh perspective on how we grasp language structure and meaning.

Outline

1

Grammatical Organization

In this chapter, I will present the grammatical structure of Cognitive Grammar, taking a closer look at how the different pieces of a language come together to express meaning. This exploration involves two key components: linguistic units and cognitive mechanisms. **Linguistic units** are symbols that link a semantic structure (the meaning) with a phonological structure (the sound). In simpler terms, a linguistic unit can be any expression, whether simple or complex, that we frequently use and have become comfortable with, almost like a habit. The primary aim of language is to connect our conceptual ideas with the forms we use to express them. When we communicate, we are sharing our experiences by transforming our thoughts into these linguistic structures. On the flip side, a **cognitive mechanism** serves as a guide that helps weave together the different parts of a linguistic expression. Together, these elements form the foundation of grammatical organization, showing how all grammatical components are meaningful and interconnected, ultimately boosting our ability to communicate effectively.

1.1 Linguistic Units

According to Cognitive Grammar, grammar is not simply a set of rigid rules dictating how we should construct sentences. It is more like a structured inventory of linguistic units that people use and understand in everyday language. When we refer to it as **structured**, we mean that these units are all interconnected in meaningful ways. The term **inventory** denotes a comprehensive list of all the linguistic elements that speakers rely on to form their sentences. A linguistic unit essentially links a semantic component (the meaning) with a phonological component (the sound). These units can vary from morphemes and words to phrases, clauses, and entire sentences. With sufficient practice, they become second nature to us, stored in our long-term memory for easy retrieval during conversations. This inventory is something that all speakers of a given language have in common, facilitating smoother communication. It encompasses not only the units themselves but also the rules for governing how they can be combined. This inventory is not fixed; it evolves over time as new units emerge and others disappear. These units are shaped by syntax and function as symbols guiding how we create and interpret language.

1.1.1 *Status*

In Cognitive Grammar, linguistic units are viewed as inherently symbolic; they carry meaning and serve as the fundamental building blocks of communication. These units are essentially patterns of action that we abstract from real-life usage events. Over time, they can become entrenched through repeated use in language events, gaining a unit status and forming a shared set of resources within a speech community. These units can range from simple to complex, and any part of a usage event can emerge as a linguistic unit if it is something that occurs frequently. For example, the word *love* symbolizes feelings of affection or deep attachment, the phrase *under the table* indicates a specific location, and the sentence *She dances gracefully* conveys both an action and a manner of doing it. We combine these units to create larger structures, following certain constraints. Morphemes come together to form words, words connect to create phrases, and phrases build into sentences. Cognitive Grammar takes a holistic view of language, considering it as a whole rather than separating syntax from semantics. This perspective shows that meaning and structure are inseparable, making structure meaningless without meaning.

1.1.2 *Tenets*

To truly delve into language analysis, Cognitive Grammar relies on a few essential **grammatical tenets**. These tenets are the fundamental beliefs about the nature of language, and guide our communication of linguistic structures. They emphasize the significance of meaning, demonstrating that language primarily serves as a tool for sharing and comprehending ideas, rather than adhering strictly to rigid rules. These tenets lay a strong groundwork for investigating language, bridging our thoughts, communication, and the utilization of language. Let's explore the key grammatical tenets:

- Grammatical classes are defined more by their meaning than by strict syntactic rules. Essentially, a **grammatical class** is a method of categorizing words based on common characteristics. The primary classes are nouns and verbs, with adjectives, adverbs, and prepositions also falling into these categories based on their functions and relationships with other words in a sentence. These classes are important as they reflect our cognitive experiences and how we convey ideas through grammar. By organizing words into these categories, we can identify shared features and conceptual meanings. For example, nouns represent things like *book*, *tree*, and *idea*, while verbs depict actions, such as *run*, *sing*, and *think*. Nouns and verbs differ in function but share similarities, both dividing into subcategories like countable/uncountable nouns and perfective/imperfective verbs.

- Linguistic constructions are the basic units of communication, combining form and meaning from words to sentences. These constructions capture both the predictable and unexpected ways we use language. They come in various forms, such as (1) Idiomatic expressions like *kick the bucket* meaning "to die" and *bite the bullet* meaning "to face a tough situation"; (2) Collocations, which are combinations like *fast food* (adjective + noun), *make tea* (verb + noun), *wind howls* (noun + verb), *traffic light* (noun + noun), *whisper softly* (verb + adverb), and *utterly amazed* (adverb + adjective); (3) Phrasal verbs that consist of a verb plus a particle, like *She brought up an interesting topic* and *They look after their younger siblings*; (4) Correlative pairs such as *the more, the merrier* and *the earlier, the better*. These constructions are learned as pairings rather than abstract rules. They showcase linguistic creativity and adaptability across diverse contexts and purposes.
- Cognitive Grammar emphasizes actual language use, demonstrating how patterns arise from usage events and are stored mentally. A **usage event** is a real instance or example of language used in communicative interaction, which can be anything from a single word to a full sentence. For instance, it could be just the word like *disbelief*, a phrase like *utter disbelief*, or a complete sentence like *She shook her head in disbelief*. These usage events are crucial for two reasons. First, they lay the groundwork for linguistic units. Second, they help us form generalizations, giving us the raw material to create abstract schemas. This method relies on **bottom-up** processing, where we start with the simplest elements and gradually build up to more complex structures. This is quite different from a **top-down** approach, which starts with the big picture, then breaks into smaller, manageable parts.
- Linguistic units are organized through **schema-instance** relationships. A **schema** represents a general pattern or abstract structure that captures the common features across many specific examples. **Instances**

represent the specific examples or tokens that fit into that schema. For example, from words like *classmate*, *flatmate*, and *roommate*, we can develop the schema [-MATE]. Once established, this schema becomes a template for generating new words in the language, such as *playmate*, *teammate*, *workmate*, and so on. The schema-instance relationships in linguistics are a clear example of **type-instance** relations, where the schema corresponds to the general type and instances correspond to specific realizations of that type. Grammar combines general patterns and specific units, both essential for effective language use. Like fine stitches, it holds language together. This framework is key to understanding language structure and supports recognizing and comprehending linguistic expressions.

- Cognitive Grammar takes a different approach by not relying on an abstract underlying structure. Instead, it focuses on **surface representations**, which are the actual forms of language as we use and perceive them. In formal approaches to grammar, sentences like *The museum was swarming with tourists* and *Tourists were swarming in the museum* are analyzed in terms of deep structure (underlying syntax) and surface structure (how they appear in speech or writing). Conversely, in Cognitive Grammar, the distinction lies in focus. Both sentences convey the same idea but have different surface structures. The arrangement of words and their grammatical roles play a crucial role in shaping the specific meaning. The first sentence emphasizes the museum being filled with visitors, while the second one highlights the tourists' activities inside the museum. In this framework, meaning is considered overt, emerging from conceptualization and the use of symbolic structures that reflect our cognitive processes.
- Cognitive processes play a crucial role in understanding language, and Cognitive Grammar really highlights this through the idea of **construal**. This concept refers to the various ways speakers can present and interpret their thoughts, showing how closely form (grammar) and meaning (conceptualization) are intertwined, illustrating how linguistic structures come together. Consider the sentences *I adore the beach* and *I love the beach*, for instance. Both express admiration, but they carry different nuances. In the first sentence, *adore* conveys a deep, intense admiration, focusing on how strongly the speaker feels about the beach. In contrast, *love* in the second sentence suggests a strong affection, emphasizing an emotional connection to the beach. While both phrases express positive feelings, *adore* implies a more profound reverence, whereas *love* indicates a heartfelt fondness. This shows grammar is linked to cognition, not merely rules.

- The unified approach highlights grammar as an interdependent system. It takes a **holistic** view of language, seeing it as a cohesive whole rather than breaking it down into separate parts. In this perspective, semantics, lexicon, and syntax form a **continuum**, constructing assemblies of symbolic structures. This stands in contrast to formal theories that treat these elements as separate entities. For example, consider the sentence *The red bird perches on the green branch*. From a grammatical standpoint, it follows English grammar rules, such as adding *es* to *perch* when referring to a single bird in the present tense. Looking at the lexicon, each word (like *red* and *green*) carries its own meaning and is carefully chosen to convey a specific idea. In terms of syntax, the arrangement of words ensures that *red* describes *bird* while *green* describes *branch*. All three components work together harmoniously to form a clear and meaningful sentence.
- Embodied cognition is a fascinating concept that suggests our minds are isolated; they are deeply connected to our bodies and how we interact with the world around us. When we discuss **embodiment**, we are examining how our thoughts, language, and understanding are influenced by our physical experiences. For example, the phrase *She laughs* perfectly illustrates the connection between a physical action (laughing) and an emotional state (joy). Our sensory and motor experiences play a critical role in our language comprehension. Language is closely linked to these experiences, demonstrating how our physical interactions impact our ability to understand and use words. This perspective, often overlooked in traditional grammar theories, emphasizes how our bodily experiences shape our language skills. Embodied cognition highlights how context and environment shape thought and ground understanding in reality.
- Unlike the rigid rules of traditional grammar, Cognitive Grammar emphasizes the flexibility of language, viewing grammatical patterns as adaptable rather than fixed. This flexibility stems from the cognitive processes we rely on such as attention, memory, and our ability to interpret meaning based on context and experience. Instead of following rigid rules, language use shifts according to what feels most natural and cognitively efficient for speakers. For example, we often prefer active constructions like *The chef cooked the meal* over passive ones such as *The meal was cooked by the chef* because the active form aligns more closely with how we mentally organize events, making it easier to process and understand. This illustrates how linguistic choices reflect underlying cognitive tendencies rather than prescriptive norms. Ultimately, Cognitive Grammar shows that

grammar evolves from how we think, perceive, and interact with the world around us.

- Every linguistic unit is viewed as a symbolic unit. A **symbolic unit** is a linguistic construct that inherently carries meaning, encompassing words, phrases, clauses, sentences, and even entire texts. The way we assemble these linguistic units is also symbolic, rather than strictly adhering to rules, as grammar itself is considered meaningful in this context. In simpler terms, language is seen as a system of symbolic representations, where sounds and gestures can symbolize our conceptualizations. Each linguistic unit consists of a semantic structure (the meaning) and a phonological structure (the form), which are interconnected through a symbolic structure. For example, the word *cat* links the phonological structure /kat/ with the mental image of a small, furry, domesticated animal. The relationship between phonological and semantic structures is influenced by how the speaker interacts with the world, as meaning is connected to a **concept**, which is essentially a mental representation of a symbol in someone's mind.

1.2 Cognitive Mechanisms

Cognitive Grammar introduces a sophisticated set of cognitive mechanisms that are essential for both understanding and producing language. **Cognitive mechanisms** are processes that help us piece together the different parts of a linguistic expression, whether we are talking about individual words or entire phrases. **Integration** is all about merging these smaller components of a complex symbolic structure into a smooth, linear sequence. A key player in this integration process is **valency**, which is the mechanism that allows two grammatical expressions to come together and form a composite expression. When it comes to integrating these subparts, four main factors come into play: correspondence, determinacy, elaboration, and dependency. These factors show us how grammatical and lexical items are combined to create meaningful expressions, illustrating how various parts of a sentence interact and contribute to the overall message. The presence or absence of these factors can significantly influence the semantic value of linguistic expressions. Next, I will dive into a detailed description of each mechanism.

1.2.1 *Correspondence*

This mechanism is all about making different parts of a sentence work together. Two subparts can come together to create a composite structure only if they share certain essential elements at both the meaning and sound levels. Usually, one subpart helps to further elaborate on a semantic idea found in the other. Take the composite structure *observer*, for instance; it is made up of the two parts *observe* and -er. The way these two parts fit together depends on the connections established between them. Phonologically, the -er part, when used to indicate an agent, refers to a process that gets fleshed out by *observe*. Semantically, -er signifies an agent that only makes sense when paired with the action described by *observe*. By merging these two related processes, we get the composite structure *observer*. As a noun, *observer* clearly describes someone who watches an event.

Now, let's examine the prepositional phrase *in the garden*. In this phrase, we observe a correspondence that highlights the relationship between its components. This correspondence is established through the interaction between the main participant (the trajector) and the secondary participant (the landmark). The preposition *in* profiles a relation between the trajector and the landmark. The trajector is unspecified; it could be an entity or a process. The noun phrase *the garden* functions as the landmark, providing the spatial reference. There is a correlation between the landmark indicated by *in* and the concept of the garden. The use of *in* as a spatial marker links the trajector to the landmark, *the garden*. *In* plays the role of defining or conveying the landmark relationship in this phrase. In the phrase *in the garden*, the preposition *in* signifies a spatial relationship, indicating that something is located within the boundaries of the garden. Without clearly expressing the spatial aspect of *in*, the phrase's meaning may be unclear. Understanding this spatial relationship is essential for interpreting the prepositional phrase accurately.

1.2.2 *Determinacy*

This mechanism involves specifying or limiting the meaning of a linguistic expression. Specifically, it determines which part lends its profile to the overall structure. The term **profile** refers to the specific feature or aspect of a linguistic expression that is highlighted or given prominence in shaping the overall meaning or structure. This specific part is referred to as the **profile determinant**, traditionally known as the head. The head's role is crucial because it guides the interpretation of the entire linguistic expression. For example, in the composite structure *observer*, the free morpheme *observe* indicates an action, whereas the bound morpheme -er indicates a person. The composite structure as a whole represents a person who observes something. The bound morpheme -er is important because it determines the category, establishes the core meaning, and selects the dependents. The free morpheme *observe* can be seen as one whose profile is influenced by the profile determinant -er. Both morphemes are essential to the meaning of *observer*, but the bound morpheme, acting as profile determinant, is more significant.

Take the prepositional phrase *in the garden* as an example. Here, determinacy is evident, specifying which element shapes the overall profile of the composite structure; namely, which garden is being referred to. Within this phrase, the preposition *in* expresses a relational meaning, whereas the noun phrase *the garden* represents a concrete entity. *The garden* functions as a definite noun phrase, identifying a specific location. The preposition *in* establishes the spatial relationship, making the phrase both precise and unambiguous. However, the phrase as a whole conveys a broader relational concept rather than denoting a tangible thing, since it describes a property of some entity relative to its spatial position. This interpretation arises because *in* acts as the profile determinant, imparting its distinctive relational character to the entire phrase. Consequently, the phrase is classified as a prepositional phrase, explicitly emphasizing a spatial relation.

1.2.3 *Elaboration*

This mechanism focuses on enhancing the overall meaning of a linguistic expression by adding detail. When we analyze such expressions, we can observe an A/D pattern at work. The A part can stand alone, while the D part relies on the A for context. The D contains an elaboration site or e-site—a conceptual gap that invites completion. The A fills this gap, providing the necessary elaboration. The D requires this elaboration to be fully interpretable. For example, the noun *observer* perfectly exemplifies this A/D pattern. The free morpheme *observe* represents the A part. Phonologically, it can stand alone as a complete form. Semantically, it is a fully understandable expression without needing external references. In contrast, the bound morpheme *-er* represents the D part. Phonologically, it cannot stand alone, and semantically, it does not form a complete expression by itself. Therefore, it must attach to a host that clarifies its meaning and adds detail.

Take the phrase *in the garden*, for instance. Here, you can really see how elaboration plays a role, highlighting just how detailed a concept can be. The noun phrase *the garden* gives us a clear context, while the preposition *in* points to the location within that garden. When we look at the phrase *in the garden*, it follows an A/D pattern. The noun phrase *the garden* serves as the A part, while the preposition *in* acts as the D part. The phrase *the garden* stands on its own and makes sense without needing any extra details. On the other hand, *in* relies on additional context to be fully understood. Understanding how these elements of the prepositional phrase relate to each other is key to conveying that something is situated inside the garden. Nominal concepts, represented by nouns, tend to be more independent, while relational concepts like those expressed through prepositions, adjectives, adverbs, and verbs are more dependent on context.

1.2.4 Dependency

This mechanism explains how linguistic elements combine both conceptually and functionally to create meaningful expressions. These elements form **conceptual groupings** that are guided by semantic relevance rather than rigid syntactic rules. Dependency is more than just a syntactic tool; it reflects how our minds organize meaning and how we mentally structure the messages we wish to convey. In terms of dependency, linguistic units are organized around **heads** and their **dependents**, with relationships that are fundamentally conceptual rather than merely formal. For example, consider the word *impersonal*. The conceptual dependency flows outward from the root: the root *person* serves as the semantic head, carrying the core meaning. The prefix *im-* and suffix *-al* function as morphological dependents that modify this root. At the first level, the root *person* combines with the suffix *-al* to form the adjective *personal*. Then, at the next level, the prefix *im-* attaches to *personal* to produce *impersonal*. Together, these morphemes form a **symbolic assembly**, a structured pairing of form and meaning that shapes the word's concept.

The way linguistic elements combine can vary significantly depending on how the speaker conceptualizes the situation. Some elements have only one possible integration, as seen in words like *impersonal*, where the combination is straightforward and unambiguous. Others, however, allow for multiple modes of integration, resulting in different interpretations. This flexibility is captured well by the dependency principle, which holds that each morpheme depends on a head morpheme for its meaning and function. Ambiguity arises because dependency relations can be hierarchically layered in different ways, creating distinct conceptual groupings and meanings within the same morphological form. Take, for example, the word *unlockable*. In one interpretation, the root *lock* first combines with the suffix *-able* to form *lockable*, meaning "able to be locked." Then, the prefix *un-* attaches to *lockable*, producing *unlockable*, which means "not able to be locked." In the alternative interpretation, the prefix *un-* first combines with the root *lock*, forming the verb *unlock*, meaning "to reverse locking." This newly formed verb then takes the suffix *-able*, resulting in *unlockable*, meaning "able to be unlocked."

Consider the phrase *in the garden* through the lens of the dependency principle. In this phrase, the preposition *in* acts as the head, governing the dependent noun phrase *the garden*. Together, they form a prepositional phrase, where *the garden* depends on *in* to complete its meaning and function. This hierarchical structure reflects how smaller linguistic units attach to heads to form larger constituents. The dependency between *in* and *the garden* is not merely additive; it is directional and functional. *In* determines the syntactic role of the entire phrase, while *the garden* provides the necessary complement to fulfill that role. From a syntactic view, the phrase's internal dependencies help it fit smoothly into the sentence; for example, in *She is sitting in the garden*, the phrase depends on the verb *sitting* as an adverbial modifier. Semantically, the dependency structure allows *in the garden* to convey a precise spatial concept. The meaning arises not from the words in isolation, but from their interdependent roles. The clarity and depth of the sentence hinge on these layered dependencies, which guide interpretation and grammatical function.

Summary

In this chapter, I have explored the fascinating world of Cognitive Grammar and how it organizes our understanding of grammar. Grammar isn't just a set of rules; it mirrors how we perceive reality and influences the way we articulate our thoughts. It is not random; it is deeply rooted in our conceptual frameworks and the meanings we create. When we construct sentences, we tap into our mental images to share our ideas clearly. Cognitive Grammar challenges traditional theories by emphasizing the inherent meaning within grammar and its close ties to our cognitive processes. It invites us to see language as a rich interplay of symbols and conceptual frameworks, providing a fresh lens through which to understand and use language. In this view, language is intertwined with human cognition, shaped by overarching cognitive principles rather than a distinct language module. Language works hand in hand with cognitive functions, particularly perception, attention, and memory. Cognitive linguists argue against the notion of a separate language module in our minds, insisting that any discussion about language should align with insights from related fields like psychology, neuroscience, and biology.

Exercises

Tenets

1. Evaluate the significance of grammatical classes in understanding language structure and meaning.
2. Consider the relationship between constructions and meaning, providing examples to support your explanation.
3. Analyze the role of frequency and usage patterns in shaping grammatical rules and restrictions.
4. Discuss the importance of schema-instance relationships in understanding language variability and flexibility.
5. Delve into the relationship between surface structure and meaning, providing examples to illustrate your points.

6. Review the importance of context in grammatical organization and how it influences the interpretation of constructions.
7. Investigate the advantages and challenges of adopting a unified approach in Cognitive Grammar.
8. Examine the role of embodied experience in shaping the meanings and structures of linguistic expressions.
9. How does Cognitive Grammar treat flexibility as central to linguistic structure, and what supports this flexibility?
10. Explore the role of symbolic units and how they contribute to understanding grammatical organization.

Mechanisms

1. What role does the cognitive mechanism of correspondence play in constructing meaning?
2. Describe how correspondence aids in understanding the relationship between form and meaning.
3. What cognitive mechanism ensures that expressions have determinate meanings?
4. Analyze the cognitive mechanism of determinacy and its impact on interpreting linguistic expressions.
5. How does the cognitive mechanism of elaboration contribute to the construction of meaning?
6. In what ways do elaborative processes expand meaning, illustrated through examples?
7. Explain with examples the role of dependency in understanding the hierarchy of linguistic elements.
8. Compare Cognitive Grammar's view of dependency with that of traditional syntactic theories.
9. Evaluate how cognitive mechanisms account for language variability and flexibility in linguistic expressions.
10. Discuss the role of cognitive mechanisms in supporting how people produce and understand language.

2

Semantic Organization

In this chapter, I will present the semantic organization of Cognitive Grammar and explore how meaning is structured and understood in our minds. My focus will be on two key components: Conceptual Semantics and construal dimensions. These elements work hand in hand to lay the groundwork for semantic organization, emphasizing the connections between all the different parts of meaning. **Conceptual Semantics** looks at how we derive linguistic meaning from our experiences in the world, while **construal dimensions** showcase the various ways we can perceive and describe a situation. In Cognitive Grammar, the meaning of an expression goes beyond just the conceptual content it brings to mind; it also involves how that content is framed. Together, Conceptual Semantics provides the core substance, and construal dimensions influence how that substance is conveyed and interpreted. This interaction explains how different expressions convey the same idea in distinct ways. Grasping this dynamic relationship is key to a thorough analysis of language.

2.1 Conceptual Semantics

Cognitive Grammar draws on Conceptual Semantics, which explains how meaning comes from our thoughts, mental images, and creative interpretations, not just from referring to things in the world. It highlights how our experiences and cognitive abilities shape how we understand and use language. Cognitive Grammar challenges formal approaches by arguing that grammar carries meaning, not just rules. It rejects **objective** semantics: meaning is in the world, existing independently of the speaker. Instead, it embraces **subjective** semantics: meaning comes from the speaker's personal experience. For example, consider the sentence *This book is* *important* that can be interpreted in two ways. In objective semantics, the book has historical, scholarly, and cultural qualities that make it important regardless of who reads it. In subjective semantics, the book matters to me because it fits my interests or changed my life. The examples show that meaning can be seen as either built into the object or shaped by the individual, even if the wording is the same.

2.1.1 Assumptions

Cognitive Grammar is based on fundamental assumptions that facilitate a productive discussion of meaning.

- Meaning is something we embody, indicating that linguistic meaning is not merely an abstract concept; it is rooted in our physical experiences and interactions with the world around us. Our understanding of language and its meanings is influenced by our sensory, emotional, and physical experiences. For .example, the word *up* often connotes positivity and success, while *down* typically evokes negative emotions and feelings of failure. These associations demonstrate how language is connected to our bodily experiences; we have all experienced the difference between moving up and down, which influences how we use these words. In Cognitive Grammar, our physical experiences and interactions play a crucial role in determining the meaning of linguistic expressions. This perspective highlights that language comprehension is shaped by real-life experiences and enriched by our environment.
- Meaning is something we conceptualize, shape, and organize through our mental processes. The words we use are like symbols that express these concepts, closely linked to how we perceive the world around us. For example, consider the difference between *Let's stop and rest awhile* and *Let's stop and rest a while.* While *awhile* and *a while* may sound identical, they carry subtle distinctions in meaning. Each version has its own nuance, evident in writing simply by the space between the words. The single-word *awhile* acts as an adverb, meaning *for a short time*, suggesting a brief break. On the other hand, the two-word *a while* also serves as an adverb but means *for a period of time*, indicating a longer rest. In Cognitive Grammar, the way we use language reflects the specific perspective we take on its meaning. These variations in perspective lead to variations in meaning, resulting in different forms of expression.
- Meaning is motivated: word use is shaped by cognitive and communicative needs, not random or fixed. Meaning is fluid,

shaped by our thoughts, experiences, and context. Motivation is the link between expression and meaning. Our understanding and use of language are deeply affected by our mental images and how we interact with the world around us. Take the adverbs *very* and *too*, for example. Their meanings are often shaped by how the speaker perceives the situation or the context of the conversation. *Very* carries a positive connotation, suggesting a high degree or a large amount, as in the sentence, *The box is very heavy, but I can lift it.* On the other hand, *too* has a negative implication, indicating something excessive or undesirable, as in, *The box is too heavy. I can't lift it.* In Cognitive Grammar, language structure and meaning are closely linked, reflecting our cognitive and communicative aims.

- Meaning is not something set in stone; it is dynamic, constantly shaped by our thoughts and situations. This means that the meaning of an expression can change and adapt depending on the context in which it is used. Take the -ing gerund, for instance. It can express different time relationships, like something that happened before or something happening right now. This is not just a coincidence; it reflects the fluid nature of language and how we use it. For example, in the sentence *He repents deserting his girlfriend*, the -ing gerund points to an action that took place in the past, with the complement event happening before the main event. Conversely, in *He enjoys solving puzzles*, the -ing gerund indicates an action occurring in the present, where both the main and complement events are happening at the same time. In Cognitive Grammar, meaning is viewed as something that exists in our conceptualization, which is a dynamic process that evolves over time and is shaped by context.
- Meaning is encyclopedic, going beyond simple dictionary definitions. To truly understand a linguistic item, we must access a wealth of knowledge connected to it. Take the existential *there*, for example. It not only indicates the existence of something, as in *There is a restaurant around the corner*, but it can also serve other functions. It can be used for listing items, as in *There were a dozen fire engines ringing the vault*, introducing a new topic, as in *There have been some nasty incidents recently*, or even negating or quantifying information, as in *There is nothing more that I want to see.* In Cognitive Grammar, meaning is both symbolic and encyclopedic, emphasizing the relationship between language, perception, and cognition. This perspective challenges the traditional notion that grammar is simply a set of rules devoid of meaning. Therefore, to grasp meaning, we must see how language works in context.

2.1.2 Processes

Cognitive Grammar sees language as tied to our mental processes, which shape how we create, understand, and express thoughts and emotions. The main processes involved are as follows:

- **Categorization.** This pertains to our ability to group various meanings of a word into a category. A **category** is a network of distinct yet related meanings for a particular word, centered around a prototype and its surrounding meanings in the periphery. The **prototype** represents the ideal instance, while the **periphery** includes additional meanings that stem semantic extensions. These meanings are akin to family members; they share common traits but differ in specific ways. For example, consider the modal verb *could*. Its primary meaning relates to ability, as in *She could swim before she turned five*. However, it also has other meanings: such as possibility, as in *We could see a movie later*; permission, as in *You could go to the party if you want*; politeness, as in *Could you please pass the salt*?; hypothetical conditions, as in *If it rained, we could stay indoors*; and suggestions, as in *You could take a walk in the park*. This shows that word meaning is fluid, forming a network beyond simple dictionary definitions.

  At the clause level, a sentence can be polysemous, meaning it can have a range of distinct yet related meanings. For example, a declarative sentence like *She is careful* serves as the primary example of this category. Other sentence types, such as interrogative (*Is she careful*?), imperative (*Be careful*), and exclamatory (*How careful she is*!), represent the boundaries of this category. These different sentence types differ in two main ways: their structural properties, such as word order patterns, and their functional properties, which include specific illocutionary functions. Each sentence type has a core example showing its main function, with peripheral ones extending it. Some additional functions may lack full traits of the category, creating inequality among them. Thus, a sentence type's functions need not always align with its main example. In Cognitive Grammar, flexibility shows that variations still convey meaning effectively.

- **Configuration.** This refers to our mental ability to organize various linguistic items into a cohesive cognitive domain. This domain serves as a foundation of knowledge that helps us understand meanings of these linguistic items. Each domain consists of multiple facets, each associated with a specific concept. To fully understand the meaning of a word, it is essential to compare it with other words within the same domain. For example, consider prepositions such as *at*, *in*, and *on*. These words are best understood when viewed through the lens of time. The preposition *at* is often used with specific times and mealtimes, as in *I wake up at 6:30 a.m.* or *She doesn't like to leave the office at lunchtime*. On the other hand, *in* is typically used for parts of the day and longer periods, as in *I usually relax in the evening* or *I'm always busy in December*. Meanwhile, *on* is commonly used with days and dates, as in *I have a long lunch on Friday* or *It's his birthday on October 19*. This demonstrates that linguistic items are not isolated; they are often grouped together within these domains.

When examining sentences at the clause level, expressions like *She made them go* and *She forced them to go* tap into the domain of causation but convey different meanings. In the first sentence, the verb *make* is followed by the bare infinitive *go*, indicating a direct action where the subject is actively involved in the outcome. This suggests a clear link between the main verb's action and the complement. The verb *make* signifies a direct influence in achieving a specific result, which is why it is paired with a bare infinitive. In contrast, the second sentence uses *force*, followed by the to-infinitive *to go*. Here, the action is more indirect, implying that the subject's actions lead to an effect without direct involvement. In this scenario, the subject does something that triggers the action. This shows that syntax reflects conceptual organization shaped by the speaker's scene description.

- **Conceptualization.** This refers to how we mentally frame a situation in different ways. The meaning of a word or phrase comes from both its conceptual content and how we construe it. **Conceptual content** is the usual meaning tied to an expression, while **construal** is about how a speaker interprets and articulates that meaning based on what they want to communicate. Two different phrases can convey the same idea but may express it differently depending on the speaker's perspective. For example, consider the phrases *a book* and *the book*. They point to the same entity but carry distinct meanings. This difference is linked to how definite or indefinite the reference is, which is reflected in the choice of articles. The phrase *a book* suggests that the book is not known to the listeners, while *the book* implies that it is something they are already familiar with. This shows how our conceptual choices lead to varied expressions, revealing the link between thought and language.

At the clause level, the sentences *I saw them quarreling* and *I saw them quarrel* convey the same idea but highlight different perspectives. These are structural choices that serve distinct communicative purposes. In

I saw them quarreling, the speaker adopts an internal view of the situation, capturing just a part of the action. This is why the verb is in the progressive aspect. Here, the speaker emphasizes the ongoing nature of the event, suggesting that the quarreling was still happening at the time of speaking. Conversely, in *I saw them quarrel*, the speaker takes an external view, observing the entire event. This is reflected in the use of the nonprogressive aspect of the verb. In this case, the speaker highlights the complete nature of the event, indicating that the quarreling had wrapped up by the time they spoke. Together, these choices show how aspect shapes perspective, allowing speakers to frame events as partial or complete.

- **Figuration.** This refers to the process of shaping our ideas using language. When we express our thoughts, we do not just throw words together; we actively mold and organize them through communication. This process is dynamic, constantly changing as we interact with language and its meanings. Figuration affects not only how we share our ideas but also how others grasp them. It deepens the foundational concepts we use to make sense of the world and categorize our experiences. In language, figuration includes various tools like metaphor, metonymy, and blending. These tools enrich our conceptual framework, making our language more vibrant, nuanced, and layered. They are not just fancy phrases; they are essential cognitive processes that shape how we construct and interpret meaning. These devices do more than just decorate our language; they leave a lasting mark on the way we understand concepts.

  Metaphors are fascinating because they help us connect different ideas by mapping one concept onto another. **Mapping** is the way we create links between various domains in our minds. When we say T is understood via S, we are delving into how we understand things. Here, T stands for the **target domain**, the idea we are trying to grasp or explain, while S is the **source domain**, which is usually something more tangible or familiar. For example, when we say *Love is a journey*, we map elements of a journey onto a relationship. It is a conceptual metaphor that helps us understand love through the familiar experience of traveling. It frames partners as travelers, the relationship as a path, challenges as obstacles, and shared goals as a destination, showing how we use concrete experiences to make sense of abstract emotions. The metaphor helps us understand the abstract concept of love (target domain) through the concrete domain of travel (source domain). Cross-domain mapping helps us express complex ideas more clearly.

- **Contextuality.** This refers to the importance of context in understanding and interpreting language. In Cognitive Grammar, understanding language involves considering the context in which it is used, including cultural, social, and situational factors. This approach aims to provide a deeper insight into how meaning is created and understood in everyday communication. People often adjust their language to fit different situations. For example, think about the expressions *She sits between the boys* and *She sits among the boys*, In the first case, *between* is used when there are two clearly defined entities. In this case, there are two boys, with the girl in the middle. In the second case, *among* is used when there are more than two entities that are not distinctly separated because they form a group. Here, she is part of a larger group of boys. These examples show how context shapes language, linking variation to specific situations.

  Let's break it down at the clause level. Consider the difference between the sentences *I had my car cleaned* and *I had cleaned my car*. The way we arrange the words changes the meaning completely. The first sentence implies that someone else cleaned the car for you, which is what the structure *had something done* typically indicates; you arranged for someone else to do it. On the other hand, the second sentence tells us that you took the initiative to clean your own car. In this case, you were the one doing the cleaning. So, the key difference here is who did the cleaning: someone else in the first sentence and you in the second. This demonstrates that word order is crucial, and context plays a significant role in how we interpret what is being said. Cognitive Grammar emphasizes that our context influences our language choices, making variation an essential aspect of language. It highlights the dynamic link between form and meaning, and ultimately between language and thought.

2.2 Construal

In Cognitive Grammar, **construal** refers to how language users perceive, interpret, and present a situation, shaping our understanding of the world through language. Construal encompasses the meaningful ways in which we conceptualize and present reality by selecting, organizing, and highlighting our experiences. Cognitive Grammar challenges the notion that linguistic packaging is solely dictated by the scene itself. Instead, in Cognitive Grammar, the speaker's role in creating meaning is pivotal. The meaning of an expression lies in the conceptualizing activity of individual speakers, which is fundamentally imagistic rather than purely propositional. Similarly, Cognitive Grammar challenges the idea that language is an abstract system of rules, divorced from real-world experiences. Instead, Cognitive Grammar emphasizes the inseparable link between language and cognition, rejecting rigid formalism. Meanings are not isolated in the head; they are shaped by conceptualization processes.

2.2.1 *Principles*

The construal theory is based on key principles that highlight the mental processes involved in constructing meaning.

- Meaning is not just the ideas, but also how we interpret them. When we talk about **conceptual content**, we refer to the basic characteristics of a situation. In contrast, **construal** focuses on our personal perceptions and interpretations of that content. Two phrases might seem to express the same idea, but their meanings can shift depending on how we construe them. Take, for example, the expressions *They have spent almost four million pounds* and *They have spent nearly four million pounds*. At first glance, these might appear similar, but they actually carry different nuances. Both *almost* and *nearly* indicate closeness to a target value, in this case, four million pounds, but they differ in construal, meaning the way the speaker mentally frames that closeness. In the first expression, *almost* suggests being very close to the target but not quite reaching it, with a slight sense of falling short while keeping the focus on the goal itself. In the second, *nearly* also implies closeness but carries a subtle hint of surprise or tension, as if the amount was expected to reach four million but ultimately did not.
- Grammatical **variations** are significant; different forms often convey subtle differences in meaning. Whenever the form changes, it signals a shift in meaning through a change in **construal**—the speaker's mental framing or perspective on the situation. For example, consider the phrases *Some fifty people attended the rally* and *Around fifty people attended the rally*. While both suggest an unspecified number of attendees, they are not interchangeable because they construe the situation differently. *Some* implies a construal where the actual number is likely less than the stated figure, focusing on an approximate but somewhat limited quantity. In contrast, *around* allows for a construal that includes the possibility of the real number being either less or more than fifty, portraying a more flexible range. In Cognitive Grammar, speakers do not view these expressions as identical because each grammatical form is tied to a unique meaning shaped by its construal. The structure of an expression mirrors

how the speaker mentally organizes and interprets the conceptual content.

- Various factors constrain and shape our interpretations. One factor is **context**, which includes the surrounding environment, background information, and the specific moment in which communication takes place. For example, the sentence *She is a real firecracker* can be interpreted differently without context: is it a compliment (she is energetic) or a criticism (she is aggressive)? Context is key in determining the intended meaning of such phrases. Another factor is **purpose**, which is the goal of communication. Our purpose for speaking shapes how we perceive a situation, whether the aim is to inform, persuade, comfort, or entertain. A third factor is **choice**, which reflects our point of view. For example, saying *She broke the vase* emphasizes the person performing the action, whereas *The vase got broken* focuses on the result or state of the vase. Each sentence conveys a different nuance. Together, these factors show that meaning is never fixed but shaped by context, purpose, and perspective.

2.2.2 Benefits

The construal theory offers several benefits over previous analyses and can address many of the issues that those analyses encountered.

- Construal provides speakers with the flexibility to express and perceive a situation in multiple ways, resulting in a wide variety of language expressions. It further acknowledges that meaning is subjective, shaped by individual perspectives. Linguistic meanings do not directly mirror reality; instead, they represent specific ways of construing and interpreting situations. For example, consider the sentences *He desires to achieve fame* and *He enjoys achieving fame.* Both sentences use similar wording, but the construal differs due to the use of different types of complement clauses. The to-infinitive suggests a future action, portraying the achievement of fame as a desired goal. In contrast, the -ing gerund indicates an action occurring at the moment of speaking, portraying the achievement of fame as a pleasurable activity.
- Construal plays a crucial role in determining the selection of a linguistic expression by considering context. Cognitive Grammar emphasizes that meaning does not solely stem from conceptual content but also from how that content is interpreted within specific contexts. By analyzing the relationship between language

and context, we can better understand the ever-changing nature of meaning. The meaning of a linguistic expression is influenced by the context in which it is used. Context refers to the circumstances surrounding the use of an expression. The choice of an expression shapes our mental representation of an event. Construal can vary depending on the context. The same concept or event can be interpreted differently based on the context. For example, the word *killer* has two possible interpretations. It can refer to a person as in *They found the killer* or to a thing as in *Cancer is a killer.*

- Construal explores the form (the structure) and the distribution (the use) of linguistic expressions. The form of an expression is defined by the specific construal imposed on its conceptual content. The distribution of an expression is determined by the semantic compatibility between its internal components. Within the cognitive framework, the issues of form and distribution are considered interconnected. For example, in the sentence *Working in the garden cheered him up*, the -ing gerund is coherent because it describes an actual event, which is supported by the past marker -ed. In this case, the to-infinitive is incoherent as it refers to a non-actual event. The cognitive analysis diverges from other approaches in linguistic research by focusing on distributional differences instead of just structural specificity.

2.2.3 *Dimensions*

As I mentioned before, **construal** is all about how we mentally shape and interpret our experiences. It is not just about the ideas we think of; it is also about how we perceive and make sense of those ideas. A key part of what gives a linguistic expression its meaning is the construal aspect that is applied to its content. When a speaker chooses a certain expression, they are selecting a specific angle from a variety of options to frame its conceptual content for expressive purposes. Construal is a complex concept with various dimensions that reflect some of our fundamental cognitive skills. These dimensions help us appreciate the richness and flexibility of human thought, shedding light on why we favor certain expressions, how grammar changes over time, and how our semantic descriptions connect with our cognitive processes. They show how language mirrors thought and how we interpret the world around us. Through subtle communication, they reveal the complex ways we create meaning.

Construal dimensions can be grouped into four main categories: specificity, prominence, perspective, and focusing.

2.2.3.1 Specificity

When we communicate, we often find ourselves at a crossroads between being specific or more schematic, and the choice really depends on the context and what we want to achieve with our message. **Specificity** involves adding those extra details to a concept, helping to create a clearer and more vivid picture in the listener's mind. On the other hand, **schematicity** involves using broader, more abstract terms to describe something. It is important to note that specificity and schematicity are not just black and white; they exist on a spectrum. Some phrases are super specific, while others are quite general. Take the sentence *The rose is beautiful*, for example. It is pretty vague. We understand that it is talking about a lovely rose, but it does not give us much to work with. Now, if we say, *The red rose is beautiful*, we are adding more detail and clarity. So, the second sentence definitely packs more specificity than the first. This level of specificity plays a crucial role in how we grasp and interpret meaning, ultimately influencing our communication and shaping how we see the world around us. Specificity is key when crafting sentences and organizing thoughts.

2.2.3.2 Prominence

Prominence is all about highlighting certain aspects of a concept, giving them varying levels of importance. In language, this means placing different elements in different spots within a sentence. Prominence plays a key role in understanding meaning, shapes sentence structure, and helps determine which parts are most important in a specific context. There are three main types of prominence: profiling, the distinction between trajector and landmark, and salience.

Profiling

Profiling is a mental process that focuses on a specific entity within a broader context. The entity that takes center stage in this scenario is known as the **profile**. It highlights the particular aspect that an expression points out as the main focus. By bringing certain elements to the forefront, profiling shapes how we mentally picture concepts and influences our understanding and interpretation of meaning. For example, in the phrase *To entertain Catherine is difficult*, the process *To entertain Catherine* is in profile, making it the subject and emphasizing the challenge of the action itself. On the other hand, in *Catherine is difficult to entertain*, it is Catherine who is in profile, and the focus shifts to her being hard to entertain. Understanding profiling is crucial because it sheds light on how language shapes our mental imagery and understanding. It allows us to explore how different ways of expressing things can affect our visual perception and how we conceive events. Examining profiling reveals how speakers frame experiences and communicate them effectively.

Trajector Versus Landmark

Trajector-landmark alignment is a fascinating cognitive process that helps us pinpoint the key players in a given relationship, highlighting both the main and secondary participants involved. The trajector is the star of the show, acting as the primary focus in this relationship, while the landmark takes a supporting role as the secondary focus. Think of it this way: in the expression *The book is under the table*, the *book* is the trajector, drawing our attention as the main subject, and its position is being described. The *table*, on the other hand, serves as a **reference point** for the book's location. By understanding trajector-landmark alignment, we can dive deeper into how language shapes our perception of relationships between different entities. It reveals how we think about events, spatial arrangements, and various situations. By identifying the trajector and landmark, we gain a clearer understanding of how language organizes information in our messages and how their elements interact.

Salience

Salience is all about what grabs our attention in language or concepts. It is what makes certain parts of a scene or situation pop out and catch our eye. The way we choose our words like their order, the specific words we pick, and how we structure our sentences can really boost or lessen the salience of different elements. When we have two landmarks in a relationship, they can stand out to different degrees. The main landmark gets what we call **initial salience**, which highlights the most important part of a scene. In linguistic terms, the participant that stands out from the background is positioned in a way that reflects its significance. On the other hand, the secondary landmark has the least salience. For example, consider the sentences *He sent a letter to Susan* and *He sent Susan a letter*. In the first one, the direct object *a letter* is what stands out first, while in the second, the indirect object *Susan* takes the spotlight. This means the two sentences convey different meanings, with only the second one clearly indicating that Susan received the letter. By looking at how language emphasizes certain elements, we can better understand how it shapes our communication strategies.

2.2.3.3 Perspective

Perspective is how we view a situation, shifting with our intentions. Language lets us adopt different viewpoints, emphasizing some elements while downplaying others. For example, consider the sentences *A few people can afford to buy a house* and *Few people can afford to buy a house*. The expressions *few* and *a few* both quantify a small number, but they differ in **construal**, the speaker's mental framing of that quantity. *A few* construes the situation positively, emphasizing the presence of some individuals who can buy a house. It profiles the existence of a small but meaningful group. *Few* construes the situation negatively, emphasizing the scarcity or lack of people who can afford a house. It profiles the insufficiency of the group. This difference in construal affects the emotional tone and communicative intent. The speaker using *a few* may be highlighting hope or possibility, while the speaker using *few* may be expressing concern or limitation. This illustrates how just one word can dramatically change the tone and meaning of what we say. Perspective encompasses four dimensions: vantage point, viewing arrangement, subjectivity, and dynamicity.

Vantage Point

Vantage point is all about where you are standing when you look at a situation, which can lead to different interpretations and perspectives. It is essentially the spot where the people involved in a conversation are positioned, whether it is the speaker or the listener. For example, consider the sentences *Andy is sitting to the left of Jane* and *Andy is sitting to the right of Jane*. The first sentence shows Andy's position from the speaker's perspective. Picture the speaker facing both Andy and Jane; from that angle, Andy is indeed to the left of Jane. Now, flip it around to the second sentence, which describes Andy's position from Jane's perspective. If Jane is looking in the same direction as Andy, then he is to her right. Grasping the concept of vantage point is crucial because it allows us to see how language mirrors our perspective and shapes our understanding of the world. By analyzing these different vantage points, we can gain valuable insights into how we think and improve our communication skills, as they play a significant role in how we express ourselves and visualize ideas.

Viewing Arrangement

Viewing arrangement refers to how the speaker positions themselves in relation to the situation they describe. There are two main types: the Optimal Viewing Arrangement (OVA), where the speaker remains detached from the scene, and the Egocentric Viewing Arrangement (EVA), where the speaker places themselves within the scenario. This distinction creates a contrast between expressions that feel objective and those that seem subjective. Choosing one arrangement over the other shapes the listener's perception, influencing how personal or distant the event feels. For example, consider the sentences *He strains to reach the pinnacle of his career* and *It is a strain to reach the pinnacle of a career*. The first illustrates EVA by linking the effort directly to a specific person (the subject), giving it a personal and subjective tone. The pronoun *he* signals active involvement in the action. Conversely, the second sentence exemplifies OVA by attributing the effort to a general concept, creating an impersonal, objective perspective. This type of viewing distances the speaker from the event, focusing on the abstract difficulty rather than an individual's experience.

Subjectivity

Subjectivity, is all about integrating the speaker's feelings and perspective into the fabric of language. It marks a transition from objective meanings to more subjective ones. When we discuss **objectivity**, we are talking about forming opinions that do not necessarily reveal the speaker's personal feelings or views. Objectivity pertains to a broader situation that affects many people, not just the individual sharing it. On the other hand, **subjectivity** involves forming opinions that do reflect the speaker's own attitudes and viewpoints. It is connected to specific situations or individual experiences, touching on the more personal aspects of life. For example, when someone says, *I believe that she will succeed*, it demonstrates a subjective perspective on the situation, emphasizing the speaker's personal involvement. In contrast, a statement like *It is believed that she will succeed* presents a more objective viewpoint, distancing the speaker from the event and reflecting a general perspective. Objective and subjective interpretations are essential to how syntax structures and conveys language.

Dynamicity

Dynamicity pertains to how a conceptualization unfolds over time during processing, particularly in terms of how the mind processes language. Dynamicity can be observed in three main cases: the mode of scanning, the order of presentation, and the course of direction.

In terms of **scanning mode**, the difference lies in whether the described scene is in motion or simply remains still. Speakers demonstrate flexibility by construing a complex scene either sequentially or summarily. **Sequential scanning** involves the speaker conceiving a situation as it unfolds through time, while **summary scanning** involves viewing the entire situation at once. For example, in the sentence *I remember that I fell down the stairs*, the speaker scans the process of falling as individual components, similar to a motion picture. Each component is viewed separately over time, giving the verb a temporal profile. In contrast, in *I remember falling down the stairs*, the speaker views all components of the process simultaneously, like a still picture, resulting in a verb without a temporal profile.

In terms of **presentation order**, the difference lies in the varying word order, aligning with the sequence of perceived events. Different word orders represent distinct ways of portraying a scene. For example, consider the semantic impact of placing a locative expression at the beginning of a sentence, as seen in *A dead rat lay in the middle of the kitchen floor* and *In the middle of the kitchen floor lay a dead rat*. Despite using the same words to describe the same situation, these two expressions are not semantically equivalent. The difference lies in how the situation is mentally processed. In the first expression, the mental focus starts with the subject *a dead rat*, indicating known information. In the second expression, the mental focus begins with the locative phrase *in the middle of the kitchen floor*, highlighting new information.

In terms of the **course of direction**, the difference lies in how an event is perceived. Speakers can construe a complex scene by taking different perspectives. This can be illustrated with examples such as *The hill gently rises from the bank of the river* and *The hill gently falls to the bank of the river*. Both statements share the same idea but differ in meaning, describing one layout with contrasting interpretations. The difference lies in the direction of mental scanning, which is reflected in the choice of words. The speaker creates a mental image of *the hill* by mentally following a path along it, either upward as in the first sentence or downward as in the second sentence. The direction is indicated by the words used: *rises from* suggests an upward movement, while *falls to* suggests a downward movement.

2.2.3.4 Focusing

Focusing is all about honing in on a specific part of an expression while allowing other parts fade into the background. It involves directing our attention to certain elements within an expression or conceptual idea to determine what really stands out as important or central. The choices we make with language assist us in sorting through information, highlighting specific details, and shaping the overall message of our expressions. It is a dynamic interaction between the ideas we possess and the way we convey them. Focusing also entails distinguishing between what is in the foreground and what is in the background, as well as defining the scope of our attention.

Foreground Versus Background

Foreground and background are terms that describe how we focus on different parts of a linguistic expression or concept. The foreground elements are the ones that really stand out, grabbing our attention, while the background elements play a more subtle role, providing context or additional information. The way we choose our words helps us sort information into what is in the foreground versus what's in the background. In conversation, we often distinguish between what is already known (the given information) and what is new. When we look at complex expressions, we can see how the individual parts relate to the whole (the way the expression is put together). For example, in the sentence *After a long day at work, she finally relaxed*, the foreground is *she finally relaxed*, which is the main action, while the background is *After a long day at work*, which sets the scene and gives us a time frame for what is happening. By understanding the difference between foreground and background, we can see how language emphasizes important elements and organizes information, ultimately helping us communicate more effectively. Recognizing these aspects allows us to craft our messages in a way that captures attention and conveys meaning clearly.

Scope

Scope is the range of content that an expression evokes, shaping how we understand its meaning. Linguistic expressions can involve two levels of scope: immediate and maximal. **Immediate scope** is the narrow range of content an expression directly relates to or describes. On the other hand, **maximal scope** covers the broader range of content that an expression evokes, including all the speaker's awareness. For example, consider the sentences *To argue about a trivial issue is unwise* and *It is unwise to argue about a trivial issue*. In the first sentence, the focus is on the complement or infinitival clause, which is chosen as the subject. Here, the speaker takes a narrow view, with the clause alone shaping their evaluation. In the second sentence, the pronoun *it* takes center stage as the subject. This time, the speaker adopts a broader perspective on the complement event, with *it* representing a global stimulus that includes the general circumstances behind the evaluation. Understanding scope is key to seeing how language shapes meaning and how we process information.

Summary

In this chapter, I have explored how Cognitive Grammar organizes meaning. I introduced the idea of Conceptual Semantics, which focuses on how we derive meaning from our conceptualizations. Within this framework, I took a closer look at the concept of construal and highlighted its importance in grasping meaning. In Cognitive Grammar, the meaning of a linguistic expression encompasses both conceptual content and construal. Conceptual content refers to the inherent properties of a situation, while construal is all about how a speaker interprets that content in various ways and selects the right language structures to convey it. Construal goes beyond just presenting raw information; it is about how we frame and organize that information. When we communicate, we make choices about how to represent reality, and these choices are shaped by our cognitive processes. Essentially, construal is woven into all linguistic expressions, showcasing different ways of conceptualizing ideas. In short, construal plays a vital role in how we understand the world and create meaning through language. It links abstract concepts to real life, offering a fresh view of language and meaning.

Exercises

Semantic Organization

1. Explain the concept of embodied meaning, providing supporting evidence to illustrate it.

2. Discuss the principle of motivated meaning and how expressions reflect speakers' intentions.
3. Explain dynamic meaning and how usage shapes an expression's meaning over time.
4. Analyze encyclopedic meaning and the role of background knowledge in understanding expressions.
5. Discuss conceptualized meaning and how mental processes shape language use and understanding.
6. Explain the process of categorization and how it differs from traditional linguistic approaches.
7. Define the process of configuration and demonstrate how it aids in understanding linguistic expressions.
8. How does Cognitive Grammar address the dynamic nature of conceptualization in various contexts?
9. Discuss figurative language in Cognitive Grammar with examples of its use and interpretation.
10. Analyze diversification in Cognitive Grammar and how it explains linguistic diversity and complexity.

Construal

1. Explain how construal distinguishes expressions with identical content.
2. Define schematicity and explain its inverse relationship with specificity.
3. How does profiling impact our understanding of linguistic expressions?
4. Explain the role of trajector and landmark in shaping linguistic meaning.
5. What role does salience play in shaping our comprehension of a situation?
6. Show how perspectives shape subjective and objective conceptualizations.
7. Describe how vantage point affects our view of events or scenes.
8. What is the importance of viewing arrangement in language use?
9. Distinguish foreground and background elements within a given context.
10. How does scope affect the way we perceive and interpret language?

PART TWO

Things

In Cognitive Grammar, we consider **grammatical classes**, commonly known as parts of speech, as groups of words that share similar meanings and have specific formal characteristics. The grammatical class of an expression is determined by the nature of its profile. Words are classified into different classes based on semantic distinctions rather than purely distributional criteria as proposed by formal approaches to language. While semantics is vital in this classification, Cognitive Grammar also recognizes the impact of distributional and phonological properties unique to each language. Understanding grammatical classes is crucial because they provide insights into how language, as a dynamic system, represents our conceptualization of the world. The goal of studying grammatical class is to understand the relationship between form and meaning in language. Language is a fascinating interplay of form and meaning, with each grammatical class serving a distinct purpose. By prioritizing semantics as the basis for description, Cognitive Grammar reveals how our minds systematically organize the lexicon and efficiently process language.

Cognitive Grammar identifies two primary grammatical classes: things and relations. The distinction between the two lies in the nature of an entity. **Things** are conceptually independent, meaning they can be conceptualized without considering the relationships they are invoked in. In language, things are associated with **nouns**, referring to objects or substances. For example, *tree* is a noun that profiles a thing, denoting a tangible object in our experience, while *freedom* is a noun that profiles a thing, representing an intangible concept in our experience. By contrast, **relations** are conceptually dependent, meaning they cannot be conceptualized without also conceptualizing the entities involved in them. In language, relations are associated with **verbs**, referring to dynamic or stative processes. For example, *run* is a verb that profiles a process, denoting a dynamic event, while *know* is a verb that profiles a state, representing a stable condition in our experience. Understanding the distinction between things and relations is essential for understanding how language operates.

Outline

3

Nouns

3.1 Introduction

In this chapter, I explore the conceptual category of **things**, articulated through the grammatical category of **nouns.** Nouns are mentally grouped based on shared features. This grouping goes beyond mere grammatical rules; it reflects how we cognitively organize the world around us. Typically, nouns designate **things**, entities that can be mentally individuated and profiled as bounded wholes. Nouns are perceived through **summary scanning**, meaning we grasp the entire entity at once rather than tracking its development over time, which is characteristic of how we perceive verbs. Categories of nouns are organized around **prototypes**: central examples that best represent the category, such as an apple being a prototypical fruit. Each noun category includes a general **schema**, for example, *fruit* as well as specific **instances**, for example, *apple*, *banana*, *orange*, and so on. Nouns function as independent conceptual units, occupying specific positions within particular domains. For example, *football* is classified as a thing because it refers to an independent object within the domain of sports, which also includes basketball, volleyball, handball, and others. It is conceptual because it evokes a shared mental image, and it is an entity because it signifies a specific instance in that domain.

3.2 Entities

In Cognitive Grammar, an **entity** or thing is any conceptual object that can be individuated and profiled in thought, the things we talk about, whether people, objects, places, abstract ideas, or events construed as objects. Grammatically, **nouns** profile such entities, designating both concrete and abstract referents. For instance, *mountain* is a physical thing, while *joy* symbolizes a more abstract idea. When categorizing things, we can split them into objects and substances, similar to the differentiation between count nouns and mass nouns in grammar. This classification is more focused on meaning rather than rigid grammatical rules. While some may define nouns based on their roles in sentence such as subjects or objects, Cognitive Grammar delves deeper into the inherent meanings and functions of nouns. It seeks to understand the entities or substances that nouns signify and how they relate to our mental perceptions of the world. Additionally, a noun's meaning is flexible, shifting with context and the speaker's perspective. Take the word *bank*, for example. In one context, it denotes a financial institution when we are talking money. In another context, it describes the side of a river in a natural setting.

The distinction between count and noncount nouns comes down to how we conceptualize, visualize, and incorporate them into our sentences. Count nouns, such as *apple*, *bird*, and *book*, refer to individual items that can be easily counted. In contrast, noncount nouns, like *knowledge*, *music*, and *water*, represent things that are more like masses or abstract concepts that cannot be counted individually. When we think about count nouns, we can easily visualize specific examples of objects, and they have clear singular and plural forms. Noncount nouns, however, focus on qualities or states and do not have a plural form; they do not point to specific instances. In terms of how we use them, count nouns are ideal for counting, quantifying, and making specific references, while noncount nouns are more suitable for general descriptions and discussing uncountable amounts or abstract concepts. In essence, count nouns emphasize individuality and countability, while noncount nouns focus on collectiveness and the idea of being uncountable. Grasping this difference can greatly enhance our communication.

3.3 Categories

Within the realm of things, there is a mental distinction between objects and substances. Similarly, within the realm of nouns there is a linguistic distinction between count and mass nouns. This distinction is based on the nature of nouns and emphasizes what they denote. Cognitive Grammar examines nouns in terms of construal, as speakers construe things according to their perspectives. **Construal** refers to our ability to imagine and represent a situation in multiple ways. Specifically, the choice of a noun reflects the speaker's **perspective**, and how they conceptualize a situation. The ability to distinguish between different types of nouns facilitates the expression of linguistic subtleties. Different types of nouns allow speakers to frame situations differently, enriching our understanding of how cognition influences language. Count nouns allow us to quantify and distinguish individual instances, while mass nouns represent unbounded or continuous concepts. In essence, both types of nouns enable us to express nuanced distinctions about the world.

3.3.1 *Objects*

Objects, grammatically referred to as **count** nouns, have some interesting features: they are bounded, heterogeneous, and countable. **Boundedness** indicates that these objects have clear limits, allowing the speaker to see them as complete entities. **Heterogeneity** indicates that they are made up of various elements that come together in an integrated manner. **Countability** indicates that they can be counted. It is the ability to recognize different items as part of a single category, making them countable. Due to these features, they are labeled as count nouns. Take the noun *house*, for instance. It has a defined structure and clearly marks an entity with specific boundaries. It is heterogeneous since it is made up of different components that all play a role in its overall design and function. Moreover, it can be easily counted with numbers: *one house*, *two houses*, *three houses*, and so forth. In the realm of Cognitive Grammar, count nouns stand out as a unique category of nouns that can be broken down into individual units.

Examples of count objects:

People:	teacher, student, boy, girl, friend
Animals:	cat, dog, bird, elephant, wolf
Fruits:	grape, apple, orange, cherry, kiwi
Artifacts:	table, book, chair, phone, toy
Plants:	rose, tree, daisy, lily, oak
Vehicles:	car, airplane, boat, train, bus
Clothing:	shirt, coat, blouse, scarf, sock
Crockery:	plate, dish, cup, bowl, saucer
Cutlery:	spoon, knife, fork, chopsticks, flatware
Tools:	hammer, screwdriver, wrench, axe, hatchet

The examples mentioned earlier are count nouns that refer to objects sharing common themes. These nouns represent everyday items that play crucial roles in our lives, helping us with various daily tasks in different situations. You can count them using numbers like *one book*, *two dogs*, or *three apples*. They can also be combined with determiners such as *a chair*, *an egg*, *this book*, *those oranges*, *some books*, *many pens*, *each student*, and *every day*, among others. Additionally, they exist in both singular and plural forms. For instance, singular forms include *a teacher*, *a sharpener*, and *an idea*, while their plural counterparts are *teachers*, *sharpeners*, and *ideas*. These count nouns are vital for organizing and categorizing our world, making our communication clearer and more effective.

3.3.2 Substances

Substances, grammatically referred to as **noncount** or **mass** nouns, refer to materials or abstract concepts that are typically treated as undifferentiated wholes. They are characterized by unboundedness, homogeneity, and noncountability. **Unboundedness** means without limit or bound, signifying the quality of being infinite, making them continuous rather than distinct and individuated. **Homogeneity** means consisting of elements of the same type. Substances are made up of the same material that retain its identity despite changes in size or form. Thus, they are coded as mass nouns. **Noncountability** means they cannot be enumerated individually, that is, lacking plural forms. For example, consider the mass noun *water*. It is unbounded as it lacks inherent edges. It is homogeneous because it is of the same nature and refers to the entire liquid rather than specific drops. It is noncountable because it cannot be counted or pluralized, existing as a single entity. In Cognitive Grammar, mass nouns are seen as representing broad, conceptual regions in our mental space that do not conform to typical divisions into discrete units.

Examples of noncount substances:

Concepts:	advice, luck, fun, information, peace
Activities:	homework, singing, dancing, jogging, fishing
Liquids:	coffee, petrol, blood, milk, water
Materials:	cloth, paper, cotton, wood, glass
Foods:	bread, butter, cheese, fish, meat
Particles:	flour, salt, sugar, dust, rice
Weather:	thunder, lightning, rain, heat, snow
Collective nouns:	furniture, equipment, rubbish, luggage, knowledge
Emotions:	joy, anger, excitement, bravery, intelligence
Gases:	air, oxygen, helium, nitrogen, smoke

The examples mentioned above are noncount nouns that refer to substances associated with recurring themes. These nouns represent everyday items that are essential in our lives, helping us tackle daily tasks in various situations. They do not have a plural form; they remain singular. For instance, *advice* is typically not pluralized, as in *She gave me advice before the interview*. You can quantify them with words like *some*, *much*, *a lot of*, *a bit*, or *a little*, as in, *Could you please pour me some water?* They also cannot be paired with the indefinite articles *a* or *an*. So, you would not say **an information*. It remains singular, as in *She gathered information from different sources*. You can use measurement units with them, such as *a glass of water*, *a piece of information*, or *a grain of rice*.

3.3.3 Alternation

Alternation refers to the phenomenon where different grammatical structures or linguistic forms are used to express similar or related conceptual content. These variations are not arbitrary; they reflect differences in how speakers mentally construe or highlight aspects of a situation. For example, consider count and noncount nouns, which can alternate depending on the context. Think of *a cake* (a count noun) versus *some cake* (a noncount noun). This alternation shows us that various structures can still convey the same underlying concepts. The type of noun we choose reflects how we construe the world around us. Count nouns focus on individual, countable items, while noncount nouns deal with broader concepts that cannot be easily divided. Count nouns help us identify specific instances within a category, while noncount nouns allow us to consider something as a whole, without clear boundaries. This alternation is a fascinating aspect of language that showcases our cognitive flexibility. In simple terms, count nouns emphasize individuality and limits, while noncount nouns emphasize continuity and expansiveness.

To understand the concept of countability, Cognitive Grammar utilizes two strategies: individuation and accommodation. Both strategies are essential for clarifying meaning.

3.3.3.1 Individuation

In Cognitive Grammar, individuation refers to the conceptual process of treating something as a discrete, countable entity rather than a continuous or unbounded substance. It involves reconceptualizing and reframing a noun to emphasize its countable nature. Individuation is a type of construal, where an unbounded mass is reimagined as a countable unit. This shift is not merely grammatical; it reflects a change in how the speaker conceptualizes the situation. The noun has not simply been replaced; the mental image of the entity has been reshaped. Noncount nouns typically represent broad or continuous ideas, while count nouns allow us to quantify and differentiate individual examples. For instance, we can take the noncount noun *water* and individuate it as *a bottle of water*, pinpointing specific instances within the larger category. This technique not only adds clarity but also enables us to express more nuanced meanings. Ultimately, this strategy highlights the dynamic relationship between meaning and form, showing that grammar is not just a set of rules; it is deeply meaningful and rooted in context.

Here are a few examples of this individuation: luggage becomes suitcase/suitcases, money turns into dollar/dollars, furniture can be swapped for table/tables, music can be replaced with song/songs, wine can be changed to bottle/bottles, electricity can become battery/batteries, information can be detailed as detail/details, advice can be simplified to tip/tips, travel can be expressed as journey/journeys, work can be referred to as job/jobs, and scenery can be described as view/views, among others. This process illustrates how mass or abstract nouns often require specific countable units to make them more tangible and precise in communication. By individuating these concepts, speakers provide clearer references to distinct, bounded entities that listeners can easily identify and understand. This linguistic shift clarifies expression and mirrors how we organize experiences into countable chunks.

There are several reasons why speakers may choose to alternate one type of noun with another.

The sea scenery is magnificent.	The sea views are magnificent.
I need information about the project.	I need details about the project.
I have some luggage.	I have three suitcases.
She appreciates art.	She appreciates the paintings.
He bought furniture.	He bought five chairs.
The music touched my soul.	The songs touched my soul.

In the left column, you will find sentences that feature noncount nouns, which refer to the substance itself. On the right, the sentences showcase count nouns, pointing to specific instances. The first example highlights cognitive flexibility, showing how we shift linguistic forms by context, goals, and representation. The second example focuses on contextual pragmatics. Speakers choose nouns by context and intent. The third example shows how count nouns enhance referential clarity by pinpointing specific instances. The fourth example shows how count nouns highlight individual items, boosting attention and salience. The fifth example shows how count nouns aid cognitive economy by efficiently pinpointing specific referents. Finally, the last example vividly showcases conceptual blending. Our minds seamlessly merge different conceptual frames, and both count and noncount nouns help us weave together diverse mental representations.

3.3.3.2 Accommodation

In Cognitive Grammar, **accommodation** means adjusting schemas to fit new patterns, adapting language to context and nuance. This approach allows the same noun to act as both a count and a noncount noun, depending on the situation. Countable sense marks specific objects, while uncountable sense covers substances, concepts, or mass phenomena. It boils down to how we perceive entities, whether they are bounded or unbounded. Bounded entities have clear limits and are seen as distinct items, which we express with countable nouns like *bird*, *cup*, or *table*. In contrast, unbounded entities do not have clear boundaries and are viewed as a continuous mass, represented by uncountable nouns like *juice*, *snow*, or *water*. Take the noun *cake*, for instance; it can function as both a count noun and a noncount noun. In the sentence *She baked three cakes for the party*, *cake* is treated as a count noun, referring to separate, distinct items. However, in *There is some cake left on the table*, *cake* is used as a noncount noun, representing an unbounded substance.

Several noun categories shift between count and noncount, with context guiding their dual nature.

We drink a lot of coffee.	We ordered three coffees.
The window is made of glass.	She broke two glasses.
I love cheese on my pizza.	I ordered three slices of cheese.
Traveling broadens experience.	He had many life experiences.

Let's break down the differences between noncount and count nouns in a way that feels relatable. In the left column, we are looking at noncount nouns, which refer to a whole idea or quantity. Over in the right column, we have count nouns that point to specific examples or types.

The first example contains a noun referring to liquid. The uncountable use of the noun applies when we talk about the drink in general. The countable use of the noun applies when we ask for a specific number or particular type of these drinks. Examples of such nouns are *coffee*, *beer*, *milk*, *tea*, *soda*, *water*, and so on. These linguistic shape-shifters keep our language dynamic and intriguing. Additional sentences include *Milk is an excellent source of calcium. She bought cleansing milks and gels. I like tea more than coffee. I prefer herbal teas.*

The second example contains a noun referring to physical material. The uncountable use of the noun occurs when we think of the thing as raw material. The countable use of the noun occurs when we refer to specific pieces or distinct types of things. Examples of such nouns are *paper*, *glass*, *iron*, *gold*, *wood*, and others. These flexible nouns change form to fit the situation. Additional sentences include *The sturdy table is made of wood. Lighter woods can be easily crushed. This book is made of paper. I read about it in the paper.*

The third example contains a noun referring to food. The uncountable use of the noun arises when we think of the thing as a raw material or a product. The countable use of the noun arises when we refer to specific portions, types, or servings of the thing. Examples of such nouns are *rice*, *flour*, *cheese*, *salt*, *yogurt*, and so forth. These nouns can perform dual roles, sometimes abstract and whole, other times specific and divisible. Additional sentences include *I enjoy fresh yogurt with fruits. We'll have two frozen yogurts, please. We need white rice next time we go shopping. She cooked two bowls of rice.*

The fourth example contains a noun referring to abstraction. The uncountable use of the noun denotes a general concept, while the countable use of the noun denotes specific instances or individual occurrences. Examples of such nouns are *education*, *experience*, *hatred*, *help*, *knowledge*, *life*, *love*, *sleep*, *time*, *understanding*, and so on. These nouns mark categories, highlighting concepts or specific examples. Additional sentences include *The importance of education cannot be overstated. She received a good education at the university. Reading books expands our knowledge. She has extensive knowledge of ancient civilizations.*

The preceding analysis highlights key takeaways. Unlike list-based grammar, Cognitive Grammar offers a fresh view of countability. It shows that nouns can mean more than their basic definitions. Some nouns can be both countable and uncountable, which really shakes up the rigid categories that formal approaches suggest. In Cognitive Grammar, categorization is not fixed; it can shift based on context and usage. This viewpoint emphasizes the dynamic, flexible, and context-dependent nature of language. Unlike formal approaches that often treat meaning as static and fixed, relying on rigid syntactic rules at the expense of actual usage, Cognitive Grammar emphasizes that meaning arises from our construal of situations. The relationship between count and noncount nouns reflects our cognitive flexibility, pragmatic considerations, and the cognitive motivations behind language use. In relation to prototype theory, some nouns can be more prototypical as count nouns or more peripheral as noncount nouns, and vice versa.

3.4 Cognitive Aspects

In Cognitive Grammar, the focus is on mental processes behind creating and understanding language, not rigid rules. There are three key operations at play: **categorization**, **configuration**, and **conceptualization**. Categorization involves grouping the multiple senses of a linguistic item into a category. Configuration involves grouping a number of linguistic items into a domain. Conceptualization involves describing the content of a situation in multiple ways. These processes shape perception, improve communication, and broadening understanding of the world. They are the foundation of both language and thought.

3.4.1 *Categorization*

Categorization is the mental ability to group the different meanings of a linguistic item into a category. A **category** is a network of distinct yet connected senses of a given linguistic item. At the heart of this category is a **prototype**, which is the most recognizable example that showcases the key traits that set it apart from other examples. Surrounding this prototype is the **periphery**, which includes other examples that stem from the prototype through various semantic extensions, organized by how closely they relate to the prototype. These examples share some, but not all, of the defining characteristics. In Cognitive Grammar, nouns, countable or not, are polysemous, covering distinct yet related meanings. Polysemy is a fascinating aspect of language where a linguistic item can have several related meanings. Take the noun *foot*, for instance:

foot

Prototypically, the noun *foot* is used for animate entities. In the sentence *She followed them on foot*, it refers to the body part on which a person or animal stands. In the sentence *She followed them on foot*, it refers to the specific body part on which a person or animal stands. Peripherally, the noun *foot* is used for inanimate entities. In the sentence *They built a house at the foot of a cliff*, it refers to the base or bottom of something such as a cliff, hill, mountain, stairs, page, and so on. In the sentence *He stood at the foot of the bed*, it refers to the end nearest to the feet of the person lying in it. In the sentence *The room measures 30 feet by 10*, it refers to a unit of length equal to one-third of a yard or 12 inches. This shows that the concept of *foot* has both a central meaning and some peripheral uses. The prototype is central, while the periphery includes senses arranged in terms of distance from it. The concepts of prototype and periphery in Cognitive Grammar show how we engage with surroundings, organize knowledge, and structure language.

3.4.2 Configuration

Configuration is the mental ability to group a number of linguistic items into a cognitive domain. A **domain** is a knowledge background in which the meanings of linguistic items can be properly described. A domain consists of several facets. A **facet** is a portion of a domain that is associated with a particular human experience. In Cognitive Grammar, the meaning of a noun cannot be understood independently of the domain it is linked to. While two nouns may describe the same configuration, they are not semantically equivalent. Each noun occupies a specific facet within the domain, giving it a unique meaning and purpose. This reflects the principle of meaning as conceptualization, which views linguistic expressions as inseparable from mental representations. To better understand this concept, let's closely examine the following related nouns:

instrument
implement
equipment

These nouns all belong to the *tool* domain but represent different facets and serve unique purposes. Therefore, each has a distinct meaning and application. An *instrument* is a tool or device used for precise work, often in scientific or medical contexts, as in *The scientist used an instrument to examine the light emitted by the star*. An *implement* is a tool or device used for a specific purpose, often in agriculture or gardening, as in *The gardener used a new implement to dig the flower beds*. *Equipment* refers to a set of tools or devices needed for a particular activity, often in sports, as in *The gym is filled with state-of-the-art equipment for exercising*. This analysis underscores the importance of a domain as a suitable context for interpreting lexical items by assigning each one to a specific facet. This distinction aids in understanding the specific roles and applications of each term within their respective contexts. It also reflects the cognitive principle that meaning is usage-based, shaped by how speakers apply words in real contexts.

3.4.3 Conceptualization

Conceptualization is the mental ability to construe a given situation in multiple ways. The meaning of a lexical item depends on both conceptual content and construal. **Conceptual content** refers to the typical meaning associated with a lexical item, while **construal** is about how we understand that meaning based on what we need to communicate. It is the speaker's ability to view a situation from different perspectives and express those views through various linguistic expressions. In Cognitive Grammar, nouns, whether abstract or concrete, may appear similar, but they do not come from the same underlying structure. Rather than being mere language variations, they carry unique semantic values. Semantics is closely connected to surface form, where the form of a linguistic expression reflects its meaning. To illustrate this, let's examine the following two nouns:

freedom
liberty

While the nouns *freedom* and *liberty* are often used interchangeably, there are subtle differences between them. The distinction between them lies in the construal imposed on a situation. *Freedom* refers to the right to live without constraints, which means being free from external limitations. For example, when we say, *He enjoys freedom of speech*, it emphasizes the ability to express thoughts without fear of punishment. On the other hand, *liberty* is more about being freed from past restrictions, allowing one to exercise their freedom within the framework of laws or moral principles. An example would be *The released prisoner enjoys his new liberty*. Therefore, while *freedom* is more of an internal, philosophical, and psychological state, *liberty* is a social concept that enables people to experience freedom while still respecting legal and moral standards.

3.5 Linguistic Aspects

When we think about nouns, it is not just about how our brains process information cognitively. Nouns also have a linguistic side that involves language structure, such as syntax and semantics. The syntax of nouns shows us how they function as subjects, objects, and complements in sentences, while semantics explores how their meanings combine to express ideas. By focusing on these linguistic elements, we can improve our understanding of word classes, which in turn helps us comprehend the various roles nouns play in language. Exploring these aspects of nouns not only enhances our comprehension of language, thought, and human experience but also enables us to communicate more nuanced meanings and navigate our environment more effectively. Understanding the linguistic complexities of nouns not only sharpens our communication abilities but also deepens our admiration for the intricacy and beauty of language.

3.5.1 *Reification*

In Cognitive Grammar, **reification** makes abstract ideas seem concrete, revealing how language shapes thought and reality. Reification lets us treat abstract notions such as emotions, ideas, or relationships as tangible things. Essentially, it is about making intangible ideas easier to grasp, often through language and cognitive processes. This process involves a metaphorical leap from something we cannot touch to something we can see and feel. This kind of metaphorical transformation is referred to as an **ontological metaphor**, which allows us to view situations and conditions as objects. Because of this, we can treat these concepts like count nouns, giving them singular and plural forms. We can quantify them with numbers and describe them with adjectives. Reification highlights the depth of meaning and the way we conceptualize things, bridging the divide between the abstract and the concrete. This process shows how abstract concepts gain structure through grammar, linking meaning to linguistic form. It recognizes the significance of all grammatical elements and how they interact dynamically in our use of language.

Time flies.

Love is blind.

Trust is fragile.

Let's examine each one in detail. When we say *Time flies*, we are really saying that time moves quickly, like birds darting through the air. But if we take a moment to think about it, this phrase invites us to see time as something we can hold onto, almost as if it has wings. This perspective helps us articulate that feeling we get when time seems to vanish in an instant. By giving time this kind of tangible quality, we make the idea more relatable and vivid. Similarly, when we say *Love is blind*, we are suggesting that love transcends mere emotion; it is like a person who cannot see. This metaphor emphasizes how love can be accepting and nonjudgmental, often overlooking flaws and imperfections. By reifying love in this way, we communicate that it does not always notice the shortcomings. In *Trust is fragile*, we are portraying trust as something delicate, like a physical object that can shatter easily. Reifying concepts enriches language, making it engaging and relatable.

3.5.2 *Nominalization*

In Cognitive Grammar, **nominalization** involves transforming verbs and adjectives into nouns, which helps us express complex ideas more straightforwardly. It is a fascinating concept that sheds light on how language and thought are intertwined. By allowing us to condense intricate meanings into short noun phrases, it helps bridge the gap between abstract ideas and their expression in words. For instance, in verbal nominalization, we take verbs and turn them into nouns to highlight actions or processes, such as changing the verb *decide* into the noun *decision*. Similarly, in adjectival nominalization, we transform adjectives into nouns to focus on qualities or attributes, like changing *free* into *freedom*. This shows that understanding noun semantics is crucial for analyzing language, meaning, and perception of reality. Nominalizations allow us to package complex information while still maintaining a link to our cognitive experiences.

In Cognitive Grammar, nominalization is all about capturing and expressing dynamic events and their outcomes in neat noun forms, helping us connect abstract ideas with our language usage. **Construal** is essentially how we perceive and organize our experiences. When we choose to nominalize certain concepts, it reveals our perspective on how we represent different situations. This flexibility arises from two main types of construal. The first is mass-like construal, where we view the event nominal as a unified whole. For instance, the action of exploring transforms into a stable entity known as exploration. The second type involves zone activation or a metonymic shift for result nominals. **Zone activation** focuses on a specific aspect or outcome within a broader context. For instance, the quality described by the adjective *beautiful* becomes the noun *beauty*, representing that result. This illustrates that nouns are more than just labels; they embody our cognitive processes and how we interpret the world around us.

Transforming verbs into nouns:

Original:	The house collapsed.
Nominalized:	The collapse of the house.

Both phrases refer to the same event, but they are structured differently and can convey slightly different nuances. Both structures are grammatically correct, but they subtly emphasize different aspects of the same event. The first structure is an active sentence where *the house* is the subject and *collapsed* is the verb. This structure emphasizes the action itself and is often used to report the event as it happened, focusing on the moment of the collapse without specifying any additional context. On the other hand, the second structure is a nominalization; it turns the verb *collapse* into a noun phrase. This structure is more passive and can be used to shift the emphasis to the result, often used in discussions about the reasons behind the collapse or its consequences. While both structures communicate the same event, the choice between them can depend on the speaker's intent and the context in which they are used. The active voice is typically more direct and dynamic, while the nominalized form can provide a more detached or formal tone.

Transforming adjectives into nouns:

Original:	The speaker's clothes were appropriate.
Nominalized:	The appropriateness of the speaker's clothes.

Both sentences describe the same event but do so in different ways. The first version is an active sentence where *appropriate* acts as an adjective, focusing on the act of questioning if the clothes were suitable. In contrast, the second version uses nominalization, transforming the adjective *appropriate* into the noun *appropriateness*. This shift focuses on the idea of appropriateness itself, assessing whether the clothes fit the occasion. Nominalization makes the expression more concise and shifts the focus from the action to the underlying concepts. While both versions depict the same event, they highlight different aspects. The choice between these structures often depends on what the speaker wants to convey and the context in which they are used. The first version is direct and action-oriented, while the nominalized version takes a more abstract view, focusing on the outcome.

3.5.3 *Entrenchment*

In Cognitive Grammar, **entrenchment** refers to a concept that explains how certain linguistic structures become fixed in the mind and influence language processing. It highlights how repeated exposure to specific linguistic patterns can make them deeply rooted in our cognitive functions. This idea helps us understand why certain grammatical features stick around in a language, how language evolves over time, and why some elements are tougher to change than others. Entrenchment is a key concept that underscores the dynamic nature of language and its strong ties to cognitive processes. In syntax, entrenchment influences various aspects of language, including word order, irregular verb, prepositional usage, and phrasal verbs. It is closely linked to the prominence of syntactic structures, determining how often they appear in language use. For example, in English the active voice *She wrote the letter* is more salient and thus more entrenched than the passive voice *The letter was written*, which is why we hear it used more frequently.

Entrenchment is realized in grammar through syntactic patterns of concord and collocation.

3.5.3.1 Concord

One key area in syntax where entrenchment is particularly evident is **concord**. In English, concord mainly concerns number, which refers to the agreement between the subject and the verb, commonly known as **subject-verb agreement**. This grammatical rule dictates that the verb must align with the subject in both number and person. Entrenchment is vital here because it fosters the regular use of correct subject-verb combinations through consistent exposure and practice. As we become more accustomed to certain patterns, these combinations start to feel automatic, which helps minimize mistakes in subject-verb agreement. Moreover, getting a handle on subject-verb agreement is crucial for clarity, coherence, and accuracy in both our spoken and written communication. Subject-verb agreement is a key skill that ensures clear, smooth communication. Concord fosters harmony, and mastering its subtleties ensures effective communication.

Cognitive Grammar shows that language reflects thought. It sees subject-verb agreement not just as a set of strict rules but as a dynamic mental process. Instead of being a rigid framework, concord is viewed as a flexible system that helps express meaning. The concept of construal, which is akin to how we visualize things, plays a vital role in choosing between different ways to express the same idea. The fact that we have various grammatical options for describing a situation shows the different perspectives we can take on that situation. Construal sheds light on how we understand and articulate language, linking the structures we use with their meaningful interpretations. The meaning of any expression hinges on the conceptual content it evokes and the construal it imposes. One important construal that affects concord is the foreground-background concept, which is key to how we organize grammar. Here, the **foreground** refers to the focused element, while the **background** includes the less focused element.

The following are the main concord patterns, which reveals the intricate ways in which speakers navigate meaning and coherence.

Collective Nouns

In Cognitive Grammar, collective nouns are understood as symbolic units that profile a group as a single conceptual entity, even though that group is internally composed of multiple members. Collective nouns arise from the way we mentally construe a set of individuals as a unified whole. Instead of profiling each member separately, the noun profiles the collective entity. They serve as brief snapshots in language, capturing the essence of a group in just a single word. A collective noun's meaning is the conceptualization of many-as-one. For example, *flock* profiles the group of birds as one entity, not as many individual birds. A collective noun does not simply name a group; it encapsulates the mental process of treating multiplicity as unity. Collective nouns illustrate one of Cognitive Grammar's central insights: grammar reflects how we construe experience.

Examples of collective nouns:

- Collective nouns for people:

army:	a group of soldiers marching in unison
audience:	the attentive gathering at a concert or play
class:	students learning together in a classroom
committee:	a team working collaboratively on a task
family:	relatives bound by blood or affection
jury:	individuals deliberating in a court case
orchestra:	musicians playing harmoniously
team:	athletes competing as one unit

- Collective nouns for animals:

colony:	social insects like ants or bees
flock:	birds soaring together in the sky
herd:	grazing cattle or other animals
pack:	wolves hunting as a group
pod:	whales swimming side by side
swarm:	bees buzzing busily around their hive

- Collective nouns for things:

bunch:	grapes hanging from a vine
bundle:	sticks tied together
clump:	bushes growing closely
pair:	two matching objects
set:	a collection of related items
tack:	books neatly piled
quiver:	arrows held together

Individual Construal

Some collective nouns are interesting because they are often used in a way that focuses on individuals rather than the group as a whole. Even though they appear singular, they actually refer to multiple entities, which means they need a plural verb. For instance, when we talk about collective nouns like *army*, *people*, *police*, *orchestra*, *choir*, *herd*, *cattle*, *swine*, *fowl*, *poultry*, *flock*, *vermin*, and so forth, we are really thinking about the individuals within those groups.

The police are looking for him.

The cattle are grazing in the field.

Some nouns are made up of two main components, which is what makes them multiplex. You will usually find these nouns in their plural form, and they can be counted easily. Examples include *glasses*, *trousers*, and *surroundings*. There are two main categories of these nouns: (1) Tools that come in pairs, such as *glasses*, *headphones*, *pliers*, *scissors*, *tongs*, *tweezers*, *binoculars*, *goggles*, and *sunglasses*; (2) Clothing items that also consist of two parts, like *trousers*, *pajamas*, *jeans*, *shorts*, *pants*, *panties*, *boxers*, *briefs*, and *tights*.

My glasses have plastic frames.

Binoculars are commonly used.

His trousers need changing.

Her tights were extremely shiny.

Group Construal

Some collective nouns are interesting because they take on a plural form but are treated as a single unit, which means they require a singular verb. Unlike count nouns, these plural nouns cannot be counted with numbers. Here are some examples of this group construal: (1) Diseases that end in -s like *diabetes*, *measles*, *tuberculosis*, *shingles*, *mumps*, and so forth; (2) Games that also end in -s like *draughts*, *darts*, *snakes*, *ladders*, *billiards*, *bowls*, and others; (3) Countries and cities that finish with -s like *United Arab Emirates*, *United States*, *the Netherlands*, *Wales*, *Philippines*, *Brussels*, *Los Angeles*, *Athens*, *Texas*, *Kansas*, *Buenos Aires*, and so on; (4) Fields of study that end in -ics like *politics*, *mathematics*, *physics*, *electronics*, *statistics*, *economics*, *linguistics*, *phonetics*, *semantics*, and so forth; (5) Lastly, nouns like *news* and *whereabouts*, which are plural in form but singular in content, also take a singular verb.

Diabetes is a curable disease.

Mumps causes a swollen neck.

Draughts is an easy game.

Darts is an indoor game.

The Netherlands is a nice place to visit.

Brussels is the capital of Belgium.

Politics is a complicated business.

Physics is a branch of science.

The news is hard to believe.

His whereabouts is unknown.

One of the clearest reasons to consider a single entity as multiplex is that it consists of many different parts. Take *diseases*, for instance; they manifest various symptoms in the body. Or consider games, which are composed of multiple elements. Countries are comprised of individual states; fields of study encompass a variety of branches; and news is made up of several different stories.

Dual Construal

Some collective nouns can emphasize either the group as a whole or its individual members. Depending on the context, certain collective nouns can act both singularly and plurally. For instance, collective nouns can be viewed as plural when the focus is on the individual members of the group acting on their own. It is crucial to pay attention to the context to figure out if a collective noun should be seen as singular or plural. The choice between singular and plural forms depends on the overall meaning of the sentence and the situation in which it is used. Collective nouns create a fascinating dance between unity and diversity, with examples like *team*, *family*, *jury*, *shoal*, *government*, *class*, *committee*, and so on. Essentially, Cognitive Grammar helps us understand how collective nouns function by clarifying their singular and plural interpretations. It highlights the importance of semantics and usage-based analysis, revealing some really interesting patterns in language.

The committee has reached a final decision.

The committee have expressed different opinions.

In the examples mentioned above, the noun *committee* acts as a collective entity, but it can be interpreted in different ways. The key difference lies in how we understand the noun and the context in which it is used. In the first sentence, the focus is on the committee as a single unit, while the individual members take a backseat. This suggests that the committee, viewed as a unified group, has reached a decision, implying that there's a consensus among its members. This can be seen in the use of the singular auxiliary *has*, which presents the committee as a cohesive whole. An example context would be: *After careful consideration, the committee decided to approve the budget proposal.* On the other hand, the second sentence highlights the individual members, putting the committee itself in the background. Here, it suggests that each member has their own opinion, showcasing the variety of viewpoints within the committee. The plural auxiliary *have* is used, emphasizing the individual perspectives. An example context would be: *During the meeting, committee members shared their thoughts, revealing differing perspectives on the issue.*

3.5.3.2 Collocation

Another key area in syntax where entrenchment really shines is **collocation.** This refers to the common and conventional pairing of words that tend to show up together in everyday language. These word combinations become entrenched in a speaker's mental dictionary through repeated use, much like *strong coffee.* Because of this entrenchment, they are easier and quicker to recall since they are stored as fixed units in our minds, which helps us communicate more fluently and efficiently. In Cognitive Grammar, collocations are viewed as meaningful units that reflect how speakers conceptualize and categorize their experiences. They are part of the broader web of linguistic knowledge that encompass both lexical and grammatical information. Collocations are not just random combinations of words but meaningful units that help express specific ideas and nuances. This viewpoint emphasizes the lively nature of language and the cognitive processes at play when we use it. Understanding entrenched patterns is key to grasping language's subtleties.

In Cognitive Grammar, collocations are viewed as established patterns of language that often carry meanings shaped by context, extending beyond just the individual words. They are essential for expressing those subtle nuances and cultural hints that make communication truly effective. Take, for example, the noun-noun pair *data analysis*, which refers to the process of examining data sets to draw conclusions. The way *data* and *analysis* come together creates a specific, meaningful term that is widely used in areas like statistics, research, and business. Similarly, the adjective-noun phrase *heavy rain* describes a large amount of rainfall. Here, the word *heavy* amplifies the noun *rain*, suggesting a significant downpour. These examples highlight how collocations convey meanings beyond individual words, communicating ideas and nuances vital for interaction. Alone, words lack weight; combined, they convey subtle meaning.

Patterns

Collocation patterns that become entrenched are those that we often hear together in everyday language. These patterns settle into a speaker's mental lexicon through consistent exposure and usage. Some typical types of collocation patterns that become entrenched include:

Noun + noun collocations:
Noun-noun collocations are cognitive units that become second nature through frequent use. These established patterns make communication smoother, allowing us to recall common phrases effortlessly, almost without thinking. When we come across familiar expressions, our brains automatically retrieve them. Certain nouns tend to pair with specific nouns, creating collocations where one noun enhances the meaning of the other. This habitual pairing influences how we perceive and describe objects and ideas. These combinations, shaped by repeated use and context, become so ingrained that changing them can be quite difficult. Here are a few examples of common noun-noun combinations found in English:

traffic jam	climate change	water bottle	book club
health care	job market	coffee shop	fire alarm
credit card	income tax		

Adjective + noun collocations:
Adjective-noun collocations are like mental shortcuts that we have developed over time through regular use. These familiar patterns make it easier for us to communicate, as we can recall common phrases almost automatically. When we encounter these well-known expressions, our brains pull them up without us even thinking about it. Certain adjectives tend to pair up with specific nouns, creating collocations that enhance the meaning of the noun. This habitual pairing shapes the way we perceive and describe objects and ideas. Because of their frequent use and the context in which we encounter them, these combinations become so ingrained in our minds that they are tough to change. Here are a few examples of frequently used adjective-noun combinations in English:

bright future	deep sleep	cold weather	fast car
happy ending	narrow escape	quick response	loud noise
heavy traffic	sharp contrast		

Verb + noun collocations:
Verb-noun collocations are like mental shortcuts we have developed over time through constant use. These familiar patterns make it easier for us to communicate, allowing us to recall common phrases without even thinking about it. When we hear expressions that we know well, our brains automatically retrieve them. Some verbs naturally pair with certain nouns, creating collocations that enhance the meaning of the noun. This consistent

pairing influences how we see and talk about things. These combinations, established through frequent use and the context in which we encounter them, become second nature and can be difficult to change. Here are a few examples of popular verb-noun combinations in English:

make a decision	take a break	give advice	pay attention
save money	take a risk	keep a promise	break a record
hold a meeting	raise a question		

Entrenchment in collocations has several key implications. To start, these entrenched collocations allow speakers to express themselves more fluently and efficiently. Because these word combinations are deeply ingrained in our language, they can be recalled and used effortlessly. Next, entrenched collocations create predictable patterns in language, making it easier for listeners to anticipate and grasp messages. This predictability boosts communication by reducing the mental effort required to process language. Additionally, entrenched collocations reveal how our brains handle and store language. Repeated exposure to word combinations enables automatic recall, underscoring usage-based learning in Cognitive Grammar. Moreover, entrenched collocations help maintain the stability of language by establishing conventional patterns that resist change. However, they can also evolve over time as new collocations gain acceptance through frequent use. Finally, grasping and using entrenched collocations can significantly improve a language user's ability to communicate naturally and precisely.

3.5.4 Coercion

In Cognitive Grammar, **coercion** occurs when we reinterpret mismatches between a selector and its element. It adjusts a phrase's meaning when its semantic parts do not fully align. The selector is a linguistic unit that requires a specific type of complement, while the selected element is the complement chosen to meet that need. When the two do not match, speakers may reinterpret the selected element to fit the situation. Coercion thus tweaks meaning so one linguistic element meshes with another, reshaping grammatical structure to convey a specific sense. It highlights how language flexes to express subtle meanings. Such reinterpretation shows how grammar adapts in real time, ensuring communication remains fluid and coherent. For instance, consider the following sentences:

I began the book.
She took a shower.
She ran a marathon.

In the first sentence: *I began* functions as the selector (or verb), typically requiring an action as its complement. *The book* is the selected element, designating a noun phrase, not an event. To resolve this mismatch, we perform coercion by reinterpreting *the book* as referring to the event of starting to read the *book*. Coercion transforms *the book* from a simple noun phrase into an event involving that noun. As a result, the sentence is interpreted to mean either *I began reading the book* or *I began writing the book*. In the second sentence, the verb *took* usually implies an action of acquiring or receiving something tangible. However, in this context, *a shower* is not a physical object to be taken. Through coercion, the phrase is understood as *She showered*, where *a shower* is interpreted as an event or activity rather than a physical object. In the third sentence, the noun *marathon* is typically associated with a physical distance, but in this case, it is coerced to represent the event itself. These examples of coercion reflect lexical flexibility, which enables speakers to convey nuance, adapt language, and enhance expressiveness.

Traditional theories of grammar often focus on sense enumeration, listing each verb sense separately. However, this misses language's fluid, context-sensitive nature. Cognitive Grammar, on the other hand, allows the same lexical construction to interact with multiple argument structures, yielding varied meanings without long verb lists. Coercion plays a key role here, allowing us to adjust the meanings of words to keep things grammatically correct and coherent. This shows how language users creatively adjust their expressions to fit the context, even when there is a semantic mismatch. A classic example of coercion is noun-verb coercion, where a word shifts its grammatical role based on the context. This happens when a word usually linked to one grammatical category like a noun is used in a situation that requires it to act as another category like a verb. In Cognitive Grammar, grammar is a problem-solving tool that evolves to convey meaning, rather than merely a set of rules. For instance, take a look at the following nouns:

Google
Facebook

Originally, the term *Google* refers to the popular search engine or the company itself. Interestingly, it can also be turned into a verb, as in *I'll Google that information*. In this case, *Google* acts as a verb, meaning to search for information using the Google search engine. The noun has been coerced into a verb role. Similarly, the word *Facebook* originally denotes the social media platform. It can also be used as a verb, as in *She Facebooked the event details*. Here, *Facebook* is functioning as a verb, indicating the action of posting or interacting on the platform. Once again, the noun has taken on a new role. These examples illustrate how nouns can shift into different roles depending on the context. Cognitive Grammar supports this kind of flexibility, highlighting the relationship between meaning and usage. Coercion enables us to adapt words to express our intended meaning more precisely.

3.5.5 Zone Activation

In Cognitive Grammar, **zone activation** highlights specific aspects of a conceptual domain to clarify an expression. Language often deals with linguistic underdetermination, which occurs when our linguistic representations are fuzzy, unclear, or not specific enough, leading to a less complete or vague understanding. This idea of linguistic underdetermination emphasizes that language is dynamic and changes with context. To explain how this linguistic imprecision occurs, Cognitive Grammar introduces the concept of the **active zone**. This is essentially the most prominent or active part of a concept in a given context, allowing us to grasp the overall situation even without the full picture. It demonstrates how certain parts of a concept stand out during communication, shaping our understanding of language. When it comes to nouns, the active zone points to the specific part of the noun directly involved in a relationship or action, often vaguely defined. This concept of the active zone clarifies how different aspects of a noun can be emphasized based on the context, influencing how meaning is constructed and understood in language. The sentences provided illustrate active zones in action:

The cat scratched the door.
The dog barked at the stranger.
The bird built a cozy nest.
The chef chopped the vegetables.
The student solved the math problem.

The sentences showcase active zones, highlighting the relevant parts of a concept in a specific context. Understanding active zones helps us focus on particular elements of a concept during communication. For instance, in the first sentence, the noun is *the cat*, but the active zone is its claws, since they play a key role in the action of scratching. In the second sentence, we have *the dog* as the noun, with the active zone being its mouth or vocal cords, which are responsible for producing the bark. Moving to the third sentence, *the bird* is the noun, while the active zone is its beak or claws, which it uses to build the nest. In the fourth sentence, the noun is *the chef*, and the active zone is the chef's hands or knife, which are crucial for chopping. Finally, in the fifth sentence, *the student* is the noun, and the active zone is the student's brain or mind, which is engaged in solving the math problem.

As the examples show, active zones mark the part of a noun involved in an action or relation.

Summary

In this chapter, I have delved into the conceptual category of **things**, represented by the grammatical category of **nouns**. Instead of adhering strictly to rules, nouns are explored based on their meanings. Nouns are not thought of as rigid labels, but as flexible tools that we shape through our experiences. They play a vital role in how we understand and interpret the world around us. Nouns can be divided into two main categories: divisible objects and indivisible substances. Count nouns refer to things we can count, while noncount nouns represent things that feel like an uncountable mass. Research shows that nouns go through three key cognitive processes: categorization, configuration, and conceptualization. In the categorization process, nouns can have multiple meanings that center around typical examples, leading to only slight differences in meaning. When it comes to configuration, nouns that express the same idea can create domains, each representing different aspects and roles within the language. Finally, in conceptualization, nouns that appear alike can hold distinct meanings, giving them unique roles in communication.

Nouns are fascinating because they showcase five key linguistic features: reification, nominalization, entrenchment, coercion, and zone activation. Reification is all about treating an abstract noun as if it were something solid and real. Then there is nominalization, which is the process of turning other parts of speech like verbs or adjectives into nouns. Entrenchment happens when certain linguistic patterns become so familiar that they are ingrained in our minds through constant use. Coercion refers to the way we might tweak the meaning of a word to keep everything in a sentence consistent. Lastly, zone activation is about bringing a specific aspect of a concept to the forefront for clearer and more meaningful communication. These features really highlight how dynamic nouns can be, showing their ability to adapt to various linguistic and cognitive situations. Grasping these aspects reveals how language influences thinking and communication.

Exercises

1. Classify each noun as (1) count, (2) mass, or (3) both. Check a dictionary if unsure.

1. love
2. show

3. position
4. character
5. literature

2. Give the appropriate collective nouns for the following collections of people, animals, and things.

1. a group of soldiers
2. a collection of bees
3. a group of deer
4. a number of cards
5. a number of thieves

3. These nouns can be countable or uncountable. Write sentence pairs to show both uses.

1. art
2. hair
3. light
4. room
5. sleep

4. The nouns given below exhibit multiplicity of meaning. Sketch out the semantic network for each.

1. eye
2. ball
3. fruit
4. table
5. mouth

5. The nouns below evoke the domain of leisure, each highlighting a distinct facet. What is it?

1. hobby
2. pastime
3. recreation
4. avocation
5. diversion

6. The nouns below differ semantically by the construal dimension noted in brackets. Discuss.

1. illness versus disease (specificity)
2. coast versus shore (vantage point)
3. delusion versus illusion (subjectivity-objectivity)
4. specimen versus sample (scope)
5. whole versus entire (foreground-background)

7. Convert the following verbs and adjectives into nouns, and give one example sentence for each.

1. calm
2. create
3. analyze

4. achieve
5. productive

8. Select the appropriate alternative (is or are) in each of the following sentences to ensure proper concord.

1. Draughts is/are an easy game.
2. Fifty kilos is/are a heavy weight.
3. The scissors is/are brand new.
4. A number of students is/are late.
5. One of my friends is/are absent.

9. Account for the ungrammaticality of the following sentences in terms of concord.

1. *One of my friends are here.
2. *The number of students are increasing.
3. *Learning foreign languages are difficult.
4. *Arsenal is playing well today.
5. *Eighty miles are a long way.

10. Show how the nouns below can be coerced into verbs, changing their grammatical function.

1. Email
2. Text
3. Tweet
4. Podcast
5. Zoom

4

Noun Phrases

4.1 Introduction

In Chapter 3, I discussed the conceptual category of **things**, conveyed through the grammatical category of **nouns**. In this chapter, I examine the conceptual category of **nominal expressions**, which denote predications about entities and are realized through the grammatical category of **noun phrases**. A **noun phrase** is a group of words acting as a noun, enabling more complex and varied sentences. A noun phrase unites words into a symbolic unit, profiling a specific concept within a larger context. Noun phrases are not merely formal units; they are conceptual groupings that reflect how we mentally organize experience. For example, the phrase *red balloon* profiles a particular object within the domain of balloons. Modifiers such as adjectives or prepositional phrases are mentally integrated with the head noun to form a unified concept. In this example, *balloon* and *red* are not just adjacent words; they are cognitively fused to represent a *red balloon*. Noun phrases are bundles of meaning that our minds assemble based on experience, context, and structure. In essence, nouns are language's backbone, with noun phrases enhancing its flow.

4.2 Nominal Expressions

In Cognitive Grammar, **nominal expressions** designate thing predications, that is, entities construed as stable and non-processual, and are encoded in grammar as **noun phrases**. A noun phrase is a language structure built around a noun (or pronoun) as its head, with modifiers adding detail. For example, in the phrase *small school*, the adjective *small* adds a descriptive touch to the head noun *school*. Cognitive Grammar emphasizes that the construction of a noun phrase reflects our cognitive processes and how we conceptualize things. Each part of a noun phrase plays a role in shaping its overall meaning. In the phrase *small school*, the word *small* conveys descriptive qualities, while *school* indicates the subject of discussion. At its core, a noun phrase typically focuses on a noun, serving as its head. This **head** noun is the key element in a noun phrase that determines its grammatical characteristics. Therefore, in *small school*, *school* functions as the head. From a cognitive viewpoint, noun phrases go beyond grammar, conveying semantic value and reflecting conceptualizations. They link form with meaning by combining nouns with modifiers.

The formation of a noun phrase occurs through a process known as instantiation. In Cognitive Grammar, **instantiation** refers to the translation of abstract linguistic structures into specific instances of language use. It involves transforming a broad concept into something specific. For example, the word *book* represents a general idea, but when we say *this book*, we are referring to a specific one. Understanding instantiation is crucial for comprehending how individuals create and interpret specific expressions based on broader patterns or schemas. It also enables us to recognize the diversity in language usage, as it pertains to the actual application of a linguistic expression within a particular context. Consider the word *cool*, for example. In one scenario, it may describe the temperature, like saying *It is cool outside*, while in another situation, it could characterize someone's personality, as in *He is a cool guy*. New experiences create fresh instantiations, which propel the adaptation of language. Instantiation also involves grounding, where a noun or clause is linked to a specific context or situation.

4.3 Grounding

In Cognitive Grammar, **grounding** is the process by which speakers provide information about what happened, when it happened, and who was involved. Grounding is accomplished through specific elements that help the speaker turn a general idea into specific instances that the listener can recognize. It creates a link between the highlighted entity or action and the surrounding context, including the speech event and participants. Grounding can be divided into two main types: nominal and clausal. **Nominal grounding** directs the listener's focus to a discourse referent using determiners, quantifiers, and modifiers. **Clausal grounding** sets event timing through tense and modal verbs. A grounding element clarifies the context of what a noun describes or what a verb conveys. For example, the word *car* is ungrounded, referring to a general category. With grounding elements like articles or demonstratives, as in the car, *this car*, the speaker directs the listener to a specific referent. Similarly, adding a tense marker to a verb grounds a situation in either the present or the past, as seen in *She goes/went home*.

4.3.1 *Nominal Grounding*

Nominal grounding refers to how a noun phrase connects to its context, which includes the speech event, the people involved, and the surrounding situation. This connection is made through grounding elements like possessive pronouns, articles, demonstratives, quantifiers, partitives, and modifiers. These elements are essential for making clear, fundamental specifications about what we know. They are definite, meaning they help pinpoint the exact referent, regardless of what the phrase itself says. Each grounding element has its own unique role that sets it apart from the others. Nominal grounding deals with identification questions, particularly how well participants can identify the thing being referred to in the real world. For instance, the word *car* is a noun that identifies a general type of object, while *the car* is a noun phrase that grounds it in reality with the article *the*, pointing to a specific instance of that type. It refers to one particular *car* among many. The key difference here is that a noun simply names a type, whereas a noun phrase goes further by designating a specific, grounded instance of that type.

4.3.2 *Nominal Grounding Elements*

The building blocks for noun phrases in English are the grammatical markers known as determiners and modifiers. Determiners include possessives, demonstratives, articles, quantifiers, and partitives. Possessives indicate ownership. Demonstratives point out where something is in space or time. Articles help specify which noun we are talking about. Quantifiers tell us how much of a noun there is, often in a nonspecific way. Partitives refer to a portion of a noun rather than the whole thing. Demonstratives and the definite article act as **deictic expressions**, which are like linguistic signposts that draw our attention to specific things around us. On the other hand, modifiers are the descriptive words that add extra detail about nouns. While determiners give us specific information, modifiers enrich the overall meaning of a sentence. In Cognitive Grammar, these nominal grounding elements are essential for helping us understand noun phrases. They serve as guides through the intricate world of language, making communication clearer and richer.

4.3.2.1 Possessives

Possessive pronouns are handy little words we use to show ownership or possession. They step in to replace nouns, making it easier to talk about who owns what without repeating the same names over and over. In English, some common possessive pronouns are *my*, *mine*, *your*, *yours*, *his*, *her*, *hers*, *its*, *our*, *ours*, *their*, and *theirs*. Some of these pronouns act like adjectives and modify nouns, such as *my*, *your*, *his*, *her*, *our*, and *their*. Others work more like nouns themselves, including *mine*, *yours*, *his*, *hers*, *ours*, and *theirs*. Unlike possessive forms that use an apostrophe, like *John's book*, possessive pronouns do not need one. Formal grammar models view possessive pronouns as determiners that modify nouns. For example, in the phrase *his book*, *his* is the possessive pronoun modifying the noun *book*. These models dive into the structures and transformations of syntax. On the other hand, Cognitive Grammar sees possessive pronouns as symbolic units that illustrate conceptual relationships. They capture cognitive categories like ownership or possession, whether tangible or abstract. For instance, *his book* shows ownership in a concrete way, while *our project* conveys ownership in a more abstract sense.

To understand the bond between an owner and what they own, Cognitive Grammar uses the **reference point** theory to break down possessive pronouns. This theory is a fascinating concept in Cognitive Grammar that shows how we mentally shift our focus from one thing (the anchor) to another (the profile determinant). This mental scanning is key to forming relationships and expressing meaning. In possessive phrases, the reference point theory is essential for understanding the connections between the possessor and the item being possessed. Take the phrase *his book*, for instance. Here, *his* is the possessive pronoun. The reference point is the owner (the person), while the profile determinant is the item in question (the book). When we say *his book*, our mental journey begins with the owner and moves to the book. The possessive pronoun acts as a link between these two. Similarly, in *her idea*, the pronoun *her* forges a connection between the owner (the person) and the idea (the profile determinant). All in all, the reference point theory sheds light on how possessive pronouns forge meaningful ties between entities, highlighting aspects like ownership, association, or control.

Possessive pronouns versus of-phrases:

Possession can be expressed in two ways: through possessive pronouns or through of-phrase structures. In Cognitive Grammar, the distinction between these two methods relies on the concepts of prominence and reference points. **Prominence**, in this context, refers to the importance or visibility of specific elements within a sentence. This concept helps us understand how different parts of a sentence relate to each other and which ones are essential for conveying meaning. The influence of prominence can appear in word choice, order, and intonation. For example, *vital* carries more weight than *important*. Fronting emphasizes as in *Justice we demand, not charity*. Lengthening or loudness highlights syllables, as in *This is CRItical*. As the examples show, the highlighted element draws the listener's or reader's attention most. On the other hand, a **reference point** is an entity that helps us clearly identify or find another specific entity. This idea is important for understanding how different parts of a sentence are connected. By using reference points, we can make sense of new information by linking it to things we already know, which improves our understanding of ownership and relationships.

This is her book.

This is the book of hers.

Both sentences clearly indicate ownership or association. The choice between them often depends on how formal the situation is and what you want to emphasize, the possessor or the item being possessed. In Cognitive Grammar, the first sentence is straightforward and highlights the prominence of the possessor, *her*. It uses *her* as the primary reference point to identify the book, making *her* the focal point of the sentence. On the other hand, the second sentence uses an of-phrase to convey possession. Here, the *book* is the main focus, with *hers* providing additional details about ownership. *Hers* serves as a reference point to specify who owns the book. This manner of expression may come across as more formal and indirect, prioritizing the *book* before linking it back to the owner. Cognitive Grammar shows how structures shape focus and the possessor-item relationship. The choice between structures depends on context and desired emphasis. Grasping these nuances helps craft sentences that convey meaning accurately across contexts.

4.3.2.2 Articles

Cognitive Grammar highlights how articles establish reference by defining entities. Articles build shared context, improving communication. Articles link to conceptual categories, showing how speakers classify and think about referents. Definite articles come from more specific ideas, while indefinite articles stem from broader concepts. They are essential for expressing both specificity and generality in our language. Furthermore, articles aid in conveying precision, contributing to the coherence of discourse and clarity in context. Essentially, articles are more than just grammatical tools; they influence our cognitive processes, facilitate communication, and connect specificity with generality in language. The choice of which article to use is influenced by cognitive factors, the context, and the speaker's intent. Articles exist on a conceptual continuum, where specificity and generality play a key role in shaping how we communicate. The definite article points to specific referents, while the indefinite article allows for wider interpretation.

In Cognitive Grammar, articles play a significant role in shaping language and facilitating effective communication.

In symbolic representation, articles involve both phonological (sound) and semantic (meaning) aspects. Take the definite article *the*, for instance. It has both a phonological side (the sound *the*) and a semantic side (which conveys a sense of specificity or familiarity). In terms of effective communication, articles serve several important functions. First is definiteness. The definite article *the* points to a specific referent that is already known or particular in the context, helping to clarify any confusion, as in the sentence *Bring me the book on the table*. Next is indefiniteness. The indefinite articles *a* and *an* introduce something nonspecific or general, as in *I need a pen*. Articles can also indicate a generic reference, referring to an entire class or category, as in *The tiger is an endangered species*. Additionally, articles can suggest uniqueness, as in *He's the best chef in town*. Lastly, articles aid in maintaining coherence in conversation by referring back to previously mentioned things, as in *She saw a cat. The cat climbed a tree.*

In Cognitive Grammar, articles vary in semantic generality or specificity, shaping how we organize and express information from broad to detailed experience. **Schematicity** refers to the general level associated with an expression, typically indicated by the article *a*. On the other hand, **specificity** pertains to the level of detail in an expression, usually signaled by the article *the*. Depending on how a speaker chooses to describe a situation, they can opt for either a general or detailed approach, which ultimately affects the conveyed meaning. A general description pays little attention to detail, while a detailed description focuses heavily on the finer points. Schematicity involves a more abstract way of representing information, offering less detail and a simpler overview. Specificity, in contrast, is linked to a more concrete representation, providing richer information and a more intricate description. Consequently, the same situation can be shown with different detail, each adding its own meaning.

The Definite Article

In Cognitive Grammar, the definite article *the* is seen as a key player in how we create meaning in language. It falls under the dimension of specificity in construal phenomena. **Construal** refers to the different ways we can present ideas. **Specificity** is about how detailed or granular we get with our expressions, helping us understand situations with clarity. The definite article emphasizes how much detail we provide about a situation or entity, and it is an essential part of the conventional meaning within a symbolic structure, shaping how we convey content in a precise way. When we use *the*, we are pointing to a specific instance of a noun. Cognitive Grammar views *the* as a linguistic tool that aids in cognitive tasks like reference, attention, shared knowledge, and categorization, making it vital for clear communication and understanding. Moreover, it highlights the speaker's intention to single out one entity from a broader set. In this way, *the* not only marks definiteness but also guides interpretation by narrowing the listener's focus.

The definite article *the* signals specificity under certain conditions, as illustrated in the following examples.

- Unique entities. The definite article is used for objects that are one of a kind or have no substitutes. In *The Earth orbits the Sun*, the definite article refers to unique, one-of-a-kind entities in our solar system.
- Previous mention. The definite article helps indicate that the noun it is paired with refers to something that has already been talked about. In *I bought a new book. The book is really interesting*, the definite article refers to the specific book that has already been mentioned.
- Shared knowledge. The definite article is also handy for pinpointing a specific item or group that both the speaker and listener are familiar with. In *Can you pass me the salt?*, both interlocutors know which specific salt is being referred to, likely the one on the table.
- Superlative forms. The definite article is used before superlatives, as in *She is the best singer in the choir*. This is because the superlative form implies a specific noun that is being compared to others.
- Ordinal numbers. The definite article is used with ordinal numbers, as in *This is the first time I have ridden a horse* because ordinal numbers used as adjectives imply the ordering is unique and definite.
- Category designation. The definite article is used before adjectives to refer to a group of people sharing a particular characteristic like the poor, the rich, the wealthy, the young, the old, the elderly, the gifted, the weak, and so forth, as in *The rich enjoy lavish lives.*
- Specific geographical features. The definite article is used with specific geographical features like rivers, oceans, mountain ranges, and so on, as in *They sailed across the Pacific Ocean.*
- Historical or cultural references. The definite article is used to refer to specific historical events, periods, or cultural phenomena, as in *I love reading about the Middle Ages.*
- Musical instruments. When talking about a musical instrument, the definite article is placed before the name of the instrument, as in *He plays the guitar very well.*
- Nationality names. The definite article is used before adjectives to refer to a collection of individuals having a certain trait in common, as in *The English like football.*

The Indefinite Articles

In Cognitive Grammar, the indefinite articles *a* and *an* play a key role in how we categorize nouns. These articles are linked to the concept of schematicity in construal phenomena, which is all about the various ways we can think about and represent a situation. While specificity zooms in on particular details and exact characteristics, schematicity takes a step back to look at broader patterns and high-level ideas. They give us a general sense without diving into the nitty-gritty. Indefinite articles indicate schematicity, letting us know that we're not talking about any specific item in a category, but rather a general one. Cognitive Grammar sees these articles as essential tools for introducing, categorizing, and generalizing nouns, which helps shape the meaning and structure of language in a clear and organized way. They support our cognitive processes of reference, categorization, and conceptualization, making them crucial for effective communication.

The indefinite article *a* and *an* signal schematicity under certain conditions, as illustrated in the following examples.

- Introducing new entities. Indefinite articles come into play when we want to bring up new entities or concepts for the first time in a conversation or text. For example, in *I saw a star last night*, the indefinite article helps to introduce a star that the listener or reader has not heard about before.
- Making generalizations. Indefinite articles are also handy for making broad statements about a category or class of items. Take the phrase *A dog is a loyal pet*; here, the indefinite article is used to talk about the general traits of dogs, rather than pointing to a specific dog.
- Nonspecific references. We often use indefinite articles when discussing a profession or occupation, which suggests belonging to a group rather than singling out an individual. For instance, in *She is a lawyer*, the indefinite article indicates that she is part of the lawyer category, not referring to a specific lawyer.
- Quantity expressions. Indefinite articles come into play with quantity expressions to generalize a noun, meaning it can refer to any member of a group. This emphasizes that the noun is not unique or easily identifiable. For example, in the phrase *Can I have a piece of cake?*, the term *a piece of* refers to just one portion of the cake.
- Singular reference. Indefinite articles are also used to introduce a single, unspecified item from a larger group. This makes it clear that the noun is just one example within a wider category. For instance, in *A student raised their hand*, the indefinite article shows that one student, among possibly many, raised their hand.

Instantiating Reference

In Cognitive Grammar, **reference** is the process by which language users identify and track entities in discourse. It is not just about pointing to a physical object; it also involves conjuring a mental image that includes various attributes and contexts associated with that entity. Reference can be construed in terms of specificity or genericity. **Specific reference** focuses on exact instances or particular individuals, while **generic reference** encompasses broader categories without delving into specifics. For example, definite noun phrases are part of specific reference. They point to something specific and identifiable in a given context. For example, in *The ring is expensive*, the article *the* points to a specific ring, ensuring clarity and directing attention to that particular instance. In contrast, indefinite noun phrases fall under generic reference. They refer to more general and inclusive concepts. For example, in *Rings are expensive*, the phrase is indefinite, referring to rings in general rather than to a specific one. Balancing specificity and generality enhances clarity in expressing ideas.

In Cognitive Grammar, the choices we make in language reveal a lot about how we see and talk about the world around us. When we use specific references, we are tapping into our personal experiences, pointing to something that is clear and identifiable. This happens when a noun phrase refers to a specific entity or group of entities that both the speaker and listener can easily recognize. On the other hand, generic references connect us to shared human experiences by using broader ideas without diving into the specifics of individual cases. This typically occurs when a noun phrase refers to an entire class or category of entities instead of a single instance. Understanding this difference more fully helps us grasp how language users share various types of information and how listeners interpret these references based on the surrounding context.

Compare the following sentences and notice how varying structures convey unique meanings:

A cow is a domestic animal.

The cow is a domestic animal.

Cows are domestic animals.

The sentences above all share the idea that cows are domestic animals, but they differ along the spectrum of references, each offering a distinct perspective. The first sentence talks about a single cow, using the indefinite article *a* before the noun. This establishes a general truth or universal statement about cows, emphasizing the category instead of focusing on any specific individual. This is a generic single reference. The second sentence employs the definite article *the* before the noun *cow*, pointing to a specific cow without naming it outright. This implies that there is a particular cow in mind, perhaps one that has been mentioned before or is understood from the context. This is a generalized specific reference. Lastly, the third sentence uses the plural form *cows* without any article, making a broad statement about all cows as a group. This is a generic plural reference.

4.3.2.3 Demonstratives

Cognitive Grammar views demonstratives as essential components of human language, going beyond mere linguistic markers. These demonstratives are powerful tools that help us establish shared attention, shape our language, and communicate effectively. Whether they refer to something close by or far away, demonstratives significantly influence how we understand language. They act as a bridge between the form of language and its meaning, directing our focus to specific entities in our shared surroundings. Characterized as deixis, demonstratives assist in navigating both space and time. They help coordinate attention between speakers, creating a common ground for understanding. **Deixis** involves using words or phrases to point out specific times, places, or people within a particular context. Demonstratives, as deictic expressions, anchor entities to context or highlight specific elements within a situation. They serve as signposts for clear communication.

Deictic Anchoring

Demonstratives can be understood through two distinct anchors: deictic (gestural) and conceptual (non-gestural). Both types play a vital role in our communication, helping us express meaning more clearly, fostering connections, and navigating the intricacies of language.

Gestural Use

A gestural use of demonstratives involves physical pointing or perceptual presence, that is, the visible movements we make with our hands and bodies when we communicate. For instance, when we use a demonstrative along with a gesture, it helps point out a specific object or location. Gestures really anchor our language in context, making it easier to clarify what we are talking about, the relationships between things, and the actions involved. Demonstratives, as gestures, can show how close something is, helping to identify where things are in relation to the speaker or other references. For example, *this* refers to something nearby or relevant to the current situation, while *these* is just the plural of *this*, also pointing to things close by. On the other hand, *that* is used for something that is not too close, and *those* is the plural form of *that*, referring to things that are further away. Demonstratives show where nouns are located and how close they are, ensuring clarity. They clarify context and positions relative to speaker and listener.

This is a nice cup of tea.

These are beautiful flowers.

Look at that mountain.

I like those shoes in the display window.

Non-Gestural Use

A non-gestural use of demonstratives involves communicating meaning through language without relying on any physical gestures. Rather, it involves relying on shared knowledge or discourse context. It enables us to articulate abstract ideas, relationships, and meanings using just words, helping us connect our thoughts with the outside world. This happens when we use demonstratives without accompanying gestures, depending instead on our shared understanding or context to pinpoint what we're talking about. In this context, we can identify two distinct uses.

One general use of demonstratives is to talk about time, especially when we want to highlight the difference between the present and the past. For instance, we often use near demonstratives like *this* and *these* to point to things happening right now, while far demonstratives like *that* and *those* usually refer to things from the past. These temporal demonstratives are really helpful in placing events or time periods, making it clear whether we are discussing the present, something that just happened, or events from long ago, much like how they indicate physical closeness. In this way, demonstratives act as cognitive anchors, situating experiences within a temporal framework.

This summer is going to be busy.

These are difficult times in life.

That happened longer ago.

Those were my greatest days.

Another non-gestural function of demonstratives is their use as discourse connectors. They play a crucial role in steering the conversation and ensuring it flows more smoothly. By referring back to points made earlier, they help keep everything connected. Additionally, they can signal when entirely new information is coming into play. Demonstratives also highlight specific sections of the conversation or text. By linking various parts of the discussion, they foster a stronger sense of cohesion and connectedness. This makes it much easier for listeners or readers to understand exactly which part of the conversation is being referenced, allowing them to follow along effortlessly.

This is the main point.	(referring to an idea mentioned earlier)
These are the steps to follow.	(introducing new information)
This is what I mean.	(drawing attention to a specific detail)
These are the reasons why.	(summarizing previously mentioned points)
Those were the days.	(indicating a specific time period)

To further clarify, let's compare the following sentences to illustrate the difference in meaning.

This coffee shop is restful.

This city is wonderful.

Both sentences use the demonstrative *this*, but they convey different meanings. In the first sentence, *this* is used in a gestural way. The speaker can actually point to the coffee shop and make eye contact with it. Here, the meaning is tied to the physical context of the conversation. Gestural demonstratives rely on physical movements or gestures that act as pointers in communication, helping to indicate specific things or places right in front of us. In contrast, the second sentence uses *this* in a non-gestural way. The speaker knows where the location is, and there is no need for any pointing to understand it. In this case, the meaning comes from a general understanding of the situation rather than a specific gesture. Symbolic demonstratives go further than just pointing; they are defined by their roles in communication, which can include a variety of functions like iconic and metaphoric gestures.

4.3.2.4 Quantifiers

In Cognitive Grammar, quantifiers are essential for our understanding of language. They act as symbolic structures with two sides: a phonological side, which is how they appear in writing, and a semantic side, which defines their meaning. Quantifiers can be thought of as linguistic tools in our cognitive toolbox that help us convey complex ideas and shape our comprehension of statements. What is intriguing is that quantifiers are not fixed; they change depending on context and personal preferences, adjusting to what is relevant or expected in a given situation. They also do not exist independently; they interact with other linguistic elements to convey specific meanings. In communication, quantifiers allow us to express various degrees, amounts, or extents, providing insights into quantity, scope, and specificity. Like other language components, quantifiers are influenced by how we use them in everyday communication. Cognitive Grammar views them as dynamic, usage-based phenomena linked to cognitive processes and language perception.

In Cognitive Grammar, quantifiers are utilized through construal operations that link our conceptual ideas to the words we use. Terms like *all*, *some*, *many*, and *few* are connected to the concept of scope in our understanding of these ideas. **Scope** refers to the amount of conceptual content an expression brings to mind, which is crucial to its meaning. Construal is essential here, as it demonstrates how we interpret and present our ideas. When considering the scope of a quantifier, we examine how it influences a sentence and which parts it applies to. Our choice of scope can alter our perception of quantity, degree, or extent, and the quantifier we select reflects our understanding of the scope and distribution of entities. For example, using the quantifier *all* suggests we view a group of entities as a complete set, while *some* indicates we are focusing on a portion of that group. Quantifiers extend beyond numbers, shaping conversations and arguments. The way we construe them influences how we reason about quantities in language.

The Domain of Quantification

Quantifiers evoke the domain of **quantification**, which underlies how we conceptualize and specify amounts of things, enabling us to construe entities with varying degrees of specificity and generality. It is not just a grammatical device, but a way our cognition organizes experience through language. A **domain** is a knowledge background with respect to which a quantifier is described. It is divided into **facets**, each of which represents an aspect of experience. When discussing the domain of quantification, we can break it down into two main facets: set and scalar. Each facet is associated with a specific idea. Both types of quantifiers play a vital role in grasping meaning and constructing sentences.

The domain of quantification includes two facets, each reflecting a specific type of experience, marked by its own quantifiers.

The Facet of Set Quantification

The facet of set quantification involves counting the elements within sets. Set quantifiers deal with groups of entities and indicate how many elements are part of a specific set. This concept revolves around membership, inclusiveness, or how elements are distributed within a set. In Cognitive Grammar, set quantification is significant because it reflects how speakers mentally construe collections of entities as bounded sets. It shows that grammar encodes not just individual reference but also the scope and inclusiveness of categories, allowing us to conceptualize wholes, subsets, or exclusions. The following are examples of set quantifiers, each accompanied by a definition and illustration:

all — Describes collectivity, referring to every element in a set. In *All teachers need training,* all refers to all the individual elements of a set as a collection.

some — Describes an unspecified amount or number of something. In *There is some cake in the kitchen, some* refers to a part of something that is not stated or known.

any — Describes selectivity, denoting a randomly selected element as representative for the full set. In *Any teacher needs training, any* refers to a randomly selected element as representative of the full set.

each — Describes distributiveness, referring to two or more entities as individuals. In *Each teacher needs training, each* means each teacher considered separately.

every — Describes distributiveness, referring to three or more entities as a group. In *Every teacher needs training, every* means all the teachers considered as a group.

most — Describes majority, referring to the biggest number or amount. In *He won the most votes, most* means the biggest number of votes.

The Facet of Scalar Quantification

The facet of scalar quantification expresses relative amounts or norms. It is not so much about counting things precisely; instead, it focuses on comparing them to a standard or norm. Scalar quantifiers are used to measure degrees or intensities. In Cognitive Grammar, scalar quantification is significant because it reflects how speakers mentally construe gradations of quantity or intensity rather than treating reference as absolute, thereby highlighting the flexible and context-dependent nature of meaning in discourse. The following are examples of scalar quantifiers, each accompanied by a definition and illustration:

many — Indicates a large quantity or a significant number of items. *There are many books on the shelf.*

much — Indicates a large amount or a considerable degree of something. *She doesn't have much time to spare.*

few — Indicates a small number, often with a negative connotation. It suggests scarcity or insufficiency. For example, in *She has few options left, few means not many/almost none.*

a few — Indicates a small number, but with a more positive connotation. It implies that while the number might not be large, it is sufficient or notable. In *She has a few friends, a few* means some, a small number.

little — Indicates a small amount, often with a negative connotation. It suggests the amount is less than expected or desired. In *She has little interest in sports, little* means not much/almost nothing.

a little — Indicates a small amount, but with a more positive connotation. It indicates a small amount, but one that is still significant or sufficient. In *She saves a little money every month, a little* means some or a small amount.

Properties

- Quantifiers exhibit dynamic polysemy, which means their meanings can change depending on the context. We all interpret situations differently based on what is happening around us, and quantifiers adapt to fit that. For example, *Every cat chased a mouse* versus *Every cat chased mice* changes the construal of *every* from individual mice to the set of mice.
- Quantifiers demonstrate prototype effects and graded membership. Cognitive Grammar recognizes graded membership within categories like quantifiers. Prototypical members have the most typical properties, while non-prototypical members might not fit the mold perfectly but still belong to the category. For example, *Most cats* is a prototypical example, while *Almost all cats* is a bit more on the non-prototypical side.
- Quantifiers are tied to image schemas, which are those familiar patterns we notice in our sensory and movement experiences. They utilize these schemas, particularly those related to containment like *all* and part-whole relationships like *some*. These schemas help us understand and measure our experiences and interactions with the world around us.
- Quantifiers are also grounded in cognitive models, which are mental structures that assist us in making sense of the world. In *Many people attended the concert*, the use of *many* reflects the cognitive model of abundance, suggesting that a large crowd was present. In *Many of the people attended the concert*, the use of *many* is linked to the cognitive model of specification, indicating that a significant number from a particular group showed up.
- Quantifiers exhibit scalarity, meaning they can be ranked along a scale for comparison. In *All students passed the exam*, *all* represents the highest point on the pass/fail scale, meaning every single student passed. In *Some students passed the exam*, *some* is placed in the middle of the pass/fail scale, meaning only a portion of the students passed. Lastly, in *Few students passed the exam*, *few* signifies a low point on the pass/fail scale, meaning just a small number of students passed.

Comparisons

In Cognitive Grammar, it is important to examine pairs of grammatical forms to uncover subtle differences in meaning and usage that may not be immediately apparent. These comparisons enhance our language skills by demonstrating how different grammatical choices can impact the clarity and precision of our communication. In addition, these comparisons help us grasp the appropriate contexts for using various grammatical forms.

some versus any

Do you need some help?
Do you need any help?

Both *some* and *any* are used to express a lack of specificity, but their cognitive nuances differ. In Cognitive Grammar, *some* is associated with inclusion, while *any* tends to suggest exclusion. In the first sentence, *some* refers to an unspecified quantity or part of a whole, implying that there is a positive amount or existence of something. Here, the speaker assumes that help is available and is willing to offer it. *Some* indicates inclusion, with help being one of the options on the table. In contrast, the second sentence uses *any*, which also refers to an unspecified quantity but considers all possible options. In this case, the speaker is open to providing help without assuming that it actually exists. This leaves the possibility open that no help is needed at all. Thus, *any* suggests exclusion, as it takes into account all possibilities without presuming any specific help.

many versus most

Many books are fun to read.
Most books are fun to read.

Both *many* and *most* are used to discuss quantity, but they have different meanings. In the first sentence, *many* refers to a large number of things, but it does not necessarily mean the majority. It suggests that there are quite a few books that are enjoyable to read. While it does not specify a proportion or percentage, it implies that there is a good selection of books available that offer a great reading experience. The emphasis here is on the variety of books available, highlighting that a significant number fall into the *fun to read* category. On the other hand, *most* in the second sentence indicates a quantity that represents the majority or nearly all of something. It means more than half of the total number. This statement claims that the majority of books are enjoyable, suggesting that over half of all books can be considered *fun to read*. Unlike the first sentence, which allows for some interpretation about how many books are enjoyable, the second sentence is more straightforward in asserting that most books provide a pleasant reading experience. Both phrases are positive, but the second more assertive in claiming most books are enjoyable.

few versus a few

She received few letters.
She received a few letters.

We often use the words *few* and *a few* with countable nouns, and the choice between them depends on what we want to convey. When we say *few*, we are highlighting a small number of something, and it tends to convey a negative vibe, suggesting there is hardly anything at all. That is why we do not use *not* in tag questions with *few*, as in *She received few letters, did she?* which implies she got almost none. On the other hand, when we say *a few*, we are indicating that there are some, even if it is not a large amount. *A few* has a more positive connotation, suggesting that there is a small but sufficient quantity. When we use *a few*, we do include *not* in tag questions, as in *She received a few letters, didn't she?*, meaning she got a small number. The distinction between *few* and *a few* comes down to perspective. *Few* highlights scarcity or lack, suggesting the amount is less than desired. Meanwhile, *a few* shifts that perspective slightly, acknowledging that there are some present, even if it is not a lot. It conveys optimism, stressing that something is there. The same idea applies to *little* and *a little* when discussing uncountable nouns.

4.3.2.5 Partitives

As mentioned previously, a noncount noun does not have inherent edges and therefore cannot be divided and counted. It is seen as an undifferentiated mass, lacking distinct parts. To refer to a portion of a noncount noun or a specific quantity of it, English grammar provides speakers with partitives. **Partitives** are unit nouns that allow us to divide a noncount noun into countable parts. A **partitive phrase** is a noun phrase consisting of a partitive, specifying a part, followed by the preposition *of* and a noun, denoting the whole. For example, in the noun phrase *a jar of honey*, *jar* is a partitive followed by the preposition *of* before the noun *honey*. Both the partitive and the following *of*-phrase contribute equally to the meaning of the partitive phrase. Cognitive Grammar views partitive phrases as symbolic units that indicate a portion of a whole. Partitive phrases rely on mental structures that help us perceive and discuss parts of a whole.

In Cognitive Grammar, partitive phrases form a category of distinct but related meanings. Categories help us organize and understand the world by grouping similar ideas together. The category of partitive phrases is organized in terms of prototype and periphery. A prototype is the most central or typical example of a category. Prototypically, partitive phrases are used before noncount concrete nouns, such as *a bottle of water*. The periphery includes less central or less typical instances that are extended from the core. In this context, there are two extensions. One is when partitive phrases are used before noncount abstract nouns, such as *a piece of advice*. Another is when partitive phrases are used before count concrete nouns, such as *a packet of cigarettes*. These peripheral examples illustrate how partitive phrases can be applied beyond the most central uses, showcasing the flexibility and range of partitive constructions in language.

The Domain of Partition

Partitives evoke the domain of **partition**, which involves breaking things down into smaller parts. It underlies how things are divided into distinguishable parts or subsets. Partitives are quite useful because they provide a way for us to quantify noncount nouns. Partitives create sets that highlight general similarities while also pointing out specific differences. This domain of partition consists of various facets, each representing a piece of the whole linked to a specific experience and playing a unique role in language. Understanding these facets is essential for exploring how encyclopedic knowledge associated with linguistic expressions reflects the world from a human perspective.

The domain of partition includes five facets, each dealing with a specific experience and represented by specific partitives.

The facet of container:
The facet of a container revolves around how we perceive objects or entities in relation to what they contain. It involves understanding things through their spatial or functional roles as containers. For example, when we say *a bottle of water*, we highlight the container facet, a vessel for holding liquids. The partitive *bottle* directs attention to a specific portion within that context. This way of thinking allows us to classify and categorize objects based on their capacity to contain. Some examples of container-denoting partitives include *a barrel of*, *a tank of*, *a bottle of*, *a bowl of*, *a jar of*, *a jug of*, *a pot of*, *a cup of*, *a glass of*, *a mug of*, *a tin of*, and *a tube of*.

The long journey consumed a tank of petrol.

The shopper wants a jar of jam.

She bought a tin of beans.

The facet of quantity:
The facet of quantity is all about how we perceive and measure amounts. It involves understanding numerical values, counting items, and taking measurements. For example, when we refer to *a sheet of paper*, we are specifically focusing on the quantity associated with that noun. This aspect is essential for expressing amounts and drawing comparisons between different quantities. Some examples of quantity-denoting partitives include *a bar of*, *a block of*, *a cube of*, *a plank of*, *a slab of*, *a pane of*, *a sheet of*, *a slice of*, *a slip of*, *a crumb of*, *a flake of*, *a fleck of*, *a grain of*, *a morsel of*, *a speck of*, *a drop of*, and *a fragment of*.

The fish was lying on a block of ice.

She wrote her address down on a slip of paper.

There is not a speck of dirt in their house.

The facet of measure:
The facet of measurement involves assessing and comparing different attributes, encompassing dimensions, scales, and units of measurement. For example, when discussing *weight*, we commonly refer to it in kilos. This aspect of measurement allows us to articulate attributes with clarity and precision. Some examples of measure-denoting partitives include *an acre of*, *a hectare of*, *a strip of*, *a kilo of*, *an ounce of*, *a pound of*, *a ton of*, *a gallon of*, *a liter of*, *a pint of*, *a quart of*, *a meter of*, *a mile of*, and *a yard of*.

There is a strip of sand between the cliffs and the sea.
The customer asked for a pound of minced beef.
They used a meter of wire for the table lamp.

The facet of category:
The facet of a category is all about how we sort and group things that share common traits or features. It involves putting ideas, objects, or events into specific categories or classes. This process is very helpful for us to better understand the world, as it brings out both the similarities and important differences among various items. Some examples of category-denoting partitives include *a breed of*, *a category of*, *a class of*, *a sort of*, *a species of*, *a strain of*, *a type of*, *a variety of*, *a brand of*, *a make of*, and *a model of*.

What sort of music do you like dancing to?
Scientists have discovered a new strain of virus.
They introduced a new brand of justice.

The facet of abstraction:
The facet of abstraction is all about how we take specific examples and transform them into broader concepts. It involves stepping back from the details to see the bigger picture. For example, when we think about *justice*, it is an abstract idea that encompasses many different legal cases. This way of thinking allows us to move beyond just the concrete instances and explore more general ideas. Some examples of abstraction-denoting partitives include *a piece of*, *a bit of*, *a grain of*, *a pang of*, *a glimmer of*, *a pearl of*, *a fraction of*, *a segment of*, *an area of*, *a field of*, *a branch of*, *a realm of*, *a sphere of*, *a spell of*, *a stint of*, *a stretch of*, and *a term of*.

Let me give you a piece of advice on the matter.
A glimmer of hope now appeared on the horizon.
The headmaster quit his job in a fit of depression.

4.3.2.6 Modifiers

In Cognitive Grammar, a **modifier** is essentially a word, phrase, or clause that adds extra detail about the head, which is the main word in a sentence. It is the part that has a schematic entity in its semantic structure, enhanced by the head to include non-intrinsic or additional information. The selection of different modifiers, whether they are singular or plural, reflects what the speaker intends to convey. Modifiers are seen as lively, context-sensitive elements that enrich our understanding of the world. They can act as adjectives or adverbs, sharpening the meaning of a word or phrase by offering more information, context, or subtle distinctions. According to Cognitive Grammar, language arises from our conceptualization of the world, with modifiers shaping it. They are not just standalone pieces; they are part of semantic networks that link related concepts. For instance, when we think of the word *car*, modifiers such as *fast*, *red*, or *electric* link to its core concept, each highlighting a different characteristic of the vehicle.

In Cognitive Grammar, the concepts of profile and base play a crucial role in understanding the meaning of modifiers. The **profile** represents the entity that stands out prominently against a background of related cognitive structures collectively referred to as the base. The profile is the element that receives focus or attention. The **base** comprises the related cognitive structures against which the profile is construed. In the phrase *a fast car*, for example, the base represents the central concept *car*, whereas the profile represents the modifier *fast*. Modifiers shift attention toward specific aspects of the base and exhibit polysemy, with multiple related meanings. For example, the word *bright* can refer to light intensity as in *a bright room* or intelligence as in *a bright child*. In Cognitive Grammar, modifiers change meaning depending on context. The distinction between profile and base helps us understand how linguistic expressions highlight specific elements (profile) against a backdrop of related structures (base). These concepts contribute to our understanding of meaning and construal in language.

In Cognitive Grammar, modifiers serve both symbolic representation and communication purposes, allowing us to express nuances, clarify context, and convey precise meanings.

Regarding symbolic representation, modifiers act as symbolic tools for expressing nuanced meanings. They modify or qualify other linguistic elements such as nouns, verbs, or adjectives to convey specific information. Symbolically, they enrich language by adding layers of meaning. For example, in *She is an ideal person*, the adjective *ideal* symbolically conveys the quality of the person. An ideal person is someone who is considered to be perfect. In *She walked slowly*, the adverb *slowly* symbolically represents the manner of walking. In Cognitive Grammar, the symbolic function is central. Modifiers are structures that directly manifest the symbolic nature of language.

When it comes to communication, modifiers play a crucial role in helping speakers and writers express themselves clearly. They allow us to highlight subtle differences, like saying *He is very tall* compared to *He is extremely tall*, or *She sings beautifully* versus *She sings passionately*. Modifiers add context and help clarify meaning, as seen in phrases like *The old man* (to differentiate from a young man) and *The red apple* (to specify its color). They also emphasize certain points, such as *I absolutely love chocolate* or *She was completely surprised*. Moreover, modifiers can either limit or enhance qualifications, as in *He is somewhat reliable* or *The evidence is overwhelmingly in favor*. Lastly, they help us make comparisons, as in *She is more talented than her peers* or *This book is less engaging than the last one*.

The domain of modification:
In Cognitive Grammar, modifiers can be described through the domain of **modification**, which is a conceptual area in which a modifier operates to alter the meaning of a head noun or verb. This domain is crucial because it highlights how meaning is not just a matter of combining words but involves complex interactions within our cognitive frameworks. In other words, modifiers do not just attach to words in isolation; they operate within a broader conceptual framework. Modification refers to the way in which conceptual content is presented. Specifically, it is the way in which a noun is accompanied by preceding or following modifiers to provide additional information about the noun. The process is influenced by the construal of **specificity**, which can either intensify a description and make it concrete or attenuate a description and make it abstract. Modification involves various syntactic devices that help in conceptualizing a situation with greater or lesser detail. The construal imposed on the conceptual content relative to communication purposes motivates the use of specific linguistic expressions.

The domain of modification has two main facets: premodification and postmodification. Each of these facets focuses on a specific experience and is represented by different linguistic features. In Cognitive Grammar, these two facets explain how words or phrases modify a noun within a noun phrase, enriching the meaning of the noun by clarifying its quality, quantity, or relationship. Both premodification and postmodification are essential for shaping the meaning of noun phrases and influencing how we perceive and understand language. They play a crucial role in our understanding of language and the world around us. Premodifiers, such as adjectives or noun adjuncts that come before the noun, are usually more concise than postmodifiers, which include adjectival dependent units (relative clauses) or relational predications (prepositional complements) that follow the noun. Premodifiers are often more compact, helping to streamline sentences, while postmodifiers tend to add extra detail, making sentences more descriptive.

The facet of premodification:
Premodifiers are small words that come before the main part of a noun phrase, shaping its meaning. They provide context by specifying what the noun refers to. For example, in *the heavy box*, the premodifier *heavy* points

to a specific type of *box*. Premodifiers highlight features such as color as in *the red apple*, age as in *an old book*, size as in *a tiny house*, quality as in *his brilliant idea*, origin as in *the Italian restaurant*, or material as in *a wooden chair*. For instance, in *She wore a vibrant, flowing, silk gown*, the modifiers describe its color, style, and material. When combined with the noun, they create nuanced meaning, as in *the fast car*, which merges the ideas of speed and the car itself. Cognitive Grammar examines premodifiers in terms of meaning and structure. Semantically, they add details to the noun. Structurally, their order follows specific, nonarbitrary rules.

Premodifiers can be either single or multiple, depending on how many characteristics of the noun are being highlighted.

Single modifiers:
A single modifier is a word that adds detail to a target, providing more specific information and enhancing its meaning. In the realm of Cognitive Grammar, a single modifier is considered a crucial part of how we understand phrases or sentences. This approach views language as a symbolic system where grammatical structures carry meaning and mirror our thought processes. Cognitive Grammar emphasizes the importance of modifiers in creating a vivid and detailed mental picture of a scene or object. Modifiers, whether describing attributes, quantities, or qualities, offer additional conceptual content that helps clarify and expand on the entities they modify. They are not just optional extras; they are vital components that enrich the overall meaning of a sentence. Modifiers play a key role in shaping how listeners or readers grasp information by providing more detailed insights about the noun or verb they modify. For instance, in the phrase *a green ribbon*, the modifier *green* specifies a particular quality of the ribbon.

In English, common types of premodifiers include determiners, numbers, and adjectives.

- Determiners specify which noun the speaker is referring to. Examples of determiners include:

Articles: a, an, and the	I found a pen on the table.
Possessive adjectives: my, your, his, her, etc.	This is my favorite movie.
Demonstratives: this, that, these, and those	He wants to buy this shirt.
Quantifiers: some, many, a few, a lot of, etc.	She has many friends.
Distributive adjectives: each, every, either, neither, etc.	Each student received a certificate.

- Numbers indicate quantity. They provide precise information about the quantity and order of entities, making communication more specific. Examples of numbers include:

Cardinal numbers: one, two, three, etc.	She has three albums.
Ordinal numbers: first, second, third, etc.	He finished first in the race.

- Adjectives qualify nouns. They help to paint a clearer picture by adding detail and specificity. Examples of adjectives include:

  Descriptive adjectives: smart, fast, clean, and so on.

    The fast runner won the race easily.

  Evaluative adjectives: witty, impressive, valuable, and more.

    Her witty remarks made us laugh.

  Relational adjectives: industrial, commercial, medical, and so forth.

    They produced a commercial ad.

  Proper adjectives: Shakespearean, Victorian. American, and so on.

    The house was decorated in a Victorian style.

Multiple modifiers:
Sometimes, one adjective may not be sufficient for a detailed description of a noun, so it becomes necessary to use multiple adjectives. These involve combinations of linguistic elements that modify a single target. The modifiers collectively contribute to the overall meaning of the noun. The main purpose of adjectives is to enhance the meaning of the noun and give it an additional connotation. Cognitive Grammar treats multiple adjectives in noun phrases as a reflection of our cognitive processes and the way we perceive and categorize information. Multiple adjectives are seen as integrating different conceptual aspects of the noun they modify. For example, in *a big red ball*, *big* and *red* each contribute distinct conceptual information about the *ball*. Multiple adjectives reflect the salience of certain features. The order of adjectives can reflect the speaker's focus and the relative importance of each attribute. Adjectives are grounded in experience, and Cognitive Grammar examines how this shapes their use and interpretation.

In Cognitive Grammar, the way we arrange adjectives follows a kind of conceptual hierarchy. Essentially, adjectives that are closer to the noun tend to be more integral to its identity. In *a beautiful old wooden chair*, for instance, *wooden* is more essential to what the *chair* is than *old* or *beautiful*. Adjective order reveals what the speaker emphasizes and values. Adjectives that stand out or grab attention are usually placed at the front. So, in *a beautiful, shiny, red sports car*, *beautiful* comes first because it might be the feature that catches the speaker's eye the most, followed by *shiny* and then red. This arrangement conveys the speaker's view and highlights the car's most impressive trait. The order of adjectives is rooted in experience and shaped perception. For example, we say *a big red apple* because size and color are the first things we notice. Ultimately, the order of adjectives reflects the typical characteristics of the nouns they describe. In *a sleek black sports car*, *sleek* is mentioned before *black* because the car's design and look are the standout features.

As mentioned earlier, the way we order adjectives is not simply a random set of rules; it is actually driven by how our brains work. The reason we arrange adjectives in a specific way is that they serve distinct roles in a noun phrase. Typically, we follow this order: (1) opinion (*cheap*, *ugly*, *lovely*), (2) size (*small*, *big*, *tall*), (3) age (*old*, *young*, *new*), (4) shape (*round*, *square*, *long*), (5) color (*black*, *red*, *yellow*), (6) origin (*British*, *Italian*, *French*), (7) material (*cotton*, *wooden*, *silk*), and (8) purpose (*sleeping bags*, *wedding dresses*, *flower cases*). This is not just a linguistic quirk; it is deeply tied to how we think and process information. It shows how we naturally sort what we see through experience. If we deviate from this order, it can disrupt the flow and make the description feel awkward or confusing. Without this structure, our expressions can appear quite unnatural in English. Therefore, getting the order of adjectives correct is crucial for clear and effective communication.

A lovely, big, new, round, brown, French, wooden dwelling house

The expression we discussed earlier supports the idea that the meaning of a complex phrase involves not only its overall semantic structure but also the way it is constructed. The **compositional path** of a linguistic expression is all about how a complex phrase is formed from its individual parts, arranged in a specific order. This path can vary in length and follows a natural flow from one adjective to the next. At the most basic level, the grounding element pairs with the noun *house*. Moving up a level, the adjective *lovely* combines with *house*. Here, *lovely* has a semantic gap; it serves as a point for elaboration, which is filled in by the noun *house*. Moving further up, the adjective *big* joins with *house*. The other semantic elements in the hierarchy continue to combine with the main noun until the full structure is complete. This expression illustrates how the order of adjectives before the main noun reflects the specific way we interpret the scene.

The facet of postmodification:
Postmodifiers are those helpful phrases that immediately follow the noun they describe. They add extra details and context to the noun, making it more informative. In the realm of Cognitive Grammar, these postmodifiers are viewed as essential elements that enhance our comprehension of the nouns they modify. For example, consider *the book on the shelf*. In this

case, the phrase *on the shelf* acts as a postmodifier, indicating the exact location of the book. Similarly, in *the man who is wearing a hat*, the adjectival dependent unit *who is wearing a hat* offers more insight into the man's identity. Cognitive Grammar emphasizes the significance of these postmodifiers in shaping our understanding and presenting a more complete picture of the nouns we discuss. They are not just mere additions; they are crucial components of the noun phrase that define a noun's identity and traits.

In English, we have various kinds of postmodifiers. Each type highlights a unique characteristic linked to the noun.

• Prepositional phrases:	He met the girl in the black skirt.
	I saw the woman with the umbrella.
• Present participle phrases:	People living in villages are hardworking.
	Look at the man standing over there.
• Past participle phrases:	I read the letter written by the school.
	The injured driver was taken to hospital.
• Infinitive phrases:	Smith is the lawyer to consult.
	The decision to leave early was unexpected.
• Relative clauses:	The person who was walking fell.
	The book that I bought is interesting.
• Appositives:	My friend, John, helped me with the job.
	Jon Smith, my history teacher, retires next year.

While the examples provided so far showcase single postmodifiers, it is important to note that there can be multiple postmodifiers within a sentence. In Cognitive Grammar, multiple postmodifiers are seen as a way to provide rich, layered descriptions of a noun. Each postmodifier adds a different dimension of meaning, allowing the speaker to convey a more nuanced and detailed understanding of the noun. This aligns with the concept of construal, where the speaker's perspective and focus shape how information is presented. When multiple postmodifiers are used, they can be organized in a way that reflects their relative importance or the sequence in which the speaker wants to present the information. Cognitive Grammar emphasizes that the use of multiple postmodifiers is not just a matter of adding more information, but also about how that information is structured and presented to convey the speaker's intended meaning and perspective. This cognitive approach allows for a more flexible and dynamic use of language, where the speaker can tailor their descriptions to fit the context and their communicative goals.

The book on the shelf, written by a famous author, is a bestseller.

The man standing by the door, wearing a blue jacket, is my uncle.

The house at the end of the street, with the red roof, is for sale.

Premodifiers versus postmodifiers:
In Cognitive Grammar, both premodifiers and postmodifiers play a significant role in effective communication. They emphasize the importance of the construal of specificity in syntax, intensifying descriptions and making them more concrete. **Specificity**, the mental act of detailing a situation, is crucial in communication, as it refers to the speaker's choice to describe a situation in depth, ultimately affecting its meaning. The significance of premodifiers and postmodifiers varies depending on the context and the writer's intent. Premodifiers are essential for pinpointing the key characteristics of a noun, achieving precision and clarity in communication by narrowing down the reference and providing specific details. On the other hand, postmodifiers enrich the noun phrase by adding context, elaboration, or additional details, going beyond the basic noun to bring depth and context. Postmodifiers often clarify relationships or provide additional background information, helping to specify which item or person is being discussed.

For illustrative purposes, consider the subtle difference in meaning between the following sentences:

I met a happy man.

I met a man who is happy.

Though the sentences have the same wording, each serves a specific function in language due to a different construal. The speaker selects the first modification pattern to give initial salience to the premodifier, emphasizing the adjective *happy* and attributing a permanent characteristic to the head noun. Conversely, the speaker selects the second modification pattern to give initial salience to the head noun *man* and emphasize a temporary characteristic through the postmodifier, which is an adjectival dependent unit (a relative clause). In both cases, the meaning of the expression is determined by how the speaker structures the scene, chooses a particular entity, and imposes a specific organization on the expression. This decision specifies which entity the speaker considers as initially salient and which one as secondarily salient. In Cognitive Grammar, different construals yield different structures, reflecting differences in meaning.

Summary

In this chapter, I have explored the conceptual category of **things**, expressed through the grammatical category of **noun phrases**. A noun phrase is a conceptual unit centered around a noun that organizes meaning and reference in discourse. Noun phrases are not just syntactic objects but conceptual groupings that highlight how speakers mentally construe entities. Unlike nouns which convey a general idea, noun phrases convey a more specific conception of an entity shaped by modifiers. For instance, the word *pen* refers to the concept of a writing tool in general. By adding grounding elements, we can transform it into a noun phrase that makes communication more precise and detailed. For example, the phrase *the pen* refers to a specific pen that we can identify within context. Transitioning from nouns to noun phrases enriches our language, allowing for more impactful descriptions and effective communication. Therefore, mastering grounding elements greatly enhances both clarity and depth in our conversations. Noun phrases are important because they structure how we mentally represent entities, relationships, and roles in communication, linking grammar directly to cognition and meaning.

Noun phrases are anchored by possessives, articles, demonstratives, quantifiers, partitives, and modifiers. Possessives show ownership (my pen), articles specify identity (the pen), demonstratives show placement in space or time (this pen), quantifiers express amount or quantity (one pen), partitives denote a portion distinct from the whole (a piece of advice), and modifiers offer additional information (useful pen). By analyzing noun phrases, we gain valuable insights into how language conveys detailed and nuanced information. This understanding is crucial for crafting clear and precise sentences that improve communication. Additionally, it assists in breaking down complex texts by breaking them down into individual components such as noun phrases, verbs, and modifiers. This breakdown enables a more thorough analysis of each element, helping to uncover the underlying structure and meaning of the text. Consequently, readers can achieve a deeper and more comprehensive understanding of the content.

Exercises

1. Show the meaning difference between these expressions, triggered by article use.

1. She went to school.
2. She went to the school.

2. These sentences seem similar but differ subtly in meaning. Point out the differences.
    1. A tiger hunts by night.
    2. The tiger hunts by night.
    3. Tigers hunt by night.
3. Identify the meaning difference between these sentences, caused by definite vs. indefinite articles.
    1. I will phone *the* doctor.
    2. I will phone *a* doctor.
4. Explore the difference in meaning between the following sentences, which contain quantifiers.
    1. Each child has a bicycle.
    2. Every child has a bicycle.
5. How do you interpret the underlined demonstratives in the following sentences in terms of usage?
    1. <u>This</u> hotel has a friendly atmosphere.
    2. <u>This</u> situation is unbearable anymore.
6. Fill in each blank with the most suitable partitive, indicating a part of a noun as distinct from a whole.
    1. a __________ of sand, salt, rice
    2. a __________ of milk, water, juice
    3. a __________ of beef, pizza, bread
    4. a __________ of chocolate, gold, soap
    5. a __________ of pasta, cereal, yogurt
7. Choose the correct order of the adjectives between brackets to complete the sentences.
    1. The (old, wooden, beautiful) chest stood in the corner of the room.
    2. The (cozy, red, leather) sofa was the focal point of the living room.
    3. The (Italian, homemade, delicious) pasta was served for dinner.
    4. The (metal, tiny, round) box contained priceless jewelry pieces.
    5. The (large, glass, modern) table dominated the dining area.
8. Complete the following exercise with correct quantifiers.
    1. We are going to be late. There is too (much/many) traffic.
    2. Well, I think I probably made (few/a few) mistakes.
    3. Can you bring soda to the picnic? I don't have (some/any).
    4. The polls say that there's (little/a little) support for the party.
    5. (Each/Every) one of us has to inform the boss about the plan.
9. Choose the adjective that serves as a modifier and fits the context of the sentence.
    1. She was (upset/angry) when he spilled coffee on her dress.
    2. He is a (noticeable/notable) linguist; his work won an award.
    3. The woman feels (lonely/alone) despite her active social life.

4. The movie is (classic/classical); it stays famous for many years.
5. This vaccine is quite (efficient/effective) against the disease.

10. The choice of premodifiers or postmodifiers depends on the aspect the speaker emphasizes.

1. She bought a red dress.
2. She bought a dress that is red.

PART THREE

Relations: Atemporal Relations

In the previous part, I discussed the conceptual category of **things**, represented by the grammatical class of **nouns**. In this part, I will delve into the conceptual category of **relations**, represented by the grammatical class of **verbs**. A **relation** is the way entities connect, interact, or position themselves, gaining meaning through these links. Unlike **things**, which focus on individual entities, **relations** shed light on how these entities are conceptually linked. Relations can be categorized as either atemporal or temporal, and both are crucial in shaping how we understand language. An **atemporal relation** exists outside time, summarizing states as a unified condition through **summary scanning.** For example, in *The mountain stands tall*, we view the mountain's state as a whole, not as a process unfolding moment by moment. Atemporal relations can be either **simple**, exemplified by attributive predications (adjectives), peripheral predications (adverbs), and relational predications (prepositions), or **complex** expressed by nominalized processes (gerunds), attributive processual predications (participles), and ungrounded schematic processes (infinitives). Atemporal relations help us make sense of states and conditions independent of time.

A **temporal relation**, on the other hand, focuses on time, showing sequential states of a process as it unfolds, emphasizing dynamic actions over static states. In Cognitive Grammar, this means the relation undergoes **sequential scanning**, allowing us to conceptualize a relation from one moment to the next. For instance, in *She runs quickly toward the finish line*, we view the action as unfolding step by step, with scanning capturing movement through time rather than a static state. Temporal relations can be either **simple** exemplified by processes (verbs), verbal expressions (verb phrases), and single-grounded processes (simple sentences), or **complex** expressed by **conceptual symmetry** (coordination and transition), **correspondence relations** (correlation), and **conceptual asymmetry** (subordination). **Coordination** connects ideas of equal weight, as in *He cooked dinner, and she set the table.* **Transition** moves focus from one thought to another, as in *It was raining; nevertheless, they went outside.* **Correlation** pairs alternatives or parallels, as in *Either we take the bus, or we walk to school.* **Subordination** links a main idea with a dependent one, as in *She will call you when she arrives.* Temporal relations help us make sense of the order of events and the progression of time. Distinguishing atemporal from temporal relations clarifies timeless qualities and time-bound events in language.

Outline

5

Simple Atemporal Relations: Predications in Adjectives, Adverbs, and Prepositions

5.1 Introduction

In this chapter, I discuss the first subcategory of atemporal relations, specifically the simple ones. **Atemporal relations** express stable, time-independent properties or connections, emphasizing constant features and static language patterns. They are accessed through a method called **summary scanning,** which allows the speaker to grasp an entire situation at once, forming a unified picture of time. There are two types of atemporal relations: **simple atemporal relations**, which involve a single connection between entities like attributive predications (adjectives), peripheral predications (adverbs), and relational predications (prepositions), and **complex atemporal relations**, which involve multiple elements or connections wrapped up in a single expression like nominalized processes (gerunds), attributive processual predications (participles), and ungrounded schematic processes (infinitives). Both are inherently static and do not exhibit change over time. The distribution is not random; it is driven by meaning. Atemporal relations contrast with temporal ones, which concern time-bound processes.

The first subcategory of atemporal relations pertains to simple atemporal relations. These are types of relationships that do not involve any kind of time progression or change. Instead, simple atemporal relations focus on individual word classes that convey timeless ideas, like adjectives, adverbs, and prepositions. They do not directly reference time; rather, they highlight stable qualities and static connections. For example, adjectives describe characteristics, while adverbs explain how something is done. Take the phrase *the blue sky*. Here, the adjective *blue* highlights a quality. In *She sings beautifully*, the adverb *beautifully* tells us how she sings. And in *The book is on the table*, the preposition *on* shows the spatial relationship between the book and the table. Simple atemporal relations stand in contrast to complex atemporal relations. While the former describe stable properties and fixed connections between elements, the latter encompass multiple components and layered meanings, adding depth to linguistic expression.

5.2 Attributive Predications

In Cognitive Grammar, the conceptual category of **attributive predications** is encoded in the grammatical class of **adjectives. Attributive predications** refer to how a speaker assigns a property to a thing, describing what something is like rather than what it does. These predications do not involve a separate process or action; instead, they simply characterize an entity. **Adjectives** are words that encode non-relational meanings, attributing properties to nouns or pronouns. In Cognitive Grammar, adjectives are not mere modifiers but meaningful conceptual structures. They encode properties and qualities, functioning as symbolic units that enrich how nouns are construed. Adjectives highlight a noun's attributes, shaping how we perceive and categorize the world. This perspective emphasizes that grammar is inherently meaningful, rejecting the idea of adjectives as purely formal categories. Adjectives fit into the trajectory-landmark organization, where the noun is the trajectory while the adjective is the landmark. For example, in *a beautiful sunset*, *sunset* is the trajector and *beautiful* the landmark. Adjectives function as predicates (The house is big), modifiers (a big house), and gradable terms (a bigger house).

In Cognitive Grammar, adjectives are seen as dynamic and versatile, fulfilling various roles rather than being restricted by rigid grammatical rules. They evoke personal interpretations and are involved in cognitive activities such as categorization, comparison, and our overall understanding of things. Unlike traditional views, which treat adjectives as static labels with superficial meaning, Cognitive Grammar views them as expressive entities deeply linked to our cognitive experiences. While traditional approaches often analyze adjectives in isolation, divorced from our sensory encounters, Cognitive Grammar grounds them in our perceptual and cognitive processes. Adjectives are not mere labels; they reflect how we perceive and engage with the world around us. They evoke specific dimensions of experience, often grounded in sensory, emotional, or evaluative domains. They are dynamic and versatile, shaping interpretation and supporting categorization, comparison, and understanding. For example, the adjective *warm* is rooted in our embodied experience of temperature, profiling a particular region within the conceptual space of thermal sensation. Cognitive Grammar offers a more comprehensive and conceptual approach to comprehending adjectives within the broader framework of language and cognition.

Dimensions of construal:
In Cognitive Grammar, how we interpret the meaning of an expression is just as important as the ideas it brings to mind. Adjectives do more than provide conceptual content; they also influence how we see and understand that content. Their function in shaping meaning is key to grasping context. Every symbolic structure, including adjectives, presents its content in a particular way. Adjectives embody a wide range of construal phenomena. Within the framework of Cognitive Grammar, adjectives follow the principles of specificity, focusing, and prominence.

Specificity refers to the degree of precision and detail used to characterize a situation. It is about how precisely we describe something. It is the mental act of construing a situation in detail. In terms of specificity, adjectives can vary in specificity. Some adjectives are more precise and detailed, while others are more general. For instance, consider the adjectives *crimson* and *red*. *Crimson* is more specific, evoking a vivid shade of red, whereas *red* is a broader category. Specificity influences how we perceive and describe objects or situations. More examples include *oak* and *tree*, *Spaniel* and *dog*, *violin* and *instrument*, and so forth.

Focusing is the mental act of giving attention to one particular part of an expression rather than another. It involves organizing information into foreground versus background. Foregrounding refers to the act of giving the most importance to a particular part in an expression, whereas backgrounding refers to the act of paying less attention and less importance to a part of a sentence. When we use adjectives, we often highlight certain aspects of a situation while downplaying others. For instance, consider the sentence *The old house stood at the end of the street*. Here, *old* is in focus (foreground), emphasizing its significance.

Prominence refers to the quality of being significant or noteworthy and can vary in degrees depending on the context. There are two main types of prominence at play here: profiling and Trajector-Landmark alignment. **Profiling** is essentially the mental process of highlighting a specific substructure that becomes the center of attention in a statement. Adjectives play a key role in this by emphasizing particular aspects of a situation or certain characteristics of objects. For example, in the sentence *She wore a sparkling dress*, the adjective *sparkling* draws attention to the dress's visual appeal. In a **trajector-landmark relationship**, the trajector is the primary participant, while the landmark serves as the secondary one. Adjectives help to highlight the most significant participants. Take the sentence *The tall man* (Trajector) *greeted the short woman* (Landmark). Here, the adjectives *tall* and *short* establish a relational contrast. This relational profiling creates a mental image where the man's tallness is foregrounded against the woman's shortness, anchoring the comparison in shared perceptual experience.

The way we understand perspective also extends to adjectives. **Perspective** is all about the angle or mental stance we take when we look at and make sense of information. Adjectives can express different viewpoints by presenting the content in particular ways. For instance, the word optimistic captures a positive and hopeful perspective, as in, *She has an optimistic outlook on life, always expecting the best outcomes*. Conversely, *pessimistic* conveys a negative and doubtful perspective, like in, *She has a pessimistic view of the situation, always expecting the worst to happen*. This illustrates how adjectives are essential in shaping our understanding and interpretation of language. Every adjective we choose has an impact on how we frame the information.

Language gains precision through **modification**, which Cognitive Grammar treats as a conceptual rather than purely syntactic process. Modification adds specificity by using adjectives to enrich nouns with additional detail. Speakers expand meaning through two processes: elaboration and instantiation. **Elaboration** enhances a conceptual structure by adding depth or nuance, while **instantiation** makes a broad concept more specific by selecting a concrete example from within it. Adjectives direct attention to salient qualities of a referent and may appear as premodifiers, as in *Suzan gave an outstanding performance*, or as postmodifiers, as in *Anna is looking gorgeous*, each reflecting different ways of organizing information in thought. These patterns show how modification shapes the grammatical structure of noun phrases and mirrors the mental processes through which we construe, refine, and communicate our messages. Ultimately, modification in Cognitive Grammar reflects how we mentally structure experience, highlight salient features, and express our communicative intentions.

5.2.1 Categories

In Cognitive Grammar, adjectives are seen as versatile linguistic tools that enhance nouns by adding extra information. They do more than simply modify; adjectives highlight specific qualities. This approach classifies adjectives in two ways: by their position in a sentence (attributive and predicative) and by their meaning (descriptive, evaluative, and relational). This dual classification helps capture both how adjectives function structurally and what they communicate semantically. Understanding adjectives from these two perspectives provides greater flexibility, enabling speakers to shape sentence structure and meaning to convey subtle nuances and improve clarity in communication.

5.2.1.1 Position-Based Adjectives

The position of an adjective matters because it influences both the meaning and clarity of a sentence. It is not just a grammatical rule; adjective placement helps make meaning precise, natural, and effective. Based on their position, adjectives are categorized as either attributive or predicative.

5.2.1.1.1 *Attributive Adjectives*

Attributive adjectives are those that come before the nouns they describe. Some adjectives, such as *utter*, *mere*, *main*, *chief*, *principal*, *sheer*, *former*, *latter*, *outer*, and *inner*, only appear in this attributive position. Let's take *utter* as an example. You can say *an utter disaster*, but you would not say *the disaster is utter*. According to Cognitive Grammar, these adjectives are considered constructions deeply rooted in our mental grammar. They have specific roles and constraints that we learn through our use of language. Because of their fixed placement, these adjectives play a crucial role in shaping meaning before the noun is even processed. Essentially, they help shape our cognitive framework for understanding and producing language, showing how we mentally organize and categorize linguistic information. This perspective highlights that our grasp of language is influenced by our experiences and interactions, and these adjectives illustrate how certain linguistic patterns become ingrained in our cognitive system.

5.2.1.1.2 *Predicative Adjectives*

Predicative adjectives are those that follow linking verbs like *to be*, as in the sentence *The flower looks beautiful*. Some adjectives, such as *afraid*, *asleep*, *aware*, *alive*, *alone*, *ashamed*, *awake*, *ill*, *afloat*, and *aloof*, can only be used in this predicative position. For example, you can say *She is afraid*, but you would not say *an afraid girl*. These adjectives often describe temporary states or conditions rather than permanent traits. They depend on context to convey precise meaning, showing how language interpretation adapts to situations. In the realm of Cognitive Grammar, predicative adjectives form a part of our mental grammar, learned through our use of language and woven into our cognitive framework for understanding and producing it. This perspective underscores how our language knowledge is influenced by our experiences and interactions, with predicative adjectives serving as a prime example of how certain linguistic patterns become ingrained in our cognitive system. It also emphasizes the crucial role that context and usage patterns play in shaping our understanding of language.

Dual flexibility of adjectives:
Most adjectives can actually be used in both attributive and predicative positions. In the realm of Cognitive Grammar, these adjectives are seen as flexible tools that reflect how we think and understand language. They are often tied to the idea of **construal**, which is all about how speakers choose to

present and shape their experiences and perceptions through words. These adaptable adjectives show just how flexible we can be in framing a specific concept, depending on the context and what we want to communicate. This adaptability lets speakers tweak their language to fit different situations, showcasing the ever-changing nature of language. By diving into how these adjectives work, we can better understand the cognitive processes that help us communicate in a meaningful and effective way.

A concerned parent

The parent is concerned.

In the first example, the word *concerned* is used attributively. It is used in a way that directly describes the noun, emphasizing its inherent quality. It implies a general trait or identity. The parent is characterized by concern, perhaps habitually or in a broader sense. This use often describes someone's role or persona. In the second example, it is used predicatively. It takes on a different role, focusing on the state or condition of the subject. It describes a current emotional state. The parent is feeling concern right now, possibly about a specific issue. So, the first paints a picture of who the person is; the second tells us how they feel in the moment. This difference is key in Cognitive Grammar, where position reflects not just syntax but how we mentally frame meaning. This versatility in how we use language showcases its dynamic nature and our ability to adapt our speech to fit different communication needs. It also demonstrates how context can influence our understanding and use of language. By recognizing these nuances, we can improve our communication skills and express our thoughts more clearly.

5.2.1.2 Meaning-Based Adjectives

The meaning of an adjective is important because it shapes both the clarity and overall message of a sentence. By understanding these meanings, we gain insight into how language mirrors our ideas. Adjectives are classified into three types based on their meaning: descriptive, evaluative, and relational.

5.2.1.2.1 *Descriptive Adjectives*

Descriptive adjectives are words that provide information about the characteristics or qualities of nouns. They help us describe people, animals, places, or objects. Adjectives describing appearance include *beautiful*, *handsome*, *cute*, *thin*, *tall*, *chubby*, *muscular*, and so on. Adjectives describing character and personality include *polite*, *friendly*, *honest*, *generous*, *rude*, *lazy*, *angry*, and so forth. Adjectives describing feelings and emotions include *terrified*, *exhausted*, *scared*, *nervous*, *embarrassed*, and so forth. Adjectives describing size, weight, and extent include *big*, *small*, *heavy*, *light*, *long*, *short*, and so on. Adjectives describing time and age include *annual*, *daily*, *early*, *late*, *recent*, *old*, *young*, and so forth. Adjectives describing places include *spacious*, *idyllic*, *serene*, *vibrant*, *quaint*, *secluded*, *lush*, *majestic*, *enchanting*, and so on. In Cognitive Grammar, descriptive adjectives highlight one part of a relational concept. For example, *red* relates an object to the color domain but focuses only on the specific property, its *redness*. Descriptive adjectives add essential detail to nouns. In *The long journey was exhausting*, removing *long* would leave the description incomplete and less informative.

She felt deeply embarrassed.

She is always very generous to the kids.

The chubby baby giggled as he played with his toys.

In a recent study, scientists discovered a new species of butterfly.

The vibrant colors of the sunset painted the sky in hues of orange and pink.

Descriptive adjectives allow us to express both inherent and noninherent qualities, enriching our language and communication. **Inherent qualities** are essential attributes that are permanent or intrinsic to the noun they describe, and they are not subject to change based on external factors. They help create a clear and vivid picture of the noun's characteristics in the mind of the reader or listener, enhancing communication and understanding. For example, in *golden sunsets*, the color gold is inherent to sunsets. In *round planets*, planets naturally have a spherical shape. In *living organisms*, being alive is an inherent quality. **Noninherent qualities**, on the other hand, refer to characteristics that are not permanent or essential to the noun they describe. They can indicate temporary states that may change over time. For example, the adjective *happy* in *happy child* is a noninherent quality because *happiness* is a temporary state. These adjectives add context, detail, and nuance, enabling more dynamic and varied expression.

5.2.1.2.2 *Evaluative Adjectives*

Evaluative adjectives are words that express the speaker's feelings, thoughts, and judgments about the nouns they describe. These adjectives provide insight into the speaker's viewpoint, which is essential for understanding subtle meanings in communication. Examples include *critical*, *impressive*, *exceptional*, *informative*, *witty*, *hilarious*, *smart*, *important*, *valuable*, *excellent*, and *systematic*. For instance, in the sentence *His witty remarks during the debate kept the audience engaged and entertained*, the word *witty* conveys a positive evaluation of someone's cleverness and humor. Rather than treating evaluative adjectives as fixed, purely semantic labels, Cognitive Grammar views them as expressions of subjective construal, how speakers mentally represent and assess situations. These adjectives help speakers convey opinions and emotions, shaped by context and perspective. Evaluative adjectives highlight the relation between an entity and the speaker's value judgment. For example, *a wonderful idea* relates to the speaker's positive evaluation, not the idea's objective feature.

Her insights during the meeting were incredibly valuable.
The critical analysis of the situation highlighted flaws in the plan.
His performance was so hilarious that everyone laughed uncontrollably.
The speaker's presentation was impressive, leaving the audience in awe.
The chef's skills were exceptional, resulting in a memorable dining experience.

5.2.1.2.3 *Relational Adjectives*

Relational adjectives are words that highlight a relationship between a noun and another entity. Unlike descriptive adjectives, which focus on intrinsic properties of a noun, relational adjectives point out a connection or association. They help clarify the type or category of the noun, often tying it to a specific field, domain, or context. This way, we can share detailed information about where a noun comes from, its affiliation, or its category. For instance, adjectives that narrow down the meaning of a noun include terms like *chief*, *complete*, *direct*, *entire*, *external*, *final*, *particular*, *general*, *initial*, and *internal*. When it comes to nationality or affiliation, we have adjectives like *American*, *Chinese*, *English*, *French*, *and German*. Similarly, adjectives related to specific subject areas include *chemical*, *industrial*, *commercial*, *medical*, and *social*. Take *medical*, for example. It directly connects to the noun *medicine* within the subject area. Relational adjectives are treated in Cognitive Grammar as symbolic expressions that profile conceptual relationships between the nouns and the modifying adjectives. Meaning comes from conceptual links, with relational adjectives cueing deeper cognitive associations.

They sought counseling to resolve their marital issues.
The chief engineer presented the new design to the team.
The city is known for its industrial heritage and factories.
The teacher showed a paternal concern for his students.
The medical team worked tirelessly to ensure the patient's recovery.

5.2.2 *Cognitive Aspects*

The main idea behind Cognitive Grammar is that grammar actually has meaning. It suggests that grammar and vocabulary exist on a continuum and can be understood as collections of symbolic structures, specifically pairs of form and meaning. Cognitive Grammar is quite strict in its claims. Instead of being dictated by outside rules, linguistic structures come from our cognitive processes, like how we categorize, configure, and conceptualize things. These cognitive processes play a crucial role in how we develop linguistic structures, influencing the way we perceive and organize our experiences with language. They are important because they help us understand how we structure, process, and derive meanings from our knowledge and experiences when we use language. This viewpoint sees language as a fundamental aspect of the mind, shaped by our cognitive processes.

5.2.2.1 Categorization

In Cognitive Grammar, adjectives exhibit **polysemy**, the case in which a single word is associated with a range of distinct but related senses. Through categorization, we group the senses into a category. **Categorization** is the mental process of classifying the multiple senses of an adjective into a category. A **category** is a network of different but connected senses of a given adjective. The category is made up of a prototype and a periphery. The **prototype** refers to the most typical or representative example of a category, which possesses the largest number of features common to that category. This concept is significant because it helps explain how we categorize words and concepts in our minds. The **periphery** refers to the less typical or representative examples of a category, which may share fewer features with the central members and have fuzzy boundaries with neighboring categories. This structure reveals how meanings can shift and overlap, illustrating the flexible and dynamic nature of language use. Overall, this approach highlights the crucial role of meaning and conceptualization in language structure and semantics.

Consider the adjective *strong*, to illustrate how it carries multiple meanings across different contexts.

strong

The prototypical zone of the adjective *strong* signifies strength and has different shades of meaning. It can mean (1) "having physical strength," as in *a strong swimmer*; (2) "having psychological strength," as in *a strong woman who endures hardship*; (3) "having a lot of influence," as in *a strong leader*; (4) "likely to succeed or happen," as in *a strong candidate for the job*; and (5) "not easily upset or frightened," as in *a strong personality*. The peripheral zone of the adjective *strong* signifies other meanings, such as (1) "having a lot of taste," as in *strong cheese*; (2) "containing a lot of substance," as in *strong coffee*; (3) "firmly established," as in *a strong marriage*; (4) "difficult to attack or criticize," as in *a strong argument*; (5) "having a lot of force, often causing offense to people," as in *The movie uses strong language*. (swearing); and (6) "great in number," as in *There was a strong police presence at the demonstration*. This example demonstrates how adjectives can shift in meaning based on context, emphasizing different facets. Cognitive Grammar recognizes these nuances, enriching our understanding of language.

5.2.2.2 Configuration

In Cognitive Grammar, adjectives do not exist in isolation in the mind of the speaker, but rather gather with other concepts in conceptual fields, called cognitive domains. The mental process of grouping a number of adjectives into a cognitive domain is called **configuration**. A **domain** is a knowledge configuration through which the meaning of adjectives can be understood. Each domain has specific facets of meaning. Each **facet** is associated with a particular experience and realized by an adjective. This means that adjectives derive their value by construing the content of the domain in specific ways. The domain provides the context for the conceptualization of an adjective. These domains are dynamic and interconnected, reflecting how meaning is shaped through the interaction of multiple cognitive elements. This highlights how our understanding of adjectives is deeply connected to the broader networks of knowledge and experience in our minds. This approach underscores meaning and conceptualization as central to language structure.

To better understand the topic, let's take a closer look at the following related adjectives:

accidental
fortuitous
casual

The adjectives *accidental*, *fortuitous*, and *casual* all relate to the idea of chance, but each one highlights a different aspect. *Accidental* describes something that happens by chance, suggesting it was unintentional. For instance, if you spill coffee on your shirt, that is an accidental event. On the other hand, *fortuitous* also refers to something that occurs by luck, but it carries a positive connotation, implying that the unexpected event had a good outcome. A great example of this would be finding money on the street, which is definitely a fortuitous moment. Lastly, *casual* points to an unexpected situation but focuses more on its relaxed or informal tone. For example, making a casual comment during a chat would be seen as a casual event. These examples show how adjectives create different domains, each shining a light on unique aspects. Cognitive Grammar appreciates the meaningfulness of language, allowing us to delve into various dimensions through adjectives. Choosing the right adjective prevents confusion and miscommunication.

5.2.2.3 Conceptualization

In Cognitive Grammar, adjectives serve as different ways of conceptualizing things. **Conceptualization** involves how we mentally form and organize our thoughts about the world around us. It is about perceiving and structuring our experiences, essentially creating mental images of objects, events, and relationships. One crucial part of this process is called **construal**, which is our ability to think about and express a situation in different ways. It highlights how we mentally navigate and interpret information, showcasing the fluid nature of conceptualization. Different adjectives can lead us to see the same content in unique ways. They play a significant role in shaping our overall understanding of the world, and the adjectives we choose can subtly influence how we interpret meaning. In summary, conceptualization is the broader process of forming mental images, while construal delves into how we assign meaning to those images. Both are crucial for grasping language and cognition. The meanings of adjectives depend not only on what they refer to but also on the construals we use to describe different scenes.

To deepen our understanding of the topic, let's examine the following contrasting adjectives in more detail:

jealous
envious

The two adjectives *jealous* and *envious* are often used interchangeably, but they actually have distinct meanings and are not synonymous. They construe situations differently. *Jealous* is a feeling of resentment, bitterness, or hostility toward someone who possesses something that you do not. It implies that something you already have is threatened by someone else, as in *You are just jealous of me because I got better marks*. On the other hand, *envious* is a feeling of desire to have the advantage that someone else possesses. It implies a desire to be in the other person's position, to have what they have, as in *She has always been envious of her sister's good looks*. In summary, while *jealous* can be described as malicious and uneasy, envious can be described as a mix of admiration or compliment. The examples show that adjectives are not synonymous even if they share the same proposition. They convey distinct, specific meanings. In Cognitive Grammar, context guides adjective choice, ensuring precise meaning and richer expression.

5.3 Peripheral Predications

In Cognitive Grammar, the conceptual category of **peripheral predications** is encoded in the grammatical class of **adverbs. Peripheral predications** are expressions that ascribe a secondary or supplementary property to a process or entity, without profiling a full relational structure. **Adverbs** are words that describe how an action, state, or relation is executed. Unlike adjectives that mark a noun's attributes, adverbs elaborate actions or qualities without altering core meaning. Adverbs specify the manner, degree, or circumstances of a process. For example, In *She sings loudly*, the subject *she* is the entity performing the action, *sings* profiles the process, and *loudly* indicates the manner in which the process occurs. Adverbs are symbolic elements that enrich a sentence's meaning by modifying verbs as in *She danced gracefully*, adjectives as in *The cake is extremely delicious*, adverbs as in *She spoke rather softly*, and entire sentences as in *Fortunately, I had brought an umbrella*. In each case, the adverb adds nuance or refinement, thereby demonstrating the flexibility and dynamism of linguistic expression.

5.3.1 *Categories*

In Cognitive Grammar, adverbs form a broad category that encompasses various expressions adding extra detail to verbs, adjectives, and even other adverbs. Rather than merely modifying, they highlight specific aspects such as manner, frequency, degree, and place. This approach considers both the form and meaning of adverbs, allowing greater flexibility in their placement within sentences. Such flexibility shapes the overall sentence structure and meaning, enabling speakers to convey subtle nuances and communicate with precision. Additionally, adverbs play a crucial role in reflecting the speaker's perspective and the context of an action or quality, further enriching the communicative experience.

5.3.1.1 Quantification of Process Occurrence

In Cognitive Grammar, **quantification of process occurrence** refers to how language expresses the number or frequency of times an event or process takes place within the speaker's conceptualization of time. It is a way of grounding events by indicating whether they happen once, repeatedly, or never. In grammar, this quantification is typically encoded by **frequency adverbs**, which describe how often an action occurs within a given period of time. These adverbs function as conceptual operators, shaping how the occurrence of an event is mentally construed along the temporal continuum. They act as symbolic markers that structure our mental images of events, providing information about their recurrence. Adverbs of frequency modify verbs, adjectives, or adverbs to show event regularity, thereby enhancing our comprehension of temporal patterns. For example, when we say *I always go to the park*, the word *always* is not simply adjusting the verb *go*; it is essential to how we conceptualize that action as habitual and recurring.

Frequency adverbs can express both definite and indefinite timing. Some indicate precise, regular intervals, while others convey general or vague frequency, as shown below.

Definite occurrence:
Some adverbs give us a clear sense of how often something happens, typically appearing up at the end of a sentence. They help us understand how frequently an action takes place. In contrast to indefinite frequency adverbs, which are vague about timing, definite frequency adverbs specify a particular time frame. In Cognitive Grammar, these adverbs play a crucial role in shaping our mental construal of scheduled, fixed, and measurable temporal cycles, enabling us to better conceptualize how often events occur over time. For example, in *She calls him monthly*, the adverb *monthly* clearly indicates how often she contacts her brother. By providing specific intervals, definite frequency adverbs help structure expectations and predictability in communication. They also anchor our understanding of habitual or repeated actions within a clear temporal framework.

Some common definite adverbs of frequency include *daily*, *weekly*, *hourly*, *once*, and *twice*.

She exercises daily to maintain her fitness.

They meet weekly to discuss literature.

The workers perform quality checks hourly.

Indefinite occurrence:
Some adverbs imply indefinite frequency, expressing an unspecified or uncertain frequency of an action or event. They provide a general idea of how often something happens without specifying an exact frequency. In Cognitive Grammar, these adverbs play a crucial role in describing routines or habitual actions. They help convey the frequency of events and contribute to our understanding of how actions unfold over time. For example, consider the sentence *She usually takes the bus to work*. The adverb *usually* provides information about the frequency of her behavior, allowing us to form mental representations of her commuting habits. These adverbs add vagueness that reflects real-life variability, making language more adaptable and expressive. They also allow speakers to communicate general tendencies without committing to precise details.

The following are common indefinite adverbs of frequency, arranged in decreasing order of occurrence: *always* (100 percent), *usually* (70 percent), *sometimes* (50 percent), *seldom* (10 percent), *rarely* (5 percent), and *never* (0 percent). These describe habitual actions, tendencies, or general patterns rather than fixed schedules, helping speakers convey how often events typically happen.

She never wears a dress.

I always feel happy when playing.

John sometimes drinks apple juice.

5.3.1.2 Mode of Action Profiling

In Cognitive Grammar, **mode of action profiling** refers to how speakers mentally construe the manner in which a process unfolds, highlighting aspects such as speed, intensity, style, or attitude. It shapes the conceptual image of an event by profiling *how* it happens rather than *when* or *how often*. In grammar, this mode of action is typically expressed by **manner adverbs**, which describe how an action is performed or the way in which something happens. They play a crucial role in conveying how actions unfold, functioning as symbolic operators that enrich the construal of the process by specifying its qualitative character. These adverbs reflect the speaker's subjective view of how an action is carried out. For example, in *The business expands rapidly*, the adverb *rapidly* profiles the mode of action, influencing how the expansion is mentally construed. Examples of manner adverbs include words such as *clearly*, *slowly*, *quickly*, *happily*, *sadly*, *loudly*, *rapidly*, *quietly*, and so on. These adverbs modify verbs and answer the question *how*, as exemplified below:

She closed the door quietly.

She ran quickly to catch the bus.

He spoke softly during the meeting.

She explained the instructions clearly.

The tortoise moved slowly across the garden.

Some adverbs of manner, like *hard*, *fast*, *late*, and *early*, share the same form as adjectives. In Cognitive Grammar, these adverbs shape meaning by showing how actions unfold, reflecting the speaker's construal. They enrich sentences by highlighting manner and influence interpretation within the event's context. For example, in *She took the early train to skip the rush*, *early* describes the train, functioning as an adjective. In *He came early to get a good seat*, *early* modifies the verb *arrived*, functioning as an adverb. Cognitive Grammar explains this overlap as a shift in **conceptual focus**, the same form can either describe an entity (*adjective*) or the way an event unfolds (*adverb*). The adverbs *hard* and *hardly* are often confused but have distinct meanings and uses. *She worked hard all day* describes the manner of the action with effort, while *He hardly ate anything* means he ate very little or almost nothing. The same distinction applies to *late* and *lately*. *He stayed up late last night* refers to something happening after the expected time or at a late hour, whereas *I have been feeling tired lately* refers to a recent period.

5.3.1.3 Spatial Anchoring

In Cognitive Grammar, **spatial anchoring** refers to the way language situates events, entities, or actions within a spatial frame of reference. It demonstrates how grammar reflects our embodied experience of space and perception. Spatial relations are not merely syntactic but fundamentally conceptual, shaping how we mentally construe and represent situations. This anchoring is often expressed through **place adverbs**, which indicate where an action occurs or how objects relate to their surroundings. These adverbs function not simply as syntactic modifiers but as conceptual anchors that connect linguistic meaning to embodied spatial schemas. Rather than treating them as mere modifiers, Cognitive Grammar emphasizes their role in grounding meaning and anchoring conceptualization. Through adverbs of place, speakers specify the location or direction of an action or event, thereby guiding the construal of a scene. Their interpretation hinges on perspective, discourse context, and dynamic speaker-listener interaction.

Place adverbs come in two types: **location** and **direction**, contributing to how we construe spatial relationships.

Adverbs of Location

In Cognitive Grammar, adverbs of location play a crucial role in shaping our understanding of events. They provide essential information about where someone or something is situated, pinpointing the exact place where an action occurs. Essentially, they help answer the question: where? These adverbs are viewed as more than simple spatial markers; they function as tools for construing spatial relationships within context. They enable speakers to conceptualize the location of events or entities dynamically. Their meaning is not fixed but varies depending on usage and context. For example, the adverb *above* can indicate physical elevation or a metaphorical hierarchy, depending on how the speaker frames the scene. Additionally, adverbs of location can be categorized as specific or nonspecific based on how precisely they indicate location. This choice reflects how speakers frame spatial context and guide the listener's mental imagery.

Specific location:

In Cognitive Grammar, adverbs that specify location provide clear details about where an action occurs, helping us understand and express the exact spatial relationships in our environment. These adverbs closely connect to our mental images of space and movement, reflecting how we perceive and navigate the world around us. They often anchor the listener's attention to a particular point in space. For example, words like *here* and *there* are examples of these location-specific adverbs, placing actions and events in space and making descriptions more vivid and accurate. The adverb *here* points to the speaker's location, implying it is close by, while *there* refers to a location away from the speaker. This distinction between proximal and distal reference helps shape how spatial relationships are mentally construed. The sentences below illustrate how these adverbs are used.

She is waiting for you here.

The book is on the table over there.

Nonspecific location:
In Cognitive Grammar, adverbs describing nonspecific locations point to indefinite places, adding a touch of vagueness or generality when discussing where an action occurs. They demonstrate our abstract understanding and navigation of the world around us. Examples include *anywhere*, *somewhere*, *elsewhere*, *everywhere*, *nowhere*, *indoors*, and *outdoors*. These adverbs are used when the specific location is unknown, not important, or not meant to be revealed. *Anywhere* means "in or to any place" and is often found in negative sentences or questions. *Somewhere* suggests that an object is in an unknown location. *Elsewhere* points to another place, while *everywhere* indicates that something exists in all locations. *Nowhere* means not in or to any place, essentially meaning not anywhere at all. *Indoors* refers to being inside a building or shelter, and *outdoors* means being outside of one. The sentences below illustrate how these adverbs are used.

She can't find her purse anywhere.

She has left her phone somewhere.

She looked for the key elsewhere.

She looked for the key everywhere.

There is nowhere to park your car.

She stays indoors during the rain.

She enjoys being outdoors in the sun.

Adverbs of Direction

In Cognitive Grammar, adverbs of direction are crucial expressions that depict the path or course of an action. They serve as powerful tools for expressing motion, perspective, and spatial relationships, helping speakers construct vivid mental models of events grounded in experience and shaped by viewpoint. This approach highlights the close connection between language, sensory experience, and embodied cognition. Directional adverbs are essential for understanding concepts of space, movement, and orientation, effectively linking language to our physical experiences. Rather than mere syntactic modifiers, they are meaningful elements that provide insight into the direction of an action, aiding in visualizing its trajector and destination. Common examples include terms like *upstairs* and *downstairs*, as well as many adverbs ending in *-ward* or *-wards*, such as *toward(s)*, *backward(s)*, *forward(s)*, *homeward(s)*, *eastward(s)*, *upward(s)*, *westward(s)*, and *onward(s)*. The sentences below illustrate how these adverbs function in context.

I went upstairs to retrieve my jacket.
I went downstairs to answer the phone.
He strolled toward(s) the horizon.
Watch out, the car is going backward(s)!
The car moved forward(s) along the highway.
We journeyed homeward(s).
The plane veered eastward(s).
He gazed upward(s) as the helicopter passed by.
The boat drifted westward(s).
They marched onward(s) despite the obstacles.

Spatial Anchors

Adverbs of place can be understood through two distinct anchors: **deictic anchors** (gestural) and **conceptual anchors** (non-gestural). A **gestural use** of a place adverb occurs when its meaning is anchored in the immediate speech situation and can only be fully understood by visually observing or physically perceiving the context at hand. For instance, if someone says, *The toilets are over there, dear*, the listener must look to see where the toilets actually are. On the other hand, a **non-gestural use** of a place adverb occurs when its meaning goes beyond just the words. It is derived from abstract spatial concepts or established knowledge, rather than direct perceptual access. Take, for example, the sentence, *I don't agree with you there*, which refers to a specific aspect of the discussion. The listener must recognize the metaphorical stance of the disagreement. In Cognitive Grammar, the distinction between gestural and symbolic uses of adverbs of place or between tangible and abstract locations carries deep cognitive significance because it reflects how language is grounded in both physical experience and abstract conceptualization.

5.3.1.4 Temporal Anchoring

In Cognitive Grammar, **temporal anchoring** functions to situate a process in time. It refers to the way linguistic expressions position an event or process within the conceptual domain of time. Temporal anchoring is part of **grounding**, which links the described situation to the speaker's cognitive context (time, space, modality). It ensures that a process is not floating abstractly but is tied to a specific temporal reference point, often relative to the moment of speaking. Temporal anchoring belongs to grounding expressions, situating processes in the speaker's temporal domain. It is commonly expressed by **time adverbs**, which provide explicit cues about when an event occurs. These adverbs act as conceptual operators, narrowing or specifying the temporal scope of the process. Time adverbs modify verbs, adjectives, or other adverbs to indicate the timing, duration, or frequency of an action. They provide temporal information, situating actions in relation to the present, past, or future. Examples of core time adverbs include *now*, *yesterday*, and *tomorrow*, each offering a distinct temporal reference point or scope for the event.

She is speaking now.

They left yesterday.

We will meet tomorrow.

These are examples of temporal anchoring, which refers to the process of situating an event in time relative to the speaker's perspective. It links the described process to a temporal reference point. *Now* anchors the event to the present moment, tying it directly to the speaker's here and now. *Yesterday* anchors the event to a past reference point, establishing retrospective grounding. *Tomorrow* anchors the event to a future point, projecting the process forward in time. From a cognitive perspective, temporal anchoring shows how speakers construe time as a structured domain, mapping expressions onto reference points. Time adverbs act as operators, directing attention to segments of the temporal continuum and shaping event processing. In short, time adverbs perform temporal anchoring by grounding events in the cognitive domain of time. They complement tense and aspect by adding precision about *when*, *how long*, or *how often* an event occurs, and they can express present, past, or future temporal perspectives.

5.3.1.5 Scalar Adjustment

In Cognitive Grammar, **scalar adjustment** refers to how language modifies the intensity or degree of a property, action, or relation along a conceptual scale. It is expressed in grammar through **degree adverbs**, which adjust the strength or extent of meaning. They anchor meaning by situating an event or property at a specific point on a mental scale: low → high, weak → strong, partial → complete. Instead of treating degree adverbs as mere modifiers, Cognitive Grammar views them as conceptual operators that adjust how a situation is construed. Cognitive Grammar highlights how language reflects our conceptualization of the world, with degree adverbs indicating the extent or intensity to which a quality or quantity applies to a given situation. Degree adverbs are integral to the conceptual structure of events, modifying gradable adjectives, verbs, and adverbs. In traditional approaches to grammar, the emphasis is placed on their syntactic position within the sentence. In Cognitive Grammar, however, they are conceived as conceptual tools that adjust the profiling of a property along a conceptual scale.

Adverbs of degree are typically divided into two scalar adjusters: **intensifiers** and **mitigators**.

Intensifiers:

Intensifiers are scalar adjusters that raise the intensity of a property or event along a conceptual scale. They often add a punch of emphasis or convey a stronger sense of intensity. They play a crucial role in highlighting the speaker's attitude and the subtle shades of meaning behind their words. In Cognitive Grammar, intensifiers are seen not just as grammatical modifiers, but as meaningful elements that contribute to how we conceptualize and construe experiences. They do not simply amplify; they guide how we mentally frame intensity. Intensifiers often encode **subjective perspective** or **evaluation**, revealing how strongly the speaker feels about the adjective or adverb they modify. So, in Cognitive Grammar, intensifiers are not just linguistic decorations; they are tools for shaping thought, emotion, and emphasis in nuanced ways. Common intensifiers include *very*, *really*, *extremely*, *particularly*, *absolutely*, *completely*, *totally*, *remarkably*, *incredibly*, *unusually*, and so on. Intensifiers can modify verbs, adjectives, or other adverbs.

The weather is extremely hot.

The concert was totally amazing.

The view is absolutely breathtaking.

Mitigators:

Mitigators are scalar adjusters that lower, soften, or reduce the intensity of a property or event along a conceptual scale. They make statements feel gentler and less assertive, opposite of emphasizing something. In Cognitive Grammar, mitigators are not treated as mere grammatical accessories. Instead, they are seen as meaningful tools of construal that help speakers shape how a concept is mentally represented. Mitigators reflect the speaker's **subjective perspective** or **evaluation**, signaling uncertainty, politeness, or emotional distance. So, in this framework, mitigators are not just modifiers; they are cognitive instruments that shape how meaning is constructed, perceived, and negotiated between the speaker and listener. By using mitigators, speakers can fine-tune meaning, making their language more adaptable to social contexts, emotional subtleties, or rhetorical goals. Common mitigators include *a bit*, *slightly*, *fairly*, *quite*, *barely*, *just*, *kind of*, *somewhat*, and so on.

She barely managed to catch the last train.

They are fairly certain it will rain tomorrow.

The girl in the orchestra sings quite beautifully

5.3.2 *Cognitive Aspects*

Expanding upon the insights and findings previously discussed regarding adjectives, I will now delve into the cognitive aspects of categorization, configuration, and conceptualization as they relate to adverbs.

5.3.2.1 Categorization

In Cognitive Grammar, adverbs exhibit polysemy, meaning a single adverb can have multiple related meanings. This results in adverbs forming a complex web of interconnected senses that centered around a core idea and its variations. When discussing the category of an adverb, we are examining a group of meanings that share common traits, making them somewhat comparable. The **prototype** of an adverb is the exemplar that best represents the category, serving as the gold standard or the most typical example. Conversely, the **periphery** includes less typical or borderline meanings that may not fully embody all essential characteristics of the category. This understanding of meaning suggests that words or phrases in a language are not rigidly defined but rather possesses a flexible quality, featuring a central example alongside more ambiguous one. It emphasizes the blurred boundaries and fluid nature of word meanings rather than adhering to strict defining traits. For example, consider the adverb *well.*

well

The prototype of *well* is as an adverb of manner, describing how an action is carried out. It can signify (1) "having skill," as in *She sings well*, indicating that the person has a good singing ability, (2) "healthy," as in *She is well*, meaning she is in good condition, and (3) "thoroughly," as in *The project was executed well*, meaning completely or favorably. The periphery of the adverb *well* signifies other meanings, such as (1) an adverb of degree expressing the extent or intensity of something. In *The team performed well in the championship*, it emphasizes high level of performance, (2) an interjection indicating acceptance or resignation. In *Well, I guess we'll have to try again next time*, it conveys a sense of resignation, and (3) with *as* meaning "also or too." In *She enjoys painting, and she plays the piano as well*, it indicates additional interests. These examples illustrate how context influences the interpretations of adverbs. An adverb's prototype is its core or primary function; the periphery covers extended or less central meanings.

5.3.2.2 Configuration

In Cognitive Grammar, adverbs are not seen as standalone elements in our minds; rather, they come together within conceptual fields called **cognitive domains.** A **domain** is a system of information that sheds light on what adverbs imply. It represents a conceptual space that sets the stage for how we interpret a specific adverb. Each domain holds unique facets of meaning, each tied to a particular experience and expressed through an adverb. A **facet** refers to a substructure or dimension within a domain, brought to the forefront by a chosen adverb. It is a way of organizing complex domains into more manageable parts. For example, the domain of *speed* encompasses facets such as *slowly*, *steadily*, and *quickly*. Each adverb highlights a particular aspect within this domain: *slowly* indicates low speed, *steadily* reflects a consistent pace, and *quickly* denotes high speed. The domain theory explains how language is structured in conceptual areas, showing grammar as part of cognition rather than arbitrary rules. Let's look at some examples:

quite
rather
fairly

Adverbs like *quite*, *rather*, and *fairly* all deal with intensity, but they each carry their own unique flavor. Even though they might seem interchangeable at times, they actually have distinct meanings. For instance, the adverb *quite* suggests something is complete or whole, as in *The movie was quite entertaining*. This implies that the movie exceeded expectations, but not in an overwhelming way; there is a subtle surprise there. On the other hand, *rather* means slightly or somewhat, as in *I found the book rather intriguing*. This adds a touch of preference and can express a stronger opinion or choice. Then we have *fairly*, which means nearly or practically, as in *The weather was fairly pleasant*. This suggests that the weather was good enough, but not extraordinary, hinting at a sense of moderation. These examples show just how important adverbs are in expressing different shades of meaning. While they might look similar, each one serves its own purpose. So, it is essential to think about the context when choosing the right adverb.

5.3.2.3 Conceptualization

In Cognitive Grammar, adverbs demonstrate the various ways speakers can describe situations through a concept known as **construal**. This is essentially our ability to view and articulate a situation from multiple perspectives. Within this framework, construal is incredibly important as it plays a significant role in shaping the meaning of our words. The significance of adverbs lies not only in the words themselves, but also in how we interpret the situation. Therefore, context and perspective are crucial when it comes to understanding adverbs. Depending on their reference and the context in which they are used, adverbs can take on different meanings. Their significance is derived from the context they are placed in, and various pragmatic factors can greatly influence our interpretation of them. Construal impacts how we comprehend and convey meaning, which is essential for understanding language. To truly grasp how construal operates, let's examine some examples of adverbs.

hardly
barely

Although often used interchangeably, the adverbs *hardly* and *barely* have distinct meanings. They construe events in different ways. *Hardly* means almost not at all, suggesting that something is nearly nonexistent or barely occurs. For example, saying *I hardly passed the exam* implies passing with minimal success. The focus here is on the small degree of achievement or success, emphasizing the low level of achievement. Conversely, *barely* means only just or scarcely, indicating that something is just enough or barely sufficient. For example, saying *I barely passed the exam* implies passing with a narrow margin of success, focusing on the minimal amount of achievement. These examples demonstrate how seemingly similar adverbs can convey unique dimensions of construal, influencing our understanding of situations in varying ways. Despite their visual similarities, adverbs can diverge in meaning based on the context, underscoring the significance of each adverb in shaping our perceptions.

5.4 Relational Predications

In Cognitive Grammar, **relational predications** refer to structures that profile a relationship between two entities, rather than a property of one entity alone. These predications show how one thing is located, oriented, or connected in relation to another. The conceptual category of relational predications is encoded in grammar through **prepositions. Prepositions** are words that link a noun or pronoun to other words, indicating its role in the sentence. In Cognitive Grammar, prepositions are not simply superficial elements but symbolic units with specific meanings. They represent conceptual relationships rather than just acting as connectors, shaping how we envision events and scenes based on our physical interactions with the environment. Prepositions are seen as meaningful, not empty function words. They encode spatial, temporal, and abstract relations through image schemas and conceptual metaphors. For example, in *The laptop is beside the printer*, the preposition *beside* indicates that the *laptop* is positioned next to the *printer*.

The meaning of a preposition is shaped by something called a **profile/base alignment**. Think of the **profile** as the semantic pole of a preposition, capturing the specific meaning it conveys. On the other hand, the **base** represents the phonological pole, which includes the actual sounds or the written form of the preposition. When you combine the profile and base, they define the semantic essence of the preposition, influencing its overall meaning. Take the preposition *in*, for instance. Its profile (the semantic aspect) conveys ideas related to location, containment, or inclusion, while the base (the phonological aspect) is simply the word *in*. The interaction between these two elements creates the various meanings we associate with *in*. To sum it up, prepositions go beyond just indicating spatial relationships; they are versatile tools for expressing a wide array of concepts. Their meanings stem from the complex relationship between profile and base, aiding us in navigating language and our understanding of the world around us.

5.4.1 Categories

Prepositions play a crucial role in our language by marking and highlighting relationships, often linking other words together in a sentence. What is fascinating is that prepositions can be **polysemous**, meaning a single preposition can carry multiple meanings depending on the context. Take the preposition *over*, for instance; it is a great example of this polysemy, as it can convey different ideas based on how it is used. The most straightforward meaning of *over* relates to space, indicating that something is positioned above or covering another object, as in the sentence, *The plane flew over the mountains*. From this spatial sense, we can derive other meanings through semantic extensions. For example, in a temporal context, it can refer to a duration, as in *She worked tirelessly over the weekend*. Figuratively, it can represent overcoming challenges, as in *He triumphed over adversity*. And in a quantitative sense, it can indicate exceeding a limit, as in *The temperature soared over 100 degrees Fahrenheit*. This illustrates how prepositions follow regular patterns of meaning that extend in systematic ways.

Through the lens of Cognitive Grammar, relational predications can be categorized into five key dimensions: spatiality, temporality, instrumentality, verticality, and horizontality.

5.4.1.1 Spatiality

As a dimension of relational predications, **spatiality** refers to the structuring of meaning through the positioning of entities in physical or conceptual space, typically expressed by prepositions of place. In Cognitive Grammar, these prepositions act as conceptual tools that reflect both our physical and mental experiences in our environment. They are fundamental for understanding how we perceive spatial connections between objects, places, and directions. Instead of being arbitrary labels, they are closely linked to our embodied cognition and image schemas, which encompasses concepts like containment, surface, and contact. These schemas help clarify the diverse meanings and uses of spatial prepositions by connecting them to our daily experiences and interactions with the world. For example, we use *in* to refer to denote general locations like cities, countries, and continents, as well as specific enclosed areas such as classrooms or rooms, and even the sky and outer space. On the other hand, *on* describes a location that is connected to a surface without clear boundaries. Lastly, *at* specifies a particular spot or place.

in	She lives in the city.	The book is in the bag.
on	Place the cup on the table.	The cat is sitting on the roof.
at	We met at the coffee shop.	The event was held at the park.

Spatial prepositions in contrast:

in versus at

She waits in the station.
She waits at the station.

Both *in* and *at* point to a sense of space, but they carry slightly different shades of meaning. Under Cognitive Grammar's approach, these prepositions reflect how speakers construe spatial relationships and frame the scene mentally. The first sentence implies that she is inside the station building, possibly in a waiting area or another specific location within the station's grounds, highlighting a more enclosed or interior spatial construal. On the other hand, the second sentence is more general; it could suggest that she is either inside or outside the station, but typically refers to her presence at the station as a whole location or point, reflecting a broader, less bounded conceptualization of space.

5.4.1.2 Temporality

As a dimension of relational predications, **temporality** refers to the structuring of meaning through the sequencing of entities and events in time, typically expressed by prepositions of time. In Cognitive Grammar, these prepositions play a crucial role in anchoring events within specific time frames, whether it be days, weeks, months, years, or even seasons. They help us express when something occurred or how long it lasted. Just like spatial prepositions, these temporal ones are not random labels; they are deeply embedded in our mental frameworks and cognitive processes. They reflect our mental experiences, linking thought and language, and bridge perception of time with its verbal expression. These prepositions are conceptual structures that shape our understanding of time beyond mere language. For instance, the preposition *in* is typically used for longer durations like months, seasons, and years, while *on* is reserved for specific days and dates. Meanwhile, *at* is used for pinpointing exact moments, such as clock times or mealtimes.

in	I usually relax in the evening.	She is always busy in summer.
on	I work from home on Fridays.	His birthday is on December 20.
at	The conference starts at 10:30.	He goes swimming at weekends.

Temporal prepositions in contrast:

in versus on

She submitted her work in time.
She submitted her work on time.

Both *in* and *on* relate to time, but they convey slightly different meanings. From a Cognitive Grammar standpoint, these prepositions reflect how speakers mentally construe temporal relationships and frame the timing of events. *In time* suggests being early enough, before a deadline or specific cutoff, highlighting a flexible temporal boundary. In contrast, *on time* refers to punctuality, occurring exactly at the planned or scheduled moment, neither too early nor too late, reflecting a more precise temporal construal.

5.4.1.3 Instrumentality

As a dimension of relational predications, **instrumentality** refers to the meaning shaped by the tools of an action, often shown with prepositions of means. Prepositions, viewed as conceptual structures, denote the means by which actions are executed. Like spatial and temporal prepositions, these are not merely arbitrary labels, but rather connect to mental representations of how we perceive the world. Instrumental prepositions connect physical actions to mental representations, bridging the gap between concrete experiences and abstract concepts. These prepositions have rich and diverse meanings beyond their spatial aspects. They offer a captivating insight into how our minds construct meaning, linking physical actions with abstract thought. In performing an action, the preposition *with* can signify not only physical tools but also abstract tools. The preposition *by* often indicates the means or methods used to achieve an action or the agent responsible for the action. The preposition *through* signifies the medium or channel through which an action occurs, emphasizing the pathway or mode of achieving something.

with	He cut the paper with scissors.	She solved the problem with logic.
by	He always goes to work by car.	They sent the message by courier.
through	He succeeded through hard work.	He learned the language through practice.

Instrumental prepositions in contrast:

by versus through

They communicated by email.
They communicated through email.

Both *by* and *through* indicate means of communication, but they carry slightly different connotations. In terms of Cognitive Grammar, these prepositions reflect how speakers mentally construe the means and medium of communication within a conceptual framework. *By email* emphasizes the method or tool used, email as the chosen means to convey messages, highlighting how the action is framed as accomplished via a specific instrument. In contrast, *through email* focuses on the medium or channel as a conduit, portraying communication as flowing within or across the email system itself. This framing can suggest a more continuous or ongoing exchange. Essentially, Cognitive Grammar shows how *by* and *through* guide listeners to construe communication either as using a method or navigating a medium, shaping how the event is mentally represented.

5.4.1.4 Verticality

As a dimension of relational predications, **verticality** refers to the structuring of meaning through an up-down orientation, typically expressed by prepositions of height or elevation. These prepositions describe spatial relationships along the vertical axis. They are not just linguistic markers but also conceptual structures that represent our mental and physical experiences of vertical space. These prepositions link to image schemas, showing how language extends from spatial to abstract domains. The preposition *over* marks an object directly above another. The preposition *above* denotes a higher vertical position, wider in sense than *over*. The preposition *under* marks an object beneath another or covered by it. The preposition *underneath* marks an object directly below another, implying close contact. The preposition *beneath* marks an object hidden under another. The preposition *below* marks a lower position with some distance.

over	The plane flew over the mountains.
	She raised concern over miscommunication.
above	The bird is soaring above the mountaintop.
	Her honesty places her above suspicion.
under	The ball is under the bed.
	He is under pressure to finish the project.
underneath	He wore a T-shirt underneath his sweater.
	Her calm demeanor hid the anxiety underneath.
beneath	He hid the letter beneath a pile of papers.
	She felt the criticism was beneath her dignity.
below	There's a basement below the first floor.
	His performance was below expectations.

Vertical prepositions in contrast:

above versus over

> The picture is above the fireplace.
> The picture is over the fireplace.

Both *above* and *over* suggest a higher position, but they carry slightly different meanings. Viewed through the lens of Cognitive Grammar, these prepositions reflect how speakers mentally construe spatial relationships, guiding listeners to visualize the scene with subtle differences in spatial framing. *Above* indicates that the picture is at a higher level than the fireplace but does not require precise vertical alignment, allowing for a more flexible spatial relationship. In contrast, *over* implies the picture is directly above the fireplace, emphasizing a closer and more exact vertical alignment. This distinction showcases how meaning arises from how speakers construe and communicate spatial concepts in context.

under versus underneath

The cat is under the table.

The cat is underneath the table.

Both *under* and *underneath* indicate a lower position, but they carry subtle differences in usage. Conceptualized through Cognitive Grammar, these prepositions reflect how speakers mentally construe spatial relationships and emphasize different degrees of closeness or containment. *Under* suggests the cat is positioned below the table without necessarily implying direct contact or coverage, allowing for a more general spatial relationship. In contrast, *underneath* implies a closer, more intimate relationship with the surface above, suggesting the cat is directly beneath the table and possibly in contact with it. This distinction reveals how meaning arises not only from spatial facts but also from the way speakers frame and conceptualize spatial scenes in context. Such nuanced differences show how language flexibly encodes the speaker's perspective on space and relation.

Nonspatial uses of vertical prepositions:
Traditionally, prepositions have been viewed mainly through the lens of their spatial meanings. However, Cognitive Grammar takes a broader perspective, suggesting that prepositions do much more than just organize space. It argues that our cognition is deeply rooted in our physical experiences. As linguistic tools, prepositions are shaped by these experiences, making them more than mere abstract concepts. They transcend simple syntax, firmly anchored in how we experience the world. This dual role showcases the richness and adaptability of language. To illustrate this idea, let's look at a few examples:

- Spatially, the preposition *under* refers to something physically beneath or below, as in *The dog lay under the table*. Yet, it also has an embodied extension. Nonspatially, it can denote authority or subordination, as in *She works under her supervisor*. Here, the spatial concept of being beneath translates to a hierarchical relationship.
- Spatially, the preposition *above* refers to something physically higher or over, as in *The lamp is above the table*. However, it also has an embodied extension. Nonspatially, it can denote superiority or a higher rank, as in *She ranks above her colleagues*. In this case, the spatial concept of being higher translates to a hierarchical or status-related relationship.
- Spatially, the preposition *below* refers to something physically lower or underneath, as in *The cat is sleeping below the window*. However, it also has an embodied extension. Nonspatially, it can denote a lower status or rank, as in *He is ranked below his peers*. In this context, the

spatial concept of being lower translates to a hierarchical or status-related relationship.

5.4.1.5 Horizontality

As a dimension of relational predications, **horizontality** refers to structuring meaning through the orientation of entities along a side-to-side axis, typically expressed by prepositions of alignment or extension. These prepositions describe horizontal relationships, enhancing our understanding of space and direction by indicating not only the location of objects but also concepts of spatial organization and movement. Through image schemas, they reveal how language extends beyond spatial into abstract domains. For example, *behind* means at the rear of something or someone, *beyond* indicates farther away than another object or person, *across* refers to moving from one side to the other, *through* suggests movement within a bounded area from one end to the other, along describes movement on or beside a line or path, *between* signifies being in the middle separating two entities, and *among* conveys being surrounded by or part of a group.

behind	The car is behind the house.
	I hung my coat behind the door.
beyond	Our house is just beyond the bridge.
	The park is beyond the city limits.
across	The child ran across the street.
	Many refugees fled across the border.
through	Visitors enter through a side entrance.
	They walked slowly through the woods.
along	She enjoys walking along the beach.
	They built a row of houses along the river.
between	A narrow path runs between the two houses.
	There is a train service between the two cities.
among	He disappeared among the crowd.
	She felt lonely among the strange people.

Horizontal prepositions in contrast:

behind versus beyond

He is standing behind a tree.
He is standing beyond a tree.

Both *behind* and *beyond* point to a location, but they are used in different ways. From a Cognitive Grammar perspective, these prepositions reflect how speakers mentally construe spatial relationships and boundaries. *Behind* locates the subject in a position directly at the back of or just past the reference object, emphasizing a close spatial relationship grounded in the object's immediate space. In contrast, *beyond* conceptualizes the subject as being further away or outside a defined area or boundary, highlighting an extended spatial frame that goes past the immediate vicinity. This difference illustrates how meaning emerges from the way speakers frame spatial scenes and direct the listener's mental imagery of space relative to objects.

across versus through

She walked across the tunnel.
She walked through the tunnel.

In the first sentence, the word *across* refers to moving over the top of the tunnel, like when a road runs above it if the tunnel is underground. The emphasis here is on crossing the middle of something without actually going inside. In the second sentence, *through* indicates entering the tunnel from one end and coming out the other side, highlighting the act of passing inside an enclosed space. As interpreted by Cognitive Grammar, these prepositions show how speakers mentally frame spatial paths and the space's nature. *Across* involves movement over a two-dimensional, open area, while *through* describes movement inside a three-dimensional, enclosed space. This contrast highlights how meaning arises from how speakers shape spatial experiences and guide listeners' mental imagery.

along versus across

He walked along the road.
He walked across the road.

The preposition *along* refers to movement in a continuous line following the length of something. Walking *along* a road means moving parallel to the road's course. In contrast, *across* indicates movement from one side to the other, over or through something. Walking *across* a road means moving from one side to the other, crossing the space it spans. Within Cognitive Grammar, these prepositions reflect how speakers mentally frame spatial paths and relations. *Along* construes movement as following a linear, bounded path, emphasizing continuity and alignment with the road's course. Meanwhile, *across* encodes movement that spans a boundary or barrier, highlighting the crossing of a defined space. This distinction shows that meaning arises from spatial experience and imagined motion.

between versus among

The flowers bloomed between the trees.
The flowers bloomed among the trees.

The preposition *between* comes into play when you want to describe something positioned right in the middle of two objects. For example, if you have two trees, the flowers would be right in the center. On the other hand, *among* is used when something is nestled within a larger group of objects. So, if there are more than two trees, the flowers would be surrounded by them. Essentially, *between* is for two distinct items that are clearly separated, while *among* refers to things that are part of a larger group or mass, where the separation is not as clear. According to Cognitive Grammar, these prepositions reflect how speakers mentally construe spatial relationships and groupings. *Between* marks a bounded relation of two entities, highlighting a precise midpoint. In contrast, *among* marks entities within a group or cluster. This distinction highlights how meaning emerges from how speakers conceptualize and communicate spatial conceptualizations in context.

Nonspatial uses of horizontal prepositions:
Traditionally, prepositions have been examined primarily for their spatial meanings. However, Cognitive Grammar reveals that prepositions play a much broader role than merely organizing space. This approach asserts that cognition is fundamentally tied to our bodily experiences. As linguistic constructs, prepositions arise from and are deeply rooted in these experiences. They are not just abstract linguistic entities or spatial organizers but are intrinsically linked to how we interact with the world. This dual role underscores the adaptability and depth of language. To illustrate this, consider the following examples:

- Spatially, the preposition *behind* means at or toward the back of somebody/something, as in *She hung the coat behind the door*. Nonspatially, it means responsible for or the cause of, as in *He was the man behind the success of the plan*. Here, the spatial sense of being at the back of is metaphorically transformed into responsibility.
- Spatially, the preposition *through* indicates movement from one side to another, as in *They walked slowly through the woods*. Nonspatially,

it can imply completion or exhaustion, as in *He read through the entire book*. Here, the spatial notion of traversing from one end to the other extends to the completion of the task.

- Spatially, the preposition *between* describes the space separating two entities, as in *The paper fell down between the desk and the wall*. Nonspatially, it signifies comparison or choice, as in *She couldn't decide between the two options*. Here, the spatial gap between two things metaphorically represents the choice between two options.

Schematic uses of horizontal prepositions:
Image schemas are essential in shaping our understanding of prepositional meanings. An **image schema** is a prelinguistic structure of experience that plays a crucial role in how we conceptualize and interpret various phenomena in the world. These prelinguistic structures, derived from our embodied experiences, help us conceptualize and interpret spatial relationships. They act as mental templates, guiding how we comprehend and express spatial concepts through language. When we encounter a preposition, relevant image schemas are evoked to construct meaning, accounting for the diverse senses beyond literal meanings. Here are some examples to illustrate this point:

- The preposition *across* often implies the image schema of a path. This schema represents a route that traverses from one side to another, emphasizing movement and direction. In *She walked across the bridge*, the image of moving horizontally from one side of the bridge to the other is invoked, highlighting the journey from a starting point to an endpoint.
- The preposition *along* commonly invokes the image schema of a path. This schema represents movement parallel to a line or following the length of something. In *She walked along the riverbank*, the image of movement alongside a path is invoked, highlighting the journey of movement parallel to the river.
- The preposition *among* captures the image schema of containment. This schema involves the idea of being within a bounded space or entity. In *She is respected among her peers*, the image of being surrounded by a group of entities is invoked, meaning she is held in high regard by the people who are in the same group, embodying social context.

5.4.2 *Cognitive Aspects*

Just as we discussed attributive predications (adjectives) and peripheral predications (adverbs) previously, let's now explore the cognitive aspects of categorizing, configuring, and conceptualizing relational predications (prepositions) with the same level of depth.

5.4.2.1 Categorization

In Cognitive Grammar, relational predications expressed through prepositions exhibit **polysemy**, with each potentially expressing several distinct but related meanings. This complexity results in a **category** with interconnected senses, categorized into a core prototype and a broader periphery. The **prototype** represents the most typical or central meaning, while the **periphery** consists of other meanings that have evolved from the core through cognitive processes such as metaphor, metonymy, and generalization. These meanings are interconnected, forming a complex network of meaning and associations. Unlike the Aristotelian model, where categories have strict criteria, Cognitive Grammar views categories as having more or less typical members, with overlapping features and fuzzy boundaries. They are not rigidly defined but exist on a spectrum of membership. People understand the meanings of linguistic items, whether lexical or grammatical, by associating them with a highly typical example. For example, consider the preposition *on*:

on

Typically, the preposition *on* serves as a marker for spatial relationships and it can express these connections in various ways. For instance, in *The camera is on the table*, the camera is physically resting above the table. In *The fly is on the ceiling*, although the *fly* is still in contact with the ceiling, the relationship may seem odd since the fly is actually underneath it. In *The painting is on the wall*, the wall acts as a backdrop for the painting, which is positioned in front of it. In *The leaves are on the tree*, the leaves cover the tree, demonstrating physical contact. In *The writing on the paper is clear*, the paper serves as a background for the writing, which stands out. So far, we observe that the relationship between these objects involves physical support. However, the preposition *on* also has metaphorical uses. For example, in *The house is on fire* the concept of fire transitions into a more abstract realm, almost becoming a place in itself. This illustrates how prepositions can adapt and convey various meanings depending on the context.

5.4.2.2 Configuration

In Cognitive Grammar, relational predications articulated through prepositions do not exist in isolation; they are tied to broader cognitive domains and specific aspects of those domains that shape their meanings. A **domain** is a mental map that helps us accurately grasp what a preposition means. It is like a blueprint for a particular area of knowledge that we use to make sense of the world around us. This framework is essential for learning and applying knowledge effectively. A **facet** refers to a specific part of a domain that relates to a certain experience. These cognitive domains link prepositional meaning to our broader knowledge. To understand a preposition, we draw on our knowledge. Prepositions organize experience and provide context for language. In this way, meaning is closely tied to how we conceptualize things, and the structures of meaning are defined in relation to these domains. These domains shape how we perceive content, enriching the semantic structures we use. For instance, let's take a look at some specific prepositions.

on
in
at
by
for

The prepositions *on*, *in*, *at*, *by*, and *for* all relate to the domain of time, but each one has its own unique role. *On* is used for specific days or dates, as in *They'll be here on Tuesday*, *I was born on July 1*, and *We will see you on Christmas Eve*. Meanwhile, *in* refers to a broader time frame, such as a month, season, or year, as in *We are going to Italy in April*, *Some trees lose their leaves in autumn*, and *I started working here in 1991*. The preposition *at* pinpoints a specific moment within a day, as in *There's a meeting at six o'clock*, *Are you free at lunchtime*? and *They will see each other at Easter*. *By* indicates a deadline, meaning not later than a certain time, as in *She promised to be back by five o'clock*, *We need a firm decision by the end of the week*, and *The application must be in by the 31st to be accepted*. Lastly, *for* is used to express a duration or amount of time, as in *She's out of the office for a few days*, *I'm just going to bed for an hour or so*, and *I haven't played tennis for years*. These examples show that while prepositions fall under the same category, they each have their own specific meanings and uses.

5.4.2.3 Conceptualization

In Cognitive Grammar, the concept of conceptualization is closely linked to meaning, and relational predications signaled by prepositions play a central role in this process. They show how linguistic expressions derive semantic value by presenting spatial and abstract content in specific ways. A significant aspect of this conceptualization is known as **construal**, which refers to a speaker's ability to depict a situation in various ways and communicate it through different linguistic forms. Prepositions play a vital role in demonstrating the different ways speakers can portray situations.

They are powerful language tools that can alter the meaning or perspective of a sentence. For example, consider the distinction between saying *looking at the picture* and *looking into the picture*. The first phrase implies a simple glance, while the second suggests a more thorough analysis. The meaning of a preposition is not just about what it states; it also relies on how that meaning is presented. To illustrate this concept, let's examine two different prepositions.

by
near

The prepositions *by* and *near* are utilized to indicate proximity or adjacency. Despite sharing similar characteristics, these two prepositions are still discernible in actual usage. They construe situations differently, resulting in different meanings. *By* indicates a location immediately adjacent to or touching another location, as in *She sits by the window*. In contrast, *near* implies a location that is relatively close but not necessarily touching, as in *She sits near the window*. These two prepositions construe the conceptual content differently and utilize different linguistic structures to express them in language. While *by* suggests direct contact or connection, *near* allows for a bit more flexibility in distance, indicating a spatial relationship without immediate adjacency. The examples confirm the absence of **synonymy** in language, where lexical or grammatical pairs are assumed to have similar meanings. It is uncommon for items to be interchangeable at random. Seemingly similar items are not interchangeable. The difference between them is not a result of formal rules; it is solely a characteristic of construal.

5.5 Linguistic Aspects of Simple Atemporal Relations

When we think about language, it is not only about how our brains process information; there are also clear relationships that emphasize the linguistic aspect. This involves the structure of language, such as syntax and semantics. These components assist us in understanding how attributive predications (adjectives), peripheral predications (adverbs), and relational predications (prepositions) work in various sentence structures and how their meanings combine to convey ideas. All of this enhances the richness and clarity of our language, allowing us to communicate more effectively and with greater subtlety. By mastering these components, both speakers and writers can create more vivid and precise descriptions, ultimately resulting in improved understanding and communication.

5.5.1 Entrenchment

In Cognitive Grammar, **entrenchment** refers to the process by which linguistic phrases and patterns become firmly established in the mind through repeated use. Once entrenched, these expressions are more easily accessed and processed than less familiar constructions. This process stems from the brain's tendency to minimize cognitive effort, as frequently used phrases are stored and recalled as unified cognitive units rather than as separate words. For example, when a language user consistently pairs a particular adverb with a verb, that combination becomes entrenched in their speech patterns. In English, the phrase *recommend highly* illustrates this phenomenon. Although not a complete sentence, it has become entrenched through usage as a conventional expression of approval, often employed to convey strong endorsement. Cognitive Grammar views entrenched phrases not as random word associations but as meaningful constructions shaped by experience and interaction. Entrenched patterns are more than memorized combinations; they reflect connections to our conceptual understanding of the world and demonstrate how language is deeply intertwined with cognition.

Adjective-noun combinations:
An adjective-noun combination is like a mental shortcut that we have all picked up over time. These familiar phrases help us communicate more smoothly because they pop into our heads without us having to think too hard about what they mean or how they fit together. When we hear expressions we know well, our brains can pull them up almost automatically. Certain adjectives tend to stick with specific nouns, thanks to this process of getting used to them, which creates collocations that enhance the meaning of the noun. This habitual pairing shapes how we see and talk about things. Because these combinations are so deeply rooted in our language and culture, they can be tough to change. Here are a few examples of adjective-noun combinations you might hear in English: *blind faith*, *sheer luck*, *utter nonsense*, *absolute certainty*, *complete disaster*, *prime example*, *total chaos*, *unconditional love*, *perfect storm*, *strong coffee*, and more. These collocations have become common expressions through their frequent use in language.

blind trust

The adjective *blind* does not refer to the physical inability to see but is used metaphorically to describe the nature of the trust. It implies that the trust is given without question or evidence, similar to how a blind person cannot see and must therefore trust without visual confirmation. This phrase often carries a negative connotation, suggesting a lack of critical judgment. From a Cognitive Grammar perspective, *blind trust* illustrates how meaning arises through the conceptual integration of words beyond their literal senses. The adjective *blind* is recruited metaphorically to shape how trust is construed, not merely as an abstract concept but as one experienced without sensory evidence or scrutiny. This example highlights how language users frame and construe complex ideas by mapping physical experience (blindness) onto cognitive and social phenomena (trust), revealing how meaning is dynamically constructed in context.

Verb-adverb combinations:
A verb-adverb combination serves as a mental shortcut that we create through frequent use. When a cognitive unit becomes entrenched, it means that we have mastered both its form and meaning, allowing us to use it effortlessly. Certain adverbs naturally pair up with specific verbs, forming collocations that really enhance the verb's impact. You will often find these combinations popping up in everyday conversation and writing, as they help to highlight the strength of actions or emotions. Here are some examples of verb-adverb combinations that are commonly paired together in English: *speak fluently*, *sprint swiftly*, *drive cautiously*, *cook skillfully*, *dance gracefully*, *study diligently*, *believe firmly*, *protest loudly*, *appreciate greatly*, *regret deeply*, and so on. Adverbs can also collocate with adjectives. Here are some examples of such common collocations in English: *absolutely necessary*, *bitterly cold*, *deeply affected*, *highly successful*, *ridiculously cheap*, *completely amazed*, *quietly confident*, *terribly sorry*, *utterly exhausted*, *insanely delicious*, and so on.

understand fully

The adverb *fully* intensifies the verb *understand*, indicating a complete or comprehensive grasp of a subject or situation. It suggests that there are no doubts or missing pieces in the understanding. This combination often emphasizes the depth and completeness of someone's cognitive or perceptual process. In the context of Cognitive Grammar, *fully understand* exemplifies how intensifiers shape the mental construal of an event by specifying the extent or completeness of the conceptualization. The adverb *fully* does more than amplify; it guides the listener to frame the understanding as thorough and without gaps, highlighting the cognitive scope involved. This usage illustrates how linguistic expressions encode nuanced mental representations that speakers use to efficiently convey complex meanings.

Preposition + noun combinations:
A combination of a preposition and a noun forms a cognitive unit that becomes well-established through frequent use. As this process unfolds, certain prepositions tend to pair up with specific nouns, leading to familiar phrases or collocations that are widely understood for their shared meanings. These combinations help express relationships and deliver clear information

in both spoken and written forms, weaving a rich tapestry of meanings that go far beyond just spatial references. Here are some examples of preposition-noun combinations commonly paired together in English: *at risk/stake/odds*, *under threat/pressure/fire*, *in danger*, *by chance*, *for granted*, *on purpose*, *with pleasure*, *from scratch*, *beyond doubt*, and so on. Prepositions can also collocate with verbs. Here are some examples of common collocations in English: *pay/blame/pray for*, *borrow/escape/prevent from*, *insist/elaborate/concentrate on*, *argue/worry/boast about*, *deal/acquaint/collide with*, *believe/participate/succeed in*, *adapt/react/turn to*, and so on.

in jeopardy

The preposition *in* typically indicates a state or condition, and when combined with the noun *jeopardy*, it denotes a situation where something is at risk or in danger. The phrase often conveys urgency or the potential for negative outcomes if action is not taken. In Cognitive Grammar, this phrase exemplifies how spatial prepositions like *in* are extended metaphorically to represent abstract states. Here, *in* construes being "inside" a conceptual state of risk, framing jeopardy as an enclosed condition one can be situated within. This metaphorical construal shows how entrenched linguistic units are formed by mapping physical spatial concepts onto cognitive and social experiences. It highlights the dynamic way meaning emerges from the interaction of syntax, semantics, and usage patterns in language.

5.5.2 *Coercion*

In Cognitive Grammar, **coercion** is the process of reinterpreting things when there is a mismatch between a word's typical meaning and how it is used. This concept is crucial for understanding why certain words can be used in sentences that may not align with their usual meanings. Coercion emphasizes the importance of semantic roles in how we perceive meaning within the structure of language. It helps clarify why some words can be used in contexts that deviate from their standard definitions. For example, if a verb typically requires an event as its complement but is followed by a noun phrase instead, coercion allows us to reinterpret that noun phrase to suit the verb's requirements. This is achieved through processes like selection, enrichment, and override, which aid in solving any semantic ambiguity. Coercion demonstrates how language can be flexible and how meaning can be dynamically shaped by the context. It is a fascinating aspect of language that illustrates how our minds adapt and reinterpret information to make sense of it. This flexibility enables speakers to convey complex ideas without always needing to explicitly articulate every detail.

Coercion in attributive predications:
Coercion with adjectives involves extending their meaning beyond their usual scope or typical literary sense.

The journey was hard.

The meeting was long.

In both sentences, adjectives *hard* and *long* are used metaphorically to describe abstract experiences. In Cognitive Grammar, this reflects how language users mentally construe and extend physical concepts to interpret nonphysical events. The adjective *hard* typically evokes physical resistance or solidity. However, when applied to a journey, it is metaphorically extended to describe emotional or psychological difficulty. This shift illustrates conceptual metaphor, where physical effort or resistance is mapped onto mental or emotional struggle. Similarly, *long* usually refers to spatial length. But in the context of a meeting, it is reconstrued to describe temporal duration. This reflects how speakers repurpose spatial language to conceptualize time, a common cognitive strategy known as spatialization of time. Cognitive Grammar emphasizes that meaning is not fixed but arises from construal.

Coercion in peripheral predications:
Adverbs can also be coerced to convey meanings beyond their primary function or literary meaning.

She spoke softly.

The music played loudly.

In both sentences, the adverbs *softly* and *loudly* are typically associated with sound intensity. However, their meanings shift depending on context, a phenomenon known as **coercion** in Cognitive Grammar. In the first sentence, *softly* is coerced to describe not just low volume but a gentle, perhaps emotionally sensitive manner of speaking. The adverb is reinterpreted to match the speaker's behavior and tone, not just the acoustic level. In the second sentence, *loudly* is typically about volume, but here it may also be coerced to imply energetic or enthusiastic performance. The context invites a broader construal, one that includes emotional intensity or dynamic presence, not just decibel level. This illustrates a key principle of Cognitive Grammar: meaning is usage-based and context-sensitive. Words do not carry fixed definitions; instead, their meanings emerge from how speakers conceptualize and frame experiences. Coercion allows language to remain flexible and expressive, adapting to the speaker's intent and the listener's interpretation.

Coercion in relational predications:
Coercion in prepositions involves their reinterpretation based on context. Prepositions may acquire additional meanings beyond their spatial or directional sense.

They walked through the problem.

He spoke on the phone.

Both sentences showcase how everyday language relies on **construal** and **coercion**, key ideas in Cognitive Grammar. In this framework, meaning is not fixed but emerges from how speakers mentally structure and interpret experiences. In the first sentence, the preposition *through* is typically used to describe movement within a physical space. However, it is coerced here to fit a more abstract domain—problem-solving. The verb *walked* evokes a step-by-step physical journey, and *through* reinforces the idea of navigating a complex issue. This metaphorical construal allows listeners to conceptualize the problem as a space that can be entered, explored, and exited, mirroring physical movement. In the second sentence, *on* usually denotes physical contact or location. But in this context, it is coerced to describe a communicative act via a technological medium. The phone is not a surface being stood on; it is a channel for interaction. This usage reflects how entrenched expressions evolve through repeated metaphorical extensions, allowing *on* to signal engagement with a device rather than physical placement.

5.5.3 *Zone Activation*

In Cognitive Grammar, **zone activation** is the process of bringing a specific part of a conceptual domain to the forefront, which we call the **active zone**, to make sense of a particular expression. An active zone highlights the part of an entity that stands out the most in a given context or is most directly involved in a specific relationship. The idea of active zones sheds light on how certain elements of a conceptual structure become more prominent or active in our minds based on the context, shaping how we interpret language and extract meanings from expressions. Active zones play a vital role in linguistic underdetermination, as they help us fill in the gaps and infer the full meaning from the partial information that language provides. They are key to how we, as language users, conceptualize and understand linguistic expressions. Active zones are crucial for analyzing the meanings of lexical concepts. For instance, when we say, *The kettle is boiling*, we actually interpret it as the water inside the kettle boiling, not the kettle itself. This shows how the active zone, *the water*, is inferred from the context, even when the expression is unclear.

Active zones in attributive predications:
In adjectives, the active zone refers to specific quality or characteristic of an entity that the adjective is highlighting. Here are some examples of adjectives with their potential active zones:

The silverware was shiny.
The special sauce is spicy.
The stars are bright tonight.
The old book was heavy.
The roses were fragrant.

In Cognitive Grammar, adjectives highlight a specific active zone within the entity they describe. This is the particular part or feature that the adjective brings into focus based on our sensory and experiential knowledge. For example, in the adjective *shiny*, the active zone is the reflective surface of the silverware, as that is the aspect perceived visually as glossy. The adjective *spicy* activates the taste-related zone of food, emphasizing the sensory experience on the palate. With *bright*, the active zone is the part of the stars that emit or reflect light, drawing attention to their luminous quality. When using *heavy*, the active zone is the part of the book one lifts or carries, highlighting the physical sensation of weight. For *fragrant*, the active zone is the part of the roses that emits scent, engaging our sense of smell. Each adjective directs cognitive attention to the salient sensory or physical property of the object, allowing language to efficiently convey meaning by profiling only the relevant quality or subregion of the whole entity.

Active zones in peripheral predications:
In adverbs, the active zone refers to the aspect of the action or quality that the adverb is highlighting or making salient. Here are some examples of adverbs with their potential active zones:

She walked quickly away.
He carefully handled the glass.
She laughed loudly at the joke.
They lived happily ever after.
He spoke slowly in the class.

In Cognitive Grammar, adverbs function by directing our attention to specific active zones that characterize how an action is performed or how a state is experienced. For example, the adverb *quickly* highlights the speed dimension of running, focusing on the rapidity of the motion. In *carefully*, the active zone centers on precision and meticulous attention to detail in the action. The adverb *loudly* activates the sensory dimension of sound volume or intensity, drawing focus to auditory impact. With *happily*, the focus shifts to the internal emotional state of joy or contentment accompanying the action. Lastly, *slowly* directs attention to the reduction in speed, emphasizing a deliberate or gradual pace. Each adverb, therefore, profiles a distinct aspect or quality of the event or state, allowing language to efficiently convey nuanced experiential perspectives. This focus helps speakers highlight the most important part of an action or state in any situation.

Active zones in relational predications:
In prepositions, the active zone refers to the specific part of an entity that is most directly involved in a relationship. Here are some examples of prepositions with their potential active zones:

The book is on the table.

The coffee is in the cup.

Look at the picture.

He wrote with a pen.

She read from the screen.

In Cognitive Grammar, prepositions function by highlighting specific "active zones" that define spatial or relational aspects between entities. For instance, the preposition *on* directs focus to the surface of the table where the book rests, while *in* emphasizes the interior space of the cup. The preposition *at* highlights the surface of the picture being observed, and *with* draws attention to the tip of the pen that contacts the paper. Similarly, *from* marks the part of the screen displaying text. These examples demonstrate how different prepositions selectively profile particular zones within relationships, accounting for their varied meanings depending on the context and the aspects of the entities involved. Prepositions highlight key zones to shape how we mentally understand spatial and functional relationships, flexibly adapting to different contexts to convey meaning clearly.

Summary

In this chapter, I have taken a closer look at **simple atemporal relations**. These types of relations do not directly involve time; instead, they focus on descriptions, attributes, and static connections. They include individual word classes that express timeless ideas, such as adjectives, adverbs, and prepositions. In the realm of Cognitive Grammar, these are categorized as non-processual relationships. A **non-processual relationship** does not involve any processes or changes over time. These types of relationships play a crucial role in how we structure language, convey meaning, and shape our understanding of reality by highlighting the stable or unchanging qualities of the things we encounter. They help us grasp and communicate the essential characteristics of objects and concepts. Simple atemporal relations consist of adjectives, adverbs, and prepositions, each fitting into specific categories and showcasing cognitive aspects. As symbolic structures, they enrich language by shaping how we perceive things, actions, and relationships.

Adjectives profile the qualities of nouns through a cognitive process known as **profiling**, which highlights a specific quality of a conceptual entity. In *She has a stunning dress*, the adjective *stunning* emphasizes the aesthetic quality of the noun *dress*. Adverbs, on the other hand, refine the meaning of actions through a cognitive process called **focusing**, making a particular aspect of an event more prominent. In *She ran quickly to catch the bus*, the adverb *quickly* focuses on the manner of the action, foregrounding speed in our mental representation. Prepositions function differently: they establish connections between entities or events by drawing on **image schemas**, mental patterns derived from our physical and perceptual interactions with the world. In *The bird is in the cage*, the preposition *in* invokes the containment schema, helping us understand spatial relationships. Together, these processes demonstrate how language not only describes but also structures our mental imagery and understanding of the world.

Exercises

1. The adjectives listed below have various meanings. Construct a semantic network for each one.

   1. fair
   2. fine
   3. cool
   4. clear
   5. sharp

2. The following adjectives evoke the domain of weakness, each highlighting a distinct facet. Can you identify it?

   1. frail
   2. weak
   3. feeble
   4. fragile
   5. decrepit

3. The following pairs of adjectives are nonequivalent in a certain dimension of construal. Discuss this.

   1. freaky versus freakish
   2. eccentric versus quirky
   3. clever versus intelligent
   4. gloomy versus melancholic
   5. continuous versus continual

4. The following adverbs can be used in different contexts to convey varied meanings. Can you identify them?

1. fast
2. just
3. well
4. hard
5. most

5. The following adverbs express speed, with subtle distinctions in meaning. Can you spot them?

1. quickly
2. rapidly
3. swiftly
4. hastily
5. promptly

6. The following adverb pairs are not interchangeable; each is semantically distinct. Can you show how?

1. late versus lately
2. fine versus finely
3. hard versus hardly
4. high versus highly
5. most versus mostly

7. The following prepositions convey distinct meanings in different contexts. What are they?

1. by
2. off
3. over
4. with
5. under

8. The following prepositions express manner, each highlighting a distinct facet, Can you explain how?

1. in
2. as
3. by
4. like
5. with

9. These prepositional pairs differ in meaning and are not easily interchangeable. Explain why.

1. above versus over
2. along versus across
3. under versus beneath
4. behind versus beyond
5. between versus among

10. The following words can be used as adjectives and adverbs. Construct sentences to illustrate their uses.

1. early
2. daily
3. likely
4. wrong
5. straight

6

Complex Atemporal Relations: Predications in Gerunds, Participles, and Infinitives

6.1 Introduction

In Chapter 5, I explored the first subcategory of atemporal relations, focusing on **simple atemporal relations**, which revolve around stable properties and static connections between elements. Linguistically, they involve single-element structures or word classes such as adjectives, adverbs, and prepositions. Now, in this chapter, I will delve into the second subcategory of atemporal relations, which centers on **complex atemporal relations**. These are conceptually richer, with intricate connections often involving multiple components or layers of meaning. Linguistically, they include nominalized processes (gerunds), attributive processual predications (participles), and ungrounded schematic processes (infinitives). By utilizing complex atemporal relations, we can convey timeless ideas that transcend specific moments in time. Both simple and complex atemporal relations remain constant and unaltered over time. In doing so, they significantly enrich our understanding of language and provide a framework for examining how these relations operate across different word classes. Appreciating the subtleties of such relations is crucial for achieving effective communication.

When discussing complex atemporal relationships, we briefly examine the verb in terms of **grounding**, whether it is grounded or ungrounded. A **grounded process** clearly indicates tense, person, and number. It is termed a **finite verb** in grammar. An **ungrounded process** is a type of verb that lacks a subject and does not indicate tense. It is termed a **nonfinite verb** in grammar. The nonfinite forms of verbs are introduced by the **symbolic markers** -ing or to-. In grammar, these markers are called **complementizers.** Nonfinite verbs serve different purposes in sentences. This versatility allows them to connect ideas without being anchored in time, making them part of an atemporal relationship. For example, in the sentence *Nigel vowed never to drink again*, the to-infinitive verb form *to drink* denotes an ungrounded process. It represents an atemporal event, lacking markers of person or tense. In English, the three main types of ungrounded processes, that is, nonfinite verbs, are nominalized processes (gerunds), attributive processual predications (participles), and ungrounded schematic processes (infinitives). These forms greatly enrich our language, providing us with the flexibility to express complex ideas in various ways.

6.2 Conceptual Subordination

In Cognitive Grammar, **conceptual subordination** refers to an unequal relationship in which a conceptually dependent unit is understood through a conceptually autonomous unit. The dependent unit elaborates or profiles a subpart of the relation evoked by the autonomous unit. Grammar encodes this relationship as **clausal complementation**, where a subordinate clause, or **complement clause**, relies on a main clause for its interpretation, regardless of whether the clause is finite or nonfinite. A **complementizer**, conceptually a **symbolic marker**, typically introduces the complement clause, appearing as a single morpheme or a pair of morphemes that signal its subordinate status. For example, in *They warned him that the road was icy*, *They warned him* is the main clause, and *that the road was icy* is the complement clause. This relationship extends beyond syntax: it is also semantic, since the complement clause provides essential information that completes the meaning of the main clause. By using complement clauses, speakers convey complex ideas more clearly, adding precise details or specific nuances.

In Cognitive Grammar, clausal complementation is understood as the integration of two component events into a unified conceptual event. The conceptually autonomous unit corresponds to the grammatically main clause, whereas the conceptually dependent unit corresponds to the grammatically subordinate clause. The subordinate clause is a crucial element that adds meaning to the autonomous clause by providing necessary details. The two clauses are like puzzle pieces that fit together to form a complete picture in a sentence. In Cognitive Grammar, the choice of a complement clause type is not only determined by the semantics of the main verb but also, to a large extent, by the role of the speaker in construing a situation. Meaning is intrinsically linked to conceptualization and determines the syntactic structure of a complement clause, since it originates in the speaker's mind. Language, in turn, mirrors the diverse ways in which lived experience is conceptualized. Thus, clausal complementation exemplifies the dynamic interplay between grammar and cognition in shaping linguistic expression.

Conceptual subordination involves two key elements: subordinate structures and symbolic markers

6.2.1 *Subordinate Conceptual Structures*

In Cognitive Grammar, a **subordinate conceptual structure** is a unit that depends on, or is embedded within, a larger conceptualization. Its meaning is interpreted through the higher-level structure it supports. In grammar, this kind of conceptual subordination is known as **complement clauses**, where an embedded clause functions as a dependent unit within a main clause. It elaborates a significant aspect of the relation evoked by the main clause's verb, providing additional details necessary for a complete understanding of a sentence. There are two main types of subordinate conceptual structures: temporal and atemporal. A **temporal** subordinate conceptual structure, a finite complement clause, is connected to a specific time and describes a situation that actually exists, directly associated with a certain timeframe. Finite complement clauses include that-clauses, wh-clauses, and whether/if clauses. In contrast, an **atemporal** subordinate conceptual structure—a nonfinite complement clause—is not linked to any specific time and does not establish a particular reality, lacking a clear temporal reference. Nonfinite complement clauses consist of -ing gerunds, to-infinitives, bare infinitives, and for-to clauses.

Let's analyze the difference with a few examples. In the sentence *Nigel vowed that he would never drink again*, the complement clause is grounded, meaning it is tied to a specific person and time, representing a clear event. On the other hand, in *Nigel vowed never to drink again*, the complement clause is not grounded, making it more abstract and timeless, lacking any markers of person or tense. Both clauses convey the same idea: Nigel's determination to avoid alcohol, but they do so in different ways. According to Cognitive Grammar, the way we interpret these differences can change the meaning. The first sentence emphasizes Nigel's personal commitment to not drinking in the future, clearly stating his intention. This temporal framing suggests that since making his vow, Nigel has not consumed alcohol. In contrast, the second sentence focuses more on the action itself, simply stating he won't drink anymore. Without *that he would*, it feels more direct and to the point. This atemporal view leaves room for the possibility that Nigel might drink again despite his promise. So, when we ask *Why doesn't Nigel touch a glass of wine anymore?*, the first sentence seems like a better fit than the second.

6.2.2 *Symbolic Markers*

In Cognitive Grammar, **symbolic markers** are conceptual elements that shape how an expression is understood within a larger conceptual structure. They operate by signaling relationships between units, such as profiling one unit as conceptually subordinate to another. They do not just decorate syntax; they shape how meaning is structured in the mind. In grammar, these markers are called **complementizers**, linguistic elements that signal a clause's role as a complement. A complementizer may consist of a single morpheme or a pair of morphemes. In Cognitive Grammar, elements such as *that*, *wh*-words, and *whether/if* function as finite complementizers, while *-ing* gerunds, *to*-infinitives, and *for-to* constructions serve as nonfinite complementizers. Unlike other theories that treat complementizers as semantically empty, Cognitive Grammar assigns complementizers semantic value explaining their behavior. From this perspective, complementizers add meaning, enriching the constructions they appear in. They are more than clause markers; they shape syntax and semantics, guiding structure and meaning.

In Cognitive Grammar, complementizers serve as both **profile determinants** and **structural centers**. The former function involves their crucial conceptual role in transforming a temporal relation into an atemporal one and contributing to the semantics of the associated complements. The latter function involves their placement in the central position within a construction, connecting the main verb to the complement clause. To illustrate this point, let's consider an example. In the sentence *The tourists view the exhibition*, the verb *view* profiles a grounded process. The verb requires **sequential scanning**, where the component states are processed individually and experienced successively. The conceptualizer shifts their mental focus from one point to another, similar to watching a motion picture. In the sentence *The tourists fancy viewing the exhibition*, The verb *view* requires the -ing form to create a gerund, thereby transforming the relation into an atemporal one. The -ing gerund necessitates **summary scanning**, where the component states are processed collectively and experienced simultaneously as a single gestalt. The conceptualizer views the whole path at once, like a still picture.

In Cognitive Grammar, speakers have the ability to view a complex scene in different ways, either through a temporal lens or an atemporal one. A symbolic marker creates an atemporal view of its paired structure. Symbolic markers shift clauses between temporal and atemporal, differing by reference to before, during, or after speech. For instance, in the sentence *The wealthy conceal exploiting the poor*, the gerund positions the complement clause before the main clause's temporal reference. In *He fancies taking a long walk by the river*, the gerund aligns the complement clause with the same time frame as the main clause. In *I heard the orchestra play/playing a symphony*, both the bare infinitive and the present participle refer to the same time span as the main clause. In *The government pledges to improve the economy*, the to-infinitive places the complement clause after the main clause's reference time. This shows that complementizers are not just formal syntactic markers; they play a key role in shaping meaning.

In grammar, the choice of a specific complementizer in a construction is primarily determined by the semantic compatibility between the main verb and the complementizer itself. **Compatibility** refers to the ability of two or more elements such as words, phrases, or clauses to coexist harmoniously within a sentence or context without causing conflicts or contradictions. This compatibility is based on the inherent meaning of both the main verb and the complementizer. Some verbs only work with one complementizer. For instance, in the sentence *She wants to rest/*resting*, both the main verb and the infinitive marker indicate subsequence, showing perfect agreement. In *She enjoys resting/*to rest*, both the main verb and the gerund marker indicate simultaneity, showing perfect agreement. Some verbs have multiple meanings and can therefore be used with different complementizers to convey different nuances. In *She attempts to rest/resting*, the main verb aligns with both complementizers to convey both meanings. Complementizers add meaning to constructions, serving as key tools for encoding language.

6.3 Nominalized Processual Predications

In Cognitive Grammar, **nominalized processual predications** refer to events or actions that are reclassified conceptually and treated as things rather than dynamic occurrences. This gives a process a more stable, entity-like conceptual status. In grammar, these nominalized processes are typically expressed by **gerunds**. A **gerund** is a nonfinite *-ing* form that functions as a noun, retaining the essence of the verb while taking on roles usually reserved for nouns. Gerunds allow us to discuss actions without actually performing them, referring to concrete or habitual activities in a timeless manner. In Cognitive Grammar, the gerund is seen as a symbolic structure that profiles an ongoing activity, a habitual action, or a process associated with a specific instance of that activity. The pairing of form and meaning in gerunds is not arbitrary but semantically motivated. Gerunds are significant because they show how actions can be expressed within a noun-based framework in a concise and flexible way. For example, in *Reading is my leisure*, *reading* functions as a noun and can be replaced by another noun such as *music* in *Music is my leisure*. The focus is on the activity itself, conceptualized as an atemporal entity.

6.3.1 Function

Unlike typical action verbs, gerunds represent ungrounded processes that assume a more conceptual role and fulfill diverse functions. A gerund is essentially a verbal noun, looking like a verb but behaving like a noun. Gerunds provide a neat way to express ideas, blending the traits of both verbs and nouns. They bridge the gap between the two, adding versatility to our language. Like linguistic chameleons, gerunds adapt smoothly to their surroundings, replacing nouns in different spots within sentences and enriching expression with their remarkable adaptability. Their placement can carry significant meaning, conveying subtle shades of nuance. Choosing a particular gerund can shift the focus, highlighting either the action itself or the activity involved. Gerunds let us express actions in a more abstract manner, framing them as reasons, hobbies, or the recipients of a subject's actions. Used in different patterns, they convey a range of meanings and enrich language.

Subject:	Swimming is good exercise.
Direct object:	He enjoys swimming.
Subject complement:	His passion is swimming.
Appositive:	His passion, swimming, keeps him fit.
Prepositional complement:	He is interested in swimming.
Adjectival complement:	He was busy swimming.

The examples above illustrate the functions of gerunds in various grammatical contexts. In Cognitive Grammar, the position of a gerund in a sentence significantly affects its meaning and function. As a subject, the gerund highlights swimming as an ongoing activity, turning the action into a concept that emphasizes its benefits. As a direct object, it emphasizes the action performed by the subject, highlighting the act of swimming. Common verbs that take gerunds include *abhor*, *advise*, *allow*, *anticipate*, *appreciate*, *avoid*, *celebrate*, *confess*, *defend*, *discuss*, *dislike*, *endure*, *escape*, *feel like*, *forgive*, *mention*, *permit*, *postpone*, *prevent*, *recollect*, *tolerate*, *urge*, *warrant*, and more. As a complement, the gerund adds detail, showing the subject's interest in swimming. As an appositive, the gerund renames or further identifies a preceding noun, offering additional information. When used as a prepositional complement, the gerund acts as the complement after the preposition *in*. As an adjectival complement, the gerund completes the meaning of the adjective. Gerunds are powerful tools for expressing actions, interests, and nuances, and their usage significantly impact the overall meaning of a sentence.

6.3.2 Meaning

In Cognitive Grammar, ungrounded processes, manifested linguistically as nonfinite verb forms, can be understood in relation to the **reality model,** which progresses from the past, through the present, and into the future. This model is essential for interpreting situations based on their status in reality. There are two ways to understand reality: the basic model and the dynamic model. The **basic model** consists of **immediate reality**, which refers to events happening currently, and **non-immediate (or known) reality**, which includes events that have already occurred. Linguistically, basic reality deals with ongoing or past event, where the facts are clear. On the other hand, the dynamic model distinguishes between **potential reality**, which refers to events that may occur, and **projected reality**, which refers to events that are expected or likely to occur. Linguistically, dynamic reality emphasizes future possibilities that remain uncertain. In this realm, facts are fluid rather than fixed. When we imagine scenarios, we enter the realm of *irreality*. For example, saying *I wish I could find a better job* expresses a purely hypothetical situation.

In the realm of language, understanding the reality model is crucial for explaining the syntactic phenomenon of the gerund. This form captures both the immediate and non-immediate aspects of our basic reality. For instance, in the sentence *She relishes telling stories*, the gerund reflects immediate reality, indicating an action that is happening right now. Immediate reality is all about simultaneity, where the main event and the complement event occur at the same time. So, when we say *telling stories*, it is clear that this action is unfolding as we speak, especially following verbs that express reactions. On the other hand, in *She admits making a mistake*, the gerund points to non-immediate reality, referring to events that have already taken place. Non-immediate reality is about anteriority, meaning the complement event happens before the main event. Here, *making a mistake* has already occurred, and this typically follows verbs of communication. To sum it up, immediate reality relates to what we experience directly, while non-immediate reality involves our thoughts, memories, and abstract concepts.

6.3.3 Cognitive Aspects

Cognitive Grammar provides a rich and insightful view of language, viewing it as a natural result of our cognitive abilities. It emphasizes that grammar is not simply a set of rigid rules but is deeply meaningful. The way we build linguistic structures is closely connected to fundamental cognitive processes such as categorization, configuration, and conceptualization. These processes are vital in how we construct meaning and are essential for our daily interactions, engaging various complex brain functions. They assist us in organizing information, grouping together linguistic elements, and understanding abstract ideas, ultimately enhancing the clarity and effectiveness of our communication. This clearly demonstrates that the significance of the nominalized processes goes beyond syntax; they also reflect our deeper thoughts and representations of language.

6.3.3.1 Categorization

The gerund is intrinsically polysemous, forming a category of distinct but related senses. Prototypically, it denotes the temporary ongoing nature of an activity. In *She is busy writing a letter*, the gerund indicates an activity that is currently taking place. This core meaning can be further extended into two additional values. The first extended value is simultaneity, where two ongoing events occur simultaneously. This usage is commonly seen after two types of verbs: mental verbs such as *consider*, *imagine*, *remember*, and enjoyment or preference verbs such as *enjoy*, *love*, and *prefer*. For example, in *She considers accepting the offer*, the complement event expressed by the gerund is mentally happening at the same time as the main event. Similarly, in *Kate enjoys dancing the tango*, the complement reflects present action. The second extended value is anteriority, where the complement event precedes the time of the utterance expressed by the main verb. This usage is often found after verbs related to communication such as *admit*, *acknowledge*, *concede*, *confess*, and *deny*. For example, in *He admits tripping her up*, the act of making her fall occurred before the act of admitting.

6.3.3.2 Configuration

Gerunds and to-infinitives are part of the domain of atemporality, yet they represent distinct facets within it. They are not isolated grammatical constructs; instead, they are intricately linked to our conceptual understanding of actions and experiences. According to cognitive linguists, both are form-meaning pairings. They serve similar purposes as nouns, but their forms and usage patterns differ. Their distribution is not random or arbitrary but rather semantically motivated. Language choices are not just rules to follow but reflections of conceptual patterns. In other words, the decision to use a gerund or infinitive in a specific context is influenced by the underlying conceptual meaning associated with the action. For example, when we say, *I enjoy lying in the sun*, the gerund *lying* reflects the experiential pleasure of the activity itself. When we say *I want to lie in the sun*, the infinitive *to lie* expresses the desire or intention to engage in the action of *lying*. As the examples demonstrate, their usage is not unprincipled; it is guided by the conceptual motivations behind the action, which is essential for effective communication.

I prefer living in the countryside.
I prefer to live in the countryside.

The verb *prefer* is versatile and can be followed by both the gerund and the to-infinitive. However, each form refers to a different facet of atemporality and carries a distinct meaning. In the first sentence, the gerund refers to the current action of living in the countryside, with the focus on the activity itself. The gerund is often preferred when actions occur simultaneously, indicating something that is enjoyed at the moment of speaking. It implies that the speaker generally enjoys the lifestyle of residing in rural areas. In the second sentence, the to-infinitive refers to a future action, shifting the focus to the purpose or intention of living in the countryside, indicating something that has not yet occurred. In both examples, the gerund and the to-infinitive provide additional information without specifying tense, suggesting that living in rural areas is the preferred choice for the speaker. Both sentences convey the idea that the countryside is the preferred place to live, but they emphasize different aspects. The first sentence focuses on the ongoing experience, while the second highlights the decision or desire to reside there.

6.3.3.3 Conceptualization

The gerund can be used in non-extraposed and extraposed constructions, each conveying a distinct perspective. In a non-extraposed construction, the complement clause appears before the main predicate in the sentence and acts as the subject. In an extraposed construction, the complement clause appears after the main predicate, and the subject position is filled by *it*. Previous approaches, adopted the end-weight principle, where longer or heavier clauses are extraposed or moved to the end of the sentence to enhance readability and ease of processing. In Cognitive Grammar, extraposition is a cognitive strategy that contributes to effective conveyance of meaning. In previous approaches, the pronoun *it* serves as a structural device to maintain sentence coherence. In Cognitive Grammar, the pronoun *it* helps establish a general context or background information for an event or situation. By introducing *it*, we create a reference point that allows subsequent details to be anchored within a broader frame. Accordingly, the choice between the two constructions resides in the construal of **scope**, the array of conceptual content that an expression evokes as the basis for its meaning.

Swimming is fun.
It is fun swimming.

Both sentences convey a similar idea, but the nuance comes from how the situation is construed. The key difference in meaning lies in the scope of each sentence. In the first one, the speaker takes a narrow perspective, focusing solely on the act of swimming as the main factor for their judgment. Here, the emphasis is on whether swimming is appropriate, suggesting that it is deemed suitable for a specific context. In contrast, the second sentence adopts a broader view, considering all aspects of the situation when making the assessment. The term *it* refers to a wider context that includes the overall circumstances surrounding the act of swimming. This implies that swimming is seen as fun for a more general situation. Thus, viewed through a cognitive lens, the basis for the evaluation in the second sentence encompasses a larger scope compared to the first. In short, the difference lies not in the activity itself but in how broadly the speaker frames the situation.

Instantiating Reference

Gerunds can be construed in terms of reference, either as **generic instantiations** (bare form) or as **specific instantiations** (with a determiner). This highlights the remarkable flexibility of language in expressing a wide range of ideas and nuances. In their generic instantiation, gerunds convey actions or concepts in a broad, general sense, allowing for open interpretation. They represent activities or processes in a nonspecific manner, without linking them to a particular time or instance. Conversely, in their specific instantiation, gerunds refer to a particular, identifiable action or occurrence, adding clarity and precision to communication. This duality enriches our ability to express meaning, enabling us to describe actions and processes with either a broad or focused lens depending on context. Such nuanced understanding makes communication more precise and effective. Through these two instantiations, the gerund adapts seamlessly, enhancing our language by making it more dynamic, nuanced, and impactful. Consider the examples below as evidence:

Swimming makes her lose weight.

The swimming makes her lose weight.

Both sentences express that swimming contributes to weight loss but differ subtly in focus and scope. The first sentence, without the definite article *the*, presents swimming as a generic instantiation of the activity. In cognitive terms, this reflects a more schematic mental image of swimming as an unbounded, habitual, or general activity. It refers to swimming in any form, emphasizing the activity as a whole rather than a particular instance. It suggests that swimming generally helps her lose weight by evoking a broad category of actions without pinpointing a specific occurrence. In contrast, the second sentence uses the definite article *the* before *swimming*, which narrows the conceptual focus to a specific instantiation of the activity. Cognitive

Grammar interprets this as a more bounded mental representation, where the speaker and listener share awareness of a particular swimming event, routine, or context. It might refer to a swimming class, regimen, or specific event, shaping a clear mental frame.

6.4 Attributive Processual Predications

In Cognitive Grammar, **an attributive processual predication** refers to a structure in which a verb process is used to describe a noun, like an adjective. The process is reduced to describe a property of an entity. In grammar, these attributive processual predications are realized as **participles**, as in *the running water* or *the broken window*, where *running* and *broken* both describe qualities derived from processes. Attributive processual predication can be either **imperfective participial form**, grammatically a **present participle** ending in *-ing*, or **perfective participial form**, grammatically a **past participle** ending in *-ed* or taking irregular forms. Present participles act as adjectives modifying nouns. In *The exciting ride made the children scream*, *exciting* functions adjectivally, describing the ride in an atemporal way. Past participles function adjectivally, attributing a **resultant state** or quality to a noun. In *The broken vase was mended*, *broken* acts adjectivally, describing the vase's current state in an atemporal way. In Cognitive Grammar, past and present participles function as ungrounded symbols, attributing qualities to entities without anchoring them to a specific time frame.

6.4.1 *Function*

The present participle is a distinctive verb form that defies classification as a typical verb, noun, or adjective. Instead, it occupies multiple roles depending on the context, demonstrating remarkable flexibility. It functions in forming continuous tenses, modifying nouns, or constructing participial phrases. Most frequently, it serves an adjectival role, enriching the noun it modifies with additional detail. One might argue that the present participle is a fundamental component of language. Initiating a sentence with a participial phrase allows for the condensation of information, conveying complex ideas succinctly, provided the modified word is placed immediately beside the phrase to avoid ambiguity. Beyond its grammatical function, the present participle shapes how we perceive and articulate ongoing actions, continuous states, and dynamic processes. It captures nuanced meanings and facilitates viewing actions from varied perspectives. In doing so, the present participle significantly enhances language, making it more versatile and expressive. Its diverse applications enrich both spoken and written communication.

Subject:	Buying clothes is what I enjoy most.
Direct object:	The whole family stood waving on the road.
Subject complement:	The movie is boring.
Object complement:	I heard her crying.
Attributive modifier:	It was an amazing match.
Predicative modifier:	I found the work exhausting.
Adverb after a verb:	She went shopping yesterday.
Sentence modifier:	Thinking of their safety, they traveled in pairs.

The examples mentioned illustrate how the present participle functions across various grammatical roles. The present participle is more than just a grammatical form; it is a conceptual tool that enriches meaning and allows language to express nuanced perspectives on actions and experiences. Its versatility helps us construe events as dynamic or continuous. In the first example, *buying clothes* serves as the subject of the sentence. In the second example, *waving* acts as the direct object of the verb *stood*. Present participles frequently follow verbs like *stand*, *sit*, *lie*, *go*, and *run* when functioning as direct objects. Moving on, *boring* describes the subject (*the movie*) in the third example. In the fourth, *crying* complements the direct object (*her*). The fifth example shows *amazing* modifying the noun *match*. In the sixth, *exhausting* describes the subject (*the work*). The seventh example features *shopping* functioning as an adverbial modifier, indicating the activity. Finally, the phrase *thinking of their safety* modifies the entire sentence.

6.4.2 *Meaning*

In Cognitive Grammar, cognitive models, shaped by experience, play a crucial role in understanding meaning. They provide a framework for interpreting events, actions, and intentions. When we encounter the -ing present participle, the **reality model** helps us grasp the specific facet associated with it. The use of the -ing present participle plays a role in representing **immediate reality**. It is used to describe actions that are currently happening, ongoing, or in progress. It represents events happening in the here and now, emphasizing direct experience and the immediacy of an event, situating it in the present moment. The present participle can be explained in terms of **grounding**, which refers to how language relates to the speech event and its participants. The -ing present participle grounds an action in the immediate present, connecting it to the ongoing experience of the speaker or listener.

For instance, in *She is running in the park*, the action of *running* is grounded as ongoing. This proves that language is a powerful tool for conveying our perception of reality, with the -ing participle expressing ongoing actions and experiences.

6.4.3 Cognitive Aspects

Building on our previous discussions of nominalized processes, that is, the gerunds, let's now delve into the cognitive aspects of categorization, configuration, and conceptualization in imperfective participial form, that is, the present participle. We will approach the topic with the same level of careful attention as before. The aim is to demonstrate how the present participle serves not only as a grammatical device but also as a cognitive tool that shapes perspective, framing experience through continuity and modification.

6.4.3.1 Categorization

The present participle is polysemous, encompassing a category of varied yet interconnected meanings. Its prototype lies in the continuous aspect, an ongoing, unbounded process of activity. In *She is reading a book*, the present participle profiles a process unfolding steadily over time. It emphasizes an activity occurring concurrently with the actual moment of speaking. At the periphery, the core meaning of ongoing process extends to modifier functions, which are more abstract yet still grounded in the central notion of dynamicity. In *the flowing river*, the present participle flowing acts as an adjectival modifier, clearly highlighting the continuous movement of water within the river. In *I found the task exhausting*, it reflects the speaker's experiential response to the noun, serving as a direct predicative modifier. In *I saw him crying*, it adds a simultaneous action to the object, functioning as an object-level complement. Finally, in *Thinking of their safety, they traveled in pairs*, it acts as a sentence-level modifier, shaping context.

6.4.3.2 Configuration

Both gerunds and present participles are verb forms ending in -ing, yet they serve distinct purposes. Gerunds function primarily as nouns, while present participles function chiefly as adjectives. The choice between them often depends on cognitive motivations. Our use of gerunds and participles is guided by meaning and conceptualization rather than arbitrary rules. Language choices mirror how we structure and interpret lived experience, revealing underlying thought patterns rather than simply following prescribed guidelines. Gerunds represent actions or states in a more abstract manner, encapsulating general concepts or activities. In contrast, present participles emphasize specific, immediate, and unfolding processes or states. Recognizing this distinction through the lens of Cognitive Grammar deepens our understanding of language as a powerful tool for expressing nuanced perspectives. By grasping the distinction, we gain expressive nuance, grammatical accuracy, and stylistic polish. This insight is truly fundamental to navigating the complexities of English grammar and advancing toward fluency.

Standing in the queue is tiresome.

Standing in the queue, I felt tired.

Both sentences convey a similar conceptual core, but they differ in how they construe the experience of queuing. The first sentence frames queuing as a broad, general activity, presenting it as tiresome in an abstract sense. Here, the -ing form functions as a gerund, conceptualized as a nominal entity, serving as the subject of the clause. This use conveys a generalized, objective stance, emphasizing the fatigue of waiting in line without tying it to a specific moment or perspective. In contrast, the second sentence employs the present participle as an adverbial modifier. This construction reflects a more immediate, subjective stance, where the speaker reports a personal feeling of tiredness during the act of queuing. The focus shifts from generalization to lived experience, showing how language moves from abstract categories to concrete perception. These examples show how the same verb form, shaped by context, can convey subtle shifts in meaning.

6.4.3.3 Conceptualization

In English, the same adjective roots yield two forms: those ending in *-ing* derive from present participles, while those ending in *-ed* derive from past participles. The difference reflects the construal of **perspective**, the vantage point in language that frames interpretation and expression. These suffixes reflect how meaning is constructed in language. Adjectives formed with -ing describe the quality of the subject, emphasizing the process or ongoing nature of the quality. For example, an *interesting book* is one that engages our attention through its content. On the other hand, adjectives formed with -ed describe the result or state arising from the action, often conveying a sense of passivity or completion. For instance, an *interested reader* is someone who is keen on reading. Additional adjectives are *boring/bored*, *exciting/excited*, *fascinating/fascinated*, *amazing/amazed*, *shocking/shocked*, *confusing/confused*, *annoying/annoyed*, *disappointing/disappointed*, *frightening/frightened*, and *terrifying/terrified*. The key difference is that *-ing* adjectives describe the cause of an emotion, while *-ed* adjectives describe the emotion itself.

The jokes were amusing.

We were amused by the jokes.

Both sentences express a sense of enjoyment but construe it from different cognitive perspectives. The first highlights the inherent quality of the jokes themselves, while the second focuses on the audience's experiential response. In the first sentence, *amusing* functions as an adjective that encodes the property of being entertaining or funny, capturing the conceptualization of the jokes as intrinsically humorous. This reflects a more object-centered construal, emphasizing the source of amusement. Conversely, the second sentence uses *amused*, also an adjective, but one that profiles the audience's internal experience of entertainment. Here, the focus shifts to a subject-centered construal, the mental and emotional state evoked by the jokes. This implies that the audience perceives and reacts to the humor in a personal, affective way. In summary, *amusing* describes the characteristics that generate entertainment, while *amused* reflects the subjective feeling of being entertained. This distinction reveals how language encodes differing cognitive frames based on our experience and interaction with events and objects in the world.

Prepositional and participial construals:
Consider how prepositional and participial construals reflect different conceptualizations.

He saved the boy from drowning in the canal.

He saved the boy drowning in the canal.

In the first sentence, *drowning* is construed as a gerund, serving as the nominal object of the preposition *from*. This construction profiles the conceptual event of drowning as an ongoing process, from which the boy must be rescued. The preposition introduces conceptual distance between the verbs, signaling a mediated relationship: the saving may involve indirect actions such as calling for help or throwing a lifejacket. In contrast, the second sentence construes *drowning* as a present participle, functioning adjectivally to modify *boy*. This participial construal creates conceptual closeness between the verbs, presenting the saving as immediate and embodied, direct intervention such as jumping into the water and pulling the boy out. These examples illustrate how the same verb form can instantiate distinct grammatical roles that reflect different construals of the event. In Cognitive Grammar, linguistic distance mirrors conceptual distance, while closeness mirrors proximity. From a cognitive underpinning, grammar operates not as a mechanical system but as a window into the mind's structuring of experience.

6.5 Schematic Processual Predications

In Cognitive Grammar, **schematic processual predications** are abstract events or actions that are not anchored to a specific time or participant. They represent a process in its most general, non-situated form, and are grammatically realized by **infinitives**. An **infinitive** is the base form of a verb, usually introduced by *to*, which names a process that is presented without temporal grounding, not tied to a specific subject, tense, or number. In English, it is conceptually an **ungrounded process** and, linguistically, a **nonfinite** form of the verb. Since a nonfinite form cannot stand alone, it requires a finite form to provide context. There are three types of infinitives: the to-infinitive, the bare (zero) infinitive, and the for-to infinitive. These forms are timeless, lacking a fixed moment, and each infinitive functions as a symbolic structure in sentence building. Cognitive Grammar also adopts a **conceptualist** approach to semantics, focusing on how we can interpret situations in different ways. Each type of infinitive conveys its own meaning: the to-infinitive indicates futurity, the bare infinitive implies immediacy, and the for-to infinitive suggests indirectness. Recognizing these nuanced differences is vital to communicating effectively.

6.5.1 Prospective Activity

In Cognitive Grammar, a **prospective activity** refers to an action that is construed as not yet realized but oriented toward the future, possibility, or intention. Prospective activity, in grammatical terms, is encoded as a **to-infinitive**. It signals an event not yet realized, pointing to a situation still to occur or about to happen. From a pragmatic standpoint, the success of the action is not guaranteed. Take the example of *She wants to join the club*. Here, the to-infinitive refers to something that does not exist at the moment of speaking and is not assured to happen. The to-infinitive also serves to express the purpose behind an action, highlighting the intended goal or outcome. For instance, in *He works diligently to support his family*, the purpose is crystal clear: he is putting in hard work with the specific aim of supporting his family. In Cognitive Grammar, the to-infinitive is an ungrounded process whose use is meaning-driven. More than a grammatical form, it conveys meaning, acts like a noun in a sentence and fulfills diverse roles.

6.5.1.1 Function

In Cognitive Grammar, the to-infinitive serves multiple purposes, reflecting its flexibility and versatility. Its flexibility makes it an essential part of language, allowing speakers to convey a wide range of functions in different contexts.

These multiple functions suggest that language is not just a set of rules but a dynamic system for expressing diverse meanings. The versatility of the to-infinitive affects how speakers express intentions, desires, and avoidance in English, shaping both language use and meaning. The to-infinitive plays a crucial role in **construal**, shaping how we perceive events and their temporal relationships. Its motivated form-meaning pairing contributes to our mental representations in language. This intricate interplay between form and meaning highlights the to-infinitive's role as a bridge between thought and expression. Understanding the uses of the to-infinitive enhances our ability to express ideas effectively. Using the to-infinitive logically requires an understanding of cognitive motivations.

Subject:	To play chess is fun.
Direct object:	He wants to play chess.
Subject complement:	His desire is to play chess.
Appositive:	His desire, to play chess, was granted.
Adjectival complement:	He is glad to play chess.

The examples cited above demonstrate the roles of the to-infinitive in various grammatical contexts. As a subject, the to-infinitive presents the central action or idea of the sentence. It is **reified**, conceptualized as an entity or concept. As a direct object, it conveys purpose and desire. Verbs that are followed by the to-infinitive include *arrange*, *ask*, *beg*, *care*, *chance*, *claim*, *come*, *consent*, *determine*, *elect*, *endeavor*, *expect*, *fail*, *guarantee*, *hesitate*, *hope*, *hurry*, *learn*, *manage*, *offer*, *prepare*, *prove*, *refuse*, *remain*, *say*, *shudder*, *strive*, *threaten*, *venture*, *wait*, *wish*, *yearn*, and others. As a subject complement, the to-infinitive adds information about the subject. As an appositive, it clarifies or describes the noun it follows. As an adjectival complement, it expands the adjective's meaning with added detail. These examples show the to-infinitive's versatility in taking on various roles shaped by the speaker's intent and the surrounding context.

6.5.1.2 Meaning

In traditional linguistics, meaning aligns with realism, based on truth and reference apart from the mind. Cognitive Grammar challenges this view by anchoring meaning in **idealization**, where the meaning of an expression is defined in terms of the **reality model**, which mirrors human experience across time. There are two distinct models of reality: basic and dynamic. Within the **basic model**, there are two facets: **immediate reality** referring to events in progress, and **non-immediate reality** referring to events that have already happened. Linguistically, basic reality refers to events that are happening now or have happened. In basic reality, the states of affairs are factual. Within **the dynamic model**, there are also two facets: **potential reality** referring to events that are not certain to occur and **projected reality** referring to events that are certain to occur. Linguistically, dynamic reality refers to the future course of events that could or could not happen. In dynamic reality, the states of affairs are not yet established.

In the realm of language, the **reality model** plays a crucial role in explaining the syntactic phenomenon of the to-infinitive. The to-infinitive captures both the potential and projected aspects of dynamic reality. Take the sentence *She wants to buy a new TV* as an example. Here, the to-infinitive reflects potential reality, suggesting events that are not guaranteed to happen. It hints at a future possibility, where the act of buying the TV could follow her desire but has not happened yet. This typically comes into play with verbs that express wishes or desires. On the other hand, in *She managed to finish on time*, the to-infinitive indicates projected reality, pointing to events that are nearly certain to take place. It suggests that the action of finishing on time is not just a possibility but something that has actually been accomplished. This usage often follows verbs that denote achievement. To sum up, **potential reality** refers to events that may not actually happen, while **projected reality** pertains to events that are generally expected to occur.

6.5.1.3 Cognitive Aspects

In this section, we examine the cognitive dimensions of infinitives. Specifically, we analyze how infinitives are categorized, configured, and conceptualized in detail. This discussion builds upon our earlier investigations into the cognitive aspects of other forms of complex atemporal relations.

6.5.1.3.1 Categorization

The to-infinitive is quite versatile, encompassing a range of related meanings that span both prototype and periphery uses within its semantic range. Its **prototype** suggests a sense of potentiality, where the action described is seen as something that will happen in the future. This occurs especially after verbs of desire, intention, or effort. For example, in *They hoped/planned/attempted to climb Mount Everest*, the to-infinitive indicates that the climbing has not happened yet but is something they aspire to do. Peripherally, the to-infinitive has two uses. The first relates to a sense of actualization, where the action of the complement is viewed as a result of a prior event. This occurs commonly with verbs of achievement, as in *They managed to climb Mount Everest*, or with causative verbs, as in *She forced him to reconsider his position*. Here, the to-infinitive conveys that the action has indeed taken place. The second relates to a sense of simultaneity. This occurs after cognitive verbs, which refers to states that exist at the same time as the main event. In *I believe him to be honest*, the belief and honesty coexist simultaneously. This shows that the to-infinitive extends beyond its core meaning, revealing its semantic richness.

6.5.1.3.2 *Configuration*

Both the bare infinitive and the to-infinitive belong to the realm of atemporality, each showcasing a distinct facet. In Cognitive Grammar, the choice of atemporal relation is determined not only by the meaning of the main verb but also by how the speaker construes the situation. The atemporal relation is chosen for its own reasons, rather than just being a result of rigid formal rules. Infinitives thus serve as a window into the speaker's construal, revealing how abstract meaning is mapped onto linguistic form. The syntactic behavior of infinitives reflects their conceptual organization. When deciding between the bare infinitive and the to-infinitive, it is ultimately a matter of the speaker's viewpoint. Speakers can visualize situations in multiple ways, which leads to different syntactic forms, each conveying a specific meaning. The same conceptual content can be interpreted in various ways depending on the speaker's construal and communicative goals, allowing for a rich diversity of viewpoints to be articulated in language.

He helped her carry the trunk.
He helped her to carry the trunk.

Both bare infinitives and to-infinitives fall within the domain of atemporality and can sometimes be interchanged, particularly after certain causative verbs. Although both forms are acceptable, they carry subtle yet meaningful differences. Each highlights a distinct facet within this domain. In Cognitive Grammar analysis, the bare infinitive represents the facet of **directness**, while the to-infinitive embodies the facet of **indirectness**. The bare infinitive is typically used when the helper is directly engaged in the action, actively exerting effort to perform it, offering more hands-on assistance. In contrast, the to-infinitive tends to indicate a more indirect or mediated form of help, where the helper facilitates the action more passively, like a cheerleader. In both cases, the action described in the complement is completed. However, with the bare infinitive, the main and complement verbs occur simultaneously, whereas with the to-infinitive, the complement action follows the main verb. This reflects Cognitive Grammar's view of language as an adaptive system where meaning and form are shaped by usage and context.

6.5.1.3.3 *Conceptualization*

The to-infinitive can appear in both non-extraposed and extraposed structures. In a non-extraposed structure, the conceptually dependent unit, that is, the subordinate clause, occupies the subject position directly before the main predicate. Conversely, in an extraposed structure, the dependent unit follows the main predicate, with the subject position filled by the pronoun *it*. This structure, beginning with *it*, emphasizes the broader context and provides background information about the event. It demonstrates that *it* is not merely a placeholder but carries meaningful function in all its forms. Indeed, it serves as a key example in debates over whether grammar consists solely of meaningful elements. In Cognitive Grammar, the distinction relates to the construal of **scope**, where speakers can adopt either a **narrow** or **broad** construal, conveying more specific or general meanings respectively. This interplay between form and meaning highlights how syntactic choices subtly shift emphasis and informational focus within language.

To play the piano is easy.

It is easy to play the piano.

Both sentences convey a similar idea, but the subtlety lies in which part of the statement gets the spotlight. This distinction is not merely coincidental; it reveals deeper cognitive processes linked to meaning and context. The difference in meaning hinges on **scope**. The non-extraposed version provides a more focused perspective on the conceptualizer, honing in on the activity itself and asserting that playing the piano is an easy task. Conversely, the extraposed version selects the broader field or immediate context as the subject, offering a wider perspective on the conceptualizer and highlighting the overall situation or a general truth. In essence, the first sentence stresses the specific act of playing the piano, while the second one emphasizes the general ease of doing so. In the first sentence, the to-infinitive complement clause takes center stage as the subject, whereas in the second sentence, the pronoun *it* is highlighted as the subject. Therefore, the conceptualizer's description in the extraposed sentence has a broader scope compared to the non-extraposed one.

Dual-pattern verbs:
Some verbs allow flexible complementation; they can be followed by either a gerund or a to-infinitive. However, they often convey different meanings depending on the speaker's intention. Verbs that fall into this category include *forget*, *remember*, *regret*, *stop*, *try*, *go on*, *quit*, *begin*, *can't bear*, *can't stand*, *continue*, *hate*, *like*, *love*, *prefer*, *propose*, and *start*. It is crucial to consider the context to determine which form to use. When deciding between a gerund and a to-infinitive, consider the message you wish to convey. The choice often relies on the intended meaning, context, and verb patterns. Cognitive Grammar delves into the reasons behind these choices, providing a fresh lens on understanding the distinctions. The distinction lies in **perspective**, the viewpoint or conceptual stance the speaker adopts when presenting a situation. Understanding perspective helps explain why speakers choose gerunds or to-infinitives, as the choice reflects how they

view the action. Generally, gerunds focus on the activity or process itself, while to-infinitives tend to highlight the purpose, intention, or potential behind an action.

Martha remembered to pay the bill.

Martha remembered paying the bill.

The content of these sentences is similar, but they are expressed in different ways. The key difference between the two forms is **perspective**, the way a speaker mentally frames or views a situation. The to-infinitive looks ahead, referring to an action that has not happened yet. It points to a single event that will occur after the main verb. So, in this case, the sentence suggests that she did not pay the bill. The word *but* supports this idea, indicating that the action did not happen, as in *Martha remembered to pay the bill, but she didn't.* On the other hand, the gerund looks back, referring to an action that is already been completed. It describes a single event that happened before the main verb. Since it talks about an event that took some time, it is more descriptive. Here, the sentence implies that she did post the letter and could share details about it. The absence of *but* reinforces this, as in *Martha remembered paying the bill, *but she didn't.* This contrast shows how small shifts in perspective can alter meaning and emphasis in language.

6.5.2 *Immediate Activity*

In Cognitive Grammar, an **immediate activity** is a neutral, generic action, conceived with a sense of immediacy and without future orientation or obligation. Grammatically, it is encoded as a **bare infinitive**, often appearing in simple contexts to present actions clearly and directly. For instance, in *We saw him run*, the bare infinitive captures the direct and immediate nature of the action. As a symbolic structure, the bare infinitive links a conceptual idea with its sound form. Cognitive Grammar emphasizes language as meaningful and tied to thought, highlighting the importance of context and usage in understanding linguistic elements. Within this framework, examining the bare infinitive involves considering how its role and meaning emerge in specific situations, where immediacy and neutrality are central features. By placing meaning at the forefront, Cognitive Grammar shows how the bare infinitive expresses immediacy and directness, clarifying its function in everyday speech and demonstrating the tight interplay between form and conceptualization.

6.5.2.1 Function

The bare infinitive plays a variety of roles and can appear in different positions within sentences, showcasing its flexibility and versatility in language. Its various functions highlight how it can express a wide range of actions and states, making it essential for conveying urgency in our communication. This adaptability truly demonstrates the dynamic nature of language and how it can adapt to meet different communicative needs. Additionally, the bare infinitive seamlessly fits into various grammatical structures, proving its vital role in both spoken and written forms. Whether in casual conversations or formal writing, its presence is crucial for achieving clear and effective communication. Moreover, it can be found in idiomatic expressions and common phrases, further emphasizing its foundational role in our everyday language. Throughout all its functions, the bare infinitive activates specific zones, highlighting certain aspects of a conceptual structure. While it does focus on the action itself, that does not mean it lacks context. In fact, it often brings a sense of immediacy and directness to our expressions.

Direct object:	They made him apologize.
Subject complement:	What he did was leave.
Object complement:	I heard her sing.
Object of preposition:	They had nothing to do except (to) chat.
Verb complement	You had better leave now.

The examples given above demonstrate the uses of the bare infinitive. As a subject, the bare infinitive is rarely used; instead, the to-infinitive is typically used. As a direct object, the bare infinitive occurs particularly after causative verbs like *let*, *make*, and *help*. As an object complement, the bare infinitive occurs after verbs of perception such as *see*, *hear*, *feel*, *smell*, *watch*, and *notice*. In this function, the bare infinitive activates the zone of the action perceived, focusing on the act of singing as it is experienced. Although, as a rule, prepositions cannot govern infinitives but require gerunds instead, a class of prepositions can be combined with the bare infinitive. This class includes *but*, *save*, *except*, *than*, and *besides*. The omission of *to* before the infinitive is common and preferable. After expressions like *had better*, *would rather*, and *would sooner*, the bare infinitive functions as a verb complement and is used to give strong advice or a warning. The bare infinitive enhances concise, precise expression, making it vital to clear and dynamic communication.

6.5.2.2 Meaning

The bare infinitive has multiple uses in English grammar. It is an essential component of effective language use, enabling speakers to express a wide range of ideas and intentions. After modal verbs, it expresses necessity as in *You must leave now*, possibility as in *She might come to the party*, permission as in *You can go home early*, obligation as in *You should apologize*, or ability as in *She can swim*. After verbs of perception, it indicates an action that is perceived, as in *I saw him run*. It means that the action was perceived directly and immediately. After causative verbs, it indicates an action that is caused or permitted, as in *He made her cry*. In imperative sentences, it is used to give commands or requests, as in *Please help me*. It directly conveys the action that the speaker wants the listener to perform. After expressions with *had better*, *would rather*, and *would sooner*, it indicates preference or advice, as in *You had better leave now*. In each case, the bare infinitive follows these expressions to convey a clear and direct preference or recommendation. The bare infinitive's varied uses show its versatility.

6.5.2.3 Cognitive Aspects

Extending our earlier examination, we now investigate the cognitive aspects of categorization, configuration, and conceptualization in the bare infinitive with equal depth.

6.5.2.3.1 Categorization

The prototypical meaning of the bare infinitive conveys immediacy, referring to an action that happens at once. For example, in *I saw her fall*, the bare infinitive *fall* following the verb of perception *saw* describes an action occurring immediately. It is something the speaker perceived directly and in real time, with the two verbs coinciding temporally. Beyond this core usage, the bare infinitive can take on extended meanings. The first extended meaning is coincident actualization. This occurs with verbs of causation, permission, and perception. In *She made him clean the floor*, the acts of forcing and cleaning are actualized simultaneously. Similarly, in *She let him drive the car*, the permission and the permitted event actualize at the same time. The second extended meaning is coincident potentiality. This arises with modals and certain expressions (*why [not]*, *dare/need*, *rather*). For instance, in *He could clean the floor*, the cleaning is presented as a possibility rather than an event that has already taken place.

6.5.2.3.2 Configuration

In Cognitive Grammar, the choice of an atemporal relation type depends on both the semantics of the main verb and the speaker's perspective. Atemporal relations are selected based on their communicative purposes, not solely on formal rules. Their syntactic tendencies illustrate their conceptual organizations. Different atemporal relations can converge within a cognitive domain, each representing a distinct facet of that domain. A **domain** is a conceptual area that organizes related knowledge or experiences. A **facet** is a specific aspect within a domain that highlights one part of its meaning. In the domain of perception, there are two facets: the facet of **finality**, coded by the bare infinitive, and the facet of **continuity**, coded by the present participle. Each conveys a specific nuance of meaning, influencing how information is presented and understood. This involves the perspective from which the scene is described, enabling speakers to convey subtle distinctions in communication, making language a powerful tool for expressing complex ideas.

I watched him climb the hill.

I watched him climbing the hill.

These examples show how choosing between the bare infinitive and the present participle mirrors different perspectives of the speaker. In the first sentence, *climb* is used as a bare infinitive, which highlights that the action is complete, suggesting that the speaker witnessed the whole event from beginning to end. This implies that the climbing was done, making a follow-up like *but he stumbled and fell* not quite fits. In the second sentence, *climbing* is a present participle, which emphasizes the ongoing nature of the action, indicating that the speaker saw him while he was climbing, but not necessarily the whole event. Here, it suggests that the climbing was still happening, so the follow-up *but he stumbled and fell* does not contradict anything. Essentially, the bare infinitive indicates that the event described by the verb *climb* is complete, while the present participle conveys that it is still in progress. This distinction allows speakers to subtly shape the temporal perspective and convey nuanced meanings about actions in their descriptions.

6.5.2.3.3 Conceptualization

In Cognitive Grammar, the way we think plays a vital role in how we define meaning. This approach emphasizes that language is closely linked to our cognitive processes, with meaning arising from how we conceptualize situations and interpret our experiences. **Conceptualization** involves framing situations, events, and relationships within our minds, shaping the way we perceive and communicate them. When we select different grammatical structures, we are not merely adhering to rules; we are consciously choosing how to present information. This choice reflects our **perspective**, what we intend to emphasize, and the subtle nuances we aim to convey. The same event can be expressed in multiple ways, each formulation illuminating different aspects depending on our conceptualization. Cognitive Grammar shows that meaning is fluid, shaped by thought patterns and communicative context. Language reflects thought and interaction, enriching expression.

He had them talk.

He got them to talk.

These two sentences showcase the uses of causative verbs and their impact on meaning. The distinction lies in how the situation is conceptualized. In terms of Cognitive Grammar, the difference lies in authority versus persuasion. The first sentence uses the causative verb *had* followed by the bare infinitive *talk*. It suggests that he arranged or instructed them to talk, emphasizing the action without specifying how it was accomplished or the level of effort involved. The emphasis is on the action itself. The second sentence uses the causative verb *got* followed by the to-infinitive *to talk*. It implies that he persuaded or managed to make them talk, emphasizing the effort or process required to achieve the action. The focus is on the effort needed to make them talk. In essence, the first sentence focuses on the action, while the second emphasizes the effort or persuasion involved in getting them to talk. These examples demonstrate how the choice of causative verb and infinitive form can convey different nuances in meaning.

6.5.3 Assigned Activity

In Cognitive Grammar, an **assigned activity** is an action explicitly linked to a subject, conceived as a responsibility or obligation rather than a neutral or future-oriented process. Grammatically, it is encoded as a **for-to infinitive**, where the preposition *for* introduces the subject and assigns the activity expressed by the to-infinitive to that participant. Within Cognitive Grammar, elements posited in grammar are endowed with semantic values that account for their function. In light of this, the for-to is a symbolic marker of assignment, which has its own meaning and contributes to the semantic import of the construction in which it occurs. It highlights purpose or beneficiary, underscoring subjective viewpoint. Similarly, the semantic value of a construction depends on how its content is construed. Accordingly, the fort-o, as part of its conventional value, embodies a specific way of construing a situation. In *They want for Chris to promote to senior manager*, the promotion expresses the purpose of their desire. Chris is the beneficiary of the promotion action, with the construction marking the subject's assignment of the activity. This shows how grammar encodes meaning through subjective construal.

6.5.3.1 Function

In Cognitive Grammar, the for-to infinitive is pivotal, showcasing the intricate and adaptable nature of language. In terms of intricacy, the for-to infinitive is commonly used to express purpose, providing clarity to the intended meaning. This suggests that language serves as a dynamic system for conveying a variety of meanings, rather than simply following syntactic rules. In terms of adaptability, the for-to infinitive serves multiple purposes and is applicable in diverse contexts. It can be found in different syntactic positions, allowing speakers to express a wide range of meanings and functions within sentences. For-to plays a key role in construal, shaping our subjective understanding of events and their temporal relations. Understanding the uses of the for-to infinitive enhances our ability to communicate ideas effectively. For-to infinitives illustrate the close connection between linguistic form and cognitive function in human communication.

Subject:	For the team to win is crucial.
Direct object:	She plans for her daughter to study abroad.
Subject complement:	The goal is for everyone to participate actively.
Object complement:	She suggested a solution for us to consider.
Adjective complement:	It is essential for the team to arrive on time.
Appositive:	Her suggestion, for us to start early, was well-received.

The examples mentioned earlier showcase how the for-to infinitive can be used in various ways. As a subject, the for-to highlights what is important, adding clarity and detail to the sentence and underscoring the significance of the team's victory. As a direct object, it pinpoints what she aims or plans to achieve, bringing precision to the statement. As a subject complement, it enriches the overall meaning and sheds light on what the goal really involves. As an object complement, it provides extra details about the object, explaining what the solution entails. As an adjectival complement, it clarifies what is essential, adding more context to complete the meaning of the adjective. Lastly, as an appositive, it gives further insight into the noun, elaborating on what the suggestion was all about. In essence, for-to infinitive serves as a powerful tool for shaping how events, intentions, and relationships are conceptually organized and communicated. They embody the Cognitive Grammar principle that syntax reflects thought.

6.5.3.2 Meaning

The symbolic marker for-to serves as a signal for two key ideas: potentiality and indirectness. **Potentiality** means that we cannot be sure if the action or state described will actually occur. For example, in *I am happy for Sarah to receive the award*, for-to points toward an event that is expected to happen in the future, while also suggesting the possibility of it not happening. This sentence is somewhat hypothetical because it leaves open the truth or falsity of the conceptual content. It could imply that Sarah will receive the award, but it could also imply that she might not. **Indirectness** creates distance between subjects, signaling less engagement and enthusiasm. It marks the subject as less involved and less eager about the event. In *The manager suggested for Tom to captain the team*, the use of for-to introduces a feeling of indirectness and a lack of enthusiasm. The manager's influence on Tom seems indirect, making the suggestion feel less assertive.

6.5.3.3 Cognitive Aspects

Building on our previous analysis, we now explore the cognitive aspects of categorization, configuration, and conceptualization in for-to infinitive with the same degree of scrutiny.

6.5.3.3.1 Categorization

The prototypical use of a for-to infinitive is to express purpose. For example, in the sentence *It is important for you to understand the rules*, the phrase *for you to understand the rules* directly conveys purpose or intention. The periphery includes marginal examples that still fall within this category. In some cases, the peripheral uses of the for-to may involve more complex or less direct expressions of purpose. For example, in *She arranged for the team to meet on Friday*, *for the team to meet on Friday* is still expressing purpose, but in a slightly more complex and indirect way than the prototypical example. Instead of explicitly stating the purpose, the for-to introduces an intermediary step, the arrangement, that leads to the intended outcome, the team meeting. By considering the concepts of prototype and periphery, we can observe how for-to infinitives range from clear, central examples to more complex, marginal ones. This approach helps us grasp the flexibility and range of these constructions in conveying meaning.

6.5.3.3.2 Configuration

The to-infinitive and the for-to infinitive both relate to the conceptual **domain** of purpose and intention, though they occupy different **facets** within it. Each form carries its own distinct nuance and use. The to-infinitive emphasizes the action or state itself, whereas the for-to infinitive highlights the subject performing the action or experiencing the state. By understanding these similarities and differences, one can effectively use both forms to convey precise meanings in discourse. Furthermore, the to-infinitive is often found in simpler, more direct sentences, while the for-to infinitive tends to appear in more complex constructions, adding nuance and specificity. This distinction allows speakers to tailor their language to different contexts and communicative needs, enhancing both clarity and expressiveness. These uses highlight language's flexibility, enabling speakers to adjust messages to subtle perspective shifts. These forms show how language shapes thought, enabling precise and intentional communication.

The boss asked Jim to represent the company.

The boss asked for Jim to represent the company.

These sentences show subtle differences in infinitive use, contrasting direct and indirect expressions, evidenced by the proximity principle, and shaped by the speaker's personal involvement and level of enthusiasm. In the first sentence, the to-infinitive means that the boss comes across as having a direct influence on Jim, showing a genuine interest in nominating him as a representative. The closer proximity of the two verbs suggests a stronger connection between their actions, hinting at the boss's enthusiasm. In the second sentence, the for-to infinitive means that the boss seems to have only an indirect effect on Jim, indicating less interest in nominating him. The greater distance between the verbs here implies a more mediated relationship. As a result, Jim's chances of representing the company are not as strong as in the first sentence. Interestingly, only the second sentence allows for scenarios where both participants are not in the same place, like when we say, *The boss asked for Jim to represent the company, but Jim wasn't there.*

6.5.3.3.3 Conceptualization

The for-to symbolic marker can appear in two different grammatical styles: non-extraposed and extraposed. In the non-extraposed version, the entire for-to event serves as the subject of a sentence. On the other hand, in the extraposed version, the pronoun *it* assumes the role of the subject. Unlike transformational grammars, which consider these two forms as related and semantically equivalent, Cognitive Grammar views them as conceptually distinct. The determining factor in selecting which grammatical form to use is how we construe scope. **Scope** refers to the range of conceptual content that an expression evokes to convey its meaning. In the non-extraposed version, the conceptualizer's evaluation, which is **narrow**, is influenced solely by the content of the sentence. In the extraposed version, the evaluation, which is **broad**, is influenced by both the content of the sentence and the immediate context surrounding it, as emphasized by the pronoun *it*. In Cognitive Grammar, this pronoun sets a general context, providing a reference point for details.

For Roberts to fly into a fury is wrong.

It is wrong for Roberts to fly into a fury.

Both sentences convey the same idea but do so in different ways, highlighting different aspects of scope. In the first sentence, we see the non-extraposed form, where *For Roberts to fly into a fury* acts as the subject. Here, the speaker takes a narrow scope on the situation, viewing the for-to structure as the sole reason for their judgment. This structure places the spotlight on Roberts's furious reaction. On the other hand, the second sentence employs the extraposed form, with *it* as the subject and *For Roberts to fly into a fury* postponed to the end of the sentence. In this case, the speaker adopts a broader scope, considering all elements that contribute to their evaluation. This includes not only the conceptual content of the sentence but also the wider context and ensuing consequences. This structure, marked by the pronoun *it*, shifts focus to a broader context and the surrounding circumstances, underscoring the inappropriateness of the action.

6.6 Linguistic Aspects of Complex Atemporal Relations

Complex atemporal relations, including gerunds and to-infinitives, extend beyond cognitive processing. They are connected to linguistic structures such as syntax, which determines their functions in sentences, and semantics, which influences their meanings. By delving into these aspects, we not only improve our comprehension of the intricacies of language but also refine our communication abilities, allowing us to convey more subtle and accurate messages. This thorough examination highlights the complexity and flexibility of language as well as its essential role in human expression and interaction.

6.6.1 *Parallelism*

Parallelism involves maintaining grammatical consistency in sentence construction, enhancing clarity and coherence in communication. By using consistent structures within sentences or phrases, parallelism reinforces recognizable patterns, making it easier for language users to process information. By showing how cognition favors balance, language becomes clearer and more appealing, highlighting the dynamic interplay between grammar and cognition in shaping effective and meaningful expression. Both gerunds and infinitives can be used to create parallel structures, enhancing the rhythm and clarity of writing. In Cognitive Grammar, parallelism is not merely a stylistic device; it reflects deeper cognitive mechanisms related to how we construe and organize meaning. Moreover, maintaining parallelism helps reduce cognitive load, making communication smoother for both speaker and listener. Parallelism helps maintain a consistent **profile** across clauses or phrases. This consistency guides the listener's attention and reinforces the conceptual coherence of the message.

To illustrate parallelism, consider the following examples, which demonstrate how consistent structural patterns help organize meaning and make information easier to process.

Nonparallel structure:	a. She likes reading books and to write stories.
Parallel structure:	b. She likes reading books and writing stories.
Nonparallel structure:	a. She likes to read books and writing stories.
Parallel structure:	b. She likes to read books and to write stories.

In the (b) examples, parallelism highlights conceptual equivalence by construing each activity as equally salient and part of the same domain. The first sentence in (a) lacks parallelism because it mixes a gerund (reading) with an infinitive (to write), resulting in grammatical inconsistency. The version in (b) achieves parallelism by consistently using gerunds (reading and writing), ensuring structural balance. Similarly, the second sentence in (a) disrupts parallel structure by combining an infinitive (to read) with a gerund (writing). The version in (b) restores parallelism by consistently using to-infinitives (to read and to write), producing smooth and coherent phrasing. In these examples, parallelism provides structural consistency, keeping attention on meaning while making sentences more persuasive. In addition, it aids comprehension and retention while enhancing readability through organized, predictable patterns in language.

6.6.2 *Entrenchment*

Entrenchment refers to the process by which repeated use of a linguistic structure strengthens its mental representation, making it more easily accessible and habitual in language use. It matters in language because repeated exposure to certain verb combinations makes them more firmly used by speakers. This process makes commonly used structures and expressions more easily accessible, reducing cognitive effort during communication. Entrenchment highlights the linguistic role of frequency and familiarity in shaping language use, showing how these patterns become naturalized in speech over time. This concept underscores the dynamic interaction between usage, cognition, and grammar. It is not native speaker intuition that determines whether verbs entrench with gerunds or infinitives, but the underlying semantics of the verbs and their complements. Thus, entrenchment shows how meaning and experience shape language habits. To clarify the concept, look at the examples below.

I enjoy hiking.
I hope to succeed.

In the first sentence, the verb *enjoy* is entrenched with the gerund. This is because the concept of enjoyment is associated with a continuous activity, making it naturally align with the use of a gerund. This reflects the idea that enjoyment is linked to an ongoing process rather than a one-time event, such as hiking. In the second sentence, the verb *hope* is entrenched with the to-infinitive. This is because hope is often connected to a desired outcome or goal, fitting well with the forward-looking nature of the to-infinitive. When we hope for something, we are envisioning a future action or result like succeeding. These verb-complement preferences are established through entrenchment, shaping language patterns over time. In Cognitive Grammar, language is a reflection of how we conceptualize experiences and influences how we engage with the world around us.

6.6.3 Zone Activation

Zone activation refers to the process by which specific aspects of a conceptual domain, called the active zone, are engaged during language use. The **active zone** is the part of a conceptual domain that is focused on, reflecting the most relevant meaning for both speaker and listener. In Cognitive Grammar, this concept highlights how certain areas within a broader conceptual framework become active depending on the communicative context. Zone activation is significant because it demonstrates how conceptual domains are selectively engaged during language processing. When we use or understand language, different zones of meaning within a concept are activated based on context. This process enables flexible and precise communication by highlighting only the most relevant aspects of a concept. It illustrates language as a dynamic interaction between cognition and context, emphasizing the vital role of mental representations in constructing meaning. To shed light on the concept, consider the examples below:

Writing novels requires creativity.
To write a novel is my dream.

Both gerunds and to-infinitives activate zones within the mind. In the first sentence, the gerund *writing* activates the activity zone, creating a mental image of the process of *writing* as a concept. This makes gerunds particularly effective in contexts where the emphasis is on discussing the nature of the activity itself. In the second sentence, the to-infinitive *to write* activates the goal-oriented zone, focusing on the aspiration or outcome rather than the activity. This goal-oriented framing makes to-infinitives ideal for expressing purpose or future intent. In essence, the choice between a gerund and a to-infinitive reflects a subtle yet significant cognitive shift. When we use a gerund, we draw attention to the nature of the activity itself, often in a more detached or theoretical way. In contrast, opting for a to-infinitive emphasizes the purpose or intended result, aligning the action with a broader goal or personal aspiration. This subtle distinction allows for nuanced communication, adapting the framing to suit different contexts and purposes.

6.6.4 Coercion

Coercion refers to the process by which grammatical structure or contextual cues compel the reinterpretation or adjustment of the meaning of a phrase to fit syntactic requirements. Coercion is significant in Cognitive Grammar and language because it reflects how meaning is dynamically constructed in context. When a word or phrase does not semantically fit its grammatical environment, coercion helps reinterpret it to ensure coherence. This highlights the cognitive flexibility of language users and emphasizes that meaning arises from interactions between linguistic elements and their usage context, revealing the adaptability and creativity inherent in human cognition. Ultimately, coercion demonstrates how language users actively negotiate meaning in real time, allowing for efficient communication even in novel or unexpected linguistic situations. To provide a clearer understanding of this concept, let us explore the following examples:

She began reading.

She began to read.

In the first sentence, the use of the gerund *reading* shifts the focus toward the activity itself. In this case, coercion frames the action of reading as an ongoing activity, conjuring an image of someone immersed in the act of reading. In comparison, in the second sentence the use of the to-infinitive *to read* alters the focus, highlighting the initial phase of the action. In this case, coercion frames the activity as something newly initiated or intentionally pursued. While the gerund places weight on the activity itself, the to-infinitive places weight on the point of initiation or the volitional aspect. The gerund-driven interpretation may prioritize the concept of continuity, while the to-infinitive construction steers attention toward intent or purpose. Essentially, coercion adjusts how the action is cognitively perceived, whether as an ongoing process or an intentional endeavor. These distinctions are crucial to understanding how language operates at a cognitive level, revealing the interplay of syntax, meaning, and interpretation.

Summary

In this chapter, I have examined **complex atemporal relations**, characterized by multielement structures and layered meanings. Atemporal relations are ungrounded processes, a verb expression that lacks grounding in time, reality, or speaker perspective. In grammar, ungrounded processes are expressed through nonfinite verbs. Atemporal relations are seen as a kind of **conceptual subordination**, where one unit depends on another. The dependent unit is understood through the independent unit and highlights part of the meaning that the independent unit brings up. In grammar, the independent unit corresponds to the main clause, while the dependent unit corresponds to the subordinate clause. Atemporal relations can be categorized into gerunds, participles, and infinitives. These relations are not merely rigid grammatical patterns; they are conceptual structures that show how one unit is understood in relation to another, independent of time. Their meanings extend beyond literal wording, reflecting different perspectives.

A gerund acts like a noun, as in *Swimming is a great way to stay fit*, where *swimming* serves as the subject and represents the activity itself as a concept that promotes fitness. A present participle functions differently, serving as an adjective to describe nouns, as in *The running water was cold*, where *running* modifies *water* to highlight its ongoing action or state. The *to-infinitive* also functions as a noun, as in *To read is to expand one's mind*, where *to read* acts as the subject, emphasizing reading as a valuable intellectual activity. Gerunds and infinitives differ in their level of specificity, and our construal influences how we perceive these forms. Gerunds typically express general or ongoing activities in a schematic way, as in *Running is great exercise*, where the focus is on the activity itself or the general action of running. In contrast, *to-infinitives* are usually more precise, often emphasizing intention or specific circumstances, as in *To run is great exercise*, where the focus is on the decision or intention to *run* being beneficial.

Exercises

1. Choosing a gerund or to-infinitive signals a semantic difference. What is that difference?

   1. She forgot locking the door.
   2. She forgot to lock the door.

2. Both the gerund and to-infinitive can function as subjects but convey different meanings. Explain how.

   1. Traveling broadens the mind.
   2. To travel broadens the mind.

3. The pronoun *it* adds meaning to a sentence. Explain how *it* shapes interpretation in context.

   1. Breaking a promise is disrespectful.
   2. It is disrespectful breaking a promise.

4. What difference in meaning do the *-ing* and *-ed* forms create in the following adjectives?

1. The loud music is annoying.
2. I am annoyed by the loud music.

5. The verb *had* takes both bare and to-infinitives. What meaning difference do they show here?

1. I had the gardener plant some trees.
2. I had the gardener to plant some trees.

6. The following sentences share the same content, but differ in construal. Can you explain the difference?

1. I heard the orchestra play a symphony.
2. I heard the orchestra playing a symphony.

7. The sentence is syntactically ambiguous: the *-ing* form may be a participle or a gerund. Explain how.

1. Ringing bells can be disturbing.

8. Identify each verb's complement: bare, to-infinitive, or gerund. Then, give an example sentence.

1. agree
2. relish
3. fancy
4. prefer
5. decide

9. Use the appropriate type of nonfinite complement clause to complete the sentences below.

1. Don't let him (wait) so long.
2. I don't fancy (go) out tonight.
3. She promised (help) her friend.
4. They hardly go (swim) nowadays.
5. He doesn't mind (work) the night shift.

10. The two sentences use similar wording but differ in meaning. Can you explain the difference?

1. I want Sarah to excel in the race.
2. I want for Sarah to excel in the race.

PART FOUR

Relations: Temporal Relations

In the previous part, I talked about **atemporal relations**, a non-processual type of relation in which evolution through time is not the focus. In this part, I delve into temporal relations, a processual type of relation in which evolution through time is the focus. Understanding temporal relations lets us express events and sequences across time, enriching communication with clarity. Temporal relations can be either simple or complex. **Simple temporal relations** involve processes (verbs), verbal expressions (verb phrases), and single-grounded processes (simple sentences). **Complex temporal relations** involve **conceptual symmetry** (coordination and transition), **correspondence relations** (correlation), and **conceptual asymmetry** (subordination). **Coordination** links equal units into a balanced structure, as in *She went to the store, and he stayed home*. **Transition** shifts attention from one unit to another, as in *She was tired; however, she continued to work*. **Correlation** pairs units to highlight parallels or proportionality, as in *Either she will arrive early, or the meeting will be postponed*. **Subordination** links unequal units where one depends on the other for meaning, as in *After she finishes her homework, she will go to the gym*.

Temporal relations are tied to **finite clauses**, which are essential for expressing when events happen and the order in which they occur. A **finite**

clause, or **grounded process**, contains a subject and tense-marked verb, expressing a complete thought as either an independent or dependent clause. Finite clauses come in various forms: simple, compound, or complex. They can serve as noun, adjective, or adverb clauses, each playing a unique role in the sentence that enhances the overall meaning and structure of the text. A crucial element of Cognitive Grammar is recognizing the conceptual motivations that underlie the different structures of finite clauses. In contrast, a **nonfinite clause**, conceptually called an **ungrounded process**, is an embedded clause that is not bound by tense and lacks a subject. Nonfinite clauses show up in subordinate clauses and can take the form of gerunds, participles, or infinitives. They serve as complements or modifiers in sentences, adding extra information or detail about an action or state, which enriches the overall meaning. Nonfinite clauses are quite flexible and can really enhance the depth and complexity of writing.

Outline

7

Simple Temporal Relations: Processes in Verbs

7.1 Introduction

In Chapter 3, I discussed the first conceptual category of **things**, expressed by the grammatical class of **nouns**. In this chapter, I will delve into the second conceptual category, **relations**, which encode processual predications in grammar through the class of **verbs**. Verbs function as carriers of **temporal relations**, which refer to how time is expressed and understood in language, including the sequence of events, their duration, and their overlap. They are foundational for expressing time in language and are accessed through **sequential scanning**. This process unfolds over time, with elements of an event processed one after another, never simultaneously during the scanning process. Within temporal relations, a distinction is made between **simple temporal relations** designated by verbs, and **complex temporal relations** designated by grounded processes, expressed in grammar as **finite clauses**. Simple temporal relations focus on the sequencing, simultaneity, and duration of events. In contrast, complex temporal relations involve dependencies between events, multiple layers of time, and temporal subordination.

7.2 Processes

In Cognitive Grammar, **processes** are understood as dynamic events or changes that unfold through time. These processes can involve actions, movements, mental activities, or any situation that can be conceptualized as ongoing rather than static. In language, processes are typically expressed through **verbs**, as verbs are the grammatical category that highlights temporal evolution, something that is happening, changing, or being carried out. Unlike nouns, which mainly focus on **things**, verbs emphasize processes as they progress over time. Rather than being solely defined by their grammatical roles, verbs are interpreted based on their meanings and how they influence our perception of the events they represent. As powerful tools for conveying temporal relationships, verbs allow us to conceptualize actions, events, and states, essential elements for understanding and expressing experiences. They connect sentence parts, bridging language and lived reality. Each verb has a form, whether spoken or signed, that is paired with a meaning that captures its semantic or conceptual essence.

7.3 Categories of Verbs

When we talk about simple time relationships, we often draw a distinction between a state or condition and a dynamic action, much like how we differentiate between dynamic and stative verbs in language. The focus here is on the essence of verbs and what they truly represent. While verbs can be complex, understanding their nuances greatly enriches our experience with language. Cognitive Grammar delves deeper at verbs through the lens of **construal**, which means that speakers interpret events based on their own perspectives and experiences. Construal involves our mental ability to visualize and express a situation in various ways. The verb we choose indicates how we perceive an event in our minds. Categorizing verbs lets us express diverse temporal nuances in language. Diverse verb types enable us to view situations from distinct perspectives. This cognitive approach broadens our understanding of how language reflects our thoughts.

Cognitive Grammar closely examines verbs by analyzing their meanings and roles in sentences.

7.3.1 Semantic Categories

Semantically, verbs can be understood as either process-profiling or state-profiling. This distinction reflects how language construes time, either as an unfolding process or as a stable situation. These categories show how speakers conceptualize, represent, and express events.

7.3.1.1 Process-Profiling Verbs

In Cognitive Grammar, **process-profiling verbs** are verbs that profile an event unfolding through time. They suggest change, energy flow, or evolution rather than stability. The verb highlights the event's process, development, and impact over time. Traditionally, these are typically referred to as **dynamic verbs**. Consider the verb *run*: it profiles an activity that unfolds through time, highlighting change and ongoing motion. Process-profiling verbs highlight an event's temporal flow, guiding us to track its development. In *She is running a marathon*, the form *running* evokes a continuous process extending over time. From a cognitive perspective, these verbs require **sequential scanning**, we mentally follow the event as a series of evolving stages. In the sentence *The artist painted a mural*, we can imagine the painting emerging step by step. Such verbs evoke vivid imagery of movement, change, and interaction. When we read *The tree is growing*, we effortlessly envision the gradual, ongoing change that defines the scene.

In terms of usage, process-profiling verbs are highly flexible. They appear across simple, perfect, and progressive constructions, as in *She walks*, *She has walked*, *She is walking*, allowing speakers to construe events with different temporal textures. Because they profile actions and unfolding processes, they are central to narrating experiences, as in He builds houses for a living. They also commonly express changes of state, as in *The weather is changing rapidly*. Process-profiling verbs combine naturally with modal verbs to convey possibility, necessity, or obligation, enriching the speaker's ability to express stance and intention, as in *She might be running late* or *They must finish the project by tomorrow*. Their versatility reflects how dynamically they adapt to communicative needs, enabling speakers to represent events in nuanced and context-sensitive ways.

Process-profiling verbs divide into aspectual classes: activities, accomplishments, and achievements, which Cognitive Grammar views as distinct ways of construing how a process unfolds over time.

Activity verbs

An activity is an ongoing process that unfolds over time without a predetermined endpoint, requiring the viewer to mentally follow the event as it progresses. Activity verbs denote actions that can continue indefinitely. Some common examples of these verbs are *walk*, *run*, *drink*, *eat*, *ride*, *talk*, *fight*, *read*, *play*, *listen*, *sing*, and *write*.

I love to ride my bike on sunny days.

They had to fight to protect their rights.

She can sing beautifully in three languages.

Accomplishment verbs

An accomplishment verb profiles a process that unfolds over time and culminates in a conceptually significant endpoint. Accomplishment verbs express actions that result in a clear and logical conclusion. Examples of such verbs include *analyze*, *approve*, *arrange*, *author*, *build*, *boost*, *calculate*, *chair*, *coach*, *compile*, *collect*, and *complete*.

She authored a new book on the history of architecture.

The experienced player coached the junior team on weekends.

The team needs to compile the latest code before the deadline.

Achievement verbs

An achievement verb profiles an almost immediate change of state, capturing the moment when a new condition is established. Achievement verbs express actions that occur in the blink of an eye. Here are some instances of these verbs: *choose*, *produce*, *raise*, *increase*, *reduce*, *choose*, *win*, *master*, *establish*, *attain*, *exceed*, and *attain*.

She chose the red dress without hesitation.

They won the match with a last-minute goal.

He attained the highest score in just one attempt.

7.3.1.2 State-Profiling Verbs

In Cognitive Grammar, **state-profiling verbs** depict stable, unchanging conditions rather than unfolding processes. Traditionally, these are expressed by what are commonly called **stative verbs**. For example, the verb *know* profiles a stable state of knowledge rather than an unfolding process. State-profiling verbs convey timeless situations without clear beginnings or ends. In *She knows the answer*, the knowledge is construed as an ongoing condition. Cognitively, these verbs invite **summary scanning**, allowing us to apprehend the state as a whole rather than tracking it through sequential stages. In *He owns a car*, ownership is understood as a steady, enduring condition. Such verbs prompt static mental imagery, as in *The soup tastes delicious*, which evokes a consistent sensory experience. State-profiling verbs usually express being, thought, emotion, possession, or perception. *She feels happy* profiles an emotional state rather than an action. Because they denote stability, State-profiling verbs rarely occur in progressive constructions. They are essential for describing situations that remain constant over time, as in *The house appears old*, which conveys a stable visual impression.

State-profiling verbs fall into four classes: emotion, cognition, perception, and possession, which Cognitive Grammar interprets as alternative ways of construing conditions that persist without temporal progression.

Emotion verbs

Emotion verbs profile an internal emotional state that is construed as stable and enduring rather than unfolding through time. They express strong feelings. Representative verbs in this category include *dislike*, *hate*, *like*, *love*, *loathe*, *envy*, *fear*, *prefer*, *want*, and *wish*.

I hate it when people are late to meetings.

They love traveling to new countries every year.

Children often fear the dark until they grow older.

Cognition verbs

Cognition verbs profile a stable mental state such as knowing, believing, or thinking, construed as an enduring condition rather than a process unfolding through time. They express thoughts. Typical examples of these verbs include *agree*, *believe*, *doubt*, *guess*, *imagine*, *know*, *recognize*, *remember*, *think*, and *understand*.

Can you guess the answer to this riddle?

I doubt we will finish the project on time.

Did you recognize the person who waved at you?

Perception verbs

Perception verbs profile a stable sensory state, such as seeing, hearing, or tasting, construed as an ongoing condition rather than a process unfolding through time. They express awareness of things through the senses. Here are some standard examples of these verbs: *appear*, *feel*, *hear*, *look*, *notice*, *see*, *seem*, *smell*, *taste*, and *watch*.

You seem very happy about the news.

I can smell cookies baking in the oven.

Can you see the bird perched on the tree?

Possession verbs

Possession verbs profile a stable ownership or relational state, construed as an enduring condition rather than a process unfolding through time. They express having, owning, or controlling something. Common instances of these verbs are *belong*, *have*, *hold*, *own*, and *possess*.

She possesses a rare talent for music.

They own a small coffee shop downtown.

The old photo album belongs to my grandmother.

7.3.1.3 Adaptability

One of language's most valuable qualities is its versatility, its capacity to adapt to a wide range of functions and contexts. Many grammatical elements display remarkable flexibility, allowing them to convey subtle distinctions and integrate smoothly into different constructions. In Cognitive Grammar, this adaptability reflects the dynamic way language evolves to meet the cognitive needs of its users. It emerges from how speakers conceptualize their experiences, shaped by bodily interaction with the world. Adaptability involves the continual reshaping of linguistic structures to fit new contexts, solve communicative challenges, and express shifting perspectives. It captures the ongoing interplay between cognition and expression, showing how language adjusts as our experiences and conceptual demands change. Through this continual evolution, language remains a powerful and responsive tool across cultures and generations.

Some verbs display remarkable flexibility, allowing them to function differently depending on how the speaker construes the situation. In Cognitive Grammar, they fall into two broad categories: process-profiling verbs, which highlight unfolding action, and state-profiling verbs, which highlight stable conditions. Verbs such as *think*, *mind*, *have*, *taste*, *smell*, *sound*, and *see* can shift between these profiles depending on the speaker's intended construal. When the speaker wants to foreground an event as something that unfolds through time, the verb is used in a process-profiling way. For example, in *She learned the answer*, *learn* profiles the temporal progression of acquiring knowledge. When the speaker instead construes the situation as a stable condition, the verb functions as state-profiling. In *She knows the answer*, *knows* profiles an enduring state of knowledge. This flexibility reflects how speakers conceptualize experience, either as a dynamic process requiring sequential scanning or as a stable state apprehended holistically.

I think it is too early to buy a car.

I am thinking about buying a new car.

The verb *think* can shift between process-profiling and state-profiling meanings depending on context. In the first sentence, *think* profiles a stable opinion, so it functions as a state-profiling verb and appears in the present simple. It conveys the speaker's settled belief that it is not the right time to buy a car. In the second sentence, *thinking* profiles an unfolding mental activity, so it functions as a process-profiling verb and appears in the present progressive, highlighting active consideration of purchasing a new car. In Cognitive Grammar, this shift does not reflect a change in the verb's grammatical class but a change in how the situation is construed—whether the speaker invites summary scanning of a stable state or sequential scanning of an evolving process. The verb *think* itself remains the same; what changes is the speaker's perspective and the conceptualization they wish to foreground. State-profiling verbs present conditions or states of being, while process-profiling verbs present actions or processes unfolding through time.

In Cognitive Grammar, language provides symbolic resources, but it is the speaker who applies them with intentional conceptualization. Adaptability is found not only in linguistic structures but also in the speaker's ability to adjust how an event is construed in response to discourse needs. The choice between using a process-profiling or state-profiling verb reflects the speaker's perspective and communication goal. Meaning is not fixed; it emerges from how the speaker mentally organizes the scene, determining what to focus on, which aspects to highlight, and how the situation should be understood within the current context. This dynamic interplay between linguistic form and cognitive construal allows speakers to craft their expressions with great precision, reflecting the fluidity of thought and the subtleties of the situation. Through flexible conceptualization, language conveys complex, context-specific meanings. In interaction, speakers adjust language to refine meaning and meet shifting communicative demands.

7.3.2 Syntactic Categories

In Cognitive Grammar, **transitivity** describes how verbs relate to sentence structure by profiling participants in an event. It is often explained through **valency**, which examines how many arguments a verb requires for completeness. Verbs may profile events with one participant (intransitive), two-participants (monotransitive), or three-participants (ditransitive), depending on how the speaker construes the situation. Transitivity is seen as a matter of conceptualization, with patterns that reveal the ideologies conveyed in a message. These patterns reflect experiences beyond language by indicating who is performing an action, who is affected, and what is participating in the event. They show how individuals use language to represent their understanding of the world. In linguistic analysis, especially in studies of mind style, transitivity patterns are crucial because they demonstrate how an author conceptualizes events. Each pattern represents a specific way of thinking and influences how actions and relationships are interpreted. Within clause structure, transitivity patterns shape meaning and influence event representation.

In Cognitive Grammar, the **billiard-ball model** explains transitivity by viewing objects as energy-driven balls that move and collide. The way this energy is passed along follows an **action chain**, a conceptual framework illustrating how energy or action flows from an agent, the one doing the action, to a patient, the one receiving it, in a sentence. It outlines a series of events involving different participants and their roles. In this chain, the first object makes contact and sends energy into the second object, which then interacts with a third one, continuing the energy transfer. This process keeps going until the energy fades away and everything comes to a halt. We refer to it as the billiard-ball model because our understanding of how actions unfold resembles the way a billiard ball moves. Essentially, this model allows us to understand the world as a network of energetic interactions between entities, which trigger changes in their characteristics.

Cognitive Grammar views language as a mirror of human thought, treating verbs not as standalone elements but as deeply connected to our cognitive patterns. This perspective suggests that verb categories are not just arbitrary labels; they actually reflect our mental images, helping us express subtle meanings. Verbs can be understood as collections of symbolic structures that arise from how we use them, echoing the cognitive framework of language. By choosing different verb categories, we can express various viewpoints, showcasing how we perceive events. This fluidity of verbs emphasizes the complex link between language and thought, enriching our understanding of how we organize and interpret our experiences. Transitivity, a key feature of verbs, defines how many objects a verb can take, categorizing them as intransitive, monotransitive, or ditransitive based on syntax and argument number. This approach shows language as dynamic, shaped by thought and interaction for nuanced expression.

What follows is a description of the different transitivity patterns, showing how verbs profile events with varying numbers of participants.

7.3.2.1 One-Participant Events

In Cognitive Grammar, **one-participant events** are situations that involve only a single conceptual participant—an entity engaged in an action, change, or state without interacting with another participant. They represent the simplest event schema, where the verb profiles just one participant within the conceptual scene. In grammar, these events are expressed by **intransitive verbs**. For example, in the sentence *He slept*, the intransitive verb *slept* stands on its own without requiring an object, profiling a simple one-participant event. This illustrates how speakers conceptualize and express situations in language: the verb invokes an event involving only a single participant, even though it still requires a subject to anchor that participant in the scene. From a cognitive view, intransitivity is not merely a grammatical pattern but a reflection of how we construe certain actions as complete without the involvement of another participant. Intransitive verbs convey complete events with a single participant, symbolizing an action or state.

Below are examples of intransitive verbs that profile complete one-participant events and do not require a direct object to complete their meaning.

She will arrive at noon.	He sleeps peacefully.
They laughed at the joke.	Accidents happen.
The magician disappeared.	She fainted from the heat.

The fog vanished by morning.	The event occurred unexpectedly.
A whale emerged from the sea.	The plants flourished in the garden.

7.3.2.2 Two-Participant Events

In Cognitive Grammar, **two-participant events** involve an actor performing an action and another being affected. The verb profiles this relational structure, highlighting the connection between the two participants within the conceptual scene. In grammar, these events are expressed by **monotransitive verbs.** These verbs require only one direct object to fully convey their meaning, as they show the action moving from the subject to the object. These verbs are part of what we call symbolic assemblies, where the verb and its object come together to create a meaningful unit that mirrors how we mentally represent actions that affect objects. Consider the sentence *She ate an apple*. Here, the verb *ate* profiles an interaction between two participants, with *an apple* completing the event's conceptual structure. This shows that transitivity is not merely a grammatical pattern but a reflection of how we mentally construe actions as involving both an initiator and an affected participant.

Below are examples of monotransitive verbs that profile twoparticipant events and require a direct object to complete their meaning.

He builds a house.	He loves the song.
He fixed the car.	I finished the project.
They need a break.	We prefer coffee.
He explained the lesson.	She solves the puzzle.
She admires the painting.	He designs a website.

In Cognitive Grammar, some verbs exhibit **flexible profiling,** meaning they can profile either a oneparticipant event or a twoparticipant event depending on how the speaker construes the scene. Traditionally, these are known as **ambitransitive verbs.** They can function intransitively or transitively, offering flexibility in sentence construction and allowing speakers to shift focus between the action itself (intransitive) and the participant affected by it (transitive). For example, in *I read all night*, the verb *read* profiles a one-participant event, whereas in *I read the book* it profiles a two-participant interaction. The verb's flexibility reflects how speakers choose to structure the scene, highlighting different facets of the same activity. These patterns show that transitivity is not merely a grammatical distinction but a reflection of how we conceptualize and present events. Such flexibility underscores the dynamic link between grammar and cognition in shaping meaning.

Below are examples of verbs that can profile either a oneparticipant or a twoparticipant event, functioning with or without a direct object depending on how the scene is construed.

One participant	Two participants
We sing loudly.	We sing a song.
Birds fly in the sky.	She flies a kite.
He eats slowly.	He eats an apple.
The vegetables grow.	I grow vegetables.
The glass broke.	He broke the glass.
They write often.	They write a letter.
She runs every morning.	She runs a marathon.
She reads every night.	She reads a magazine.
The door opened.	They opened the door.
She watches quietly.	She watches the show.

7.3.2.3 Three-Participant Events

In Cognitive Grammar, **three-participant events** involve an interaction among three conceptual participants, typically an agent, a recipient, and an entity being transferred or affected. The verb profiles this triadic relational structure within the conceptual scene. In grammar, these events are expressed by **ditransitive verbs**, which take two objects: a direct object and an indirect object. Ditransitive verbs profile three-participant events in which an action is directed toward a direct object while also affecting a recipient. The verb and its two objects form a symbolic assembly that reflects our mental construal of an action involving multiple entities. For example, in *She gave him a gift*, the verb *gave* links the subject to both the recipient *him* and the item transferred *a gift*. This pattern shows that ditransitivity is not merely a grammatical feature but a reflection of how we conceptualize complex events and interpret the relationships among participants.

Some ditransitive verbs undergo **dative shift**, allowing the two objects to appear in different arrangements. In the **oblique dative** form, the verb takes a noun phrase plus a dative prepositional phrase, with the latter not treated as a core argument. However, in the **double-object** construction, the verb takes two core objects, placing the indirect object, typically a person, before the direct object, usually a thing. This pattern is common with verbs of giving, sending, or showing actions that inherently involve transferring something between participants. In Cognitive Grammar, double-object constructions are analyzed as triadic symbolic assemblies that profile a three-participant event. They reflect a meaningful alignment between form and conceptual structure, allowing speakers package a complex, multi-participant event into a single, cognitively economical expression. Placing the indirect object closer to the verb highlights the recipient as the focal participant, mirroring the strong conceptual link between the action and the person affected by it.

To illustrate the point, consider the following pair of sentences that appear in double object and oblique dative forms:

Felix sent Lily a postcard.

Felix sent a postcard to Lily.

According to the theories of autonomous syntax, both sentences share the same origin, with the second one being a variation of the first. Since they stem from the same source, they essentially convey the same meaning. However, in Cognitive Grammar, there is a nuanced difference in meaning that comes from how we perceive **salience**. When two landmarks (or objects) are involved in a relationship, they can vary in how much attention they draw. The primary landmark gets what we call **initial salience**, which highlights the most important participant in a scene. On the other hand, the secondary landmark has the least salience. In the first sentence, there is no dative shift, so the direct object, *a postcard*, is the one that stands out initially. In contrast, the second sentence does include a dative shift, making the indirect object, *Lily*, the one that captures our attention first. This leads to the two sentences having different meanings, as only the first one suggests that Lily has received the postcard. There is also a structural difference: the first sentence places the noun directly, while the second uses *to*.

Below are examples of ditransitive verbs that require both an indirect object and a direct object.

Double-object form	Oblique-dative form
He sent her a letter.	He sent a letter to her.
I lent him my book.	I lent my book to him.

Double-object form	Oblique-dative form
They told us a story.	They told a story to us.
She offered me a job.	She offered a job to me.
He gave her a present.	He gave a present to her.
I showed her the photos.	I showed the photos to her.
They brought us some food.	They brought some food to us.
She baked her friend a cake.	She baked a cake for her friend.
She bought her parents gifts.	She bought gifts for her parents.
He taught the students a lesson.	He taught a lesson to the students.

7.3.3 *Aspectual Categories*

Verbs have a unique way of expressing different aspects, such as perfective and imperfective. The key difference between these two lies in how we perceive actions, demonstrating how language reflects our understanding of the world around us. While these aspects primarily focus on meaning, they also impact how we structure sentences. In terms of meaning, perfective describes actions that are viewed as completed, while imperfective refers to actions that are still ongoing. On the syntactic side, they influence verb conjugation and sentence formation. The distinction between perfective and imperfective is somewhat akin to the variance between count and mass nouns. Similar to count nouns, perfective actions are clearly defined, with a specific beginning and end. In contrast, imperfective actions are more fluid, lacking a distinct start and finish. For example, saying *write a poem* is perfective, implying the action is complete once the poem is finished, whereas *write poems* is imperfective, suggesting a more indefinite timeframe.

What follows is a description of each aspectual category along with its various subcategories.

7.3.3.1 Perfective Verbs

In the perfective aspect, we look at a situation in its entirety, from beginning to end. The perfect or bounded aspect can be divided into two categories: punctual and durative. These terms assist in describing the timing of actions in grammar. Understanding this difference is crucial in understanding how different languages express aspect, which refers to the internal timing of an action or state indicated by a verb. Cognitive Grammar emphasizes the importance of viewing verbs not only as grammatical forms but also as conveyors of meaning and the mental images they evoke. Within this framework, verbs are analyzed based on their semantic roles and how they influence our comprehension of the events they depict. Punctual verbs capture swift, instantaneous actions, while durative verbs portray processes that unfold gradually over time. This perspective in Cognitive Grammar aids in our comprehension of how we perceive and communicate time through language. By exploring the distinction between punctual and durative verbs, we gain an understanding of how actions are mentally visualized.

Punctual Verbs

Punctual verbs are all about timing; they occur at a specific moment. These verbs describe actions that are quick and fleeting, happening in the blink of an eye. They do not have any internal time structure since they take place in just one instant. You won't find these actions lingering; they're all about that brief moment. Adverbs like *instantaneously* or *all at once* can really highlight the swift nature of these verbs. For example, in the sentence *He kicked the door open*, the verb *kick* is punctual because it captures a quick, momentary action, just a single event. In contrast to durative aspects that stretch over time, punctual aspects are all about that specific moment. Some common examples of punctual verbs include *sneeze*, *cough*, *blink*, *die*, *arrive*, *jump*, *finish*, *begin*, *knock*, and *reach*. You can also use time-related adverbs like *now*, *then*, or *today* to give a clearer picture of when these actions happen. Here are a few more examples of punctual verbs:

> The hunter shot the deer.
>
> Someone knocked on the door.
>
> The cat jumped onto the windowsill.
>
> They won the game in the last minute.
>
> The car stopped suddenly at the red light.

Durative Verbs

Durative situations are those that last for a specific amount of time, regardless of how short that time may be. They involve actions or events that occur gradually over a period. Durative verbs depict actions or events that unfold over time, giving them a sense of duration, even if only momentarily. For example, in the sentence *She wears jeans*, the verb *wear* is considered durative because it implies a continuous action, indicating a persistent state. This differs from punctual aspects, which occur at a precise moment. Examples of durative verbs include *clean*, *draw*, *run*, *sing*, *sleep*, *play*, *write*, *build*, *read*, *walk*, and many others. Durative verbs can be modified with adverbials such as *all day*, *for ages*, or *forever*, which offer additional information about the duration of an action, as seen in *She studied all day for the exam.* The choice of adverbial can emphasize the duration associated with a durative verb. These verbs often highlight the ongoing nature of an action, creating a sense of continuity and flow. This aspect is crucial for conveying the timing of activities in language. Here are a few more examples of durative verbs:

She read the book for hours.

He runs every morning to stay fit.

We waited for the bus in the rain.

She cooked dinner for the family.

She works at the office from nine to five.

7.3.3.2 Imperfective Verbs

In the imperfective aspect, we examine a situation from within its time frame. It focuses on those moments that appear to stretch continuously or occur repeatedly as time passes. This imperfect or unbounded aspect can be divided into two categories: habitual and iterative. Both of these types involve repetition and are essential for understanding how language conveys habits or recurring situations. Cognitive Grammar delves into how we mentally frame these habitual and iterative events, giving us a clearer picture of the cognitive processes influencing our verb choices. This exploration illuminates the structure and meaning of language. Differentiating between habitual and iterative verbs is important because it enables us to express recurring actions and time patterns accurately. By making this distinction, we can communicate with greater precision. The imperfective aspect offers a detailed view of actions, emphasizing their ongoing or repeated nature. This viewpoint is vital for capturing the fluidity and continuity of events in our language.

Habitual Verbs

Habitual verbs focus on actions or events that occur regularly, almost like a routine. They emphasize consistency and continuous behavior. What's intriguing is that habitual verbs typically do not include specific time markers; instead, they convey a sense of timeless regularity. This sets them apart from iterative verbs, which emphasize the repetition of specific events. Habitual verbs, in contrast, convey ongoing regularity without pinpointing exact moments. For example, when we say, *She calls her best friend every day,* the verb *call* is in the simple present tense, indicating that this is a regular occurrence for her. Similarly, in *She reads a book before bedtime*, the verb *read* implies that this is a common practice for *her*. Some examples of habitual verbs include *attend*, *eat*, *exercise*, *cook*, *go*, *practice*, *speak*, *run*, *visit*, and *write*. You can enhance habitual verbs with adverbs of frequency like *often*, *usually*, *never*, or *rarely*. These adverbs indicate how frequently something occurs, as in *She rarely walks to work*. Here are a few more examples of habitual verbs:

He watches the news every night.

They walk their dog every morning.

He waters the plants every other day.

He studies for his exams every weekend.

He exercises at the gym three times a week.

Iterative Verbs

Iterative verbs are all about actions that happen repeatedly, creating a sense of cycles or repetition. Interestingly, these verbs do not always need to specify times. They can refer to time frames or suggest repetition without pinpointing exact moments, depending on the context and the speaker's intent. For example, in the sentence *The ball bounced repeatedly on the floor*, the verb *bounce* indicates an ongoing action, showing that the ball is bouncing multiple times. Similarly, in *He coughs*, the verb *cough* suggests a recurring action, indicating that he coughs again and again. Common examples of iterative verbs include *chatter*, *patter*, *stutter*, *babble*, *cackle*, *gamble*, *rattle*, *joggle*, *fizzle*, and *sizzle*. You can enhance these verbs with adverbials like *over and over again*, *constantly*, *incessantly*, or *repeatedly*. For instance, *She chattered incessantly during the meeting* emphasizes the ongoing nature of her chatter. Overall, iterative verbs highlight the repetitive nature of actions, giving a rhythmic or cyclical feel to what is happening. This characteristic is essential for expressing the frequency and regularity of events that occur in our language. Here are a few more examples of iterative verbs:

The steak sizzles on the hot grill.

He blinked rapidly in the bright light.

The birds chattered noisily in the trees.

He stuttered nervously during his presentation.

She tapped her fingers on the table while thinking.

In addition to iterative verbs, English also has **inchoative verbs**, which enrich the language by showcasing processes of change and repetition. These inchoative verbs, sometimes known as **inceptive verbs**, focus on the beginning or initiation of a process or state. For example, in the sentence *The flowers bloomed in the spring*, the verb *bloomed* signifies the start of the blooming process. In English, inchoative verbs are often formed by adding the suffix -en to a base verb, creating words like *blacken*, *brighten*, *thicken*, *harden*, *darken*, *lighten*, *soften*, *ripen*, *flatten*, *sweeten*, and many more. Some verbs can also take on an inchoative meaning with the -ify ending, such as *modify*, *solidify*, *petrify*, *purify*, and others. Additional examples of inchoative verbs include *decay*, *thaw*, *melt*, *rust*, *fade*, *sour*, *toast*, *roast*, *burn*, *warm*, and so on. These inchoative verbs play a crucial role in how we express events and states in language, helping us understand how information about these occurrences is represented and utilized in our linguistic expressions.

7.4 Cognitive Aspects

Basic mental processes shape how we perceive and understand the world. They build the foundation for our thinking and guide how we engage with our environment. These processes help us organize information, see relationships, and form mental pictures of our experiences. In the end, they improve our understanding and add meaning to everything we encounter.

7.4.1 Categorization

Instead of adhering to rigid categories, Cognitive Grammar acknowledges that verbs can have a primary meaning along with additional, related meanings. Verbs are adaptable, allowing them to adjust based on context and usage. Understanding a verb's meaning becomes clear when examining its various applications in different situations, enhancing the depth of our language and communication. The different meanings of a verb form a category, with a central or core meaning surrounded by related, less common meanings. The **prototype** represents the most typical example of a category, showcasing its essential features. Conversely, the **peripheral** meanings are less typical examples, sharing fewer characteristics. The core meaning of the verb serves as the focal point, while the peripheral meanings extend beyond a straightforward interpretation. Understanding these categories is important because it aids in comprehending how language and meaning are structured in our minds. To illustrate this concept, let's delve into an example.

run

The verb *run* is highly versatile and encompasses a range of meanings. At its core, it typically denotes moving swiftly on foot, as in *She runs every morning around the park*. This meaning is very common in usage. Nonetheless, the verb also carries peripheral meanings. Some of these are closely related to physical movement. In *The water runs down the hill*, it still involves physical movement, but of liquid. In *The engine runs smoothly*, it implies ongoing mechanical motion or activity. In *The train runs hourly*, it describes the movement of a vehicle or system over time. In *The path runs through the woods*, it suggests moving in a specific direction. Other meanings are more abstract or metaphorical. In *She runs the business*, it indicates metaphorical control or direction. In *He is running for office*, it signals pursuit or engagement. In *They ran the story in the paper*, it points to symbolic transmission or dissemination. Finally, in *The contract runs until next year*, it implies temporal extension. This gradation demonstrates how the verb *run* evolves from concrete physical motion to abstract conceptual domains, reflecting the cognitive flexibility of language.

7.4.2 Configuration

In Cognitive Grammar, language is seen as a fundamental part of how we think. This means that you cannot really grasp grammatical elements on their own; they are all connected, each one influencing how we perceive the world in its own way. Verbs, for instance, are categorized into cognitive domains, and their meanings are shaped by the different facets within those domains. A cognitive **domain** is essentially a framework of knowledge that helps us understand a particular semantic unit. Meanwhile, a **facet** is a specific angle of cognition tied to language and its usage, reflecting a part of our experiences. Understanding cognitive domains is key to grasping the meaning behind language structures because, in Cognitive Grammar, meaning is closely linked to how we conceptualize things. Semantic structures are defined in relation to these cognitive domains and gain their significance by interpreting the content of these domains in a particular manner. This interconnectedness highlights how deeply language is woven into our mental processes, shaping not just communication but our very understanding of reality.

banish
discharge
dismiss
expel
evict

The verbs cited above evoke the domain of dismissal, with each representing a distinct facet within that domain. Each is used uniquely and conveys its own specific meaning. The verb *banish* involves exiling, excluding, or sending someone away from a place or community, as seen in the sentence *He was banished from New Zealand for political reasons*. The verb *discharge* refers to releasing or permitting someone to leave a location or position such as a patient from a hospital or a soldier from military duty, as illustrated by *He was discharged from hospital after recovering from illness*. The verb *dismiss* signifies ending someone's employment or position, as shown in *She was dismissed from the firm for calling her boss a liar*. The verb *expel* involves forcing someone out of a place or organization such as expelling a student from school for misbehavior, as in *She was expelled from school for starting a fire in the library*. Lastly, the verb *evict* pertains to legally removing someone from a property, typically due to nonpayment of rent or other legal issues, as in *They were evicted from the apartment for failing to pay the rent*.

7.4.3 Conceptualization

In Cognitive Grammar, we examine the meaning of a linguistic expression through two lenses: conceptual content and construal. **Conceptual content** refers to the specific meaning that an expression conveys, while **construal** is how a speaker mentally organizes that content. Verbs, in particular, have dual aspects: one related to the conceptual content and the information it conveys, and the other linked to construal, which is how the speaker structures that content mentally. Construal operations are crucial processes in language that influence how we comprehend different situations. Verbs play a significant role in these operations, shaping our mental images and influencing how we perceive events or emphasize specific aspects from a particular perspective. By understanding both conceptual content and construal, we can truly appreciate the depth and versatility of verbs in language. This view of linguistic semantics highlights the role of human cognition in interpreting language. To illustrate this point, let's delve into an example:

fear
frighten

The verbs *fear* and *frighten* both relate to the emotion of fear, but they serve different functions and reflect distinct conceptual perspectives of the speaker. *Fear* describes an internal emotional state; when you fear something, you experience that anxiety within yourself, as in the sentence, *He fears losing his job*. On the other hand, *frighten* involves causing fear or alarm in someone else. Therefore, when you frighten someone, you are inducing fear in them, as in *The horror movie frightened the children*. In summary, *fear* is about feeling afraid, while *frighten* is about making someone else feel that way. This demonstrates the significant impact verbs can have on shaping our perceptions of the world. They enable us to view events from multiple perspectives and articulate our personal experiences. Verbs are essential in how we understand and interpret actions and events, aiding us in framing situations in our minds based on factors like specificity, focus, prominence, and perspective.

7.5 Linguistic Aspects

When we think about verbs, it is not just about the cognitive side, how our brains perceive and process information. There is also a rich linguistic side connected to the structure of language, involving elements like syntax and semantics. The cognitive aspect reveals how people mentally organize and interpret the world around them, while the linguistic aspect deepens our understanding of how language functions and is used in communication. These linguistic features of verbs are essential for clear and precise expression. They allow us to convey when an action occurs (tense), the nature and duration of the action (aspect), the speaker's attitude or intention (mood), and whether the subject performs or receives the action (voice). Together, the cognitive and linguistic dimensions of verbs strengthen our ability to communicate effectively, whether speaking or writing. They enrich our interactions by enabling us to express complex ideas, emotions, and relationships with subtlety, ultimately helping us navigate the complexities of daily life and human experience with greater clarity and connection.

In the upcoming sections, I will delve into the world of verbs and explore their linguistic features. We will cover topics such as coercion, zone activation, mood marking, and participant roles.

7.5.1 Coercion

In Cognitive Grammar, **coercion** involves bending grammatical rules to suit particular situations, opening the door to more flexible and context-sensitive interpretations of language. It helps explain why certain words can appear in phrases that do not quite match their usual meanings. Coercion is key to understanding how words can fit into structures that deviate from their expected semantic roles. For instance, when a verb typically requires an event as its complement but is followed by a noun phrase, coercion allows that noun phrase to be reinterpreted to meet the verb's needs. This concept illustrates how language can adapt and create meaning dynamically, tailored to specific contexts. It offers linguistic flexibility, enabling speakers to express complex ideas without being overly explicit. This highlights the importance of how we conceptualize meaning within language and shows how our cognitive processes actively adjust and reinterpret what we hear for better understanding.

Coercion in verbs occurs when a verb's meaning extends beyond its usual sense, often influenced by context or usage.

He buttered up the boss.

The man drank the pub.

In the first sentence, the verb *butter* is cleverly twisted to mean *flatter* or *compliment*. Here, it is used metaphorically instead of its literal sense, connecting the world of cooking (like buttering bread) with our social interactions. By mixing words from different areas, fresh meanings can be created. In the second sentence, the verb *drink* usually requires a liquid to act upon, but here, *pub* is a place. This twist allows us to interpret that the man drank a lot at the pub, maybe even all the drinks available. These examples demonstrate the flexibility of language and the creativity that comes with human communication. Language is a powerful tool that can be easily shaped for various purposes, including playful manipulation. This adaptability highlights the lively nature of how we express ourselves, emphasizing the limitless ways we can share and understand meaning.

7.5.2 Zone Activation

In Cognitive Grammar, there is an interesting idea called the **active zone** that relates to verbs. Essentially, the active zone of a verb pinpoints the specific part of an action that truly matters in a certain context. It highlights the key aspect of what the verb means in that situation, showing how verbs can draw attention to particular elements of an action or process. When we use a verb, we mentally engage with an active zone that represents the entity actively involved in the action. Take the verb *touch*, for instance. In *She gave the fabric a gentle touch*, the active zone would be the fingertips, as they are directly engaged in the act of touching. Understanding active zones is crucial for grasping meaning. They showcase the dynamic nature of language and how we interpret and utilize verbs. This concept shifts our perspective from rigid categories to more fluid processes, helping us analyze how speakers mentally visualize actions. Active zones highlight the adaptability of language and meaning, as well as the interplay between verbs and their context.

She kicked the ball.
He heard the music.
She tasted the soup.
They built a house.
He wrote a letter.

In the first sentence, the verb is *kicked*, while the active zone is the *foot*, as it is the most relevant part of the body in performing the action of kicking. In the second sentence, the verb is *heard*, while the active zone is the *ears*, as they are involved in the act of hearing. In the third sentence, the verb is *tasted*, while the active zone is the *tongue*, as it is the part involved in the act of tasting. In the fourth sentence, the verb is *built*, while the active zone is the *hands* or the *tools* used in the construction process. In the fifth sentence, the verb is *wrote*, while the active zone is the *hand* or the *pen*, as these are the parts involved in the act of writing. These examples demonstrate how different parts of an action can be highlighted depending on the verb and the context, helping language users focus on specific aspects of an action in various contexts. This understanding of active zones can enhance clarity and precision in communication. It also illustrates the intricate relationship between verbs and the physical or conceptual tools used to perform actions.

7.5.3 Mood Marking

In Cognitive Grammar, **mood** refers to the form a verb takes to express the speaker's attitude, intention, or perspective toward the action or state described. This view highlights that every use of language is inherently subjective. When speakers choose their words and grammatical structures, they are sharing their unique interpretation of reality. Language consists of symbolic connections between forms and meanings, extending beyond vocabulary into the realm of grammar. Because of this, verb moods are essential symbolic elements that reveal the speaker's perspective. Their importance lies in serving as linguistic tools for expressing **subjectivity**, a way of construing meaning that reflects the speaker's attitudes or viewpoints through the verb. Verb moods enable speakers to convey beliefs and emotions, shaping how listeners interpret the message. Within Cognitive Grammar, verb moods go beyond mere grammatical forms; they provide insights into how speakers perceive and communicate their reality. Different verbs can express various moods, each carrying its own distinct attitude or function.

Below is a description of each mood, which is determined by the speaker's perspective.

Indicative Mood

The indicative mood is a verb form used to express statements of fact, opinions, or questions about real-world situations. Cognitive Grammar views the indicative mood as a crucial element in how we use language to convey factual information and describe reality. It serves as a way to make statements that we believe to be true or to pose questions that seek factual answers, anchoring our conversations in a shared understanding of reality. We use the indicative mood to state facts, share opinions, or ask questions as if they were facts, conveying a sense of certainty. This aligns with the Cognitive Grammar perspective that language mirrors our mental images of the world. By using the indicative mood, speakers can assert facts, describe observations, and inquire about the real world, fostering a common ground for effective communication. This shared understanding is essential for meaningful interactions. The indicative mood helps establish clarity and trust between speakers and listeners. Here are a few examples to illustrate this idea:

Berlin is the capital of Germany.	(stating a fact)
His baby brother is really cute.	(expressing an opinion)
Have you finished your homework?	(asking a question)

Imperative Mood

The imperative mood is a verb form used to give commands, requests, instructions, or advice. It typically addresses the listener directly and uses the base form of the verb, often without stating the subject, which is usually implied as *you*, whether singular or plural. Cognitive Grammar sees the imperative mood as a powerful way to influence the behavior of others through commands, requests, or instructions. It reflects the speaker's desires for a specific outcome. This mood serves as a tool for social interaction, aiding in achieving particular goals by encouraging actions. This method of expression is crucial in daily conversations, ensuring clear and direct communication. It aligns with Cognitive Grammar, as the imperative mood engages the listener's mind to prompt response. Ultimately, the imperative mood shows how language functions as a tool for shaping behavior and relationships. Here are a few examples to illustrate this idea:

Sit on the sofa.	(command)
Let me go to bed.	(request)
Keep reading.	(instruction)

Subjunctive Mood

The subjunctive mood is a verb form used to express wishes, hypothetical situations, suggestions, or conditions contrary to fact. The verb reflects something imagined, desired, or uncertain rather than a concrete reality. Cognitive Grammar views the subjunctive mood as a way to express hypothetical situations, wishes, demands, or suggestions. This mood helps convey desires or imagined scenarios that may not be real or true, often reflecting the speaker's intentions. It is more complex than the indicative mood, as it often communicates statements that contradict reality. Verbs are often in forms that differ from the indicative mood, such as using *were* instead of *was*. This allows speakers to explore scenarios that are not bound by reality, enabling abstract thinking. The subjunctive mood explores possibilities, aligning with Cognitive Grammar's focus on language and thought. Here are a few examples to illustrate this concept:

I wish I were rich.	(expressing a wish)
I demand he be removed!	(expressing a demand)
If I were her, I would ask Jane to drive.	(hypothetical)

7.5.4 Participant Roles

As I mentioned earlier, verbs capture how we think about processes, while nouns focus more on the things themselves. Verbs are not just random forms put together by grammar rules; they are meaningful expressions that blend both meaning and structure. They originate from specific instances of use and, over time, become ingrained in our minds as standard units. In Cognitive Grammar, we view language as a well-organized set of these conventional units, with verbs linking to other parts of language in various ways. These connections are not just abstract grammatical ties; they are deeply connected to how we think and perceive the world, showing how we understand and express our experiences. Verbs play a crucial role in depicting events and states within our mental framework of meaning. They relate to their arguments, which are the participants involved in the action or event that the verb describes. This framework outlines how many arguments a verb can have, with each participant taking on a specific role in the event.

In Cognitive Grammar, **participant roles** are the conceptual functions that entities take on within an event as it is mentally represented. They reflect how a speaker construes the relationships among the participants involved—who is acting, who is affected, who is experiencing something, and so on. Crucially, these roles are not fixed grammatical categories but cognitive structures that arise from how humans understand and conceptualize events. They capture the way our minds organize interactions rather than prescribing a rigid set of labels. This conceptual organization is central to understanding how participants in an event relate to one another and to the actions they take or experience. Participant roles show how we mentally structure an event, linking the verb to the participants we conceptualize as involved in it. The verb profiles a particular facet of the event and guides how its participants are organized within that conceptual scene. It highlights the structure we notice, shaping our sense of participants and their interaction.

The following are the most widely used participant roles and the notions that characterize them.

- Agent: The animate or volitional doer of an action.

  The **chef** cooked the meal.

- Patient: The entity that is affected by the action.

  Jim wrote a **letter**.

- Causer: The inanimate, non-volitional doer of action.

  The **storm** destroyed the house.

- Experiencer: The animate participant who experiences an emotion unintentionally.

  Lily felt sad.

- Benefactive: The animate recipient who benefits from an action.

  She sent **Leo** a postcard.

- Possessor: The entity that owns something.

  Alice has two mobile phones.

- Instrument: The inanimate, concrete or abstract, tool used by an agent to carry out an action.

  The **key** opened the door.

- Goal: The entity toward which something moves.

  She went to the **store**.

- Source: The entity from which something moves.

  She left **home** early.

- Location: The place where an action occurs.

  They met at the **station**.

- Time: The temporal dimension in which an action is carried out.

  Tomorrow is her birthday.

- Theme: The entity that is the topic of the conversation.

  They discussed **politics**.

Semantic roles play a vital role in helping us understand the function of each noun in a sentence, especially in relation to the main verb. This understanding provides us with a deeper insight into the sentence's underlying meaning. In Cognitive Grammar, these roles are essential for comprehending how different parts of a sentence interact. By identifying the contribution of each noun to the main verb, Cognitive Grammar improves our understanding of the sentence's fundamental semantics. This perspective emphasizes the significance of grammar, portraying it as a fundamental aspect of human cognition that intersects with our perception, focus, and memory. Such analysis allows for a thorough interpretation of a sentence's meaning, illuminating the relationship between its various elements. Understanding semantic roles is not only crucial for breaking down complex sentences but also for applying them in natural language processes.

Summary

In this chapter, I have probed the conceptual category of **relations**, represented by the grammatical category of **verbs**. Semantically, verbs can profile either unfolding processes or stable states, expressed through the distinction between dynamic and stative verbs. Dynamic verbs express change or movement, while stative verbs denote stability or existence. Syntactically, verbs organize events by structuring the roles of participants. They can profile one-participant events (intransitive verbs), two-participant events (monotransitive verbs), or three-participant events (ditransitive verbs). Aspectual distinctions further enrich the meaning of verbs by specifying how an event unfolds in time. Perfective verbs present events as bounded and complete, while imperfective verbs portray them as ongoing or unbounded. Within these categories, finer distinctions emerge: perfective verbs include punctual verbs, which denote instantaneous actions, and durative verbs, which extend over time. Imperfective verbs, by contrast, encompass habitual verbs, which describe repeated actions, and iterative verbs, which emphasize recurrence.

Verbs display cognitive and linguistic aspects. In cognitive aspects, verbs undergo three cognitive processes: **categorization**, **configuration**, and **conceptualization**. **Categorization** allows verb meanings to extend from prototypical cases; **configuration** groups related verbs into domains that highlight different facets of events; and **conceptualization** shows how similar verbs can still profile distinct aspects of a situation, offering alternative perspectives on the same situation. These processes reveal how verbs are not static labels but dynamic tools for shaping thought. On the linguistic side, verbs are influenced by four mechanisms that govern how verbs function in discourse. **Coercion** is the process by which context forces a verb or expression into a specific interpretation. **Active zone** refers to highlighting the relevant part of a concept in meaning construction. **Mood marking** encodes the speaker's stance toward an event. **Participant roles** define the semantic functions entities take in an event. Together, these mechanisms show how verbs structure meaning and guide our understanding of events.

Exercises

1. The verbs below demonstrate the versatility of the English language. Explore their various meanings.

1. pass
2. take
3. turn
4. bring
5. break

2. The verbs below relate to cleaning, each highlighting a distinct facet. Can you identify it?

1. brush
2. scrub
3. sweep
4. wipe
5. scour

3. These verb pairs differ by how their content is construed. How can this be shown?

1. pick versus select
2. imply versus infer
3. allude versus refer
4. gather versus collect
5. accuse versus charge

4. Classify each verb as a one-, two-, or three-participant predicate within cognitive analysis.

1. The wind was howling loudly.
2. She lent her friend some money.
3. They danced at her wedding party.
4. I advised him to consult a physician.
5. I heard a beautiful melody this morning.

5. Use each verb in one- and two-participant predicates; write sentences to show the difference.

1. eat
2. run
3. walk
4. drive
5. break

6. Provide example sentences illustrating the perfective and imperfective use of each verb.

1. lie
2. rise
3. read
4. look
5. have

7. Some verbs are versatile, profiling either a process or a state. Show this with sentences.

1. see
2. taste
3. mind
4. smell
5. sound

8. State the type of semantic process that the verb in each of the following sentences denotes.

1. The apples ripened.
2. He poured the milk.
3. He found a parking space.
4. John rides his bike to work.
5. You're sniffing. Do you have a cold?

9. Identify the specific mood of the verb in each sentence and its effect on meaning.

1. I wish it would stop raining.
2. Let's go out to dinner tonight.
3. Have you finished your work?
4. May you live long and prosper.
5. He lives abroad most of the year.

10. Choose the correct verb form in each sentence, which conveys the intended meaning.

1. He (has/is having) a party tomorrow night.
   I (have/am having) a lot of work to do today.
2. She (sees/is seeing) the person she met on holiday.
   I (see/am seeing) what you mean.
3. Nancy (thinks/is thinking) scary movies are stupid.
   Nancy (thinks/is thinking) about what to do this weekend.
4. I (felt/was feeling) tired so I went to bed early.
   I (feel/am feeling) like a walk. Do you want to come?
5. The soup (tastes/is tasting) delicious.
   The chef (tastes/is tasting) the soup.

8

Simple Temporal Relations: Processes in Verb Phrases

8.1 Introduction

In Chapter 7, I explored the conceptual category of **relations**, represented grammatically by **verbs**. In this chapter, I examine the conceptual category of **verbal expressions**, which encode processual predications in grammar through **verb phrases**. A **verb phrase** is essentially a combination of an auxiliary verb and a main verb. Verbs and verb phrases are language's backbone, adding depth and subtlety to communication. Verb phrases are groups of words that act as verbs in a sentence, adding layers of complexity and variety in terms of syntax, including aspects like tense, aspect, voice, and modality. They serve two main functions in language: reference and specificity. When it comes to reference, they pinpoint the exact timing of an action. For example, in *She studies*, the action is happening now. In *She studied*, it is in the past, and in *She will study*, we are looking at the future. As for specificity, they offer more details. In *She came*, it is pretty vague, but in *She came at seven*, it gives a clearer picture of when that action took place. To sum it up, verbs are language's core; verb phrases enrich expression.

8.2 Verbal Expressions

In Cognitive Grammar, a **verbal expression** is a conceptualization that profiles a temporal process. In grammatical terms, it is encoded through a **verb phrase**. This is a grammatical unit built around a main verb and any words that expand or complete its meaning. It expresses an action, event, or state, and can include auxiliary (helping) verbs, modals, objects, complements, and adverbials. In each case, **the main verb** carries the core meaning, while the other elements shape tense, aspect, voice, or modality. For instance, in *She has studied hard*, the verb phrase is *has studied*, where the main verb *studied* acts as the head because it determines the core meaning and grammatical function of the entire phrase. The auxiliary verb *has* supports the main verb but does not define the phrase's structure. Verb phrases are more than just grammatical structures; they blend both semantic (meaning) and syntactic (structure) elements, showcasing how form and meaning are intertwined. They transcend grammar, shaping how we frame actions through cognitive processes like perspective, attention, and focus.

In Cognitive Grammar, there are several important ideas that relate to verb phrases, highlighting the theory's focus on meaning and how we conceptualize things. Verb phrases are viewed as inherently symbolic, connecting the sounds we use (the form) with the meanings they convey (the meaning). This connection is straightforward and doesn't need a separate syntactic system to bridge the gap. Instead, verb phrases are seen as patterns that have become established through frequent use in communication. Unlike traditional approaches that view grammatical forms as just syntactic, Cognitive Grammar asserts that all grammatical forms, including verb phrases, carry meaning. They play a vital role in shaping the overall meaning of sentences by reflecting how the speaker perceives events. Cognitive Grammar also blurs the lines between words and grammatical structures, seeing them as part of a continuum, with verb phrases being a key element in this cohesive system of meaning. Essentially, verb phrases are more than mere words; they embody the speaker's interpretation of a situation.

A verb phrase is derived from a process called **instantiation**. In Cognitive Grammar, instantiation is the process of how a general concept (or type) is realized or exemplified by a specific example (or instance). A **type** is an abstract category in language, while an **instance** is a particular example of that type. In grammar, instantiation involves turning a general verb concept into a specific example or occurrence. For example, the verb *jog* represents the overall action of moving at a slow, steady pace, usually for exercise. However, when we say, *She jogs every morning*, we are referring to *jogs* as a specific instance of the broader concept of jogging. Instantiation is important in Cognitive Grammar because it connects abstract ideas to real-life examples. It shows how we use general concepts in daily situations, how people understand and organize language, and how meaning is created in different contexts.

8.3 Grounding

A verb phrase is formed through **grounding**, a linguistic mechanism that links the subject of discussion to its context, including the speech event and participants involved. Grounding ties words to time, place, and experience, clarifying meaning and sharpening communication. There are two main types of grounding: nominal and clausal. **Nominal grounding** connects nouns to a specific context using fundamental grounding elements like possessive pronouns, articles, demonstratives, quantifiers, partitives, and modifiers. For instance, in the sentence *This picture is new*, the demonstrative *this* grounds the noun *picture* in the immediate context. On the other hand, **clausal grounding** links clauses to a specific context through elements such as tense, aspect, voice, and modality. For example, in the sentence *She will arrive tomorrow*, the auxiliary verb *will* grounds the action of arriving firmly in the future. Grounding is also tied to **subjectivity**, which influences how linguistic expressions are mentally visualized and interpreted from individual viewpoints, enabling effective communication of meaning.

8.3.1 Clausal Grounding

In Cognitive Grammar, finite clauses arise as a result of **clausal grounding.** This process involves connecting a finite clause to a specific context, making it meaningful and relevant to both the speaker and the listener within their shared reality. This anchoring is achieved through various grounding elements such as tense, aspect, voice, and modality. These elements serve to ground linguistic expressions in a particular context, providing them with temporal, spatial, and experiential significance. They work to clarify and specify the meaning of sentences by placing actions or states within a specific timeframe, manner, or set of circumstances. Each grounding element plays a unique role in adding context and clarity to the clause. For example, the verb *visit* emphasizes a process by indicating a type of action. However, in the sentence *She visited her aunt*, the verb is anchored in reality by the past tense, indicating a specific instance of that action. This informs us about a particular visit that occurred in the past.

8.3.2 Clausal Grounding Elements

The key grammatical markers that form the foundation of verb phrases in English include tense, aspect, voice, and modality. In the realm of Cognitive Grammar, these markers are essential for shaping our comprehension of verb phrases. This approach reveals how language captures these markers, offering valuable insights into how speakers express time, the structure of events, and their personal viewpoints. Tense tells us when an action or state occurs whether it is in the past, present, or future. Aspect highlights the nature of the action, indicating if it is completed or ongoing. Voice shows the connection between the subject and the action, distinguishing between active and passive constructions. Modality reflects the speaker's attitude toward the statement, whether it is about possibility, certainty, permission, or obligation. Lastly, modification adds extra details about the action or state through various words, phrases, or clauses. Together, these grounding elements act as linguistic tools that enhance our understanding of the information being communicated, making conversations richer and more meaningful.

8.3.2.1 Tense

The first way to establish clausal grounding in a verb phrase is by using tense. In Cognitive Grammar, the relationship between tense and our **reality model** offers a fascinating perspective on how we understand language. We assess situations against reality as it unfolds from past to present to future. There are two models of reality: the basic model and the dynamic model. The **basic model** consists of two aspects: **immediate reality**, which refers to events happening right now, and **non-immediate reality**, which pertains to events that have already occurred. In basic reality, the states of affairs are factual. The **dynamic model** also consists of two aspects: **potential reality**, which involves events that might happen, and **projected reality**, which includes events that are expected to happen. In dynamic reality, the states of affairs are not yet certain. Imagining scenarios belongs to the realm of irreality, exemplified by the hypothetical wish, *I wish I could find a better job*, which reflects possibilities rather than factual states of affairs.

Tense in Cognitive Grammar is the way language expresses the timing of an action or event, highlighting when it is located in relation to the speech moment or other reference points. It revolves around the verb's time frame, which includes the present, past, and future. Tense helps us understand how a situation is situated in time from the speaker's perspective, with the moment of speaking acting as a reference point that connects us to these three time frames: past, present, and future. When we use the past tense, we are talking about something that happened in a reality that is not immediate, referring to a time that lies behind us. It looks back and places a situation as occurring before we speak. On the other hand, the present tense is all about immediate reality, indicating that what we're describing is happening right now, at the same time as we are speaking. Then there is the future tense, which points to a reality that has not happened yet, referring to a time that lies ahead of us. It looks forward and places a situation as occurring after we finish speaking. Overall, tenses ground situations, revealing reality and clarifying context.

Let's now analyze examples that demonstrate the three spheres of time: past, present, and future.

I attended the conference.

I attend the conference.

I will attend the conference.

The expressions mentioned above represent different time frames and facets of reality. They indicate that by selecting a specific tense, the speaker is informing the listener about the type of reality in which the situation is grounded. In the first expression, the speaker anchors the situation in non-immediate reality, occurring before the time of speaking. This is linguistically shown through the use of the past tense with the verb *attended.* In the second expression, the speaker anchors the situation in immediate reality, happening at the time of speaking. This is indicated by the use of the present tense with the verb *attend.* In the third expression, the speaker anchors the situation in projected reality, occurring after the time of speaking. This is shown through the use of the future tense with the modal verb *will attend.* In Cognitive Grammar, tense is not a strict timeline; it serves as a flexible lens through which we perceive events. It goes beyond just objective time, intertwining with **subjective construal**, reflecting how speakers perceive and interpret events.

Tenses are considered **deictic expressions**, which are linguistic elements that point to aspects of the communicative situation. Their interpretation relies on knowing who is speaking, when, and where. These expressions heavily rely on context to make their meaning clear. In the realm of Cognitive Grammar, they hold a lot of importance for a few key reasons. First, they anchor actions and events in time from the speaker's perspective. Second, they help listeners place actions in the correct temporal context. Third, they indicate the relevance of actions to the current discourse. Fourth, they convey the speaker's involvement or emotional connection. Lastly, they aid in understanding the speaker's perspective and context. The diverse functions of deictic expressions underscore their crucial role in effective communication and cognitive processing. By grounding language in context, they bring clarity and precision to our conversations. Understanding these nuances can really enhance both our writing and speaking skills.

Non-Immediate Reality

In Cognitive Grammar, **non-immediate reality** refers to situations that are no longer part of the speaker's immediate experiential ground. In grammar, this is expressed through the **past tense**. The past tense is used to talk about events or situations that have already happened. Essentially, the past tense describes actions, events, or states we perceive as completed or situated in the past, creating a temporal distance from the here and now. Using the past tense draws a clear boundary between our current experience and the narrative we recount. The past tense can be categorized into four main forms: simple past, past continuous, past perfect, and past perfect continuous. These forms combine tense and aspect, enabling us to frame past events with nuance, reflecting not only when something happened but also the nature and duration of the event. This layered approach enriches our storytelling, offering deeper insight into how we relate to our past experiences.

He trained yesterday.

He was training at 8:00 a.m. yesterday.

He had just trained.

He had been training for an hour.

The first sentence uses the simple past tense, which is used to describe actions that have been completed in the past. Time markers such as *yesterday*, *ago*, *formerly*, *previously*, *last week*, or even *in 1985* may be used. Moving on to the second sentence, it is in the past continuous tense. This tense describes actions that were in progress at a certain moment in the past, often accompanied by words like *while*, *when*, and *as*. Now, the third sentence shifts to the past perfect tense, which highlights an action that was finished before another action took place in the past. Adverbs like *already*, *yet*, *just*, *until that day*, and *by the time* are commonly used here. Finally, the fourth sentence is in the past perfect continuous tense. This tense illustrates an action that was ongoing in the past and continued right up to a specific moment. Look for time markers like *for*, *since*, and *the whole day* to identify it.

To avoid any mix-ups with past tenses, it can be really useful to look at them side by side in pairs of sentences.

The fire started when the firemen arrived.

The fire had started when the firemen arrived.

Both sentences are grounded in the past, placing them outside the immediate scope of the speech event. They rely on memory rather than direct perception, a key marker of non-immediate reality. However, they do so in slightly different ways. The first sentence, using the simple past tense, indicates that the fire broke out exactly when the firemen arrived, highlighting the immediate connection between their arrival and the fire's start. This past event lies beyond the speech moment, which reflects the speaker's perspective that is shaped by memory or prior knowledge. In contrast, the second sentence employs the past perfect tense to sequence events, showing that the fire had already started before the firemen arrived. This construction profiles the fire as occurring prior to another past event (the firemen's arrival), adding a layer of temporal distance that creates a more complex form of non-immediate reality. It reflects a retrospective viewpoint, where the speaker looks back from a past reference point. The past perfect (*had started*) introduces a higher stratum of conceptualization; it is not simply past, but past relative to another past event.

I had waited a few days for the reply.

I had been waiting a few days for the reply.

Both sentences describe an action in the past, representing non-immediate reality, but there is a difference in meaning. In the first sentence, the focus is on the fact that the waiting happened and ended. The verb phrase is instantiated as a finished process. It is grounded in a past reference point, removed from the present speech event. The speaker conceptualizes the waiting as bounded, with a clear start and end. In the second sentence, the focus is on the duration and ongoing nature of the waiting up to a certain point in the past. It suggests that the waiting was still in progress or had just ended when something else happened. The verb phrase is instantiated as an unbounded, ongoing process. It is grounded in the same past reference point, but the speaker's subjective viewpoint highlights the experience of waiting rather than its completion. This adds a layer of temporal texture, showing how the speaker mentally construes the situation. In short, the first sentence (*had waited*) simply reports that the waiting occurred and ended, whereas the second (*had been waiting*) invites the listener to imagine the experience and passage of time.

Immediate Reality

In Cognitive Grammar, **immediate reality** refers to situations directly accessible to the speaker at the moment of speaking. In grammar, this is expressed through the **present tense**. The present tense is used to describe actions or states occurring right now. It creates a sense of urgency and relevance from the speaker's perspective. The present tense can be divided into four main forms: simple present, present continuous, present perfect, and present perfect continuous. These forms combine tense and aspect, revealing different nuances of meaning. Each form reflects how the speaker perceives the situation, including the nature and duration of the event. This layered approach enriches communication, making the speaker's message more vivid and impactful. It also allows speakers to highlight the immediacy or ongoing nature of their experiences, drawing listeners into the moment as if it were unfolding in real time, enhancing engagement.

He trains every day.

He is training now.

He has trained already.

He has been training for an hour.

The verb in the first sentence is in the simple present tense, which we use to talk about habits, scheduled events, or general truths. Adverbs that fit here include *always*, *usually*, *never*, *occasionally*, *often*, *seldom*, *sometimes*, *once*, *twice*, and *every day*. Moving on to the second sentence, the verb is in the present continuous tense, which we use to talk about actions happening right now. Relevant adverbs here include *now*, *at the moment*, *currently*, and *right now*. In the third sentence, we find the present perfect tense, which we use to describe actions that started in the past and are still relevant today. Suitable adverbs here include *already*, *recently*, *yet*, *just*, *ever*, *never*, *so far*, and *up to now*. Finally, the fourth sentence uses the present perfect continuous tense, which we use to highlight actions that began in the past and are still ongoing, focusing on how long they have been happening. Adverbs appropriate here include *for*, *since*, *the whole week*, and *all day*.

To avoid confusion with present tenses, it is important to compare them side by side in pairs of sentences.

She lives with her parents.
She is living with her parents.

Both sentences describe an action in the present, representing immediate reality, but they do so in different ways. The first sentence presents the situation as a stable, ongoing fact: living with her parents as a habitual state. The verb phrase is instantiated as a bounded but stable situation. It is grounded in the present moment, reflecting immediate reality. The speaker conceptualizes the situation as unchanging and general, without emphasizing duration or transition. The second sentence shows a temporary, ongoing state; she lives with her parents for now, due to circumstances. It is also grounded in the present, yet highlights change, duration, or temporariness. The progressive aspect invites the listener to imagine the flow of time and the possibility of change. So, while both describe immediate reality, the second adds a layer of temporal texture and subjectivity, suggesting that the situation is in progress and possibly not permanent.

I have written the essay.
I have been writing the essay.

Both sentences are grounded in the present perfect tense, but they differ in how the speaker chooses to construe the situation. The first sentence is anchored to the present but profiles a completed event in the recent past. The verb phrase is instantiated as a completed action with relevance to the present. The speaker frames essay-writing as a finished, result-focused process. This construction reflects non-immediate reality in terms of time, as the writing occurred earlier, but remains grounded in the present through the perfect tense. In contrast, the second sentence is also anchored to the present but profiles an ongoing process or recently completed process. The speaker emphasizes the ongoing effort and duration of writing, possibly unfinished. The verb phrase is instantiated as an unbounded, dynamic process, focused on time flow and engagement over completion. This construction reflects immediate reality by emphasizing an ongoing or recently completed action that is still relevant or connected to the present moment.

Potential/Projected Reality

In Cognitive Grammar, **potential/projected reality** refers to situations that are anticipated or expected, but not yet actualized. In grammar, this is expressed through the **future tense.** The future tense is a way to communicate situations expected to unfold after the present moment. It shows how the speaker envisions events or actions happening in the future, often based on their current intentions, plans, or predictions. The future tense can be divided into four main types: simple future, future continuous, future perfect, and future perfect continuous. These types integrate tense and aspect, revealing subtle semantic distinctions. Each category enables the speaker to express their thoughts uniquely, emphasizing their perspective and the timing of the event, and this provides a more detailed way to convey time and intention, adding clarity and depth to the message.

He will train tomorrow.

He will be training in two hours.

He will have trained before he goes to work.

He will have been training for an hour.

The verb in the first sentence is in the simple future tense, used to describe actions set to happen later on. Common adverbs with this tense include *tomorrow*, *tonight*, *later*, *soon*, *next*, *in a few days*, *in the future*, and *in 2030*. In the second sentence, the verb is in the future continuous tense, which describes actions that will be in progress at a specific time in the future. Common adverbs with this tense include *all day long*, *in two hours*, *tonight*, *soon*, and *later*. In the third sentence, the verb is in the future perfect tense, indicating an action that will be completed before another future action takes place. Common adverbs with this tense include *by*, *before*, and *by the time*. Lastly, the verb in the fourth sentence is in the future perfect continuous tense, describing an action that will be ongoing in the future until a specific moment. Common adverbs with this tense include *for*, *since*, and *how long*.

To clear up any confusion about future verb forms, we need to compare them in pairs of sentences.

She will buy a new dress.

She is going to buy a new dress.

The first sentence refers to a potential reality that is not yet realized. The verb phrase is instantiated as a bounded future event, conceptualized from the speaker's current viewpoint. The speaker construes the situation with less connection to present evidence; it is more abstract and speculative. The action is presented as a prediction, decision, or intention made at the moment of speaking and is often spontaneous or unplanned. The second sentence refers to a projected reality, often based on prior plans or observable evidence. The speaker presents the action as intended or already decided, possibly with signs that it will happen soon. The verb phrase is instantiated as a future process that is conceptually unfolding from the present. The speaker sees the situation as happening right now, imagining the action already underway. This conveys a more personal and planned view, making the future seem closer and more real. In brief, while both sentences express future events: *will buy* is speculative or spontaneous, while *is going to buy* is planned or anticipated.

You're not staying out all night, are you? Well, I am going to, yes.

You're not staying out all night, are you? Well, I was going to, yes.

The first sentence is construed as a projected reality tied to a present mental state. The speaker frames the plan as active, intentional, and unfolding from the present, showing strong commitment to staying out all night. This means the person is definitely planning to stay out all night. The second sentence is construed as a non-immediate reality tied to a past mental state. The speaker presents the action as something that was once intended but is no longer certain or active. The intention is now tentative or discontinued, often signaling a change of mind or outside interference. This means that the person had the intention to stay out but might have had a change of heart. Both use the *going to* construction to express intention, yet there is a difference in meaning. The present tense *am going to* reflects a live, unfolding plan, whereas the past tense *was going to* signals a shift in intention, often implying that the plan may no longer be valid.

8.3.2.2 Aspect

The second way to achieve clausal grounding in a verb phrase is through **aspect**. In Cognitive Grammar, aspect refers to how speakers mentally construe the temporal structure of events, how they unfold, persist, repeat, or conclude. It is not merely a grammatical form but a way we conceptualize time and action through language. Cognitive Grammar emphasizes that grammar is not arbitrary; rather, it serves as a window into thought. Aspect, therefore, reveals how speakers mentally organize time, action, and experience. Unlike traditional grammars, Cognitive Grammar treats aspect as a meaningful reflection of how we mentally represent events, rather than just a formal category. Aspect is part of how we construe or frame an event. Aspectual markers are seen as grounding predications that express the speaker's viewpoint on events over time. English distinguishes two main aspects: **perfective** and **imperfective**. The perfective aspect relates to actions considered as completed wholes, whereas the imperfective aspect relates to actions that are ongoing or in progress. We often express the perfective aspect using the nonprogressive form for states and the imperfective aspect through the progressive form for activities.

To illustrate, let's examine the difference in meaning between the two modes of aspect.

She has slept.

She is sleeping.

The two expressions of *sleep* show different views of the event, grounding it in time in distinct ways. Though both mean sleeping, they evoke different images and purposes, reflecting how the speaker construes the situation. The aspect in the first sentence is perfective, expressed through the present perfect tense. The speaker construes the event of sleeping as a bounded whole; it is completed. The auxiliary *has* connects the past event to the present in the speaker's mind. In contrast, the aspect in the second sentence is imperfective, expressed through the progressive form. The speaker construes the event of sleeping as an ongoing process. The auxiliary *is* situates the clause in the present moment, making the action immediate and experiential. This contrast illustrates how grammar reflects how we think, not just how we structure sentences. It highlights the interplay between language and cognition. Aspect is not just grammar; it reflects perspective.

In some situations, the nonprogressive form contrasts with the progressive form. The key difference here is **scope**, which refers to the range of content that a linguistic expression applies to or evokes. It shapes how we interpret meaning by deciding what elements enter the speaker's construal. Scope can be either broad or narrow. **Broad scope**, or maximal, includes all the content an expression triggers, covering everything the speaker considers to grasp its meaning. On the other hand, **narrow scope**, or immediate, hones in on the specific area of focus that is relevant for interpreting an expression. To put it simply, broad scope shows the big picture; narrow scope zooms in on the specific focus. Broad scope takes an external view, seeing the whole and using the nonprogressive form. The speaker perceives the entire act in its completion. In contrast, narrow scope takes an internal view, showing a partial glimpse with the progressive form. The speaker focuses solely on the internal dynamics of the activity.

By way of illustration, let's consider the difference in meaning between the two sentences:

I saw him climb the wall.

I saw him climbing the wall.

The two sentences look alike but show different aspects and perspectives. Both describe the same physical action, but they activate distinct mental images and serve different communicative purposes. In the first sentence, the nonprogressive form, indicated by the word *climb*, highlights the entire event. The speaker views climbing as a complete act, beginning, ascent, and finish, packaged as a finished episode. Therefore, adding a follow-up like *but he stumbled and fell* would disrupt the sentence's integrity. In this construal, credibility is full because the speaker is certain he reached the top. A follow-up like *but he fell* would therefore disrupts the sentence's coherence. In the second sentence, the progressive form, shown by *climbing*, shifts the focus to the ongoing action. The speaker views climbing as ongoing, without focusing on its start or finish. The speaker may have seen only part of the climb, perhaps just the middle or a moment during the ascent. In this construal, credibility is partial since the speaker is not sure he reached the top. That is why a follow-up like *but he fell* fits without contradiction.

8.3.2.3 Voice

The third way to establish clausal grounding in a verb phrase is through **voice**. In Cognitive Grammar, voice, sometimes referred to as **diathesis**, refers to how a speaker construes the prominence and roles of participants in an event, typically the agent (doer) and the patient (receiver). It reflects the speaker's conceptualization of who is foregrounded in the action. Voice is the grammatical system that allows speakers to shift focus between participants in a clause based on how they mentally structure the event. Voice can take two patterns: the **unmarked voice**, referred to in grammar as the **active voice**, and the **marked voice**, referred to in grammar as the **passive voice**. The first places focus on the agent rather than the patient, whereas the second shifts focus to the patient instead of the agent. These different voice patterns reflect various ways of understanding events. In language, voice patterns arise from how we conceptualize relationships between participants, highlighting the dynamic interplay between agents, patients, and focus. Each voice serves its own communicative purpose, and the choice between them often depends on the context and the emphasis the speaker wishes to convey.

To demonstrate this, consider the following examples that illustrate the two voice patterns.

The hunter killed the lion.

The lion was killed by the hunter.

Both active and passive sentences use the same words, but they differ in structure because of where the focus lies. In the first sentence, we have the active voice, where the subject, the hunter, takes center stage by performing the action of killing. Here, the spotlight is on the doer. In contrast, the second sentence is in the passive voice, where the subject, the lion, receives the action of being killed. This time, the focus shifts to the recipient of the action. Regardless of the voice, both types of sentences feature a main verb, and in the case of passive voice, there is also an auxiliary verb involved. The passive construction typically uses the verb *be* followed by a past participle. Choosing between active and passive voice really comes down to what the speaker wants to highlight. Active voice tends to be more straightforward and dynamic, while passive voice can be handy when the doer is either unknown or less significant than the action itself. The choice of voice shapes clarity and impact, making it vital for effective communication.

Attenuation

Voice can be seen as **attenuation**, the softening of impact within a linguistic expression, shaping how we process information. In Cognitive Grammar, attenuation is a construal strategy: speakers choose to present information in a way that reflects lower epistemic commitment or reduced emotional intensity. This idea is key to grasping how speakers can adjust the emphasis in what they say. Attenuation in syntax lets speakers soften emphasis, downplay details, or convey ideas more gently. There are various linguistic tools to achieve this, and one of them is the passive voice. By opting for the passive voice, speakers can redirect attention from the doer of the action to the action itself or the recipient of that action. This approach is especially handy when the speaker wants to minimize the subject's importance or when the subject is either unknown or not particularly relevant. This technique enables speakers to share information in a more subtle and indirect way, which can be quite useful in certain communicative situations.

To make this clearer, let's examine some sentences that illustrate the difference in meaning between active and passive voice:

> The manager rejected the proposal.
>
> The proposal was rejected.

These two sentences describe the same event but differ in **voice**, which in Cognitive Grammar reflects how the speaker construes the focus, agency, and prominence of participants in the scene. In the active voice, the manager is clearly the agent and is foregrounded. The speaker construes the event as intentional and direct, emphasizing who made the decision. This version may carry more accountability or personal attribution. In contrast, in the passive voice, the agent is either absent or backgrounded, which can soften the tone, avoid assigning blame, and emphasize the outcome rather than the actor. The focus shifts to the proposal and the fact of its rejection. This construal minimizes the importance of who performed the action, which can be useful in formal, diplomatic, or impersonal contexts. Though describing the same event, the sentences evoke different images, goals, and intentions. In Cognitive Grammar, voice is not just a grammatical choice; it is a conceptual strategy shaping how listeners perceive events.

8.3.2.4 Modality

The final, or fourth, way to achieve clausal grounding in a verb phrase is through modality. Modality consists of linguistic tools that indicate how likely or unlikely a proposition is, whether it is possible, impossible, probable, improbable, or certain. It reflects the speaker's or writer's **attitude** toward what they are expressing. In Cognitive Grammar, modality captures a person's stance or viewpoint on a situation through their choice of words. We express modality primarily using modal verbs, which act as **grounding elements** that link the meaning of a phrase to its context. These modal verbs mark modality and are closely tied to **subjectivity**, representing the speaker's perspective shaped more by personal feelings and opinions than by objective facts. The choice of modality can produce distinct effects, significantly influencing the tone or mood of the expression. For example, selecting between *must* and *should* conveys different degrees of obligation or certainty, highlighting varying levels of subjective interpretation.

Cognitive Grammar often uses the concept of **force-dynamics** to explain how modal verbs function. Force dynamics is a framework describing how opposing or supporting forces between entities shape our understanding of causation, resistance, and agency. Within this framework, attitude includes both deontic and epistemic modality, both linked to force. Take the modal verb *can* as an example, which combines force dynamics and modality. Force dynamics considers how forces interact in a situation. When we say, *She can lift the heavy box*, we refer to the physical capability or force involved—her strength or ability to lift. Modality, on the other hand, reflects the speaker's attitude and interpretation, conveying either possibility or permission. The speaker acknowledges her capability to lift the box, but interpretation depends on context. If the context emphasizes her strength, it signals possibility, as in *She has the strength to lift the box*. If the focus is on permission, it suggests allowance, as in *She is allowed to lift the box*. Thus, the interplay between force dynamics and modality shapes how we understand the sentence.

In Cognitive Grammar, modality is divided into deontic and epistemic categories, which express attitude and perspective. This makes language a powerful tool for conveying subtle meanings.

Deontic Modality

Deontic modality in Cognitive Grammar refers to how a speaker expresses obligation and permission based on social norms, authority, or the speaker's intent. It reflects the speaker's construal of what should, must, may, or could happen, often shaped by external forces like norms, expectations, or standards. Deontic modality encompasses two key areas: obligation and permission. Obligation is expressed using modal verbs such as *must*, *have to*, *need to*, *ought to*, and *should*. Permission, on the other hand, is conveyed through modal verbs like *can*, *could*, and *may*. When an action is obligatory, it signifies a duty or moral imperative to perform it. When an action is permitted, it indicates that the person has the right or approval to proceed. Unlike deontic logic, which studies the abstract relationships among obligation, permission, and prohibition, deontic modality focuses on how these concepts are expressed in language, reflecting rules and social norms.

Let's explore the two aspects of deontic modality—obligation and permission—through some examples.

> They must hand in their homework on Tuesday.
>
> You can use my car if you have an urgent task.

Both sentences illustrate the concept of deontic modality. The first denotes obligation, something necessary and mandatory. It is often expressed with the modal verb *must*, signaling a compelling external force like rules or deadlines. The speaker construes the action as nonnegotiable, emphasizing duty and necessity. The agent is under pressure to act. In contrast, the second sentence conveys permission, indicating what is allowed but not obligatory. It is usually expressed with *can*, removing barriers and enabling free action. The speaker construes the situation as optional and supportive, highlighting possibility rather than obligation. In Cognitive Grammar, modality is not just about grammar; it is about how speakers mentally construe relationships between forces, agents, and actions. These two sentences demonstrate how different modal verbs shape our understanding of attitude. Each modal verb reflects the speaker's viewpoint and feelings.

To grasp modal nuances, it is useful to study them in pairs, as shown in the following examples.

> You have to take the medicine.
>
> You must take the medicine.

The sentences above highlight deontic modality, which is all about expressing obligation. When discussing obligation, the driving force comes from the speaker's social authority, essentially imposing their will on the listener. Here, the speaker exerts the force, while the listener is required to comply. Both *have to* and *must* suggest that something is necessary, but they have slightly different meanings. In the first case, *have to* refers to rules, laws, or instructions. It implies that someone else has deemed it necessary for me to take the medicine. This obligation is external, arising from regulations. For example, a doctor might say to a patient, *You have to take this medication three times a day*. On the other hand, *must* conveys the speaker's own desire to take the medicine, emphasizing a personal obligation. Here, the speaker emphasizes the importance or urgency of taking the medicine, as it does not come from someone else's instruction. A concerned family member might say, *You must take this medication to recover*. In summary, *have to* relates to external requirements, while *must* pertains to internal ones.

Epistemic Modality

Epistemic modality in Cognitive Grammar refers to how a speaker conceptualizes the likelihood or truth of a situation. It reflects the speaker's mental assessment of reality, how confident they are that something is or might be true. Epistemic modality encompasses two key areas: possibility and certainty. We express possibility using modal verbs like *may*, *might*, and *could*, while certainty is conveyed through verbs such as *must*, *can't*, and *couldn't*. We differentiate between possibility and certainty based on what we know and the evidence we have. Epistemic possibility refers to something that could be true, given the relevant knowledge constraints, while epistemic certainty relates to something that must be true based on the information we have at hand. In Cognitive Grammar, epistemic modality is not just a grammatical category; it is a conceptual strategy that reveals how speakers mentally navigate knowledge, inference, and uncertainty. This modality shapes how speakers convey confidence, doubt, or speculation, influencing how listeners interpret the speaker's stance toward the information presented.

Let's examine the two facets of epistemic modality—possibility and certainty—using some examples.

> He might get there in time, but I can't be sure.
>
> Schools cannot function without teachers.

Both sentences showcase epistemic modality, but each conveys a different speaker attitude toward the proposition. This contrast highlights how modal verbs shape meaning beyond mere grammar. In both cases, the speaker clearly communicates their stance through the choice of modal verb. In the first sentence, the speaker expresses uncertainty about a future event. The modal verb *might* signals possibility. The mental force is tentative; the speaker is not strongly pushed toward belief or disbelief. The attitude is highly subjective, foregrounding the speaker's limited knowledge or evidence. In contrast, the second sentence presents a structural necessity, a general truth about how institutions operate. The modal verb *cannot* expresses certainty and implies a strong barrier or inherent limitation; functioning is blocked without a key component. The attitude here is more objective, as the speaker asserts a widely accepted reality rather than personal doubt.

To understand modal differences, it is helpful to examine them in pairs, as shown below.

I will go to the gym tomorrow.

I would go to the gym tomorrow.

The modal verbs *will* and *would* both refer to the future but convey different nuances in meaning based on how speakers construe events and their likelihood. Using *will* signals a strong commitment or determination to perform an action. It frames the future event as highly certain or almost guaranteed. For example, saying *I will go to the gym tomorrow* reflects a confident mental construal, where the speaker sees the event as definite and intends to follow through. In contrast, *would* introduces a conditional or hypothetical stance. It expresses willingness to act, but only under specific circumstances. For example, *If I had more time, I would go to the gym* presents a scenario that is contingent and uncertain, shaping the future event as possible but not assured. From a Cognitive Grammar perspective, *will* constructs a future reality grounded in strong internal or external forces driving the action forward, while *would* frames the event within a hypothetical landscape where conditions modulate agency and outcome.

To deepen our understanding of the differences in meaning, let's examine another pair of examples.

The restaurant may close.

The restaurant might close.

These sentences illustrate epistemic modality, which expresses the speaker's judgment about possibility. In the first sentence, *may* signals fact-based possibility with higher certainty. The speaker mentally construes the event as plausible and supported by available information, for example, *Due to financial difficulties, the restaurant may close next month.* The speaker views the closure as likely, showing stronger belief. In the second sentence, *might* signals a hypothetical or uncertain scenario, reflecting weaker conjecture over strong evidence, for instance, *The lease is expiring, and the restaurant might close if negotiations don't go well.* This frames the event as conditional and less certain, opening a mental space for alternative outcomes. From a Cognitive Grammar perspective, *may* indicates a more likely possibility, while *might* suggests a weaker, more uncertain one. Essentially, *may* carries greater weight in expressing epistemic commitment, whereas *might* invites openness and hesitancy in the speaker's stance.

Polysemy

One key feature of modal verbs is their **polysemy**, the ability to take on multiple, related meanings depending on context. In Cognitive Grammar, polysemy is seen as a reflection of how language mirrors the flexibility of human thought. Polysemy enriches communication by adding nuance and reflecting conceptual frameworks, as modal verbs evoke various mental spaces, demonstrating grammar's deep connection to thought beyond formal rules. Additionally, polysemy links language and cognition, as modal verbs are used to guide norms (*should*), make inferences (*must*), and discuss hypotheticals (*might*). In Cognitive Grammar, meaning is derived from the speaker's construal of a situation, rather than from fixed definitions. Modal verbs are influenced by discourse, intention, and shared knowledge, making them powerful tools for adaptive and context-sensitive communication. They illustrate how grammar is dynamic, constantly negotiating meaning in interaction. Modal verbs serve as a bridge between thought and social practice.

Examples of polysemous modal verbs show how meanings shift with context and construal.

She can swim.	Ability
She can leave.	Permission
It can rain tomorrow.	Possibility
You may go now.	Permission
It may rain later.	Possibility
You must finish your homework.	Obligation
He must be at home.	Deduction
She will travel to Paris next week.	Future
I will help you.	Volition
It will rain tomorrow.	Prediction

In Cognitive Grammar, word choices subtly alter meaning, and understanding these nuances can prevent misunderstandings. To illustrate this point, let's analyze a couple of sentences:

It can rain.

It may rain.

Both sentences express the possibility of rain, but they differ subtly in meaning based on how speakers mentally construe that possibility. The first sentence, containing the modal verb *can*, suggests that rain could occur under certain conditions, indicating the condition if the environment, climate, or situation allows for it. On the other hand, the second sentence, containing the modal verb *may*, provides a specific prediction about the likelihood of rain, often indicating a more immediate or specific chance. While the first is more general and discusses the potential for rain in a broad sense, the second is more focused and is typically used in weather forecasts. In terms of certainty, the first implies that rain is just one of many possible outcomes, while the second suggests a more immediate and probable chance of rain. Understanding these distinctions enables speakers to select modals that accurately reflect their intended level of certainty and scope, whether expressing general potential (*can*) or a specific probabilistic forecast (*may*). This awareness enriches communication by making intentions clearer and more context-sensitive.

8.4 Modification

In Cognitive Grammar, **modification**, conceptually referred to as **conceptual elaboration**, is a symbolic relation in which the modifier enriches or narrows the conceptual content of the head. Language is inherently meaningful and rooted in human cognition; modification is therefore deeply semantic, not merely syntactic. Modification involves adding or adjusting components of a verb phrase to reflect different conceptualizations of an event or action. These modifiers may include adverbs, adverbial phrases, adverbial clauses, and prepositional phrases. Cognitive Grammar interprets such modifiers as conceptual choices: speakers select grammatical forms that best match their intended mental representation of an event. The choice of modifier often depends on how the speaker conceptualizes the event, which is shaped by personal experience and perspective. Ultimately, modification in verb phrases illustrates how grammar functions not merely as a set of rules, but as a dynamic toolkit for expressing rich, multifaceted meanings. It reflects the way we mentally structure events, time, agency, and emotion.

In Cognitive Grammar, language reflects how we frame meaning to match our intent. One way this is achieved is through **specificity**, which refers to the level of detail and precision used when describing a situation. It shows how finely we adjust our language to paint a clear and precise image of an event or experience. Specificity improves clarity, and precise verb phrases help bring details into focus. On the other hand, when these details are less crucial, we choose more general expressions. In contrast to specificity is **schematicity**, which involves more abstract or generalized representations. For example, the sentence *She sprinted across the field* is more specific than *She moved*. Taken together, this view shows that grammar is not a rigid set of rules, but a flexible tool we use to mold meaning based on how we think and what we want to communicate. In Cognitive Grammar, being specific plays a significant role in construal, which is the process of mentally visualizing a situation and conveying it through language.

Expanding verbs with modifiers:
Turning a verb into a full verb phrase involves adding adverbs, adverbial phrases, adverbial clauses, or prepositional phrases. These elements function as elaboration, refining and enriching the verb's meaning.

Adverbs

Single-word adverbs are among the most frequently used modifiers of verbs. They typically indicate how, when, where, how often, or to what degree an action occurs. Adverbs add details that make actions more precise and engaging. In Cognitive Grammar, **trajector** and **landmark** show how sentence elements relate. Here, the verb acts as the trajector, the main action, while the adverb acts as the landmark, enriching it. Adverbs also play a role in **scanning**, a cognitive process that reflects how we mentally process events. Adverbs ending in *-ly* typically involve **sequential scanning**. In *She walked quickly* the adverb *quickly* describes how an action unfolds over time. By contrast, adverbs that offer a general overview of an action often involve **summary scanning**. In *He always arrives on time*, the adverb *always* summarizes his punctuality without detailing each individual occurrence. In Cognitive Grammar, distinguishing sequential from summary scanning is essential as it reveals how adverbs contribute to the overall meaning of a sentence.

Consider the contrast between the following sentences, which illustrate schematicity versus specificity.

He drives.

He drives carefully.

The first sentence presents a **schematic construal** of the action. It offers a minimal representation without detailing how the activity is carried out. It simply presents a basic template for motion, with the verb *drives* lacking specificity about the manner of driving, cautious, reckless, or routine. In contrast, the second sentence offers a more **specific construal** of the action, by adding the adverb *carefully* to enrich the verb phrase, indicating attentiveness, safety, and caution. This specificity transforms a general action into a more detailed event, encouraging the listener to conceptualize the action more precisely. From a Cognitive Grammar view, this contrast shows how specificity enhances meaning: the first sentence is schematic, while the second sentence adds depth. Grammar functions as a flexible tool for shaping conceptual content, allowing speakers to adjust their descriptions to match their communicative goals and reflect their mental representations of events.

Adverbial Phrases

Adverbial phrases are clusters of words that function like adverbs, providing a more detailed description of the action or state expressed by the verb. In

Cognitive Grammar, these phrases can shed light on how, when, where, or why something occurs, altering our perception of a sentence. For example, they can convey manner, showing how an action is performed, such as doing something with great care. They can indicate place, specifying where an action occurs, like in the park. They can also denote time, pinpointing when something happens, such as after the meeting. Additionally, they can offer a reason, explaining why an action is taken, like to avoid traffic. Similar to single-word adverbs, these phrases are symbolic units that enhance the overall meaning of a sentence, helping us visualize the action or state by providing additional context. By offering more detail and specificity, they enable speakers to communicate events with varying degrees of precision.

Adverbial phrases, like single-word adverbs, add nuance by expressing evaluations or attitudes. In *She ignored the instructions to a great extent*, the phrase *to a great extent* highlights the depth of her disregard, showing not just that she ignored but how strongly she did that. Such phrases enrich context by vividly expressing emotions, judgments, or perspective beyond a simple adverb. In Cognitive Grammar, adverbial phrases can be analyzed through the **trajector-landmark** framework: the verb represents the trajector, while the adverbial phrase serves as the landmark, adding grounding and complexity. These constructions involve two types of scanning: **sequential**, which tracks an action over time as in *He spoke with increasing confidence*, and **summary**, which presents a holistic view of an action as in *She finished the project with ease.* These patterns demonstrate how speakers use adverbial phrases to express meaning more precisely.

The following examples highlight the difference between schematic and specific construals.

He arrived.

He arrived in a hurry.

The distinction between the two sentences lies in the additional conceptual detail introduced by the second. The first sentence presents a minimal scene. It is structurally simple and semantically sparse, offering no insight into the manner, motivation, or emotional tone of the event. It merely states that he reached a destination, without any indication of speed or urgency. In contrast, the second sentence enriches the scene by profiling the manner of arrival. The phrase *in a hurry* conveys urgency, hinting at haste driven by lateness, stress, or significance. This added detail invites the reader to imagine not just the endpoint but the dynamic process leading up to it. Thus, while both sentences describe the same basic event, the second construes it with greater specificity and emotional texture. It transforms a neutral statement into one charged with implied motivation and context.

Let's compare an adverb with an adverbial phrase to highlight the distinction in their meanings.

He ran quickly.

He ran with great speed.

Both sentences describe the same basic event—running—but differ in how they profile the action and its qualities. The first sentence uses the adverb *quickly* to directly modify the verb *ran*. This compact construction is typically processed as a single conceptual unit, foregrounding the action with speed as an inherent feature, but offering minimal elaboration. In contrast, the second sentence employs an adverbial phrase that shifts attention from the verb to the quality of the action. This phrasing distinguishes the motion from its intensity, allowing for a richer mental simulation and deeper appreciation of the speed involved. It construes the event with greater emphasis and vividness, inviting the listener to conceptualize not just the act of running but its impressive nature. In Cognitive Grammar, this contrast illustrates how different linguistic forms shape our mental imagery: the adverb integrates the quality into the action, while the adverbial phrase highlights it as a distinct conceptual element. Through such variation, language guides how we visualize and interpret different facets of the same experience.

Adverbial Clauses

Adverbial clauses are dependent constructions that modify the main verb of an autonomous unit by providing additional conceptual context. They play a crucial role in how we mentally organize and interpret complex scenarios, typically introduced by conceptual asymmetry markers such as *after*, *although*, *because*, *if*, *since*, *until*, *unless*, *when*, and *while*. In Cognitive Grammar, adverbial clauses are meaningful constructions that link events through relations like cause, condition, concession, time, or purpose, shaping how listeners understand connections between situations. In this framework, the autonomous unit profiles the main process, while the adverbial clause gives supporting background. In *She left because it was late*, leaving is foregrounded while lateness is backgrounded. Clause type reflects the speaker's construal. For instance, *If you study* sets up a hypothetical scenario, inviting the listener to mentally simulate a possible outcome. Adverbial clauses often use **sequential scanning**, linking events by time, contingency, or contrast.

To solidify the points we have covered, let's take a closer look at two illustrative examples.

She waited.

She waited until he came.

The difference between these two sentences lies in the conceptual richness introduced by the second. The first sentence is narrower in scope, profiling waiting abstractly, without context or detail. The second sentence is broader in scope, adding conceptual richness, as emphasized by the phrase *until he came*. From a Cognitive Grammar perspective, the autonomous unit *she waited* remains the profiled process, while the adverbial clause *until he came* provides backgrounded information that shapes how the waiting is construed. The adverbial clause not only enriches the temporal scope but also establishes a conceptual link between the two events: her waiting and his arrival. In short, the first sentence is general and open-ended, while the second offers specificity and depth, illustrating how even a small addition can significantly alter the mental representation of an event. This subtle shift in construal demonstrates how grammar functions not merely to structure language but to shape meaning. Such examples highlight the role of grammar as a cognitive tool for organizing and interpreting experience.

Prepositional Phrases

Prepositional phrases are groups of words that consist of a preposition, its object, and any modifying words. When these phrases modify a verb, they function as adverbials, adding extra details about where, when, or how something occurs, enriching the meaning of the sentence. Cognitive Grammar views prepositions as context-dependent, with meanings that shift based on surrounding words and discourse. Prepositional phrases function as modifiers, adding not just grammatical structure but meaningful depth to sentences. In terms of trajector-landmark alignment, the noun or noun phrase that follows the preposition is known as the **landmark**, while the entity it relates to is referred to as the **trajector**. Cognitive Grammar sees prepositional phrases as conceptual tools that structure experience, guide attention, and express nuanced relationships. They are not just glue for syntax, but meaning-makers shaping how listeners mentally interpret events.

To reinforce our understanding of the topic, let's examine a pair of examples more closely.

They met.

They met at the park.

The first sentence provides a basic conceptual structure: it simply states that an encounter occurred, without specifying when, where, or how. This offers a broad and abstract view of the interaction. In contrast, the second sentence is more specific, clearly stating that the meeting took place *at the park*. This spatial detail transforms the event from a vague occurrence to a specific experience. By adding *at the park*, the location of the encounter is made clear, allowing the listener to imagine the scene more vividly. From a Cognitive Grammar standpoint, the prepositional phrase *at the park* acts as a background modifier that enhances the meaning of the main action *they met*. It establishes a trajector-landmark relationship, where the meeting (trajector) is conceptually located relative to the park (landmark). This spatial connection clarifies the setting and enhances comprehension, showing how even short prepositional phrases can alter mental representations of events and highlight grammar as a tool for shaping thought and meaning.

8.5 Verb Phrases Versus Phrasal Verbs

Within the framework of Cognitive Grammar, a crucial distinction is drawn between verb phrases and phrasal verbs, grounded both in their structural composition and semantic function. This distinction is theoretically significant, as it highlights two fundamentally different mechanisms through which linguistic meaning is organized and conceptualized. A **verb phrase** is a unit made up of a main verb and its auxiliary (helping) verbs. Verb phrases are compositional: their meaning comes from the interplay of main and auxiliary verbs. The main verb gives core meaning, while auxiliaries add detail like tense, mood, aspect, or voice. For example, in the sentence *She is dancing beautifully*, *dancing* is the main verb, and *is* functions as the auxiliary. On the other hand, a **phrasal verb** combines a verb with one or more particles, usually prepositions or adverbs. The meanings of phrasal verbs can be complex, as they may be either compositional or non-compositional. Non-compositional phrasal verbs, in particular, often require deeper mental simulation and context-based interpretation to be fully understood.

Compositional phrasal verbs have literal meanings from the direct combination of verb and particle. For example, in *She picked up the book*, *pick* and *up* together mean to physically lift something. In contrast, **non-compositional** phrasal verbs are often idiomatic: the meaning of the whole cannot be predicted from the individual parts. These expressions create new meanings that are unrelated to the original verb, forming a single semantic unit in which the preposition or adverb significantly alters the verb's meaning. Such interpretations are frequently shaped by cultural norms or historical usage. For instance, when we say *She ran into an old friend*, it does not refer to literal running or colliding, but to unexpectedly meeting someone. Similarly, *They broke up last month* does not imply physically breaking something, but rather ending a romantic relationship. While many phrasal verbs follow regular patterns, some evolve into idiomatic expressions, making their meanings less transparent and more dependent on context.

Object placement in phrasal verbs:
In Cognitive Grammar, phrasal verb objects are flexible, appearing after the particle or between verb and particle. This variability reduces cognitive load, letting speakers choose the order that best fits intent and ease. When constructing sentences, our minds tend to prioritize the most **salient** information. In phrasal verbs, the particle typically draws more attention

because it conveys how or where the action unfolds. The object may appear before or after the particle, depending on what the speaker chooses to foreground. This flexibility reflects the dynamic nature of language as a tool for conceptualization, where form adapts to meaning, and structure follows cognitive priorities. In cases where the phrasal verb is idiomatic or less transparent, object placement may influence how easily the listener can parse and interpret the intended meaning. Thus, object positioning serves not only grammatical function but also cognitive and communicative strategy.

To solidify our grasp of the topic and sharpen our sense of the contrast, let's examine a pair of examples.

She picked up the key.

She picked the key up.

Both sentences are grammatically correct, yet they subtly differ in **construal,** the way the event is mentally represented. In the first version, the focus leans toward the physical action of lifting the key, highlighting the process. In the second, the emphasis shifts slightly toward the completion of that action, highlighting the result. A similar contrast appears in the pair *She took out the rubbish* versus *She took the rubbish out.* The first highlights the rubbish's movement, while the second stresses the outcome, the rubbish is now outside. Cognitive Grammar accounts for this flexibility by recognizing that language reflects our attentional and conceptual priorities. Importantly, when the object is a pronoun, it must appear between the verb and the particle, as in *She picked it up.* This placement aids **processing efficiency,** helping the listener quickly connect the pronoun with the verb-particle unit. These examples illustrate how phrasal verb flexibility aligns with cognitive preferences, shaping expressions by salience, focus, and framing.

Summary

In this chapter, I have explored the conceptual category of **verbal expressions,** encoded in grammar via **verb phrases.** In Cognitive Grammar, a **verb phrase** is understood as a symbolic unit that links a verb (often with auxiliaries) to the conceptual structures it evokes, rather than just a syntactic slot. It is a conceptual structure imbued with meaning rather than a purely formal device. Verbs provide schematic, generalized representations of actions, which can be elaborated into more precise verb phrases by adding contextual elements. This shift, from a verb like *write* to a fuller expression such as *write a letter*, allows speakers to communicate situations with greater clarity and specificity. Understanding how verb phrases refine meaning is essential for effective communication, as it enriches expression and enhances the precision of our descriptions. Cognitive Grammar situates verb phrases within a broader view of language as a dynamic, usage-based system shaped by conceptualization and human experience.

Verb phrases undergo grounding, which refers to how linguistic expressions are tied to the speaker's perspective and the communicative situation. A verb phrase does not merely describe an action; it is grounded by auxiliaries and inflections that specify when, how, and under what conditions the action occurs. Grounding transforms abstract verb meanings into situated events, making them interpretable in real-world communication. Verb phrases are anchored to the speech event through tense, aspect, voice, and modality, each contributing a distinct layer of meaning. **Tense** locates an action in time, **aspect** shows how it unfolds, **voice** indicates whether the subject performs or receives the action, and **modality** reflects the speaker's stance through expressions of obligation, permission, possibility, or certainty. Together, these components demonstrate how verb phrases illuminate the link between language and our interpretation of events, revealing the rich and nuanced meanings conveyed by linguistic choices.

Exercises

1. Identify the verb phrase in each of the following sentences, noting how it functions within the clause

1. She spoke in a polite way.
2. Anne will sit in the corner.
3. He was walking to work today.
4. She ran quickly to catch the bus.
5. The author is writing a new book.

2. Turn each verb into a verb phrase, adding the needed elements to complete the constructions.

1. He drives.
2. She sings.
3. They paid.
4. She dances.
5. The dog barks.

3. Identify the finite and nonfinite verbs in the following sentences, noting each form's role in the clause.

1. Her brother likes to watch TV for hours on end.
2. The hawkers shouted so loud to attract customers.
3. I expect you to finish the job before you go home.
4. She does not want to waste her time watching TV.
5. The injured mountaineers were taken to the hospital.

4. In each sentence that follows, state whether the aspect of the verb is perfective or imperfective.

1. The kids are playing outside.
2. She has left her purse in the car.
3. They have seen this film already.
4. He has been studying for his exam all week.
5. The whole class is going to the theater tonight.

5. The sentences below use similar wording but convey different meanings. Can you spot the difference?

1. I saw him cross the street.
2. I saw him crossing the street.

6. Identify the tense used in each sentence by matching it to the corresponding verb form.

1. I live in the countryside.
2. We are visiting the castle.
3. I haven't had breakfast yet.
4. She phoned her aunt yesterday.
5. Were you working at nine o'clock?
6. She had finished the assignment.
7. Will you be in London tomorrow?
8. Will he be traveling this evening?
9. They will have painted the fence.
10. She is going to speak to the manager.

7. Compare how each sentence pair reflects different timeframes through tense, highlighting shifts in meaning.

1. I drive to work.
   I am driving to work.
2. I live in London.
   I have been living in London.
3. I traveled to London.
   I have traveled to London.
4. I have done my homework.
   I have been doing my homework.
5. The teacher corrected the test.
   The teacher had corrected the test.

8. Choose the correct verb tense to fill in the blanks, matching the intended conceptualization or meaning.

1. This time tomorrow, I __________ on the beach. (lie)
2. She said that she __________ help me. (will)
3. She usually __________ her dog in the evening. (walk)
4. I'm tired. I __________ for five hours. (study)
5. You __________ an accident if you drive fast. (have)

6. When you phoned, I __________ in the garage. (work)
7. I __________ all my childhood in a mountainous area. (spend)
8. The phone __________ while I was watching TV. (ring)
9. I tried a little of the soup to see how it __________. (taste)
10. I can't walk because I __________ my leg. (break)

9. Fill in the blanks with the correct modal verb form, picking the option that aligns best with the situation.

1. __________ I use your laptop for a moment?
2. We __________ obey the traffic rules.
3. You __________ take a break and relax.
4. You __________ apologize for your behavior.
5. He __________ swim like a fish.
6. I __________ come if I have more time.
7. He hasn't studied well. He __________ fail his exam.
8. We __________ finish the project by Friday.
9. She __________ play the piano when she was young.
10. I __________ give you a lift home after the party.

10. The following pairs of modal verbs may occur in the same sentence but convey different meanings. Explain.

1. The doctor said I must/have to rest.
2. The concert will/might start at 7:00 p.m.
3. John can/may attend the party tonight.
4. He might/should take the earlier flight.
5. You should/must call your grandparents.

9

Simple Temporal Relations: Single-Grounded Processes in Simple Sentences

9.1 Introduction

In Chapter 8, I discussed how verbs can expand into verb phrases. Now, in this chapter, I will delve into how we express simple temporal relations in **single-grounded processes**, grammatically called **simple sentences**. We can categorize sentences into three main types: simple, compound, and complex. Each of these types plays a unique role in how we convey information and express our ideas. Cognitive Grammar sees these sentence types not only as grammatical structures but also as meaningful expressions that are linked to our thought processes. They carry inherent meaning, reflecting the speaker's perception of a situation. Additionally, they are polysemous, meaning they can take on various functions and convey different meanings depending on the context and the speaker's intent. In Cognitive Grammar, linguistic expressions, including different sentence types, are more than just formal structures; they have meaning on their own. The choice of a specific sentence type is influenced by how the speaker interprets the content. Essentially, these sentence types are dynamic tools that help us structure our thoughts and communicate them to others, shaped by our individual experiences. This perspective highlights the importance of understanding the cognitive processes that underlie our use of language.

9.2 Single-Grounded Processes

In Cognitive Grammar, a **single-grounded process** is a dynamic event anchored to one point of reference, usually the speaker's here and now. It involves a straightforward conceptualization of an action or event as it unfolds in time, without additional layers of grounding such as modality, negation, or complex temporal framing. In grammar, single-grounded processes are typically expressed by **simple sentences**. It is a one-verb sentence that conveys a complete thought. It typically includes two main components: the subject and the predicate, which together form a finite clause. For example, the sentence *She laughs* presents a single-grounded process. It features an autonomous unit that describes a habitual action. Here, the verb *laughs* indicates an ongoing activity without any additional information. In terms of function, there are four main types of single-grounded processes: statement, question, imperative, and exclamatory. Each type serves a distinct purpose in language: making statements, asking questions, giving commands, or expressing strong feelings. Single-grounded processes act as foundational units of language, laying the groundwork for more complex expressions.

In Cognitive Grammar, a single-grounded process is not just a collection of words linked by grammar rules; it is actually a lively interaction of meaning and form, all shaped by how we think. It is more than just words strung together; it is a meaningful creation that mirrors our mental processes and how we see and engage with the world around us. A single-grounded process serves as a way to express conceptual ideas, influenced by how the speaker interprets it. The way a sentence is crafted is affected by the speaker's viewpoint, what they choose to highlight, and the emphasis they place on certain parts. This means that the structure and use of a sentence carry deep meaning and are understood through the lens of cognitive processes. Cognitive Grammar suggests that grammatical elements are part of a spectrum that includes the lexicon, existing within groups of conceptual frameworks alongside phonological structures. Consequently, the meaning of a sentence is adaptable and can shift depending on the speaker's intention and context.

9.3 Categorization

In Cognitive Grammar, **categorization** refers to the cognitive skill of organizing the various functions of a sentence type into a category. A **category** is a network of linguistic expressions that consist of various meanings with subtle differences. The category is structured around a prototype and a periphery. The **prototype** represents the member with the essential properties of the category, while the **periphery** includes members that share some, but not all, of these properties. They conform to the category's general characteristics but vary in specific details. In Cognitive Grammar, the analysis of a one-verb sentence follows a similar process. A **one-verb sentence** is argued to be polysemous, and therefore encompasses distinct yet interconnected types. The statement serves as the prototype within the sentence category, while question, imperative, and exclamative sentences function as peripheral members. These peripheral sentences arise from changes applied to the statement, such as changes in word order, or subject-auxiliary inversion. This approach highlights the fluidity and interconnectedness of linguistic categories.

Each sentence type, in turn, exhibits **polysemy**, meaning it has multiple meanings. These multiple meanings form a category, which is organized into prototype and periphery. The category exhibits properties of two kinds: structural properties including word order patterns and functional properties including specific illocutionary functions. The prototype of a sentence type contains the direct, primary function, serving as the most salient example of the sentence type category. It assembles the key properties of the sentence type category. The periphery of a sentence type contains other indirect functions derived from the prototype via dynamic processes of semantic extensions. The remaining functions contain some, but not all, of the properties of the sentence type category. The different functions of a sentence type are not equal, as they do not rigidly conform to the prototype but gain membership in the category based on similarity rather than identity. This network allows for the flexible and dynamic use of language, reflecting the cognitive processes involved in understanding and producing sentences.

When analyzing sentence structure, we focus on how sentences are constructed in a language to form grammatically coherent expressions. When analyzing sentence function, we focus on the intended purpose a sentence serves within communication. Depending on their purpose, sentences can be categorized into four main types: statement, question, imperative, and exclamative. Each sentence type reflects a distinct function, and speakers choose the form that best conveys meaning. This means that there is not a simple one-to-one correspondence between the appearance of a sentence and its functions. Since different sentence types can fulfill various roles, we should consider them in relation to each other rather than in isolation. This classification is based on the notion that our use of language reflects our perception and understanding of the world around us. When it comes to using and interpreting these linguistic forms, speakers often rely on the context. The situation in which a sentence is uttered can significantly influence its interpretation, providing extra clues that help clarify the speaker's intended meaning.

Sentences are more than just words; they are speech acts that play a vital role in communication. In Cognitive Grammar, a speech act links an expression to a communicative action shaped by the speaker's view of the interaction. It is part of the construal, the way a speaker mentally structures and presents a situation. Like any other linguistic unit, every speech act is a pairing of form and meaning. A speech act is an utterance that serves a purpose, revealing how meaning and form reflect our thinking. Speech acts are learned patterns of use, not abstract logical categories. They can be divided into two main types: direct and indirect. A **direct speech act** has a locutionary effect, conveying the literal meaning of the words chosen. In contrast, an **indirect speech act** carries an illocutionary force, conveying a nonliteral meaning shaped by context. For example, a sentence like *It is cold in here* can function as a simple statement or, indirectly, as a request to close a window. These differences reveal how language operates not only as a tool for conveying facts but also as a medium for negotiating social intentions and interpersonal dynamics.

The following sections outline the four main sentence types: statement, question, imperative, and exclamative, along with their key features. In Cognitive Grammar, these are seen not as rigid categories but as grounding predications: conventional ways of shaping speaker-addressee relations and information flow. Each serves a distinct communicative function.

9.3.1 Statements

In Cognitive Grammar, a **statement,** also a declarative, is a symbolic construction whose conventional function is to present a situation as a grounded, objective description. Its meaning is not just propositional content but the speaker's construal of the event as information to be shared. The default construal of a statement is information presentation, and its conventional discourse function is assertion. Importantly, its illocutionary force arises from usage and context rather than a separate syntactic layer. Statements typically follow **canonical** or standard word order patterns in grammar. A canonical word order is the usual, most typical arrangement of elements in a sentence for a specific language: Subject-Verb-Object in English. For example, in *He repaired the bike*, the subject (the doer) comes first, followed by the verb (the action), and then the object (the receiver of the action). This canonical arrangement reflects a basic cognitive tendency to conceptualize events as an agent acting upon something, mirroring how we mentally structure everyday experiences.

In Cognitive Grammar, word order is not simply a rigid rule but a reflection of our thought processes. It serves as a way to link our thoughts to the words we use, conveying a specific perspective. When this order is altered, it becomes **noncanonical.** Cognitive Grammar views these deviations from the usual structure as intentional strategies used to create specific effects in conversation. Such variations are deliberate choices that reveal how the speaker perceives a situation. Word order is also linked to the concept of prominence, which refers to the importance assigned to certain elements in a statement. This prominence influences how we understand and organize information, allowing us to highlight certain aspects over others and shaping how the listener mentally constructs and interprets the described event. Departures from the expected pattern draw attention to the rearranged element, signaling that it carries special communicative weight. They let speakers shift focus and steer the listener's interpretation.

The following are instances of language usage that deviates from canonical constructions.

Fronting

In Cognitive Grammar, **fronting** is understood as a form of **focal adjustment,** where an element is moved to the clause-initial position to increase its conceptual prominence. It is a noncanonical word order choice used to give an element greater prominence by placing it at the beginning of the clause. It is understood not as a syntactic transformation but as a construal strategy that highlights what the speaker wants the listener to focus on. In cognitive terms, **fronting** is considered a versatile tool in language that demonstrates the evolving way we structure information and express emphasis in communication. It is not just a stylistic choice; it is closely connected to how we think and process information. When speakers highlight certain elements, they reveal both their communicative intentions and the cognitive processes guiding how they structure meaning. In essence, fronting is a product of construal, revealing the speaker's deliberate focus on a specific part of the sentence for clearer communication, as evidenced by the sentences below.

She goes for a run every morning.	Canonical
Every morning, she goes for a run.	Adverbial fronting
He won the trophy at last.	Canonical
The trophy, he won at last.	Object fronting

Dislocation

In Cognitive Grammar, **dislocation** is understood as a form of **focal adjustment,** where an element is placed outside the canonical clause structure to increase its prominence or clarify its role in the conceptualization. It is a noncanonical word order which entails placing a noun phrase outside its typical position in the sentence, either at the beginning or the end. **Left dislocation** involves placing a phrase at the beginning of a sentence, whereas **right dislocation** involves placing it at the end. Right dislocation is used to provide clarification or additional information, often in an afterthought-like manner. In cognitive terms, dislocation is seen as a strategy for managing information flow and maintaining coherence. It helps structure sentences to reflect the speaker's focus and the informational structure of the discourse. The canonical structure remains unchanged, but the dislocated element is utilized for emphasis, contrast, or introducing new information. Therefore, dislocation is not viewed as a syntax device but as a construal strategy for adjusting prominence and guiding interpretation, as evidenced by the sentences below.

I have never read that book.	Canonical
That book, I have never read.	Left dislocation
I have never read it, that book.	Right dislocation

In Cognitive Grammar, there is an interesting concept known as a **double-subject construction.** This refers to a sentence structure that features two subjects, both involved in the action described by the verb but playing different roles. The main subject is the one who performs or experiences the action, while the secondary subject adds extra context. This is often viewed as a **topic-comment structure.** The **topic**, which is the first noun phrase, tells us what the sentence is about and sets the scene for the information that follows. The **comment**, represented by the second noun phrase, provides us with more details about the topic. In cognitive terms, a topic-comment structure is understood as a prominence-based construal, where the topic serves as the conceptual anchor and the comment profiles the new or focal information. This kind of construction reflects a cognitive strategy for organizing information, allowing speakers to foreground a key element as the conceptual anchor before introducing new or focal content.

This book, its content is interesting.

The sentence above is organized into two conceptual parts: the **topic** and the **comment.** The topic, *This book*, serves as the **conceptual anchor**, establishing what the sentence is about and orienting the reader to the domain of discourse. The comment, *its content is interesting*, provides the **focal information**, elaborating on the anchored concept by profiling what is noteworthy about it. In Cognitive Grammar, this topic-comment structure reflects a construal strategy in which the speaker foregrounds a particular element before introducing new or more detailed information. By placing the topic first, often through fronting, the speaker increases its prominence and guides the listener's attention toward the intended conceptual focus. The sentence highlights the book as the anchor and then directs attention to its content as the focal point. Organizing information in this way provides context upfront, supports clearer mental processing, and enhances precision in communication. This shows that the mind prefers to anchor first and add details later, starting with something familiar or already established before integrating new or more specific information.

Clefting

In Cognitive Grammar, **clefting** is analyzed as a form of **profiling**, where a specific element is conceptually highlighted by giving it a dedicated structural frame. Typically, this frame starts with the pronoun *it*, followed by a verb phrase, usually *be*, then the element to be profiled, and finally the rest of the sentence. Clefts can also be formed with *wh*-words such as *what*, *where*, *why*, *who*, and *how* to create emphasis. A cleft sentence uses a non-canonical word order to split a single idea into two clauses, thereby spotlighting a specific piece of information. Its main purpose is to link what the listener already knows with new, focal information, drawing extra attention to that highlighted detail. In cognitive terms, clefting is not a syntactic operation but a strategy to enhance prominence. It directs attention to a specific element by isolating it in the autonomous unit, often for purposes of contrast or clarification. Cleft sentences are powerful tools for adding emphasis and making communication more impactful. When speakers use clefting, they highlight a chosen element to shape how their message is construed, revealing their communicative intentions.

Jerry went to the movie yesterday.	Canonical
It was Jerry who went to the movie yesterday.	It-clefting
I needed a laptop.	Canonical
What I needed was a laptop.	Wh-clefting

Inversion

In Cognitive Grammar, **inversion** is understood as a form of **prominence-adjustment**, where shifting the usual word order highlights a particular element or reorganizes the conceptual scene for communicative effect. Inversion uses a noncanonical word order that places the verb before the subject to create specific effects. In cognitive terms, inversion is not merely a stylistic choice but a way to highlight particular elements within a sentence. It is not treated as a purely syntactic anomaly but as a motivated construction grounded in conceptual organization and discourse function. By placing a negator or negative-like adverbial in initial position, inversion draws attention to the action or situation that follows. This strategy allows new or surprising information to take center stage right at the beginning of a sentence, offering fresh perspectives. Essentially, inversion functions as a prominence-adjusting construal that speakers strategically use to highlight or foreground particular elements for communicative effect. Language is more than just words; it is also about how we express and share our experiences.

I have never been more insulted in my life!	Canonical
Never have I been more insulted in my life!	Negative inversion
I rarely go outside.	Canonical
Rarely do I go outside.	Adverbial inversion
The cat is hiding under the bed.	Canonical
Under the bed is the cat hiding.	Adverb phrase inversion
If you study diligently, you will pass the exam.	Canonical
Only by studying diligently will you pass the exam.	Conditional inversion

Raising

In Cognitive Grammar, **raising** is analyzed as a form of **transparency in profiling**, where a higher–clause subject directly reflects the conceptual structure of the lower clause without any implied syntactic movement. It is understood as a construal strategy: an element conceptually belonging to a lower clause is profiled in a higher clause, giving it greater prominence while preserving the same underlying conceptual relationships. In Generative Grammar, by contrast, raising is treated as a syntactic process that moves a nominal argument from a lower clause into the autonomous unit. Although raised and non-raised expressions differ on the surface, they are assumed to share the same underlying structure. This view underscores the distinction between deep and surface structures and the flexibility of syntactic operations. Cognitive Grammar, however, does not treat raising as movement at all. Instead, it sees raising as a reflection of how speakers construe and conceptualize a situation, emphasizing the tight integration between meaning and form.

Three patterns can be distinguished: subject-to-subject, subject-to-object, and object-to-subject. What these patterns reflect is not actual movement but different ways of construing which participant is profiled in the higher clause. In subject-to-subject raising, the participant conceptually associated with the lower clause is profiled as the subject of the higher clause. In subject-to-object raising, that same participant is profiled as the object of the higher clause. In object-to-subject raising, a participant that functions as the object in one process is reconceptualized as the subject in the higher-level construction. In Cognitive Grammar, each grammatical structure corresponds to a particular way of construing a situation, so the choices available to a speaker are not interchangeable. Raised and non-raised constructions are therefore understood as distinct construals rather than variants of a single underlying structure. Each offers a different perspective on the same scene and serves its own communicative purpose. The difference lies in profiling, the mental process of selecting and highlighting one element as the focal participant.

I expect that Anna will leave.	
I expect Anna to leave.	subject-to-object raising
That Anna will resign is likely.	
Anna is likely to resign.	subject-to-subject raising
To entertain Anna is difficult.	
Anna is difficult to entertain.	object-to-subject raising

The difference between a raised construction and its non-raised counterpart reflects two distinct ways of construing the same conceptual content. The difference lies in which element is profiled and how the roles of trajector and landmark are assigned. Consider the pair *To entertain Anna is difficult* and *Anna is difficult to entertain*. Both express the same basic situation, yet they direct attention differently. In the non-raised version, *To entertain Anna is difficult*, the entire complement clause functions as the subject and is profiled as a single, undifferentiated unit. No individual participant is highlighted. In the raised version, *Anna is difficult to entertain*, the focus shifts: Anna becomes the profiled participant, the trajectory, while the rest of the clause recedes into the background. This shift illustrates a change in construal, where meaning emerges through attentional focus and the selective profiling of conceptual elements.

Existential Constructions

In Cognitive Grammar, an **existential construction** is treated as a **presentational construction** that introduces a new figure into the discourse. It typically begins with *there*, followed by a form of *be* and an indefinite noun phrase. The grounding element *there* directs the listener's attention toward a specific region of conceptual space. Crucially, the construction relies on **figure-ground alignment**, in which the newly introduced entity is profiled as the **figure** emerging against a **ground** established by the spatial or situational setting. The construction profiles a relational predication that highlights the presence of an entity in a particular location. In essence, it is a grounding construction that profiles the existence or emergence of an entity within a conceived scene. Such constructions present the whole clause as new information, shifting attention from individual parts to a single statement about an entity's existence or absence.

Nobody is at home.	Canonical
There is nobody at home.	Existential there

Both sentences convey the same core message but emphasize different aspects and are structured differently. In Cognitive Grammar, the distinction between them lies in how information is framed and how the scene is conceptually organized. The first sentence places *nobody* in the subject position, making it the figure against the background of the situation. By foregrounding *nobody*, the sentence directly communicates the idea of absence as the central point. In contrast, the second sentence uses the existential phrase *There is*, which sets up a conceptual space before introducing the figure. Through **figure-ground alignment**, the home setting functions as the ground, and the entity *nobody* emerges as the figure within that space. This shifts the attentional focus: the listener is first oriented toward the location, and only then is the absence of people revealed. These examples illustrate how Cognitive Grammar highlights the role of framing and construal. Different grammatical choices shape how a situation is conceptualized, what is treated as figure or ground, and which aspects of the scene are brought into prominence. Ultimately, the chosen construction reveals how the speaker structures and presents the situation.

It-Constructions

In Cognitive Grammar, **it-constructions**, a type of **subject-setting construction**, are sentences that begin with the impersonal pronoun *it*. *It* functions to establish a presentational frame for introducing an event or situation. It signals the relevance of the upcoming discourse by providing a conceptual frame in which the profiled event occurs. Metaphorically, *it* can be viewed as a **container** holding content. Moreover, *it* operates as a **global setting** or **host**, acting as a **subject marker** that identifies the **immediate scope** of interpretation. In Cognitive Grammar, **setting** refers to the conceptual region in which an event unfolds or a situation exists, while the **immediate scope** focuses on the specific event being profiled. **Profiling,** as a construal operation, highlights the particular facet of the scene that the speaker chooses to make prominent. The setting-subject *it* indicates the general circumstances of the event, serving as a **reference point** for its location and interpretation. Overall, it-constructions illustrate how speakers structure meaning by anchoring events within a conceptual setting and highlighting what is most relevant in the discourse.

To finish the project on time will be difficult.	Canonical
It will be difficult to finish the project on time.	It-construction

When comparing a canonical sentence with its noncanonical construction, the difference lies in how each organizes the conceptualization of the event. In the canonical form, the complement clause functions as the subject and is immediately profiled as the figure of the clause. In the noncanonical version, the impersonal *it* serves as a setting-subject that establishes a presentational frame before the event is introduced. This shift means that the canonical sentence highlights the action directly, whereas the it-construction foregrounds the speaker's evaluation and places the event within that evaluative frame. By creating this abstract setting, the construction draws attention to the broader circumstances that make the situation significant. It encourages the conceptualizer to consider not only the challenge of finishing the project on time but also the potential consequences such as missing the deadline, increased pressure on the team, the need for additional resources, and a possible decline in quality. Through this framing, the *it-construction* guides the listener to interpret the event within a wider context that clarifies why it matters.

9.3.2 *Questions*

In Cognitive Grammar, a **question,** also called an interrogative, is a symbolic construction with the conventional function of requesting the addressee to supply missing information. Unlike statements, which present a situation as known by the speaker, questions present a situation as unknown to the speaker. In a statement, the speaker is the epistemic authority; in a question, the addressee becomes the epistemic authority. The speaker profiles a knowledge gap and directs the addressee to fill it, indicating that the speaker is seeking knowledge rather than asserting it. This involves a grounding predication that identifies the clause as a request for information rather than a statement. questions typically involve restructuring the sentence or using specific question words, as in *Does she come?* or *When does she come?* The meaning of questions emerges from how speakers use them in real communicative contexts, rather than from abstract syntactic rules. In essence, questions signal missing information and prompt the addressee to voluntarily provide it, allowing speakers to clarify details, narrow down options, and guide the interaction.

Questions can be categorized into various types, each serving a unique role in communication.

Yes-No Questions

In Cognitive Grammar, **yes-no questions** are not understood as a special syntactic pattern but as a symbolic construction that conveys the speaker's epistemic stance in a particular way. A yes-no question, often referred to as a polar question, is a type of question that expects a simple answer: either yes or no. The main purpose of polar questions is to confirm or deny something, and they usually end with a rising intonation. They are designed to elicit a direct yes or no response, making them essential for social interactions and information exchanges. Polar questions highlight a binary uncertainty in the speaker's knowledge and asks the listener to confirm or deny a specific proposition. The listener is seen as the epistemic authority who can resolve the uncertainty. This serves as a grounding predication, indicating that the speaker is seeking confirmation rather than making an assertion. Yes-no questions prompt binary answers. For example, in *Is it raining?* the focus is on the presence or absence of rain, leading to a clear yes or no answer.

A yes-no question can be either positive or negative, each serving a distinct function in language.

Is Cathy your neighbor?	Yes, she is.
Can you play the piano?	No, I can't.

A positive question is formed by placing an auxiliary or modal verb just before the subject. The listener typically responds with a simple yes or no. When we ask positive questions, we often raise our intonation at the end. A negative question is created by placing *not* after an auxiliary or modal verb. When we talk about negative questions, we usually use a falling intonation. These questions serve different purposes: (1) to express surprise, as in *Didn't you hear the bell? I rang it four times*, (2) to verify information, as in *Aren't you Peter? Nice to meet you*, (3) to seek confirmation, expecting the listener to agree, as in *Isn't it a great day?* (implying it is sunny and the sky is blue), (4) to share opinions more politely, as in *Wouldn't it be better to put the heating on?* (which sounds nicer than saying *It would be better to put the heating on*), and (5) to extend urgent offers, invitations, or complaints, as in *Wouldn't you like something to drink? Thank you, that's very kind of you*, or *Won't you sit down? No thanks, I can only stay a minute.*

Let's take a closer look at how positive and negative yes-no questions differ, revealing the distinct construals they evoke.

Does she have a car?

Doesn't she have a car?

While both are structurally questions, they reflect different mental representations. They reflect different ways of construing the same conceptual content. The first, a positive question, presents a neutral inquiry. Its interpretation allows for either affirmation or denial. The speaker is unsure and seeks confirmation, without assuming an answer. On the other hand, the negative question implies an expectation: the speaker expects a *yes* response and uses the question to confirm what they already believe to be true. This form often conveys surprise, disbelief, or emphasis, subtly influencing the listener's understanding. In Cognitive Grammar, these differences go beyond just syntax; they reveal how speakers mentally structure and present information. The choice between positive and negative questions depends on the speaker's communicative intent, contextual expectations, and interactional goals. Each structure profiles a different aspect of the conceptual scene and directs the listener's focus accordingly. Recognizing these differences improves communicative accuracy and helps us tailor questions to our intentions.

Wh-Questions

In Cognitive Grammar, **wh-questions** are not treated as unique syntactic patterns but as symbolic constructions that profile a missing conceptual element and prompt the listener to provide it, thereby enriching the shared mental representation of a situation. Unlike yes-no questions, wh-questions seek detailed information and encourage the listener to offer specifics. They typically start with a question word, often involve subject-verb inversion, and aim to uncover particular details in the response. Forming a wh-question directs attention to the exact information needed in a given context. For example, posing the question *Where are the keys?* foregrounds spatial information, with location serving as the relevant dimension. Wh-questions go beyond grammatical function in language; they engage cognitive processes that aid in interpreting and navigating situations. As potent cognitive tools, they enhance understanding, spark curiosity, foster creative critical thinking, and deepen exploration by honing in on specific information.

Below is a curated list of wh-questions, each accompanied by its meaning and illustrative examples.

Who: asks about a person in subject position.	Who came? Tom came.
Whom: asks about a person in object position.	Whom did you see? I saw Tom.
What: asks about things in subject position.	What makes you angry? Dishonesty
What: asks about things in object position.	What did you buy? I bought books.
What: asks about profession.	What are you? I am an engineer.
Which: asks about choice.	Which color do you like? I like blue.
Whose: asks about possession.	Whose car is broken? Tom's car is broken.
When: asks about time.	When did he arrive? He arrived yesterday.
Where: asks about place.	Where is the pen? It is on the desk.
Why: asks about reason.	Why does he study? He studies to succeed.
How: asks about manner.	How does she drive? She drives recklessly.
How: asks about means.	How does she come? She comes by bus.
	How did he open the door?
	He opened the door with a screwdriver.
How much: asks about quantity.	How much money did it cost? It cost £100.
How many: asks about number.	How many people did come?
	Twenty people came.
How old: asks about age.	How old is the building? It is one hundred years old.
How long: asks about length of time.	How long will you stay?
	I will stay for a week.
How often: asks about frequency.	How often do you visit your aunt?
	I visit my aunt once a week/twice a month.
How far: asks about distance.	How far is the city center?
	It is 4 kilometers far.

Statement Questions

In Cognitive Grammar, **statement questions** are question forms that adopt the syntax of a statement but function pragmatically as genuine questions. They preserve the assertive nature of statements (making a claim) while simultaneously incorporating a question aspect (seeking information), thereby blending the roles of statement and question. Rather than being treated as a syntactic anomaly, they are understood as symbolic constructions that pair statement form with question function. Such questions profile conceptual content as if asserted, yet leave it open for validation, engaging the listener to provide confirmation or correction. This reflects how language encodes both conceptualization and communicative intent. Statement questions are often used to convey surprise or to seek confirmation, and the typical response is agreement or affirmation. In short, they illustrate grammar's focus on form-meaning pairings, not rigid sentence types.

She isn't married?

Although this question may appear as a straightforward statement in form, it is distinguished by a rising intonation at the end and the use of a question mark, signaling that it is indeed a question. This type of question, often referred to as a statement question, blurs the boundary between statement and inquiry, relying heavily on prosody and pragmatics to convey its questions intent. In terms of meaning, the speaker is seeking validation for a belief or assumption they hold. The use of a negative form often implies that the speaker anticipates a positive response, and they may be surprised or skeptical if that assumption is proven wrong. Context and the speaker's intention play a crucial role here. In this scenario, the speaker may be expressing surprise or attempting to confirm someone's marital status. The rising intonation transforms the statement into a question, prompting the listener to either agree or disagree with the assumption. The combination of the negative form and the rising intonation links the question to the speaker's existing knowledge and expectations. Understanding these elements illuminates how statement questions operate in conversation, emphasizing the relationship between form, meaning, and context.

Rhetorical Questions

In Cognitive Grammar, **rhetorical questions** function as conceptual tools for making a point rather than eliciting an answer. They offer a distinctive way of conveying information and engaging the audience. Rhetorical questions are not merely syntactic structures; they are conceptual devices that reflect how speakers construe and communicate their mental representations. The speaker frames information to highlight a perspective or emphasize a key concept, often implying the answer within the question itself. Although questions in form, rhetorical questions carry assertive or evaluative meaning and are frequently used to express disbelief, irony, or emphasis. While they resemble typical questions, they do not require an answer because the response is usually evident. More than a request for information, they serve as statements in disguise. In conversation, rhetorical questions spark critical thinking, highlight key points, invite alternative viewpoints, and stress the obviousness of something already mentioned.

Do you think I am stupid?	(I cannot be cheated or fooled.)
Do you think I was born yesterday?	(I am not naive or gullible.)

These are presented as questions, but they function primarily as rhetorical devices. They are not intended to elicit a genuine response; rather, they serve to assert the speaker's stance emphatically. The first question, for instance, is posed not to seek information but to highlight the speaker's disbelief or frustration at the suggestion that they could be easily deceived. In doing so, the speaker is essentially declaring their awareness and intelligence, rejecting any implication of gullibility. This rhetorical strategy allows the speaker to maintain control of the conversation while signaling emotional resistance. Such rhetorical questions are commonly used to express indignation, challenge assumptions, or push back against belittling attitudes. They underscore the absurdity of the implied belief and compel the listener to reconsider their position. Moreover, rhetorical questions like these are powerful tools in persuasive communication: they engage the listener by prompting reflection, reinforcing the speaker's argument, and delivering emphasis more effectively than a direct statement might. They reflect a construal in which the speaker foregrounds emotional stance or evaluative judgment rather than genuine inquiry.

Tag Questions

In Cognitive Grammar, **tag questions**, also known as question tags, are symbolic constructions that combine a statement with a short question tag. A tag question is essentially a statement followed by a brief question tag, serving as a way to express uncertainty or seek confirmation. They convey attitudes such as surprise, doubt, or disbelief, adding emotional nuance to language. Tag questions do not constitute a separate sentence type but function as a constructional category that blends assertion with inquiry. Conceptually, they profile information as asserted while leaving it open for validation, engaging the listener to confirm, deny, or align with the speaker's stance. Depending on how the situation is construed, tag questions allow speakers to soften assertions, invite collaboration, or challenge assumptions. They also help align speaker and listener by checking mutual understanding, negotiating belief, or managing politeness. Generally, if the autonomous unit is positive, the tag will be negative, and vice versa. Moreover, if there is an auxiliary verb in the autonomous unit, the same one will be used in the tag.

She comes, doesn't she?

She does not come, does she?

Both examples illustrate how tag questions function to seek alignment with the listener. The speaker is not merely stating a fact but inviting confirmation or reassurance. In the first sentence, the speaker anticipates agreement that she is coming; in the second, the negative form signals uncertainty or doubt, prompting the listener to affirm or clarify. Tag questions enhance conversational interactivity by encouraging engagement and mutual understanding. From a Cognitive Grammar perspective, tag questions are not just grammatical ornaments; they are dynamic, context-sensitive tools that reflect how speakers shape meaning, manage relationships, and guide interpretation. They are not just syntactic add-ons; they are meaningful constructions that integrate a statement with a question tag to convey a nuanced communicative intent. Each component, the autonomous unit and the tag, forms a symbolic assembly, working together to express the speaker's stance, emotional tone, and expectations. Tag questions mix statements with questions to guide communication, serving the purpose of encouraging listener participation.

Closed-Choice Questions

In Cognitive Grammar, **closed-choice questions**, often referred to as alternative questions, are symbolic constructions that present a limited set of options. Unlike open Wh-questions, they do not aim to gather detailed information but instead highlight a specific, defined set of choices, prompting the listener to select from among them. Conceptually, they combine question form with restricted choice, demonstrating how grammar encodes both inquiry and decision-making within specific contexts. These questions are typically distinguished by their intonation: rising on each option until the final one, which then drops. Closed-choice questions set the stage by narrowing down possible answers and guiding the listener toward specific choices, with the expectation that one of the provided options will be chosen. Because they come with predetermined answers, they restrict responses and steer conversation toward clear communication goals. This style is useful in surveys and interviews, guiding discussions toward clear objectives.

Do you want tea or coffee? I want tea.

Would you like orange, grapefruit, or tomato juice? I like orange juice.

The closed-choice question narrows down the scenario by presenting just two options: tea or coffee. This setup limits the possible responses and nudges the listener to choose between the given choices. The way the speaker frames the question reveals their viewpoint on the matter. By providing clear options, the speaker shapes how the listener perceives and responds to the question. The listener interprets the question within the boundaries set by the speaker and is expected to select one of the options presented. In this case, the listener opts for tea, which is one of the choices presented. Typically, the intonation of the question features a slight rise on *tea* and *coffee*, followed by a drop at the end, signaling to the listener that they need to make a choice. Overall, the closed-choice question effectively serves its purpose of determining the listener's preference between the two specific options, ensuring clarity and precision by limiting the range of possible answers. Closed-choice questions reduce cognitive load by limiting the range of responses, unlike open-ended ones that afford the respondent more freedom.

Echo Questions

In Cognitive Grammar, **echo questions** are symbolic constructions in which the speaker repeats or reformulates part of a prior utterance as a question. They are typically used when the listener did not fully hear or understand what was said, or when the content is too surprising to believe. Echo questions are usually spoken with rising intonation and strong emphasis, often on a wh-word. Conceptually, they profile previously introduced content while leaving it open for confirmation or surprise. They function as tools for reactivation and negotiation, reflecting attempts to reconstrue prior utterances. As metalinguistic expressions, echo questions repeat prior utterances with questioning intonation, showing how speakers adjust focus and interpretation in context, often to seek clarification or confirmation. By repeating the statement with a wh-word at the end, they highlight the speaker's interest or surprise and emphasize a particular aspect of the original utterance. This aligns with the concept of construal, in which the same situation can be viewed and expressed differently depending on the speaker's perspective.

He is a pilot.	(Original statement)
He is what?	(Echo question)

The initial statement, *He is a pilot*, sets the scene by sharing details about someone's job. When someone replies with an echo question like *He is what?*, they are seeking clarification or affirmation of the information just presented. This suggests that the person asking the echo question either did not catch the original statement or did not fully grasp it. They want the original speaker to repeat or explain what was said. Typically, the response would be a straightforward repetition of the original statement, *He is a pilot*, to confirm or clarify things. We often notice that the intonation of the echo question rises at the end, which signals a request for more information. This rising tone shows that the speaker is eager for additional details or confirmation. Ultimately, the echo question plays a crucial role in making sure everyone is on the same page. It helps clear up any confusion or miscommunication, making it easier to exchange accurate information. Thus, echo questions are not just syntactic repetitions; they are cognitive strategies for managing interaction and meaning. They recycle linguistic material to spotlight a specific conceptual element.

9.3.3 *Imperatives*

In Cognitive Grammar, **imperative sentences** are symbolic constructions that encode directive meaning, linking a speaker's intention to a hearer's expected action. They usually start with the base form of a verb and end with either a period or an exclamation mark, depending on the urgency or forcefulness of the command. Unlike statements, which describe states of affairs, imperatives are directive constructions that activate the hearer's role within the cognitive model of communication. They are not just syntactic forms but conceptual instructions that guide the hearer's attention toward performing an action. Imperatives are symbolic because they combine a specific form with a corresponding conceptual function. Instead of presenting reality as a description of events, they present it as an instruction for the hearer to act. The subject *you* is typically implied, reflecting how grammar is deeply rooted in usage and mental processes rather than abstract rules. Ultimately, imperatives clearly demonstrate that grammar serves as a dynamic tool for coordinating social and cognitive activities rather than existing solely as static structure.

In English, commands can be expressed in various ways, each reflecting a distinct construal.

Commands Without a Subject

In Cognitive Grammar, **commands without a subject** express a directive construal. The verb appears in its base form, without any endings for number or tense. The person being addressed is left implicit but conceptually understood to be *you*. The absence of an overt subject reflects the fact that the hearer's role is already cognitively and pragmatically presupposed in the directive act. Grammar here is symbolic: the form (bare verb) pairs with the function (directive meaning). These commands do not describe reality but instead construe reality as a potential action to be carried out by the hearer.

The construal at work here is backgrounding or defocusing of the subject. The speaker's intention is foregrounded, while the hearer's participation is activated through the implicit subject. This construal is interactive and performative: language is used as a dynamic tool to coordinate social and mental activity rather than to represent states of affairs.

Shut the door.

Clear the table.

Leave me alone.

These imperative constructions imply the subject *you*, creating a direct and unambiguous directive through backgrounding or defocusing of the subject. From a cognitive perspective, these forms foreground the intended action while minimizing interpersonal negotiation, presenting reality not as a description but as an instruction for the hearer to act. Although inherently forceful, speakers often soften imperatives by adding politeness markers like *please* as in *Please shut the door* or *Shut the door, please*, which effectively reduce the directive's intensity. To further mitigate the command's force and promote social tact, the directive can be reframed as a question or indirect statement, as in *Will you shut the door, please?* or *I wonder if you would kindly shut the door.* Such reformulations shift the construal from obligation to cooperation, linking linguistic form with social cognition and emphasizing language's interactive role.

Commands with a Subject

In Cognitive Grammar, **commands with a subject** are imperative constructions in which the subject is overtly expressed. The explicit mention of the subject makes it clear who is being directly addressed, shifting the focus from the action itself to the actor's responsibility. This is essentially a matter of focal prominence or profiling. By explicitly stating the subject, the speaker profiles the agent of the action. Such commands function as symbolic structures used to convey emphasis, contrast, or urgency. For example, in *You sit down right now!*, adding *you* emphasizes the command and makes it more forceful than simply *Sit down!*. In *You stay here, and I'll go*, the subject *you* highlights the contrast between the roles of speaker and listener. In *Somebody call an ambulance!*, the subject *somebody* assigns urgency and responsibility to those present. Therefore, these commands are typically not paired with the politeness marker *please*.

You close the door.

Jack, close the door.

Somebody, close the door.

These imperative constructions vary in how they construe the subject, shaping both the interpersonal dynamics and the communicative clarity of the command. In the first example, the explicit use of *you*, though typically implied in imperatives, foregrounds the addressee and reinforces directness through subject profiling. In the second, the vocative *Jack* functions as a noun of direct address, anchoring the command to a specific individual and enhancing referential precision via profiling of the addressee. The third command introduces a third-person subject, *somebody*, which shifts the directive toward an unspecified agent. This broadens the scope of responsibility, signaling through profiling that any available participant may fulfill the action. Each variation reflects a distinct construal strategy, balancing specificity, urgency, and social tact.

Commands with the Verb Let

In Cognitive Grammar, **commands with *let*** are considered directive speech acts that prompt action rather than describe events. They follow the structure *let + subject (first or third person) + base verb*, and when used with plural pronouns (*let's*), they function as suggestions that include both the speaker and the addressee, creating a sense of collaboration and politeness. The construal responsible is causative/directive, as *let* frames the addressee as controlling access to an action and directs them to release that control. When using *let's*, the construal shifts toward inclusive joint action, inviting co-participation. Overall, these constructions highlight the addressee's enabling role, whether granting permission or joining in, while carrying a collective or cooperative nuance. Commands with the verb *let* are often used to express various meanings as shown below.

Let's watch television tonight.	Suggestion
Let her explain her point of view.	Permission
Let me handle this situation.	Request
Let's try our best in the competition.	Encouragement
Let the paint dry.	Enablement

These constructions employ the verb *let* to signal inclusion, permission, or facilitation, engaging the speaker and others in a shared or authorized action. Cognitively, *let* functions as a schematic prompt that foregrounds agency while modulating interpersonal dynamics. The subject, whether *us*, *her*, *me*, or *somebody*, helps shape the construal of responsibility and involvement. When expressing negation, *let* combines with *not* followed by the base form of the verb, as in *Let's not argue about this*, *Let her not go alone*, or *Let's not make any hasty decisions*. These forms maintain the collaborative framing while introducing restraint or caution. From a Cognitive Grammar standpoint, such constructions are analyzed in terms of the speaker's intention, perspective, and the symbolic assembly of form and meaning. They reflect how grammar encodes not just structure, but also social cognition, inviting, permitting, or enabling action through nuanced construal.

Negative Commands

In Cognitive Grammar, **negative commands** are understood as prohibitive directives that instruct the addressee to refrain from performing an action. Structurally, they are formed with *don't*, followed by the base verb. The responsible construal is directive/prohibitive, as the speaker profiles the addressee's potential action and explicitly blocks or restricts it. Unlike commands with *let*, which enable or permit, negative commands construe the addressee's control as something to be withheld. This highlights the speaker's authority to prevent an action rather than facilitate it. Such commands are often used to avoid unwanted outcomes; for example, *Don't take the highway* helps prevent the inconvenience of getting stuck in traffic. By giving reasons, they help comprehension and show grammar as a tool for clear communication.

Don't take the highway. There is too much traffic.

Don't smoke. It is very bad for your health.

In these examples, the imperative *don't* introduces a negated directive, while the following clause provides a cognitively salient justification. The construal is directive/prohibitive: the command *Don't take the highway* construes the action as undesirable due to contextual information, too much traffic, which shapes the listener's mental representation of the situation. Similarly, *Don't smoke* invokes a health-related conceptual frame to reinforce the prohibition. These constructions rely on the listener's ability to integrate negation with background knowledge and pragmatic inference. In Cognitive Grammar, grammatical constructions inherently carry meaning, and negative imperatives serve as clear examples of how linguistic form encodes speaker intention. Negative commands are more than syntactic prohibitions. They are symbolic constructions that encode both the action to be avoided and the conceptual motivation behind it.

Persuasive Commands

In Cognitive Grammar, **persuasive commands** are imperative constructions that not only instruct the listener to perform or avoid an action but also aim to persuade through justification or appeal. Structurally, the use of *do* before the main verb can soften the tone and make the command more compelling rather than merely obligatory. Prohibitive forms such as *don't* frame the action as undesirable. These commands are symbolic units rather than simple grammatical formulas, as they depend on the listener's integration of context and inference. The construal responsible for persuasive commands is directive/prohibitive with justificatory elaboration. The directive construal frames desired actions, the prohibitive construal frames actions to be avoided, and justificatory elaboration adds persuasive force by linking the command to background knowledge, values, or consequences such as efficiency, comfort, or convenience.

Do have some more coffee.	(request)
Do forgive me. I didn't mean to offend you.	(apology)
Do try to keep the noise down, gentlemen.	(complaint)

In these examples, the use of *do* in imperatives illustrates how commands operate through a directive/prohibitive construal enriched with justificatory elaboration. In the first command, the speaker frames the request positively, making it more inviting and less forceful, with *do* signaling genuine encouragement for the listener to enjoy more coffee. In the second command, the situation is construed as one requiring an apology, and *do* emphasizes the sincerity and urgency of the appeal for forgiveness, reinforced by the explanation *I didn't mean to offend you*. In the third command, the speaker addresses a problematic noise level, and *do* adds emphasis and politeness to the complaint, while the respectful address further softens the directive. In each example, the use of *do* makes the command sound persuasive, enhancing the likelihood of compliance.

9.3.4 *Exclamatives*

In Cognitive Grammar, an **exclamative** expresses a strong emotional reaction to a situation, where the speaker's evaluative stance is highlighted through interpersonal construal. Structurally, these sentences typically end with an exclamation mark (!), signaling that something intense or emphatic is being conveyed. Exclamatives often use anastrophe, a technique that plays with word order by shifting the usual arrangement for added impact. Unlike statements, which simply present facts, exclamatives introduce excitement, emphasis, or urgency. They are not just syntactic forms but conceptual construals, ways of presenting and highlighting a situation. Rather than neutrally describing an event, they foreground the speaker's perspective and emotional involvement. The construal is subjective with heightened prominence achieved through profiling and focusing on remarkable aspects. Crucially, interpersonal construal aligns speaker and hearer, directing attention to the extraordinary quality of the event or entity.

Exclamative sentences can be formed by using *how* or *what* followed by an adjective in the following ways:

How clever a student she is!

What a clever student she is!

These exclamations exemplify subjective construal with heightened prominence, using profiling and focusing to highlight remarkable aspects of the situation. However, they differ in how admiration is construed. The how-construction intensifies the attribute of cleverness, foregrounding it as a scalar property and inviting the listener to marvel at the remarkable degree of the quality itself. In contrast, the what-construction profiles the entity, the student, as the central focus, with cleverness presented as an attributed trait, drawing attention to both the person and the quality. From a Cognitive Grammar perspective, these subtle structural differences reflect distinct construal strategies: *how* emphasizes the intensity of the attribute, while *what* emphasizes the entity possessing it. Yet, both rely on subjective construal to foreground the speaker's evaluative stance and emotional involvement. Together, they illustrate how grammatical choices shape meaning and frame emotional evaluation in discourse.

Interpretation

In Cognitive Grammar, meaning arises from both compositional structures and non-compositional patterns shaped by usage. Some single-grounded processes exhibit **compositionality**, where the overall meaning is derived from the individual words and their grammatical arrangement. For example, *The bird sings beautifully* conveys a straightforward interpretation built from lexical content and syntactic structure. Yet not all sentences follow this principle. Some display **non-compositionality**, where meaning cannot be inferred directly from the words themselves but instead emerges from convention and context. A familiar case is the phrase *Break a leg!*, which functions as a wish of good luck despite its literal wording suggesting harm. Thus, linguistic meaning in Cognitive Grammar is grounded not only in compositional rules but also in entrenched usage patterns. Ultimately, meaning reflects how speakers conceptualize experience, relying on mental imagery and construal rather than abstract propositional content.

Non-compositionality encompasses a range of linguistic structures, including idioms, metaphors, and metonymies; forms where meaning cannot be fully derived from the individual components alone.

- Idioms:

  Idioms carry a figurative meaning that is quite different from their literal interpretation. You cannot simply figure out what they mean by looking at the individual words. Take the phrase *keep a straight face*, for instance; you would not guess its meaning just by breaking it down. It actually means to hold back laughter. The essence of the idiom is more than just the words themselves. Similarly, in *get hitched*, the literal meanings of *get* and *hitched* do not really explain what it means: to get married. The key mechanism in idioms is **non-compositional meaning**, where the meaning of the whole expression cannot be directly inferred from the meanings of its individual parts. Idioms are stored in our minds as single units and understood through common usage and shared knowledge. This approach highlights how crucial context and cultural background are when interpreting idioms, showcasing the fascinating connection between language and thought.

- Metaphors:

  Metaphors are all about taking ideas from one area and applying them to another. They play a crucial role in helping us grasp abstract ideas by connecting them to experiences we know well. The real meaning comes from this connection, rather than just the words themselves. Take the phrase *Time is money*, for instance. Here, *time* and *money* do not just blend together to form a meaning; it is really about the concepts of value and scarcity. Similarly, when we say *Time is a thief*, we are comparing time to a thief, suggesting that it robs us of precious moments. This comparison digs deeper than the straightforward meanings of *time* and *thief*, highlighting a feeling of loss. The key mechanism is **conceptual mapping**, the projection of structure from a source domain onto a target domain. In the realm of Cognitive Grammar, metaphors are not merely phrases we use; they actually reflect the mental processes that influence how we see and understand the world around us.

- Metonymies:

  Metonymies are all about swapping one word or phrase for another based on their contextual ties. The meaning comes from these connections. Take the sentence *The crown will announce new laws tomorrow*. Here, *the crown* stands in for the monarchy or ruling authority, not just a physical crown. Similarly, when we say *Hollywood released a new blockbuster*, we are really talking about the American film industry, not the place itself. In these cases, metonymy hinges on the relationship between the two ideas. In Cognitive Grammar, metonymy is viewed as a mental process where one entity (the source) stands in for another (the target) based on a relationship of **contiguity**. The key mechanism is a **profiling shift**: we mentally access one concept (e.g., *the crown*) but focus on another related one (*the monarchy*). Metonymy showcases how our language and thought processes work hand in hand to express meaning through these connections.

From the preceding discussion, several insights emerge. Meaning extends far beyond the literal interpretation of individual words, exemplifying the principle of **non-compositionality**. These expressions play a cognitively rich role in language, serving as vivid illustrations of how linguistic form encodes complex, culturally embedded conceptualizations. Non-compositional constructions enrich communication with nuance and expressiveness, often drawing on shared experiences and background knowledge to foster interpersonal resonance. From a Cognitive Grammar standpoint, such expressions are not anomalies but conceptually grounded linguistic patterns, **entrenched** through repeated use and enriched by mental imagery. Their effectiveness lies in how they activate familiar mental frames, enabling speakers to convey layered meanings both efficiently and evocatively. Mastering these forms enhances communicative competence and deepens one's appreciation for the intricate interplay between language, thought, and culture.

9.4 Configuration

Cognitive Grammar revolves around the idea of domain theory, which posits that the meaning of a linguistic item is best understood in relation to the domain it fits into. A **domain** can be thought of as a knowledge structure that helps define the meaning of a linguistic item. Each domain consists of various facets, and understanding these facets is crucial for using words accurately. A **facet** is a specific concept within a domain that is expressed through different language forms. Domains are made up of linguistic items, and to fully understand the meaning of one item, it is necessary to consider the meanings of others within the same domain. In this discussion, different types of sentences that convey the same idea create domains, with each one representing a unique facet and serving a distinct purpose in language. The meaning of a single-grounded process is influenced by the domain it belongs to and the specific facet it represents within that domain. There are five domains where sentence types converge, as they are conceptually linked and elaborate on the same idea, while also emphasizing key elements of social interaction.

9.4.1 *The Domain of Advice*

Advice is a pool of knowledge offering guidance on possible actions in given situations. How it is perceived depends on the relationship between giver and receiver, the context of delivery, and the choice of words. In Cognitive Grammar, advice reflects how a situation is framed. Advice is treated as a conceptual phenomenon, showing how linguistic structures reflect different levels of speaker evaluation and stance. Advice can have different facets, each with its own level of intensity. Weak advice is unassertive, lacking the firmness or enthusiasm to make an impact. It often comes across in straightforward statements, which are suitable for everyday situations. Then there is mild advice, which is gentle and kind, striking a balance in its effectiveness. This type often appears in questions, making it suitable for more moderate contexts. On the other hand, strong advice is bold, clear, and assertive, leaving a noticeable impact. It typically takes the form of imperative sentences, perfect for high-stakes moments. Regardless of the sentence type used, it is essential to consider the strength of the advice when giving it.

Now, let's analyze some data to see if the sentence types behave in semantically distinct ways within the domain.

Our colleague is unwell.

1. You should visit him.
2. Why don't you visit him?
3. Consider visiting him.

The sentences mentioned represent different types of advice, each highlighting a unique facet. In (1), we have a statement. Using *should* gives weaker advice, more like a suggestion or ideal. In (2), we see a question. The question form offers gentler, more polite advice, softening tone and giving space for reflection. In (3), we encounter an imperative sentence. The imperative gives strong, casual advice, stressing importance and prompting immediate action. Another way to offer advice is by using the phrase *If I were you*. For example, saying *If I were you, I would visit him* is a softer approach than the imperative and shows more empathy than the statement. By putting yourself in someone else's shoes, this structure allows you to share what you would do in their situation. From a Cognitive Grammar perspective, these variations reflect distinct construals of intention and social interaction, each forming a meaningful unit shaped by context and use.

9.4.2 *The Domain of Request*

Request revolves around asking someone for something or asking them to perform an action. How we perceive a situation can significantly shape the way a request is phrased and interpreted. In Cognitive Grammar, requests are grounded in how situations are perceived and framed. Rather than being treated as abstract rules, requests are understood as conceptual phenomena, shaped by usage, perspective, and speaker-hearer alignment. Each linguistic structure reflects a distinct conceptualization of interaction. Perspective plays a crucial role in shaping both the form and interpretation of requests. In English, requests vary in politeness and can be categorized as least polite, impolite, or polite. A least polite request is the most direct, often perceived as disrespectful, and is typically expressed through an imperative sentence. An impolite request tends to be rude and is usually framed as a statement. By contrast, a polite request is more considerate, making it the least direct, and is generally presented as a question. This account of requests highlights the interplay of grammar, meaning, and construal, rather than treating them as purely syntactic.

Let us now check the data to see if the sentence types have different semantic preferences within the domain.

I bought a present.

1. I want/need you to wrap it for me.
2. Could/Would you wrap it for me, please?
3. Wrap it for me.

The sentences mentioned earlier fall within the domain of requests, each highlighting a distinct facet. Example (1) uses a statement with *want* or *need* to express the speaker's state directly, though it may seem abrupt or impolite. Example (2) uses a question with *could* or *would* to frame requests politely, reducing imposition and suiting sensitive or unfamiliar contexts. By contrast, *can* and *will* are more casual and less polite. Example (3) uses an imperative, giving a direct command that is forceful but potentially rude. It fits informal contexts and close relationships, conveying authority and urgency for immediate action. In Cognitive Grammar, these variations are symbolic constructions that help speakers show what they mean, how urgent it is, and how they relate to others. Together, they reveal the subtle choices speakers make to balance clarity with social appropriateness. Such choices underscore how grammar is inseparable from interaction and meaning.

9.4.3 The Domain of Compliment

Compliments are a fascinating aspect of communication, expressing praise, admiration, or approval. The way we perceive a situation can greatly influence how a compliment is delivered and received. In Cognitive Grammar, compliments are rooted in construal, most notably perspective, which is the conceptual viewpoint or angle from which a situation is construed. Compliments are seen as conceptual phenomena, shaped by usage, alignment, and context. Compliments are generally categorized into three facets: formal, semiformal, and informal. A formal compliment is typically more serious and is usually reserved for official settings. When giving a formal compliment, it is important to ask for permission first to ensure your intentions are clear, often in the form of a question. On the other hand, a semiformal compliment is suitable for everyday conversations with colleagues and is usually a straightforward statement. Informal compliments are more spontaneous and are often shared among close friends, usually expressed in an excited or exclamatory manner.

Now, let us carry out a check on some data to see if the sentence types occur in different environments within the domain.

She is wearing a new dress.

1. May I say how elegant your dress is?
2. Your dress is really elegant.
3. What an elegant dress!

These sentences fall within the domain of compliments, each highlighting a distinct facet of expression. Sentence (1) is formal, which is highly polite, deferential, and carefully phrased. The compliment shows respect and humility, framing the compliment as permission-seeking rather than direct assertion. Sentence (2) is semiformal, which is direct and polite, but less ceremonious. The compliment is clear and respectful, but it does not add extra layers of politeness or distance. Sentence (3) is informal, which is casual, spontaneous, and enthusiastic. The compliment feels genuine and lively, often strengthening social bonds. In short, the differences mainly lie in tone: The sentence (1) uses a courteous framing, the sentence (2) is direct but polite, and the sentence (3) is casual admiration. From a Cognitive Grammar standpoint, each sentence type reflects a different **construal** of speaker intention, social proximity, and communicative tone. These symbolic constructions not only convey admiration but also shape interpersonal dynamics. Recognizing such nuances improves communication competence, fosters positive social harmony, and promotes empathy.

9.4.4 *The Domain of Suggestion*

Suggestion involves sharing ideas or plans for others to consider. A suggestion offers a possible way forward, whether helpful, practical, or simply enjoyable. The framing of a situation can significantly influence how a suggestion is presented and how seriously it is received. In Cognitive Grammar, suggestions rely on construal, with situational framing shaping their form and meaning. Suggestions are seen as conceptual phenomena, shaped by perspective, stance, and speaker-hearer alignment. Suggestions can vary in strength, ranging from weak to strong. A weak suggestion often lacks enthusiasm or firmness and is typically expressed in straightforward statements. A mild suggestion is gentle and considerate, showing attentiveness to the listener's choice, and is often phrased as a question. By contrast, a strong suggestion carries greater weight, approaching the force of an order, and is usually delivered in a commanding form. The type of sentence chosen thus becomes a powerful communicative tool, reflecting both the intended persuasiveness and the degree of influence the speaker seeks over the listener's decision.

Let us now examine some data to see if the sentence types are associated with distinct patterns within the domain.

He feels tired.

1. You could take a rest.
2. Why not take a rest? / Why don't you take a rest?
3. Take a rest.

These sentences illustrate different facets of making suggestions, each shaped by its syntactic form and pragmatic force. In (1), the statement with *could* conveys a weak suggestion. It presents rest as a possibility rather than a directive. In (2), the question form offers a mild suggestion. *Why not* tends to introduce general ideas, while *Why don't you* is slightly more specific and personal. Related expressions like *How about* and *What about* are often used in casual contexts, especially when suggesting food or drink, as in *How about some lunch?* or *What about a coffee?* Sentence (3) employs the imperative form, delivering a strong and direct suggestion. It is typically used in informal settings or among close acquaintances, where immediacy and clarity are valued. From a Cognitive Grammar perspective, these variations are not merely structural; they reflect different construals of speaker intent, social proximity, and the degree of imposition. Recognizing these subtleties enhances communicative effectiveness, allowing speakers to tailor their suggestions to context and relationship, and fostering clearer, more empathetic interactions.

9.4.5 The Domain of Apology

Apology is a complex area that involves accepting responsibility, recognizing harm, and expressing sincere remorse. In Cognitive Grammar, apologies are viewed as conceptual phenomena shaped by usage, speaker-hearer alignment, and emotional framing, with context and perspective central to their interpretation. The delivery of an apology shapes its impact; considering both parties' feelings makes it authentic. In English, apologies can take different forms, each conveying a distinct level of sincerity. A fake or insincere apology lacks genuine regret and is often expressed as a simple statement, typically using *sorry* followed by *if*. A genuine apology reflects true remorse, where the speaker feels genuinely sorry, disappointed, or upset about their actions, and is often phrased as a question. An empathetic apology is a heartfelt expression of sorrow, in which the speaker conveys deep regret through a command or request.

Now, let us peruse some data to see if the sentence types really have different usages within the domain.

1. I am sorry if I hurt your feelings.
2. May I offer my apologies for hurting your feelings?
3. Please accept my apologies for hurting your feelings.

These sentences illustrate different facets of apologizing, each shaped by its syntactic form and pragmatic tone. Sentence (1) is a statement, offering a conditional apology that may come across as emotionally detached or insincere. The use of *if* introduces ambiguity, suggesting the speaker is unsure whether offense occurred, which can dilute the perceived sincerity of the apology. Sentence (2) employs a question form, framing the apology as a polite offer. This structure implies that the transgression was likely unintentional and positions the speaker as respectful and considerate. It softens the act of apologizing by inviting the listener's acceptance, making it suitable for formal or delicate situations. Sentence (3) uses an imperative construction, delivering a direct and emotionally resonant apology. This form is often reserved for close relationships, where the speaker's vulnerability and sincerity are more readily accepted. The imperative here does not impose but rather expresses earnestness, signaling a genuine desire for reconciliation. From a Cognitive Grammar viewpoint, different apology types reveal how intent, emotion, and context shape meaning, enriching communication and empathy.

Before we move forward, let's briefly summarize our exploration of sentence types. These constructions share underlying features yet operate across distinct **domains**, each serving a unique communicative function. While a single sentence type can express multiple meanings depending on context, different types may also compete to represent the same situation, offering alternative construals. This leads us to the concept of **construal**, the speaker's cognitive framing of an experience and their linguistic choices in expressing it. The interpretation and use of a sentence type are shaped not only by grammatical form but also by how the speaker perceives and prioritizes aspects of the situation. When sentence types compete, they reflect divergent perspectives on the same event, highlighting the dynamic interplay between language and cognition. We will delve deeper into this cognitive framework in the next section.

9.5 Conceptualization

Cognitive Grammar is based on the concept of **construal** theory, which suggests that the meaning of a linguistic expression involves not only its conceptual content but also the unique way that content is framed. **Conceptual content** refers to the inherent meaning of a situation, while construal is how we describe and represent that meaning through language. It is about how a speaker perceives that conceptual content in different ways and chooses the appropriate structures to express it. In this context, the selected sentence type corresponds to the particular perspective adopted toward the situation. The speaker's **perspective** is the particular way someone views a situation, shaped by their experiences, beliefs, or context. It is like the mental lens through which we understand the world. As a result, different sentence types that express the same content have different meanings. They differ in how speakers interpret shared content, leading to various meanings in language. Each sentence type carries a unique linguistic meaning.

9.5.1 *Individual Sentence Types*

In certain instances, linguistic expressions are unambiguous and yield a single, straightforward interpretation. When only one construal is available, the risk of miscommunication is effectively eliminated. However, language often permits multiple interpretations, and in such cases, the intended meaning cannot be derived from the utterance alone. Instead, comprehension relies on contextual cues, shared knowledge, and the dynamics of the conversational exchange. This inherent ambiguity, rather than being a flaw, can enhance communicative efficiency, allowing speakers to convey nuanced meanings that are refined and clarified through context. Ultimately, the illocutionary force of an utterance emerges from these surrounding cognitive and social factors. This interaction between form and context shows how communication relies on inference.

To clarify and substantiate this point, we will now examine several examples that highlight its practical implications.

The police are coming.

At face value, this sentence functions as a straightforward statement, conveying the imminent arrival of law enforcement. However, its interpretation is far from fixed. In Cognitive Grammar, this variability reflects **construal**, specifically **subjective construal**, where meaning depends on the speaker's evaluative stance and the framing of the situation. Depending on the context, the sentence can carry distinct illocutionary forces. In one scenario, it may serve as a warning, perhaps uttered in a tense moment where someone is engaged in illicit activity. In another, it might express reassurance or relief, such as in the aftermath of an accident or emergency. These divergent readings illustrate how a single linguistic form can encode multiple layers of meaning, shaped by both semantic content and pragmatic inference. The sentence thus exemplifies the dynamic interplay between form, context, and speaker intention in human communication.

Can you pick me up later?

At first glance, this sentence appears to be a straightforward yes-no question. However, its communicative intent is more ambiguous. In Cognitive Grammar, this variability reflects **construal**, specifically **interpersonal construal**, where meaning arises from the alignment between speaker and hearer. The phrasing suggests a request cloaked in question form, and its true function depends heavily on contextual interpretation. In English, such constructions often imply more than their literal meaning. In this context, the speaker is more likely requesting help than simply posing a question. This sentence exemplifies how linguistic form alone does not determine communicative force. Instead, meaning emerges through shared context, speaker intention, and listener inference. This example shows how one expression can serve multiple pragmatic functions.

Sit here.

On the surface, this sentence functions as a directive, a command that might elicit a response such as *Yes, sir*. Yet its communicative force is highly context-dependent. In Cognitive Grammar, this variability reflects **construal**, specifically **interpersonal construal**, where meaning emerges through the dynamic alignment between speaker and hearer. In one scenario, it may be interpreted as a polite request, prompting a casual *Okay*. In another, it could be perceived as an offer, met with a *No thanks*. It might also serve as advice, *What a good idea*, or as encouragement, leading to a grateful *Thank you*. These varied interpretations demonstrate how a single linguistic form can encode multiple intentions. The pragmatic meaning of the sentence arises not solely from its grammatical structure, but from the interplay of context, speaker intent, and listener inference. This flexibility shows how meaning is shaped by shared interpretation.

Oh, what a great job you've done!

At first glance, this sentence functions as an exclamatory remark, typically signaling praise. However, its interpretation hinges on prosody and context. In Cognitive Grammar, this variability reflects **construal**, specifically **subjective construal**, where meaning depends on the speaker's evaluative stance and the way the situation is framed. In one reading, it conveys genuine admiration, a sincere compliment often marked by a falling intonation that reflects surprise or delight at the listener's exceptional performance. In another, it adopts a sarcastic tone, where the speaker uses exaggerated praise to express criticism. This ironic usage is usually accompanied by a more dismissive or flat vocal delivery. This sentence shows how intonation and context shape meaning, allowing one form to convey opposite intents. This variability highlights the listener's crucial and active role in using tone and context to interpret intent.

To summarize, sentence interpretation relies heavily on context, both explicit and implicit. Verbal cues such as speaker intent, shared knowledge, interpersonal relationships, and prior discourse shape how meaning is constructed. Nonverbal cues, including physical setting, cultural norms, and body language, further influence interpretation. These elements work in concert to guide understanding. Additionally, subtle features like tone, timing, and pauses enrich communication by signaling emotion, emphasis, and intent. Recognizing how these cues interact enhances our ability to interpret language accurately and respond appropriately across diverse communicative situations. Ultimately, effective communication is not just about decoding words but about navigating the rich interplay of linguistic, social, and contextual signals that give those words life.

9.5.2 *Pairs of Sentence Types*

In certain situations, two distinct types of sentences can coexist within the same context. However, they are not interchangeable and cannot be treated as mere paraphrases of one another. Structural variation signals a shift in meaning, with form shaped by semantic and pragmatic factors. Semantics pertains to the explicit, literal meaning conveyed by a sentence type, while pragmatics delves into the subtler, implied meaning that the listener infers. These layers of meaning often interact, creating nuanced interpretations that go beyond the surface structure. **Inference** plays a pivotal role in this process, as it reflects the listener's cognitive ability to decode the speaker's intent using contextual cues and situational knowledge. The conclusions drawn are not solely based on linguistic input; they hinge on the listener's grasp of the event being described, their assumptions about the speaker's goals, and the broader conversational setting. This dynamic interplay between form, meaning, and context underscores the complexity of human communication and the sophistication of our interpretive mechanisms.

To illustrate how subtle shifts in syntax can produce significant differences in meaning, let's explore the following sentences:

She was wearing blue jeans.

She was wearing blue jeans!

The core idea in both sentences is that she was wearing blue jeans. However, each one conveys that idea in a unique way, giving it a distinct meaning. In Cognitive Grammar, this variability reflects **construal**, specifically **subjective construal**, where meaning is shaped by the speaker's evaluative stance and emotional framing of the situation. The first sentence is a straightforward statement, where the speaker neutrally asserts something they believe to be true and shares it with the listener. On the other hand, the second sentence is an exclamation that expresses surprise, with the speaker emphasizing their belief and using a falling tone to convey emotion. Even though the words are arranged the same way, the sentences have different meanings because they serve different purposes. When a language has two forms that express the same idea but are structured differently, they are not interchangeable; they differ based on the speaker's intent. This subtle shift reveals a key principle in Cognitive Grammar: in language, meaning shapes form. Whether spoken or written, form reflects thought. The speaker's intent guides how meaning unfolds: a statement tone signals neutrality, while an exclamation conveys emotion.

Shouldn't you use another route?

You should use another route.

Both sentences revolve around the same conceptual content: suggesting an alternative route. Yet, they differ significantly in how that suggestion is framed and interpreted. In Cognitive Grammar, this variability reflects **construal**, specifically **interpersonal construal**, where meaning emerges from the interaction between speaker and hearer. The first is phrased as a question, which, despite its question form, functions as a polite advisory. It invites the listener to consider the suggestion without imposing it, allowing space for disagreement or negotiation. The second is a statement, more direct and assertive in tone, presenting the advice as a fact or recommendation. This contrast illustrates a key insight from Cognitive Grammar: form emerges from meaning. The speaker's intent, whether to advise gently or assertively, shapes the grammatical structure. These sentence types are not interchangeable, even if they share propositional content. Each reflects a distinct **interpersonal construal** of the situation: the question implies uncertainty or openness, while the statement conveys confidence or urgency. Thus, language is not merely a tool for transmitting ideas; it is a window into how those ideas are cognitively shaped.

Isn't Nancy clever?

How clever Nancy is!

Both sentences celebrate Nancy's cleverness, yet they do so in distinct ways that reflect different communicative intentions. In Cognitive Grammar, this variability reflects **construal**, specifically two different types: **interpersonal construal** in the first case and **subjective construal** in the second. The first, framed as a rhetorical question, invites agreement. Though it appears as a question, it functions more as a compliment cloaked in conversational engagement. The speaker subtly seeks validation from the listener, reinforcing the shared admiration, an instance of **interpersonal construal**, where meaning emerges through speaker-hearer alignment. The second sentence, by contrast, is an exclamatory statement. It does not ask for confirmation; it declares surprise or admiration outright. The speaker expresses a personal emotional response, not expecting any reply, an example of **subjective construal**, where meaning is shaped by the speaker's evaluative stance. This aligns with the typical function of exclamations: to convey strong feelings rather than elicit interaction. The key takeaway is that meaning shapes structure. Though similar in wording, these expressions differ. Their grammatical forms, question versus exclamation, mark distinct pragmatic roles, showing that language depends on construal.

Summary

This chapter explores the fascinating world of **simple temporal relations** expressed through **single-grounded processes**; namely, **one-verb simple sentences** in grammar. Such sentences are captivating because they can convey a wide range of ideas, adding richness and depth to language. By examining their patterns and interrelations, we can enhance our ability to construct coherent and meaningful discourse. To characterize these sentences, I draw on three theories of Cognitive Grammar. The first is **prototype theory**. A single-grounded process is polysemous, capable of serving multiple functions. These functions form a complex category that can be understood in terms of prototypes and peripheries. Within this framework, **statements** act as the prototype, while **questions**, **imperatives**, and **exclamatives** occupy the periphery. Statements present information as grounded facts. Questions seek missing information by directing attention to a conceptual gap. Imperatives prompt or instruct action by invoking the hearer's agency. Exclamatives highlight intense evaluation or emotional salience within a situation. This demonstrates that meaning is organized around *best examples* (prototypes) rather than strict definitions.

The second is **domain theory**, which demonstrates that single-grounded processes denoting the same concept can form distinct domains. Within these domains, they represent different facets and fulfill various roles in language. The meaning of a sentence type is shaped by the domain it belongs to, as each highlights a particular aspect. Single-grounded processes may tap into domains such as advice, requests, compliments, suggestions, or apologies. This shows that meaning depends on broader cognitive structures, background knowledge, and mental frameworks. The third and final theory is **construal**, which emphasizes that single-grounded processes evoking similar content are not identical in meaning or interchangeable in use. They differ according to how the speaker interprets their shared content, leading to distinct conceptualizations expressed linguistically in unique ways. Each sentence type thus carries its own meaning. This demonstrates that meaning varies depending on how a situation is conceptually framed, and that mental choices govern linguistic structures. Taken together, these cognitive theories reveal that meaning is not fixed but dynamically shaped by human cognition.

Exercises

1. Illustrate how each of the following sentence pairs differs in both structure and meaning.

1. She needs a holiday.
   What she needs is a holiday.
2. Nobody is outside.
   There is nobody outside.
3. She seldom takes a day off work.
   Seldom does she take a day off work.
4. Can you help me for a moment?
   Can't you help me for a moment?
5. Follow the instructions.
   Do follow the instructions.

2. Create questions for which the answers would be the underlined words, highlighting both structure and usage.

1. Jill is a hostess.
2. This bike is Mary's.
3. They voted for Mark.
4. She slept well yesterday.
5. He bought the new version.

3. Fill in the appropriate wh-word based on the answers provided, showing understanding of meaning and context.

1. ___________	is his father?	Estate agent
2. ___________	suit do you like?	The light grey
3. ___________	does he study?	To succeed
4. ___________	did she get hurt?	Ran into a tree
5. ___________	turn is it to drive?	Your nephew

4. Turn each of the sentences below into an exclamation. Refer to the underlined words with *what* or *how*.

1. She baked a delicious cake.
2. The sunset is beautiful.
3. He gave an outstanding performance.
4. She sang the song perfectly.
5. The view is breathtaking.

5. Provide original example sentences illustrating each of the following concepts, showing how form reflects meaning.

1. Command with the verb *let*
2. Negative command
3. Command without a subject
4. Command with a subject
5. Persuasive command

6. The sentences convey a similar idea but differ in emphasis and tone. Can you spot the nuances?

1. How delicious this cake tastes!
2. What a delicious cake this is!

7. There are two ways of reading the following sentences: semantically and pragmatically. What are they?

1. The doctor is arriving
2. Could you lend me a hand?

8. Despite sharing the conceptual content, the sentence pairs differ in construal and communicative role.

1. She was wearing a red dress.
2. She was wearing a red dress!
3. Couldn't you arrive earlier?
4. You should arrive earlier.

9. Both sentences show the same action, but subject presence creates a difference in meaning.

1. Close the door.
2. You close the door.

10. The two sentences share meaning, but raising transforms the first into a different interpretation.

1. To solve this puzzle is challenging.
2. This puzzle is challenging to solve.

10

Complex Temporal Relations: Conceptual Symmetry in Coordination

10.1 Introduction

In Chapters 7–9, I examined **simple temporal relations**. These relations involve a single clause anchored in time and situate one conceptualization without creating a dependency structure. They are typically expressed through verbs, verb phrases, or one-verb sentences. In this chapter and the next, I turn to **complex temporal relations**. These are linguistic structures that link two events in time. They involve conceptual symmetry and conceptual asymmetry. **Conceptual symmetry** is expressed through **coordination**, which refers to the formation of a new symbolic structure by combining independent units of equal weight. **Conceptual asymmetry** is expressed through **subordination**, which refers to the formation of a new symbolic structure by combining units of unequal weight, where one unit depends on another for its semantic interpretation. These processes illustrate how the mind organizes discrete elements into higher-order structures, reflecting our ability to build complexity from simplicity. They show the mind's natural tendency to integrate meaning across units, thereby shaping both language and thought.

In grammar, **compounding** is analyzed as a complex process that encompasses three interrelated mental operations: conceptual symmetry, conceptual shift, and correspondence relation. **Conceptual symmetry**, traditionally called **coordination**, links two cognitively equal units, forming a balanced, nondependent structure. For instance, in *She studied hard, and she passed the exam*, the conceptual symmetry marker *and* simply connects two parallel actions. **Conceptual shift**, traditionally called **transition**, links two units by reorienting attention, moving from one conceptualization to another. For example, in *She studied hard; therefore, she passed the exam*, the discourse connector *therefore* highlights a cause-and-effect relation, enriching the connection between studying hard and passing the exam, while ensuring the information flows smoothly. **Correspondence relation**, traditionally called **correlation**, pairs linguistic structures to highlight parallels, construing them as a unified meaning. For example, *Not only is she smart, but she is kind*, the paired correlative *Not only ... but also* integrates two qualities into a single conceptual scene. These operations organize meaning through equality or progression, connecting not only units but also guide the flow of thought, ensuring coherence and continuity in discourse.

10.2 Conceptual Symmetry

In Cognitive Grammar, **conceptual symmetry** refers to the way two or more elements in a construction are treated as conceptually equal. Both elements are equally salient, processed in parallel, and foregrounded without hierarchy in the conceptual structure. Traditionally, conceptual symmetry is often discussed under **coordination**, the grammatical process of linking two or more units of the same rank, such as words, phrases, or clauses, so that they are treated as equally important in the sentence structure. It involves merging two autonomous units using parallel structures in a sentence without subordinating one to the other. This results in a **compound sentence** consisting of two autonomous units that profile parallel events or ideas, linked by a conceptual symmetry marker such as *for*, *and*, *nor*, *but*, *or*, *yet*, and *so*. For example, the sentence *He is poor, but he is honest* contains two autonomous units connected by the conceptual symmetry marker *but*. Conceptual symmetry opposes conceptual asymmetry. Conceptual symmetry treats linked elements as equal in status, while conceptual asymmetry establishes hierarchy, where the autonomous unit is primary while the dependent unit is secondary.

In Cognitive Grammar, conceptual symmetry is not just a mechanical linking of clauses but a mental operation that organizes how concepts are accessed, activated, and related. When we coordinate elements, we treat them as conceptually equal, aligning them within our mental representation to build a coherent structure. This involves accessing distinct conceptual units, activating them in working memory, and recognizing their overlap or compatibility so they can be integrated. For example, in *He studied hard and he passed the exam*, the two events are accessed as separate actions, activated as salient, and coordinated through their shared conceptual domain of academic effort. Conceptual symmetry thus highlights similarities as in *He cooks a lot, and he often tries new recipes*, or contrasts as in *Jack prefers tea, but Mark prefers coffee* by placing ideas side by side in mental space. In Cognitive Grammar, conceptual symmetry aligns equal structures, enriching communication by unifying ideas and clarifying meaning.

In Cognitive Grammar, conceptual symmetry is viewed metaphorically, highlighting how concepts are dynamically accessed, activated, and overlapped. This approach helps us mentally connect and associate various elements in language. When discussing **access**, we are referring to the mental process of bringing together different elements for comparison and combination, with each element acting as a unique conceptual shelf. Once we have accessed these elements, we activate them in our mental representation. **Activation** involves mentally highlighting these elements so we can effectively compare and combine them. **Conceptual overlap** occurs when entities share certain conceptual features, enabling conceptual symmetry. For example, consider the sentence *She runs in the park and swims in the lake.* Here, three processes are at work. First, we access the two activities: *running* and *swimming*. Next, we can compare and combine them as both are active pursuits. Finally, they both share the conceptual feature of physical activity. These processes allow us to mentally integrate and relate different parts of a sentence.

10.2.1 *Mechanisms*

Two essential components sustain conceptual symmetry. **Markers of conceptual symmetry** signal balance, while **coordinate processes** structure that balance in language. Together, they form the operative mechanisms through which conceptual symmetry is both realized and accounted for.

10.2.1.1 Markers of Conceptual Symmetry

In Cognitive Grammar, **markers of conceptual symmetry** are linguistic cues that signal the mental alignment of clauses or phrases with equal conceptual weight, creating balance without hierarchy. Cognitively, they reflect how the mind organizes parallel concepts in mental space, highlighting their equality and allowing them to be processed as coordinated units. Traditionally, these markers are referred to as **coordinating conjunctions**, words that join elements of equal grammatical importance, such as words, phrases, or autonomous units. They act as joiners, linking like with like, for example, noun + noun, clause + clause, and so on. They signal that the connected elements have equal status in the sentence. Therefore, to craft a compound sentence, we typically rely on conceptual symmetry markers like *and*, *but*, *or*, *nor*, *for*, *yet*, and *so*. These conjunctions act as bridges that connect sentence parts and enhance flow. Markers of conceptual symmetry join related ideas into one sentence, showing equal importance and structure.

These conjunctions are crucial in shaping sentence structure and conveying meaning effectively.

In Cognitive Grammar, punctuation plays a crucial role in shaping how we mentally construe relationships between clauses. When crafting compound sentences, certain conventions guide how conceptual connections are signaled. A comma before a conceptual symmetry marker, as in *He exercises regularly, so he stays fit*, highlights the mental alignment of two events, with the conjunction marking their conceptual symmetry. A semicolon between autonomous units, as in *He exercises regularly; he stays fit*, signals a looser but still coordinated relationship, presenting the facts side by side without emphasizing causality. This creates a more neutral construal, allowing the reader to process each clause independently while still recognizing their connection. When clauses are not closely related, a period as in *She loves painting. He enjoys playing the guitar* separates them entirely, reflecting distinct conceptual domains. Thus, punctuation is not merely mechanical; it directs how readers access, activate, and integrate ideas, clarifying conceptual relationships and ensuring coherence in communication.

Functions of Markers of Conceptual Symmetry

Cognitive Grammar offers a richer insight into how these structures function within language. Markers of conceptual symmetry serve several purposes:

- Joining words: When a marker of conceptual symmetry joins two or more individual words, those words should be the same part of speech: a noun with a noun, a verb with a verb, an adjective with an adjective, and so forth.

  She likes sandwiches and cakes. (Joining two nouns)

  She will sing and dance. (Joining two verbs)

  He is a small but aggressive dog. (Joining two adjectives)

  He typed the letter quickly but accurately. (Joining two adverbs)

- Joining phrases: Markers of conceptual symmetry can also link phrases of the same grammatical type: noun, verb, adjective, or preposition.

  She can sing like a rock or dance like a ballerina.

  She likes reading books and watching movies.

- Joining clauses: When two autonomous units are closely related, it often makes sense to combine them into a compound sentence with a marker of conceptual symmetry and a comma.

I am going to the shop, for I have run out of sugar.

She wanted to go for a walk, but it started raining.

10.2.1.2 Coordinate Processes

In Cognitive Grammar, **coordinate processes** refer to two or more dynamic events conceptualized as occurring at the same level of prominence. They are linked side by side in the speaker's mind, with neither ranked below the other. Each event is independent, yet they are mentally grouped together as part of a larger, coordinated scene. Traditionally, coordinate processes are typically expressed through **coordinated sentences.** A **coordinated sentence** is composed of two or more independent clauses connected by coordinating conjunctions, forming a compound sentence. Each clause can stand alone as a complete thought. Coordinate processes allow us to combine related ideas while keeping them separate; each part of the sentence requires its own subject and verb. For example, consider the sentence *The sun came out, and the birds started singing.* Traditionally, this construction is classified as a compound sentence, in which two independent clauses are joined by *and.* From a cognitive perspective, it can be described as comprising two coordinate processes: *came out* and *started singing.* These processes are linked by the marker of conceptual symmetry, *and*, which places them on equal footing. Neither clause is backgrounded; rather, both are profiled as equally significant events within the scene.

In Cognitive Grammar, understanding coordinate processes is crucial for a number of reasons.

- Coordinate processes bring together two or more autonomous units. By analyzing their structure, we gain insight into how our minds handle complex information and juggle multiple ideas at once. For example, consider the autonomous units: *The concert was fantastic* and *The crowd cheered loudly.* When we connect them with *and* to show addition, it transforms into: *The concert was fantastic, and the crowd cheered loudly.* This change highlights how coordinate processes can blend various thoughts into a unified expression.
- Coordinate processes also help us articulate relationships between ideas, contrast different viewpoints, or emphasize particular points. Grasping their patterns boosts our ability to communicate nuanced meanings effectively. For example, look at the autonomous units: *He studied hard* and *He aced the exam.* When we link them with *so* to indicate a result, it becomes: *He studied hard, so he aced the exam.* This transformation shows how coordinate processes can clearly and concisely convey complex relationships between ideas.

- Coordinate processes are great for explaining intricate concepts, emphasizing key thoughts, and ensuring a smooth flow of information. This fosters a sense of coherence and unity in writing. For example, consider the autonomous units: *He went surfing* and *She went snorkeling*. When we connect them with *but* to express contrast, it turns into: *He went surfing, but she went snorkeling.* This change illustrates how coordinate processes can effectively communicate complex relationships while keeping clarity and cohesion intact.
- Coordinate processes add variety and depth to your writing. Instead of relying solely on simple sentences, using compound structures makes your prose more engaging and dynamic. For example, consider the autonomous units: *She will text him* and *She will call him*. When joined with *or*, they become: *She will text him, or she will call him*. This not only enhances readability but also introduces a natural, conversational rhythm that reflects how we think and communicate in everyday life. So, it keeps your writing lively and captivating.

10.2.2 *Cognitive Aspects*

In Cognitive Grammar, coordinate processes are understood as the product of three fundamental cognitive mechanisms: **categorization, configuration,** and **conceptualization.** Through categorization, coordinate processes are organized around prototypes that serve as cognitive reference points, guiding how we classify and interpret them. In configuration, these processes form patterned groupings within cognitive domains, highlighting relationships between clauses expressed through addition, contrast, choice, or causality. In conceptualization, coordinate processes reflect our mental representations, showing how we access, activate, and integrate diverse elements of thought to construct coherent meaning. Taken together, this interplay demonstrates the dynamic adaptability of language, revealing how conceptual symmetry enables us to articulate complex and nuanced ideas with clarity and precision.

10.2.2.1 Categorization

Categorization is a mental skill that identifies common traits by examining how structures relate. Markers of conceptual symmetry, that is, coordinating conjunctions, exemplify this process by forming a group of distinct yet connected meanings defined by shared characteristics. The member that best represents the key traits of this group is called the **prototype**; essentially, it is the one that comes to mind the quickest. The other members, which share some but not all of these traits, are known as **periphery**. The peripheral members still align with the category's specifications but add their own unique twists. The senses in a category act like family members: they share some general features but differ in specific ways. These markers reflect different conceptual relationships and attentional frames. This variation within the category illustrates how language mirrors cognition, not through rigid boundaries but through graded membership. In Cognitive Grammar, gradience reflects how we organize language by salience, frequency, and clarity.

When it comes to markers of conceptual symmetry, *and* stands as the prototype. It is the most basic and frequently used marker, linking equal elements in an easy-to-understand way. Moreover, it is acquired early in language development and used in almost all contexts, reinforcing its central role. Moving away from the prototype, *but* introduces contrast. Though common and clear, it shifts framing from similarity to opposition, demanding more effort. *Or* implies alternatives or choices, introducing a decision-making element that is cognitively more demanding than *and* or *but*. Moving further from the prototype, *so* signals consequence, shifting to causality and becoming more abstract. *For* expresses reason, but its rarity and complexity make it less direct than *and*, as it requires deeper inferential processing. *Nor* is rare, used after negation, and structurally demanding, making it cognitively distant from the prototype. Lastly, *yet* conveys contrast or concession, akin to *but*, though rarer and more peripheral.

She likes both coffee and tea.

The weather is sunny but windy.

He can swim or dive.

She doesn't like coffee, nor does she enjoy tea.

I was tired, so I went to bed early.

He was tired, yet he kept working.

She stayed home, for she was feeling unwell.

10.2.2.2 Configuration

Configuration is a cognitive skill that organizes linguistic items into different domains, with each item fitting into a specific aspect. This means that to truly grasp the meaning of a word, we cannot just look at it on its own; we need to consider the domain it is part of. The **domain** is a framework of knowledge that sheds light on what a word means, while a **facet** represents a particular angle of that domain tied to a specific experience. We can categorize markers of conceptual symmetry according to cognitive domains based on their meanings, which helps us understand them better. Cognitive domains are like collections of knowledge that shape how we interpret semantic units, acting as the backdrop for our understanding of markers of conceptual symmetry. These domains create mental contexts that affect how we perceive and express meaning, much like mental landscapes where our understanding of language is grounded. The way we group the markers shows their vital roles in crafting cohesive and well-structured language. Each marker has its unique function, and we can sort them based on what they do.

Here are the domains that illustrate the distinct functional roles of the markers of conceptual symmetry.

Addition: and

And is used to join two equal elements. It means "plus."

Alex bought a book. Ellen bought a new doll.

Alex bought a book, and Ellen bought a new doll.

Contrast: but, yet

But is used to indicate a contrast or contradiction. It means "in contrast."

Andrew likes green. Frank likes blue.

Andrew likes green, but Frank likes blue.

Yet is used to introduce an unexpected contrast. It means "but at the same time."

She suffered from a knee injury. She won the match.

She suffered from a knee injury, yet she won the match.

Choice: or, nor

Or is used to mean one or the other of two alternatives.

You must study hard. You will fail the exam.

You must study hard, or you will fail the exam.

Nor is used to express a negative condition or choice.

My sister doesn't like to study. She does not take notes in class.

My sister doesn't like to study, nor does she take notes in class.

Cause and effect: for, so

For is used to introduce a reason or explanation for an action. It means "because."

She eats healthy food. She wants to stay in shape.

She eats healthy food, for she wants to stay in shape.

So is used to indicate a consequence or result. It means "therefore."

William was sleepy. He went to bed early.

William was sleepy, so he went to bed early.

10.2.2.3 Conceptualization

Conceptualization is a mental skill that enables individuals to view a situation from different angles and express those views in various ways. Selecting the right expressions is not only about conveying ideas but also about how those ideas are construed. **Construal**, or framing, involves how a speaker considers a situation and conveys its meaning through language. The choice of markers is linked to the specific construal of the situation. Even if two markers of conceptual symmetry appear to convey similar ideas, each one adds its own nuance to the meaning, leading to subtle distinctions. While some markers may seem interchangeable, a closer examination reveals that they are not truly substitutable. The selection of a marker can significantly impact the tone and meaning of a compound sentence, influencing the understanding of the relationships within that sentence. This variance in meaning arises from the speaker's **perspective**, the mental viewpoint a speaker adopts to represent and describe a scene. It shapes how meaning is constructed: not just what is said, but how it is mentally framed.

Let's now compare some pairs of expressions to substantiate the role of construal in bringing about differences in meaning.

He studies hard, but he failed.

He studies hard, yet he failed.

Both sentences highlight a contrast, but they carry slightly different meanings. They are both grammatically sound and share similar information, yet the choice between *but* and *yet* subtly shifts the tone. The sentence with *but* suggests a cause-and-effect relationship: the person worked hard, but despite their efforts, they still failed. This emphasizes the stark contrast between their hard work and the unfortunate result of failure, introducing a conflict between the two ideas. On the other hand, the sentence with *yet* brings in an element of surprise or unexpectedness. It suggests that even though the person studied hard (which you would typically expect to lead to success), they still ended up failing. This highlights the surprising or contradictory nature of the outcome. In short, the first sentence zeroes in on the cause-and-effect dynamic, while the second one underscores the unexpected result despite the effort put in. These examples illustrate how we interpret information is not just about the content itself but also about the way we construe that content.

He was hungry, so he ate all the cake.

He ate all the cake for he was hungry.

Both sentences point to a cause-and-effect relationship, but they carry a subtle difference in meaning. Both constructions are grammatically correct, yet the choice of the markers (so vs. for) changes the nuance a bit. The first sentence, using *so*, highlights a direct cause-and-effect link: the person's hunger prompted them to devour the entire cake, showcasing the logical outcome of being hungry. On the other hand, the second sentence employs *for*, which functions similarly to *because*, shedding light on the reason behind the action and highlighting hunger as the driving force for eating the cake. In summary, the first sentence emphasizes the outcome of hunger, eating the cake, while the second highlights hunger as the underlying motivation for the action. In Cognitive Grammar, subtle shifts in conceptualization and alternative framings of the same content give rise to variations in linguistic expression and distinct encodings. This phenomenon shows how construal links cognition and grammar, enabling speakers to shape meaning through nuanced choices.

He can choose the white shirt and the blue one.

He can choose the white shirt or the blue one.

The way we interpret the two sentences really comes down to perspective. The choice between using *and* or *or* makes a subtle but important difference in meaning, leading to either a dual option or a single choice. In the first sentence, the word *and* implies inclusivity, suggesting that he can choose both the white shirt and the blue one, giving him the freedom to pick both at the same time. On the other hand, in the second sentence *or* implies exclusivity, indicating that he must decide between the white shirt and the blue one; he can only choose one, not both. So, the key difference here is whether he can select one item, both items, or just one of the two. To sum it up, the first sentence allows for a dual choice, while the second one limits the selection to a single item. This distinction is not just grammatical; it reflects how language encodes conceptual structure. Using *and* portrays the scenario as additive, emphasizing the possibility of accumulation, while *or* portrays it as selective, highlighting a decision point. This demonstrates that even a simple shift in conjunction can reshape the listener's understanding of the options available.

10.2.3 Linguistic Aspects

When it comes to syntax, two key processes really stand out: **ellipsis** and **parallelism**. In Cognitive Grammar, these are not treated as purely syntactic phenomena but as conceptual processes. Ellipsis is explained through profiling, domain activation, and conceptual economy, while parallelism is understood in terms of conceptual symmetry, alignment, and schematicity. Understanding these syntactic processes is crucial because it sheds light on how sentences are built and how we convey meaning. Both ellipsis and parallelism are like windows into the way our minds work, helping us use language in a more efficient and effortless manner. **Ellipsis** allows speakers to drop information they believe the listener can easily fill in based on the context. It is a way of zeroing in on what is new or important while assuming that the listener shares some background knowledge. On the other hand, **parallelism** shines a light on the similarities between ideas or elements. This technique can emphasize the connections between concepts, create a sense of balance, or simply make the information easier to digest and remember.

10.2.3.1 Ellipsis

One interesting linguistic aspect of coordinate processes is **ellipsis**, where certain elements are omitted because they can be understood from context. Ellipsis refers to the omission of linguistic elements that are recoverable through shared knowledge, allowing speakers to focus attention on what is most relevant or prominent in discourse. In Cognitive Grammar, ellipsis is not merely a syntactic omission but a conceptual and usage-based phenomenon grounded in how speakers manage shared knowledge and mental processing. It highlights the collaborative nature of communication, where the speaker's perspective and the listener's ability to infer meaning work together. Ellipsis reflects our cognitive processes of language comprehension and construction, enabling speakers to convey thoughts more efficiently and concisely while relying on the listener to fill in missing details. Cognitive Grammar views language as adaptable, with ellipsis showing how speakers adjust to context. By omitting redundant or easily inferred information, speakers enhance clarity and focus on the essential aspects of their message.

In Cognitive Grammar, ellipsis exemplifies three core cognitive principles: **economy**, **activation**, and **profiling**. Economy is achieved as speakers streamline communication by omitting predictable material, reducing processing effort. Activation occurs because omitted elements remain mentally accessible and recoverable through shared context. Profiling highlights meaning by interpreting expressed material against what is left unsaid, avoiding full repetition. Ellipsis is not missing syntax but an interpretive strategy grounded in shared conceptual structures, demonstrating language's adaptability to context and the dynamic construction of meaning in interaction. It underscores how linguistic form is inseparable from cognitive processes, revealing the intimate link between grammar and thought. Ultimately, ellipsis shows that communication is not a mechanical transfer of syntax but a cooperative act of meaning-making.

To substantiate the role of ellipsis in shaping meaning and structure, let's have a look at an illustrative example:

She can play the guitar, and he can [play the guitar] too.

The sentence above exemplifies an elliptical structure, where both the speaker and listener rely on shared contextual knowledge to construct and interpret meaning. The speaker intentionally omits the repeated verb phrase *play the guitar* in the second clause, expecting the listener to mentally fill in the missing information. This omission reflects the principle of **economy**, as language use is streamlined by avoiding unnecessary repetition. The listener then infers the meaning by drawing on prior context and cues, which demonstrates **activation**, since the omitted material remains cognitively accessible within the discourse domain. Building on the context provided in the first clause, the listener interprets *he can too* as *he can play the guitar too*. What is overtly expressed is thus understood in relation to the background of what is left unsaid, exemplifying **profiling**, where meaning emerges through contrast between expressed and omitted elements. This interaction shows a cognitive partnership: speakers streamline speech while listeners fill gaps with knowledge, reflecting Cognitive Grammar's link between form, representation, and shared understanding.

Ellipsis takes different forms. In each case, the omitted elements are understood from the context.

Gapping or verbal ellipsis is the omission of only the verb in the second of two coordinated clauses.

John likes coffee and Susan [likes] tea.

Stripping is the omission of all but one constituent in a clause.

Would you like tea, or [would you like] coffee?

Sluicing is the omission of constituents after a wh-word in interrogative clauses.

Jane is planning something, but I don't know what [she is planning].

Nominal ellipsis is the omission of a noun or pronoun that has already been mentioned in the sentence.

I have two dogs, and John has three, so he has more [dogs].

Clausal ellipsis is the omission of an entire clause in a sentence.

I went to the shop and then [*I went*] to the park.

The patterns and examples of elliptical structures demonstrate the dynamic nature of language. They reflect the mental processes that help us communicate more efficiently and effectively. These structures highlight a key cognitive principle in which we tend to minimize effort while maximizing understanding. They also underscore the importance of context in both using and understanding language. By cutting out repetitive or obvious information, speakers can make their communication more efficient, making it easier for listeners to grasp and process what is being said. This economy of expression not only streamlines interaction but also showcases the speaker's ability to anticipate the listener's inferential skills, reinforcing the idea that language is a collaborative cognitive activity shaped by shared knowledge and expectations. Ultimately, ellipsis exemplifies how linguistic form is guided not just by grammatical rules, but by cognitive strategies that prioritize relevance, coherence, and mental economy in real-time communication.

10.2.3.2 Parallelism

Another intriguing linguistic aspect of coordinate processes is **parallelism.** This concept involves using similar grammatical structures within sentences to create a sense of balance and rhythm in our language. Parallelism is closely linked to the idea of construal, as it demonstrates how speakers actively organize their thoughts and shape their expressions to enhance clarity, coherence, and aesthetic appeal. In Cognitive Grammar, parallelism is viewed as a reflection of our cognitive processes, highlighting how we structure information in our minds to facilitate understanding of language. The use of parallel structures underscores the relationship between linguistic form and cognitive function, illustrating our brain's innate inclination to simplify and organize information for clearer and more efficient communication. Ultimately, parallelism illustrates how similar structures can establish balance and coherence in sentences, mirroring our cognitive preference for patterns and symmetry. Parallelism is not merely a stylistic embellishment; it serves as a cognitive strategy that enhances comprehension and supports mental efficiency.

In Cognitive Grammar, parallelism exemplifies three core cognitive principles: symmetry, alignment, and efficiency. **Symmetry** arises when clauses or constructions share similar conceptual structures, making them easier to process. The use of consistent forms helps listeners understand more readily. **Alignment** occurs as parallel structures organize and connect mental spaces, drawing attention to similarities or contrasts in meaning. Parallelism also taps into our natural tendency to notice patterns and connect ideas, which is vital for thinking. **Efficiency** emerges as predictable patterns reduce cognitive load, reinforcing coherence in discourse. Because our brains favor efficiency, we grasp and remember information more easily when it is presented clearly and systematically. In short, parallelism adds balance and coherence to language, enhancing clarity and effectiveness while making messages more persuasive and memorable by reinforcing key ideas through repetition and conceptual symmetry.

Let's look at an example to see how parallelism functions in language and enhances clarity.

She likes reading, writing, and painting.

In the sentence above, the gerunds *reading*, *writing*, and *painting* create rhythm and balance, reflecting **symmetry**. The clauses share similar conceptual structures, making them easier to process. **Alignment** occurs when parallel forms link mental spaces, highlighting similarities and contrasts to improve coherence. **Efficiency** emerges because predictable patterns reduce cognitive load, allowing listeners to grasp and remember information more readily. Profiling highlights the expressed items against potential alternatives, emphasizing their equal importance and guiding interpretation. Together, these principles show that parallelism is not merely stylistic but a cognitive strategy that reinforces coherence, boosts clarity, and strengthens memorability. The way the sentence is built matches how we naturally organize ideas in our minds.

Below are some common patterns of parallelism along with examples using markers of conceptual symmetry:

Parallel words:

You can have tea or coffee. Nouns

She is young, yet she is wise. Adjectives

I studied hard, so I passed the exam. Verbs

He studied quietly and carefully. Adverbs

Parallel phrases:

She enjoys reading books, writing stories, and painting pictures. Gerunds

He likes to swim in the lake, run in the park, and bike through the city. Infinitives

Parallel clauses:

He works hard, but he also takes time to relax.

They went to the park, and they played soccer.

These examples of parallel structures illuminate the dynamic interplay between linguistic form and cognitive function. They underscore our innate tendency to recognize patterns, optimize mental effort, and appreciate aesthetically coherent communication. From a Cognitive Grammar standpoint, parallelism reflects how conceptual structures are shaped and construed through language, enhancing clarity, foregrounding salient ideas, and engaging the audience by aligning with familiar mental schemas. When speakers maintain consistent syntactic patterns, they activate entrenched cognitive routines, allowing messages to be processed more fluently and retained more effectively. This alignment between linguistic structure and cognitive architecture demonstrates how language use mirrors the way we think, revealing our preference for well-structured, harmonious input. Moreover, parallelism serves as a cognitive scaffold, directing attention and reinforcing meaning through repetition and symmetry, mechanisms that facilitate conceptual integration and reduce processing load in real-time communication.

10.3 Conceptual Shift

In Cognitive Grammar, **conceptual shift** refers to the change in how a situation or event is mentally construed, for example, shifting focus from one participant, action, or perspective to another. It highlights the dynamic nature of meaning construction as speakers guide listeners through different viewpoints or aspects of a scene. A conceptual shift between discourse spaces involves moving from one idea to another, whether within a single sentence or across multiple sentences. It merges linguistic elements in a way that guides the hearer from one mental frame to another, ensuring cohesion and continuity in the unfolding discourse. This shift is important because it shows how meaning is dynamically constructed; the listener must continuously adjust mental representations as the discourse unfolds. Traditionally, this phenomenon is commonly referred to as **transition**, emphasizing the structural or rhetorical move from one part of discourse to another. This smooth movement uses linguistic tools like **discourse connectors**, traditionally referred to as conjunctive adverbs, which link two autonomous units and help create a seamless flow of thoughts.

In Cognitive Grammar, conceptual shift is not just a mental exercise; it also maps onto linguistic structure, as mental processes correspond directly to patterns in language. Conceptual shift guides mental processing by helping the brain move from one idea to another and recognize connections. When we use conceptual shifting, our minds actively shift between concepts, identifying how ideas relate through contrast, addition, cause and effect, or sequence. On the linguistic side, conceptual shift appears through discourse connectors, which are linking words that join ideas while indicating the logical flow of ideas. Discourse connectors signal the type of connection between sentences, whether contrast (*however*), addition (*moreover*), or cause-and-effect (*therefore*), guiding readers in understanding the links across a message. By using these adverbs effectively, we enhance the coherence and cohesion of our writing, making it easier for readers to follow our line of thought. An important detail to remember is that discourse connectors often require specific punctuation, such as semicolons or commas, to clarify how ideas are connected.

Take, for instance, the sentence *She was tired; however, she continued working.* A lot goes on mentally when we read that. First, we experience a cognitive shift. Our minds move from understanding the feeling of tiredness to recognizing the action of pushing through work, emphasizing the contrast between those two ideas. Next, we engage in conceptual integration. Our brains combine the new information *continuing to work* with what we already know *being tired*, helping us create a clear picture of the situation. Then, there is attention management. The word *however* plays a crucial role in directing our focus, indicating that an important contrast is coming. On the linguistic side, several key elements come into play. First, we observe a signaling relationship. The word *however* signals a contrast between the two parts of the sentence, demonstrating that despite being tired, she is still working. Second, coherence and cohesion are essential. Using *however* improves the overall clarity of the sentence, making the connection between the two ideas clear and logical. Lastly, punctuation and structure are vital. The semicolon before *however* and the comma after it are necessary for proper punctuation. The semicolon links the two autonomous units, while the comma helps separate the discourse connector.

10.3.1 *Mechanisms*

Two essential components sustain conceptual shift. **Discourse connectors** signal transitions and links across ideas, while **discourse relations** structure those connections within the flow of meaning. Together, they constitute the operative mechanisms through which conceptual shift is both realized and accounted for.

10.3.1.1 Discourse Connectors

In Cognitive Grammar, **discourse connectors** are linguistic devices that guide the flow of ideas by signaling relationships between autonomous units. They are devices that map mental processes onto linguistic forms, guiding how we track coherence, shift between ideas, and build meaning dynamically in discourse. Traditionally, these are commonly referred to as **conjunctive adverbs**. These are words that connect two autonomous units within a single sentence to show how ideas are logically related. Discourse connectors are seen as essential tools that aid in organizing and clarifying the connections between ideas in conversation. They not only serve as grammatical links but also convey significant meaning that influences the overall flow of the discussion. For example, the discourse connector *therefore* is used to indicate a cause-and-effect relationship. In the sentence *The weather* *forecast predicted heavy rain; therefore, the outdoor event was postponed*, the discourse connector *therefore* helps the listener or reader understand that the event's postponement is a direct result of the expected heavy rain. This demonstrate that discourse connectors do more than connect; they convey essential meaning.

Functions of Discourse Connectors

Cognitive Grammar provides a deeper understanding of how these structures work in language. Discourse connectors play a key role in

- Clarifying the relationships between ideas, making it easier for our brains to digest and grasp complex information. For example, in *She did not study for the exam; therefore, she did not pass*, the discourse connector *therefore* clearly shows a cause-and-effect link between the two autonomous units. This helps the reader see that not studying directly resulted in failing the exam, allowing for a smoother understanding of the logical connection.
- Enhancing the coherence of our communication by seamlessly linking sentences and clauses. Coherence ensures that ideas flow logically, making it simpler for the reader or listener to follow along. For example, in *The weather was terrible. However, we decided to go hiking*, the discourse connector *however* introduces a contrast between the two clauses, providing a smooth transition from one idea to the next. Without *however*, the two sentences may confuse.
- Highlighting certain points, directing the listener or reader's focus and interpretation. In the sentence *The project was completed on time. Moreover, it was under budget*, the discourse connector *moreover* emphasizes the additional positive outcome of being under budget. This draws the reader's attention to the significance of both achievements, showcasing the project's overall success. Emphasis helps prioritize information and clarify its importance.
- Reflecting our thought processes and how we organize information mentally. For example, in *She was cooking dinner. Meanwhile, her brother was setting the table*, the discourse connector meanwhile indicates that both actions were occurring at the same time. This mirrors how we perceive and arrange events in our minds, illustrating a parallel sequence of actions. It helps readers vividly visualize the scene, reflecting how we naturally process events.

10.3.1.2 Discourse Relations

In Cognitive Grammar, **discourse relations** are sentences in which two ideas are conceptually linked, structuring how events, thoughts, or statements fit within a larger mental framework. They help speakers organize information and guide the listener through the flow of meaning. Traditionally, these discourse relations are typically realized by **transitional sentences.** A **transitional sentence** serves as a bridge connecting two ideas, effectively forming a compound sentence. For example, in *He did not study for the test; consequently, he did not pass*, the discourse connector *consequently* links the two clauses, illustrating a cause-and-effect relationship. The discourse connector not only clarifies the relationship but also improves the overall flow and coherence of the writing. Discourse relations frequently weave together multiple ideas into a single sentence, adding complexity and detail to the text. A well-crafted discourse relation guides the reader through the writer's thought process, making the text more accessible and easier to follow. It ensures a smooth logical progression from one idea to the next, avoiding any jarring jumps. In punctuation, a semicolon precedes the discourse connector, which is then followed by a comma.

10.3.2 Cognitive Aspects

In Cognitive Grammar, the theories of prototype, domain, and construal are essential in helping us understand discourse relations. The **prototype** theory explains that our mental categories are based on typical examples we encounter. The **domain** theory focuses on conceptual contexts, such as physical spaces, time periods, or abstract ideas, that help us grasp linguistic expressions. The **construal** theory explores the different ways we can perceive and describe a situation. Together, these theories enrich our comprehension of discourse relations by providing diverse perspectives to analyze and interpret the connections between different parts of those sentences. They serve the foundation of Cognitive Grammar, offering crucial frameworks for describing and analyzing linguistic expressions in general and grammatical units specifically. By exploring these theories, we can gain deeper insights into the mechanics of language and how we construct meaning in our minds. These theories explain how discourse relations work and reveal how we mentally process language shifts during real-time communication.

10.3.2.1 Categorization

In Cognitive Grammar, categorization is central to how we interpret and organize the world. It involves grouping linguistic elements into categories based on their shared features. This process is deeply influenced by prototype theory, which posits that within any category, some members are more prototypical while others are more peripheral. A prototype is the most typical or central example of a category, what people instinctively recognize as representative. The periphery includes less typical members that share some traits but deviate from the core features. This structure reflects how our minds organize language and meaning based on similarity and experience. Categorization is significant because it reshapes our understanding of linguistic categories. Rather than viewing them as rigid boxes with fixed boundaries, we see them as flexible groupings centered around the most typical examples. Linguistic elements can vary in how strongly they fit a category, depending on their similarity to the prototype. This mirrors how our minds naturally organize concepts, through familiarity and experience rather than strict definitions. Categorization is not just about rules, but about how people actually think and use language.

A typical discourse relation usually consists of two autonomous units linked by a common additive marker, as in *She enjoys painting; in addition, she takes photos*. This structure represents the central member of this category and serves as a **reference point** for recognizing other relations. Discourse relations that deviate slightly from this prototype are positioned closer to the periphery, depending on how closely they resemble the core example. An example that is almost typical is a relation that shows contrast, as in *She loves city life; however, he prefers the countryside*. A bit further from the prototype is a relation that denotes cause and effect, as in *The roads were icy; therefore, the school was closed*. Moving outward toward the outer edges, we come across discourse relations that show temporal relationships, as in *She was preparing dinner; meanwhile, he set the table*. At the furthest edge, we find discourse relations that express comparison, as in *I appreciate your help. Likewise, I am grateful for your support*. This shows that additive transitions are the most central, while contrast, cause and effect, time, and comparison relations grow more peripheral with less similarity.

10.3.2.2 Configuration

In Cognitive Grammar, when we use language, we **profile** a concept against a **base**, which is typically a **domain**: a structured body of knowledge or experience. This domain often has an internal **configuration**, arranging its elements in a meaningful way for interpretation. Within the domain, each element corresponds to a **facet**, a specific aspect of the domain reflecting a particular experience. Therefore, meaning emerges from profiling a concept against a domain, highlighting a facet that aligns with the communicative purpose. Regarding discourse relations, the same mechanism provides insight into how various discourse connectors connect to different conceptual domains, facilitating a better understanding of their overall meanings. Initially, the connectors are organized within domains, which serve as the conceptual knowledge backgrounds for their comprehension. This organization demonstrates how the discourse connectors interrelate to create a coherent whole. Within these domains, the discourse connectors are positioned in a way that each corresponds to a facet of the domain tied to a particular concept. This shows how we organize information to convey and grasp language.

Here are the most common domains of discourse connectors, along with their descriptions and examples.

The Domain of Addition

The domain of addition can be understood through a hierarchy of connective expressions that vary in strength and emphasis. At the weakest level, *also* signals simple addition, introducing another point without much weight. *In addition* carries a moderate force, suggesting a more formal accumulation of ideas. *Besides* extends the discussion peripherally with moderate to strong impact, adding something that feels supplementary yet significant. *Furthermore* intensifies the progression, marking a strong continuation that builds momentum. Finally, *moreover* represents the strongest form of addition, reinforcing emphasis and underscoring the importance of what follows. Each connector clearly encodes a nuanced conceptual framing of addition.

> She loves reading; also, she enjoys writing.
>
> He is a talented musician; in addition, he is a skilled painter.
>
> I do not want to go out; besides, it is raining.
>
> The project is behind schedule; furthermore, we are over budget.
>
> The plan is risky; moreover, it is expensive.

These discourse connectors are not interchangeable; each profiles a different facet of the domain of additive discourse relations. *Also* profiles a parallel facet, adding a similar point without strong emphasis. *In addition* profiles a supplementary facet, contributing extra but balanced information. *Besides* profiles an unexpected or secondary facet, offering an additional reason to support an earlier statement. *Furthermore* profiles a reinforcing facet, strengthening the prior assertion. *Moreover* profiles a heightened facet, introducing a more compelling or persuasive point. Together, they form a configuration of additive strategies that reflect nuanced relationships between ideas. Each one plays a unique role in connecting thoughts and clarifying how different parts of our writing relate to one another. Using semicolons here really highlights the close connection between those clauses, making our writing flow better and feel more engaging. By understanding how these connectors function within domains and profile specific facets, writers can make more deliberate choices that clarify relationships between ideas and strengthen argumentative flow.

The Domain of Contrast

The domain of contrast can be mapped across a spectrum of connective expressions, each carrying a distinct force of opposition or concession. At the weakest level, *still* conveys a persistent concession, acknowledging a point while maintaining continuity. *Nevertheless* introduces a defiant concession of moderate strength, signaling resistance yet allowing the discourse to move forward. *Nonetheless* strengthens this stance into a resilient concession, occupying a moderate to strong position that underscores determination despite opposing factors. Moving into stronger territory, *instead* marks a clear substitutive opposition, directly replacing one idea with another. At the strongest end of the scale, *conversely* delivers a logical reversal, flipping the perspective entirely and emphasizing the sharpest form of contrast. Each connector highlights a unique way of framing contrast.

> She was tired; still, she continued working late into the night.
>
> The team was tired; nevertheless, they won the match.
>
> The task was difficult; nonetheless, he completed it on time.
>
> He did not go to the gym; instead, he decided to take a long walk.
>
> He is very outgoing; conversely, his brother is quite shy.

These discourse connectors are not interchangeable; each profiles a distinct facet within the domain of contrastive discourse. *Still* evokes a persistent facet, suggesting continuity despite an expected barrier. *Nevertheless* highlights a mitigating facet, introducing a fact that lessens the impact of the preceding statement. *Nonetheless* emphasizes a resilient facet, presenting a contrast that upholds the validity of the earlier idea. *Instead* draws attention to a substitutive facet, presenting an alternative action that replaces the anticipated one. *Conversely* activates a polarizing facet, offering a viewpoint that directly opposes the previous one. Collectively, these connectors form a structured network of contrastive strategies that reveal nuanced relationships among ideas. Each one serves a distinct function in linking concepts and clarifying how different elements of a text interact. The use of semicolons underscores the close conceptual bond between clauses, enhancing both coherence and rhythm. By grasping how these connectors shape domains and profile facets, writers can sharpen links, enrich texture, and strengthen flow.

The Domain of Cause and Effect

The domain of cause and effect unfolds across a continuum of connective expressions, each signaling a different degree of logical force. At the weakest level, *as a result* conveys a direct consequence, simply linking cause to outcome. *Accordingly* strengthens the connection with a moderate sense of formal alignment, showing that events follow in a structured manner. *Therefore* carries a moderate to strong weight, presenting a logical conclusion drawn from preceding facts. *Hence* intensifies the reasoning further, marking a strong deductive inference that emphasizes inevitability. At the strongest end, *thus* delivers summative reasoning, encapsulating the entire argument and underscoring the most forceful causal link. Each connector offers a nuanced view of cause and effect.

> The project was delayed; as a result, the deadline was extended.
>
> The rules have changed; accordingly, we must adjust our plans.
>
> The weather was bad; therefore, the event was cancelled.
>
> He didn't study for the exam; hence, he failed.
>
> They planned to cut costs; thus, they reduced staff.

While these discourse connectors operate within the same domain, they are not interchangeable. Each one activates a different facet of causality. *As a result* profiles an outcome facet, emphasizing the natural consequence of a prior event. It is similar to *as a consequence* and *consequently*, but the latter often carry a slight suggestion of something potentially negative, as in *He did not follow the instructions; as a consequence, the experiment failed*, and *She missed the bus; consequently, she was late for work*. *Accordingly* profiles a responsive facet, highlighting an action taken in alignment with a changed condition. *Therefore* profiles a deductive facet, presenting a conclusion logically derived from preceding information. *Hence* profiles an explanatory facet, offering a reason or justification for the result. *Thus* profiles a resultative facet, signaling a direct consequence of an intentional decision. Together, discourse connectors form a system of causal strategies that illuminate subtle connections between ideas. Each highlights cause-effect, while semicolons reinforce closeness, coherence, and cadence.

The Domain of Time

The domain of time can be expressed through a gradation of temporal connectors that mark different relationships and strengths. At the weakest level, *then* indicates a simple sequential step, moving the discourse forward in order. *Meanwhile* introduces a moderate sense of parallel occurrence, highlighting events that unfold at the same time. *In the meantime* carries a moderate to strong force, emphasizing an interim interval that bridges one moment to the next. *Subsequently* strengthens the temporal link by signaling an ordered progression, underscoring the structured unfolding of events. At the strongest end, *eventually* conveys the final culmination, marking the ultimate outcome or resolution in the temporal chain. Each connector represents a nuanced conceptual framing of time.

> We went to the park; then, we had ice cream.
>
> She was cooking dinner; meanwhile, her husband was setting the table.
>
> The meeting starts at 3:00 p.m.; in the meantime, let's review the agenda.

He graduated from college; subsequently, he started his career.

After years of hard work; eventually, she became the boss of the company.

Each of these connectors engages a different facet of temporal structure, making them noninterchangeable. *Then* profiles a next-in-sequence facet, marking a straightforward temporal transition. *Meanwhile* profiles a simultaneity facet, highlighting parallel actions happening at the same time. *In the meantime* profiles an intervening facet, pointing to activity occurring between two defined temporal points. *Subsequently* profiles a chronological progression facet, indicating a sequential development over time. *Eventually* profiles a culmination facet, emphasizing a delayed but inevitable outcome following a prolonged process. These connectors help to clarify the timing and sequence of events, making writing more precise and easier to follow. Additionally, they enhance the narrative flow by providing clear temporal markers. By using semicolons, the conceptual bond between actions is underscored, enhancing both coherence and rhythm. Knowing how connectors work helps writers clarify timing, enrich flow, and strengthen temporal understanding.

The Domain of Comparison

The domain of comparison can be traced along a continuum of connective expressions that highlight varying degrees of resemblance and evaluative force. At the weakest level, *equally* conveys balanced parity, suggesting that two elements share the same status or weight. *Similarly* introduces a moderate sense of parallel resemblance, pointing out likenesses without overstating them. *Likewise* strengthens the connection into a moderate to strong mirrored correspondence, emphasizing that one case reflects another. *Correspondingly* advances the comparison further, marking a strong proportional alignment that underscores structural or functional parallels. At the strongest end, *comparatively* delivers evaluative contrast, not only noting similarities but also weighing differences, making it the most forceful connector in the domain of comparison. Each connector evidently encodes a distinct conceptual framing of comparison.

The team worked hard to meet the deadline; equally, they maintained project quality.

The first trial was successful; similarly, the second confirmed our results.

He didn't like the movie; likewise, I found it quite boring.

The company's profits increased; correspondingly, their stock prices rose.

The new policy improved satisfaction; comparatively, it boosted productivity.

These discourse connectors serve distinct comparative purposes, each illuminating a different relational nuance. *Equally* evokes a balanced emphasis facet, underscoring that two achievements hold comparable significance. *Similarly* highlights a shared trait facet, emphasizing commonalities in outcome or process. *Likewise* profiles a parallel evaluation facet, signaling agreement in judgment or experience. *Correspondingly* reveals a harmonizing facet, indicating that one change aligns with another in a coordinated manner. *Comparatively* activates a relative assessment facet, inviting comparison across dimensions of impact. Each connector contributes to the linking of ideas, offering its own conceptual flavor. The strategic use of semicolons reinforces the underlying connection between clauses, enhancing both coherence and rhythmic flow. These connectors clarify relationships between concepts, making writing more cohesive and logically structured. By understanding how they function within domains and profile specific facets, writers can make more deliberate choices that yield clearer, more purposeful comparisons.

10.3.2.3 Conceptualization

In Cognitive Grammar, **conceptualization** refers to the mental act of creating and organizing concepts based on our experiences and perceptions. A key part of this mental journey is the concept of **construal**, which refers to the different ways a speaker can interpret and view a situation. This includes elements like perspective, focus, and the level of detail we choose to highlight. When it comes to discourse relations, construal plays a significant role in how we understand the connections between clauses. The construal theory offers us the flexibility to interpret things in various ways, allowing us to pick up on different nuances and emphases in those relationships. Our perceptions get organized into mental structures, which we then express through language. Conceptualization sheds light on how people use language to communicate complex ideas and experiences. It shows us that different discourse connectors can reflect various perspectives on the same situation, emphasizing the adaptability of our cognitive processes and how we can adjust our understanding and descriptions based on context and viewpoint.

To understand how construal influences the interpretation of meaning, let's explore a few illustrative examples.

You set up the tent; meanwhile, I will build a fire.

You set up the tent; in the meantime, I will build a fire.

Both discourse connectors *meanwhile* and *in the meantime* signal a temporal relationship between two events, yet they differ subtly in how that relationship is construed. While both expressions activate similar conceptual content, they diverge in profiling; that is, in the selective attention given to particular facets of a conceptual scene. From a Cognitive Grammar perspective, the distinction lies in which aspect of the temporal scene is foregrounded. *Meanwhile* highlights two actions unfolding together within the same time frame. In this case, while the tent is being set up, the fire is actively built alongside it. By contrast, *in the meantime* marks the interval between two events, framing it as a span for secondary action. In this case, while the tent is being set up, the fire is built within that interval. This usage conveys a more sequential perspective: the fire is constructed during the time that passes as the tent is assembled. In essence, *meanwhile* construes the overlap of processes, whereas *in the meantime* construes the intervening duration between them.

He was injured; hence, he was unable to play.

He was injured; thus, he was unable to play.

Both *hence* and *thus* signal a causal or resultative relationship between two events, yet they differ subtly in how that relationship is construed, that is, in how the speaker conceptually organizes and profiles the connection. Both expressions activate similar conceptual content, a causal link between injury and inability, but they differ in how that link is mentally structured and emphasized. *Hence* profiles a forward-looking construal, highlighting the consequence that emerges from a prior condition. It profiles the resultant state as a natural or inevitable outcome of the initial event. In this case, the injury is construed as giving rise to the inability to play. The conceptual flow moves from cause to consequence, emphasizing the temporal and logical progression. *Thus*, by contrast, profiles a retrospective construal, emphasizing the logical conclusion drawn from preceding information. It frames the inability to play as a deduced outcome, based on the prior event of injury. The construal here is more analytical, focusing on the reasoning process that connects the two events rather than the inevitability of the result. In short, *hence* profiles the forward projection of consequences, while *thus* profiles the backward inference of conclusions.

Summary

In this chapter, I have examined conceptual symmetry and conceptual shift. Both are cognitive operations because they describe how the mind organizes and navigates meaning. **Conceptual symmetry** links ideas of equal semantic weight, through markers of conceptual symmetry, by maintaining balance and equivalence between them. On the cognitive side, these markers undergo three distinct processes. **Categorization** is not merely a listing of functions; rather, it involves distinguishing prototypes from peripheral members. Among all markers, *and* clearly serves as the prototype. The periphery, arranged by distance from the prototype, includes *but*, *or*, *so*, *for*, *nor*, and *yet*. In terms of **configuration**, symmetry markers evoke the following cognitive domains: addition (*and*), contrast (*but*, *yet*), choice (*or*, *nor*), and cause-and-effect (*for*, *so*). In **conceptualization**, the choice of marker depends on how a situation is construed. Although two markers of conceptual symmetry may seem to convey similar ideas, each adds its own nuance, creating subtle distinctions in meaning. On the linguistic side, coordinate processes typically involve ellipsis and parallelism. Ellipsis, the omission of repeated elements, reduces redundancy, while parallelism, the use of similar structures, enhances clarity and balance.

Conceptual shift also links ideas of equal semantic weight, through discourse connectors, but does so by redirecting or reframing the relation, introducing a change in perspective or meaning. In cognitive terms, these connectors are subject to three distinct processes. **Categorization** involves differentiating prototypes from peripheral members, with addition serving as the prototype among discourse relations, followed by peripheral members denoting contrast, cause and effect, time, and comparison. **Configuration** involves grouping the discourse connectors into domains, structuring how ideas are processed and related, evoking cognitive domains such as addition, contrast, cause-effect, time, and comparison. **Conceptualization** influences how a situation is construed; even if two discourse connectors seem similar, each adds nuance, shaping subtle distinctions in meaning and interpretation. Together, these processes reveal how discourse connectors function not only as linguistic devices but also as cognitive tools, guiding interpretation by signaling shifts in meaning and ensuring coherence.

Exercises

1. Combine the following sentences with the markers of conceptual symmetry given in brackets.

1. Her marks were high. She was not accepted. (yet)
2. The students took notes. The teacher lectured. (and)
3. The team is strong. The fans have nothing to fear. (for)
4. I decided to major in English. I always enjoyed it. (so)
5. Carl cannot be at the meeting. Andrew cannot be at the meeting. (nor)

2. Identify the meaning that each of the following markers of conceptual symmetry signals in the combination.

1. He trained hard, so he won the race.
2. She missed the bus, for she overslept.
3. Nancy can't sing, nor can she dance.

4. He cannot write poetry, yet he keeps on trying.
5. Leave the place at once or you will be in trouble.

3. Choose the appropriate markers of conceptual symmetry to fill in the gap, balancing and differentiating meaning.

1. I wanted something to eat, _________ I looked in the fridge.

   (a) but (b) or (c) so (d) nor
2. You must hurry _________ you will miss the train.

   (a) so (b) or (c) for (d) yet
3. The man likes coffee, _________ his wife prefers tea.

   (a) but (b) so (c) for (d) nor
4. He is overweight, _________ he consumes more calories.

   (a) and (b) but (c) yet (d) for
5. He doesn't eat cake, _________ does he eat biscuits.

   (a) nor (b) and (c) or (d) yet

4. Revise the sentences by adding appropriate markers of conceptual symmetry to form compounds.

1. He was hungry he didn't eat anything.
2. She studied hard she didn't pass the exam.
3. We can go to the museum we can go to the zoo.
4. I wanted to go to the concert I couldn't get tickets.
5. The weather was nice we decided to go for a hike.

5. The following sentences share the same content but use different markers of conceptual symmetry. How are they different?

1. The weather was stormy, but they went for a hike.
   The weather was stormy, yet they went for a hike.
2. He finished his work, so he went for a walk.
   He finished his work, then he went for a walk.
3. The storm intensified, so they sought shelter.
   They sought shelter for the storm intensified.
4. She is tired, yet she persists in working.
   She is tired, still she persists in working.
5. We can go to the park, or we can go to the museum.
   We can go to the park, and we can go to the museum.

6. Join the following sentences with the given discourse connectors to show their logical links.

1. There was no coffee, I had to drink tea. (instead)
2. She is much too old for him. She is married. (besides)
3. She practiced daily. Her performance improved. (accordingly)
4. She forgot her umbrella. She got soaked in the rain. (consequently)
5. We are unable to get funding. We had to abandon the project. (therefore)

7. Fill in the blanks with the appropriate discourse connectors such as however, therefore, moreover, consequently, nevertheless.
   1. She is very talented; __________, she is also very humble.
   2. She studied hard for the exam; __________, she didn't pass.
   3. The weather was terrible; __________, we decided to go hiking.
   4. He didn't like the movie; __________, he watched it until the end.
   5. The project was challenging; __________, we managed to complete it on time.
8. Rewrite the following sentences into conceptual shift by using appropriate discourse connectors.
   1. He was hungry. He didn't eat anything.
   2. She studied hard. She didn't pass the exam.
   3. We can go to the museum. We can go to the zoo.
   4. The weather was nice. We decided to go for a hike.
   5. I wanted to go to the concert. I couldn't get tickets.
9. Form compound sentences from the following idea pairs, using symmetry markers or discourse connectors.
   1. He was tired / He kept working.
   2. I love to travel / I don't have much time.
   3. She is very talented / She is also very humble.
   4. The cake was delicious / It was too sweet for my taste.
   5. We could go to the beach / We could stay home and relax.
10. The following statements have the same substance, but they are different. How do the connectors distinguish them in?
   1. She is very talented; besides, she is very hardworking.
      She is very talented; furthermore, she is very hardworking.
   2. She wanted to go to the beach; conversely, he preferred to stay home.
      She wanted to go to the beach; instead, he preferred to stay home.
   3. He didn't study for the exam; hence, he failed.
      He didn't study for the exam; thus, he failed.
   4. She was preparing dinner; eventually, they sat down to eat.
      She was preparing dinner; subsequently, they sat down to eat.
   5. The new model is faster; comparatively, the old model is more reliable.
      The new model is faster; equally, the old model is more reliable.

11

Complex Temporal Relations: Correspondence Relations in Correlation

11.1 Introduction

In Chapter 10, I examined **conceptual symmetry** and **conceptual shift**. Conceptual symmetry, traditionally called **coordination**, shows how speakers construe elements as equal within one structure, creating balance. Conceptual shift, traditionally called **transition**, highlights how discourse moves from one mental representation to another, creating movement. In this chapter, I will examine **correspondence relations**, traditionally called **correlation**, the conceptual links speakers establish between elements of a construction, aligning them so they match or map onto each other in meaning or structure. These relations involve mental mappings that connect parts of a construction into a coherent conceptual whole. Within the framework of Cognitive Grammar, important distinctions emerge between conceptual symmetry and correspondence relations. The first integrates two or more independent units into a single unit, typically through conceptual symmetry markers such as *and*, *but*, *or*, *nor*, *so*, *yet*, and *for*. In contrast, the second operates at the phrasal level, linking words or expressions through paired correlatives such as *either … or*, *neither … nor*, *both … and*, *not only … but also*, and *whether … or*. Paired correlatives highlight relationships of equivalence or opposition between elements, creating balance, rhythm, and precision.

11.2 Correspondence Relations

A correspondence relation maps component structures in a complex expression, linking symbolic units into larger expressions by highlighting conceptual connections, scalar, proportional, or parallel, so each element is interpreted relative to the other. Correspondence relations are not merely syntactic devices; they emphasize conceptual links such as addition, choice, or exclusion, and reflect cognitive operations like highlighting or balancing ideas, showing how language elements interact in real time. Rather than functioning as mechanical rules, they are motivated by how speakers conceptualize relationships. Traditionally, correspondence relations are referred to as **correlation**, using correlative conjunctions to join words, phrases, or clauses while ensuring grammatical parallelism. Each conjunction introduces an element, and together they show the logical relationship. In this way, correspondence relations reveal both the structural and cognitive dimensions of language, showing how grammar and thought converge. They show how expressions form and how meaning is constructed.

In Cognitive Grammar, correspondence relations are not simply a mechanical process for cohesion and balance, but rather conceptual mappings that illustrate how different symbolic structures align with each other in the mind. For example, consider *She is not only smart but also diligent*. In cognitive terms, this represents a correspondence relation of addition. This can be seen as a conceptual blend, in which the speaker highlights two qualities that together define the person. The speaker establishes two mental spaces: one *smartness*, another for *diligence*. Each clause corresponds to one attribute, and the paired correlatives indicate that they are conceptually linked and jointly emphasized. The meaning arises from their interdependence: neither quality exists in isolation, and the correspondence is established through the paired correlatives. The paired correlatives map the two conceptual structures, smartness and diligence, into a unified profile of the subject. This demonstrates that correspondence relations are not only about syntax but also about conceptual mapping, in which linguistic structures mirror cognitive connections.

11.2.1 *Paired Correlatives*

In Cognitive Grammar, a **paired correlative** involves two elements working together to link clauses or phrases. It highlights how two linked expressions form a conceptual unit in meaning construction. They are paired structures that function as a single conceptual unit. Each part of the pair contributes meaning, but the full relational meaning only emerges when both are present. They are not merely connectors; they carry meaning and reflect how we mentally process and relate various pieces of information. They guide the speaker and listener to mentally coordinate two alternatives, emphases, or parallel ideas. They are cognitively processed as linked units that highlight balance, contrast, or reinforcement. Examples include *both ... and*, *either ... or*, *not only ... but also*, and *whether ... or*. Traditionally, paired correlatives are called **correlative conjunctions**. A correlative conjunction is a conjunction that comes in pairs to connect equal grammatical elements. Correlative conjunctions always come in pairs, establishing a connection that shapes both the structure and meaning of the sentence. They are like a dynamic duo, as one cannot function without the other. They ensure syntactic parallelism. Both parts must connect similar structures like two nouns, two adjectives, two clauses, and so on.

For example, *both ... and* is a pair of words that work together to connect elements within a sentence in a parallel manner, as in *Both Ali and Sara attended the meeting*. In this sentence, the paired correlative profiles the two participants, Ali and Sara, as equally salient. Each participant is given the same grammatical weight, shifting the focus from one individual to the collective presence of both. This balance creates a cognitive symmetry, where the listener perceives the sentence as a joint effort by the two agents. The verb *attended* is depicted as the shared action, but the *both ... and* construction ensures that the emphasis is on their combined participation. This correlative pair signals that the construction is not just about adding two subjects together but integrating them into a single unit of attendance. Overall, *both ... and* showcases equal profiling of two agents, establishes a framework for joint inclusion, maintains balance in conceptual and syntactic structure, and emphasizes the completeness of participation.

Punctuation:
When it comes to punctuation, there are a few key rules to keep in mind for paired constructions. The first rule is that when you use paired correlatives, you should place a comma right before the second part of the pair, as in *Either you come to the party, or you stay home*. The second rule is that in more complex sentences, you can swap the comma for a semicolon before the second element. This is especially true when each part of the pair has its own internal commas or other punctuation, as in *She enjoys hiking; both the mountains and the forests attract her*. On the other hand, in short and simple sentences, you can skip the comma altogether, as in *Neither the cat nor the dog likes rainy weather*. Proper punctuation is really important when using paired correlatives. A well-placed comma clarifies how elements relate, ensures correct understanding, and enhances rhythm. It also shapes balance and emphasis. While missing punctuation may not be strictly ungrammatical, it can hinder readability. Small details make a big difference in writing.

Functions of Paired Correlatives

Cognitive Grammar provides a more profound insight into the functioning of paired correlatives. They are utilized to join:

- Single words:
  He is both a doctor and a pharmacist. (single nouns)
  He not only smokes but also drinks. (single verbs)
  She is neither rich nor famous. (single adjectives)
  He speaks neither slowly nor clearly. (single adverbs)

- Phrases:
  Both the manager of the project and the lead designer attended the meeting. (noun phrases)
  He can either stay at home or go to the gym. (verb phrases)
  All of these clothes are either too small or worn out. (adjective phrases)
  He worked not only with great precision but also under intense pressure. (adverb phrases)

- Clauses:
  I believe both that he is honest and that he is capable. (noun clauses)
  He will either bring snacks, or he will bring desserts. (verb clauses)
  She hired both the designer who won the award and the one who created the viral campaign. (adjective clauses)
  He succeeded not only because he worked hard but also because he believed in himself. (adverb clauses)

An examination of the examples provides insight into the cognitive treatment of paired correlatives. In Cognitive Grammar, paired correlatives are more than just syntactic connectors; they also reflect conceptual relationships between elements. Paired correlatives activate mental spaces that highlight addition, choice, condition, sequence, and comparison, showing how language mirrors cognitive processes. These constructions encourage both speaker and listener to engage in **parallel processing**, mentally aligning two linguistic units while evaluating their semantic roles. This dual activation increases awareness of relational meaning, whether balancing alternatives, emphasizing dual attributes, or negating multiple possibilities. From a cognitive standpoint, paired correlatives demonstrate how grammar shapes and is shaped by our mental architecture. They rely on conceptual symmetry, prompting the brain to map one element onto another in a structured, comparative framework. This aligns with a fundamental principle of human cognition: the tendency to organize information in pairs. Therefore, paired correlatives are not just grammatical tools but cognitive scaffolds for constructing meaning in language.

11.2.2 *Paired Constructions*

In Cognitive Grammar, a **paired construction** refers to a construction in which two linked expressions function together as a single conceptual unit. It employs **paired correlatives** to connect elements of equal importance. The two parts jointly express one unified relationship rather than two separate statements, creating balance and parallelism that make the message clearer and more coherent. Paired correlatives can express addition and inclusion (*both … and*), alternatives (*either … or*), exclusion (*neither … nor*), emphasis and comparison (*not only … but also*), or conditional contrasts (*whether … or*). Each element adds meaning, yet the complete sense arises only when both occur together. Paired correlatives make both parts equally important, set up a framework of inclusion or contrast, and create a sense of balance so the listener processes the sentence smoothly and symmetrically. Paired correlatives guide the hearer to mentally coordinate alternatives, emphases, or parallel contributions. Traditionally, paired constructions are referred to as **correlative sentences.** A correlative sentence uses paired conjunctions to connect equal grammatical elements, with the emphasis on syntactic parallelism rather than conceptual profiling.

Consider *Either you apologize or you leave.* Traditionally, this example is classified as a correlative construction, consisting of the two independent clauses *you apologize* and *you leave* joined by the correlative markers *either … or*. In Cognitive Grammar, however, the sentence is not simply a syntactic combination of clauses but a paired construal of two parallel processual predications. Conceptually, the two clauses are of equal prominence, with neither being subordinated to the other. The markers *either … or* establish a relationship of mutual exclusivity, presenting the addressee with a binary choice in which only one process can be actualized. This construction is viewed as a conceptual integration rather than a mechanical joining of clauses. The two processes share the same discourse frame, with *either … or* functioning as a conceptual operator that structures alternatives. Instead of just labeling the sentence as correlative, Cognitive Grammar highlights how it organizes meaning: foregrounding the speaker's imposition of choice and profiling the exclusivity of the options. In this way, the sentence illustrates how grammar reflects not only formal structure but also the conceptual dynamics of construal.

Cognitive Grammar highlights the diverse functions of paired constructions. This overview explores their roles.

- Paired constructions create a sense of parallelism and balance by linking semantically similar elements. For instance, in *She neither called nor sent a text message*, the construction foregrounds a conceptual contrast between two actions. This parallel structure aids processing by aligning mental spaces, enhancing comprehension and reinforcing cognitive links.

- Paired constructions serve to emphasize multiple focal points within a sentence. In *Not only did she win the race, but she also set a new record*, the pairing draws equal attention to both achievements. Cognitive Grammar interprets this as a mechanism for distributing salience across conceptual domains, allowing the listener to process and retain both pieces of information with equal weight.
- Paired constructions are excellent at combining related elements. Consider *Both the sun and the moon illuminate the night sky*. Here, the paired correlative activates a shared conceptual frame, grouping two celestial bodies under a common function. This reflects the cognitive tendency to categorize and associate elements based on functional or thematic similarity.
- Paired constructions can structure choice and possibility. In *We could either hike up the mountain or swim in the lake*, the construction delineates two distinct mental scenarios. Cognitive Grammar views this as a way of mapping alternative conceptual paths, guiding the listener through a decision-making framework that is both linguistically and cognitively coherent.
- Finally, paired constructions contribute to the rhythmic and aesthetic quality of language. In *Whether it rains or shines, we will have a picnic*, the repetitive structure creates a pleasing cadence. From a cognitive perspective, this rhythm supports fluency and ease of processing, reinforcing the sentence's semantic unity while enhancing its expressive appeal.

11.3 Cognitive Aspects

In Cognitive Grammar, a correspondence relation is not just about following formal rules; it is more about understanding three key ideas: prototype, domain, and construal. This approach emphasizes meaning, allowing us to connect these concepts to compound sentences. A **prototype** involves pinpointing the central member of a category, the real-world example that truly embodies it. The **domain** focuses on choosing conceptual content tied to a specific area, highlighting its various aspects through representative compound sentences. This selection process affects how we interpret meaning and adjust it to fit different contexts. **Construal**, on the other hand, deals with how we perceive and express a situation in language. It involves making specific lexico-grammatical choices to communicate meaning effectively. Essentially, it shows that the way we describe a scene reveals our understanding of it. These concepts shed light on how language influences our thinking and helps us communicate better. They serve as powerful tools for enhancing correlation, shaping how we view and understand the world, and guiding our linguistic decisions.

11.3.1 *Categorization*

In Cognitive Grammar, **categorization** is the process of mentally grouping individual experiences into a category. This process is key to understanding the relationships between different language structures. Paired correlatives form a category that includes related yet distinct meanings. Within this category, overlapping defining properties apply to its members. The **prototypical** sense, which embodies the core characteristics of the category, is the one that usually comes to mind first. Other members share some traits but are considered **peripheral** senses because they do not have all the defining features. In correspondence relation, the prototype is represented by *both ... and*, which connects equal elements. On the other hand, the periphery includes elements that are related but not equal, adding extra information. Closest to the prototype are paired correlatives like *not only ... but also*, which emphasizes the second element as even better, and *either ... or*, which presents a choice between two options. Moderate distance is realized by the paired correlatives *neither ... nor*, which dismisses both options, and *rather ... than*, which favors the first alternative. Furthest from the prototype are the paired correlatives *whether ... or*, which accepts any of the alternatives; and *if ... then*, which introduces a condition.

The audience both clapped hands and stomped feet.
He is not only a stellar student, but also a great athlete.
I will either go for a hike or stay home.
He neither submitted his essay nor asked for an extension.
I'd rather leave now than wait for all the speeches.
I can't decide whether to go out or stay in.
If it rains tomorrow, then we will stay indoors.

11.3.2 *Configuration*

In Cognitive Grammar, **configuration** is the process of organizing elements into a domain that identifies meaning and supports interpretation. Meaning arises through the process of profiling a concept against a base, typically a **domain**, which represents a structured body of knowledge. Each element within a domain highlights a **facet**, a specific dimension that reflects a particular experience. This cognitive mechanism applies to the use of paired correlatives. These correlatives are initially grouped into domains, which serve as conceptual backgrounds for their interpretation. Within each domain, individual paired correlatives correspond to distinct facets, each reflecting a unique conceptual function such as symmetry, contrast, exclusion, or conditionality. This organization showcases the cognitive architecture behind how we interpret, connect, and communicate meaning through language. By categorizing paired correlatives into domains, we not only enhance clarity in meaning but also reveal the mental strategies speakers use to structure relationships between ideas. Such categorization reflects the dynamic interplay between linguistic form and conceptual structure, reinforcing how grammar is deeply rooted in cognition.

The Domain of Addition

The domain of addition is linguistically encoded using the paired correlatives *both ... and* and *not only ... but also*. These correlatives show how ideas are layered and how speakers organize and emphasize them in discourse. They reveal the cognitive tendency to structure meaning through parallelism and reinforcement.

Both ... and

The paired correlative *both ... and* presents two ideas of equal importance. *Both* implies inclusion: one element plus another, while *and* signals continuation, extension, or expansion of meaning within the expression.

She is intelligent. She is beautiful.

She is both intelligent and beautiful.

This construction cognitively frames *intelligence* and *beauty* as coexisting qualities, without prioritizing one over the other. The construction encourages the listener to conceptualize the subject as possessing equally salient attributes.

Not only ... but also

The paired correlative *not only ... but also* introduces two ideas, but with greater emphasis on the second. *Not only* emphasizes the truth value or significance of the first idea, while *but also* intensifies the second, making it appear more impressive, more shocking, or more consequential.

He is arrogant. He is selfish.

He is not only arrogant but also selfish.

This construction frames selfishness as an intensification of arrogance, guiding the listener to view the second trait as more striking. Beyond conveying information, the additive structure influences the listener's interpretation by layering ideas to emphasize their cognitive and rhetorical impact.

The Domain of Choice

The domain of choice is linguistically marked by the paired correlatives *either* ... *or*, *neither* ... *nor*, *rather* ... *than*. These correlatives reflect how speakers conceptualize alternatives, negations, and preferences, organizing meaning to mirror cognitive decision-making and emphasize evaluation and selection.

Either ... or

The paired correlative *either* ... *or* introduces a choice between two alternatives. It is typically used in affirmative statements. It signals that the speaker is considering two viable options, and only one may be selected.

We can hike up in the mountain. We can swim in the lake.

We can either hike up in the mountain or swim in the lake.

This construction cognitively frames the two activities as mutually exclusive possibilities, clearly guiding the listener to perceive a distinct decision point or moment of choice between them.

Neither ... nor

The paired correlative *neither* ... *nor* is used in negative statements. It indicates that both options are being rejected or deemed untrue. It is employed when none of the mentioned alternatives apply.

She is not going to the party. She is not staying home.

She is neither going to the party nor staying home.

This construction cognitively excludes both scenarios, strongly emphasizing the absence of expected outcomes and subtly prompting the listener to infer a third, unstated possibility or alternative.

Rather ... than

The paired correlative *rather* ... *than* expresses a preference for one thing over another. It highlights the speaker's intentional choice, favoring the first alternative. It is often used to contrast desirable versus less desirable actions or states.

She'd watch TV. She'd solve riddles.

She'd rather watch TV than solve riddles.

This construction cognitively frames *watching TV* as the preferred activity, while *solving riddles* is presented as the less favored alternative. The construction reflects the speaker's evaluative stance and prioritization.

The Domain of Condition

The domain of condition is expressed linguistically through the paired correlatives *whether* ... *or* and *if* ... *then*. These correlatives show how speakers structure conditionality, uncertainty, and causal logic in discourse.

Whether ... or

The paired correlative *whether* ... *or* introduces a conditional scenario involving two alternatives. It is typically used to indicate that either option is possible, and the outcome does not depend on which one is chosen. This structure often appears in contexts of uncertainty, indecision, or neutral evaluation.

He bikes to work. He drives to work. He is unsure.

Whether he bikes or drives to work is unsure.

This construction cognitively frames the two transportation methods as equally plausible options, explicitly emphasizing the speaker's uncertainty and hesitation rather than the choice itself.

If ... then

The paired correlative *if* ... *then* establishes a conditional relationship between two propositions. The *if* clause sets the condition or triggering event. The *then* clause presents the result, consequence, or logical outcome.

You get a cut. You will bleed.

If you get a cut, then you will bleed.

This construction reflects a cause-and-effect relationship, cognitively organizing the information as a general truth or predictable outcome. It is used to express factual knowledge, logical reasoning, or hypothetical scenarios.

The Domain of Sequence

The domain of sequence is linguistically conveyed through the paired correlatives *no sooner* ... *than* and *scarcely* ... *when*. These correlatives reflect how speakers cognitively structure the temporal relationship between events, particularly when one action closely follows another.

No sooner ... than

The paired correlative *no sooner ... than* indicates that one event immediately succeeds another in the past. Immediate succession implies no delay between the two events. The event following *no sooner* occurs just before the event introduced by *than*.

I had finished cooking. The guests arrived.

No sooner had I finished cooking than the guests arrived.

This construction cognitively frames the arrival of the guests as instantaneous, occurring the moment the cooking was completed. It emphasizes the tight temporal link between the two actions.

Scarcely ... when

The paired correlative *scarcely ... when* indicates that one event rapidly follows another in the past. Rapid succession suggests speed, though it allows for minor pauses. *Scarcely* conveys the idea of *only just*, implying that the event following *scarcely* was barely completed before the event introduced by *when*.

She had finished reading. She fell asleep.

Scarcely had she finished reading when she fell asleep.

This construction cognitively frames the transition from reading to sleeping as swift and seamless, with minimal temporal separation.

Additional paired correlatives that convey near-immediate succession include *hardly ... when* and *barely ... when*. These are less formal and more commonly used than *scarcely ... when*. They often describe actions that occur with minimal effort or delay, reinforcing the perception of quick transitions.

Dad had arrived. You left for school.

Hardly had dad arrived when you left for school.

I had finished my meal. The waiter brought the bill.

Barely had I finished my meal when the waiter brought the bill.

These constructions help speakers cognitively organize events in a tight temporal sequence, emphasizing how quickly one action follows another.

The Domain of Comparison

The domain of comparison is linguistically realized through the use of the paired correlative *as ... as*. This conjunction reflects how speakers cognitively assess and equate the qualities of two entities, emphasizing their similarity in degree or importance. The paired correlative *as ... as* is used to compare things of similar proportion or equal significance. It is typically employed when the speaker wishes to highlight that two ideas or attributes carry equal weight. The first *as* functions as an adverb, modifying the adjective or adverb that follows. The second *as* can function either as a preposition or a conjunction, depending on the structure of the sentence: As a preposition, it is followed by a noun or pronoun. As a correlative, it is followed by a clause.

She looks lovely. Her mother looks lovely.

She looks as lovely as her mother.

This construction cognitively frames the speaker and her mother as possessing equally lovely appearances, thereby reinforcing the idea of a balanced comparison. The construction allows the listener to conceptualize both individuals as jointly sharing the same degree of the described quality.

11.3.3 Conceptualization

In Cognitive Grammar, **conceptualization** is a mental process that helps speakers form ideas and choose the right language to express them clearly. When picking a linguistic expression, two important concepts come into play: conceptual content and construal. These concepts are essential for grasping meaning. **Conceptual content** gives us the fundamental meaning, while **construal** shapes how we interpret and communicate that meaning. It is like looking at a scene from different viewpoints, where each angle reveals something unique. Construal determines not only how meaning is framed but also which linguistic forms are most appropriate for expressing it. The selection of a paired correlative depends heavily on the specific construal applied to the conceptual content. This means that just having the conceptual content is not enough to fully understand the meaning; it needs to be interpreted in a certain way. Even if two paired correlatives seem similar, each one can impart a different meaning to the content. In Cognitive Grammar, sentences that appear alike can actually convey different meanings because of variations in construal, highlighting the subtle nuances based on the speaker's perspective.

To demonstrate how construal operates in practice, let's examine an illustrative example.

We enjoy neither mountains nor beaches.

We do not enjoy either mountains or beaches.

The sentences may appear similar on the surface, but they differ significantly in construal. While the conceptual content, a lack of enjoyment for mountains and beaches, is shared between the two, the construal, or the way this content is mentally framed and linguistically expressed, leads to distinct interpretations. The first sentence employs *neither* ... *nor*, which construes the speaker's attitude as a rejection of both options simultaneously. It presents a unified conceptualization of disinterest, emphasizing that neither alternative holds appeal. In contrast, the second sentence uses *either* ... *or* within a negative construction, which construes the situation as a lack of enjoyment for at least one of the two options, leaving room for ambiguity. This framing suggests that one option may be acceptable, but the speaker is not committed to enjoying either. Thus, although both sentences communicate a general lack of enjoyment, the construal applied through the choice of paired correlatives influences the nuance of the meaning. This example illustrates how linguistic form interacts with conceptual structure, showing that subtle changes in construal can alter how conceptual content is expressed.

Paired correlatives and markers of conceptual symmetry each play unique roles in how we construct sentences. Paired correlatives have a stronger impact than symmetry markers, emphasizing the connection between the ideas they link. They work together to pair contrasting or complementary thoughts, adding both emphasis and structure to our writing. In contrast, symmetry markers focus on bringing related information together but with a lighter touch. Paired correlatives link balanced elements within a sentence, drawing attention to their relationships and creating a sense of symmetry. Meanwhile, symmetry markers simply join similar elements, helping to maintain balance and smooth flow. Together, they illustrate how language not only conveys meaning but also shapes the cognitive organization of ideas, guiding readers toward clarity and coherence.

Let's explore a couple of examples to distinguish the roles of paired correlatives and conceptual symmetry markers.

Cats and dogs make good pets.

Both cats and dogs make good pets.

The sentences share the same conceptual content, the idea that cats and dogs are suitable as pets. However, they differ in construal, which refers to how this content is mentally framed and linguistically expressed. The first sentence uses the conceptual symmetry marker *and*, which presents the information in a neutral, unmarked way. It simply states that cats and dogs, individually or collectively, make good pets, without drawing attention to their relationship or grouping. The construal here is broad and nonspecific, leaving the listener to interpret the connection between the two animals. In contrast, the second sentence uses the paired correlative *both* ... *and*, which construes the content with emphasis on inclusion and pairing. It highlights the combined suitability of *cats* and *dogs*, suggesting that the speaker views them as equally valuable and worth considering together. This construal foregrounds the idea of joint companionship, subtly shifting the focus from individual qualities to collective appeal. This distinction illustrates how the choice of linkers can reshape the listener's interpretation, even when the underlying conceptual content remains the same. Through construal, speakers can fine-tune the meaning they wish to convey.

Felix or Henry found my bicycle.

Either Felix or Henry found my bicycle.

The sentences share the same conceptual content, the idea that one of two individuals located the bicycle. However, they differ in construal, which refers to how this content is mentally framed and linguistically expressed. The first sentence uses the conceptual symmetry marker *or*, which presents the information in a neutral and somewhat ambiguous way. It suggests that either Felix or Henry but not both found the bicycle, leaving room for the possibility that only one of them discovered it. This construal is less committed, allowing for multiple interpretations. In contrast, the second sentence uses the paired correlative *either ... or*, which explicitly frames the situation as a binary choice, asserting that one of the two individuals definitely found the bicycle. This construal eliminates the possibility that neither did and emphasizes the certainty of one outcome, even if the speaker is unsure who it was. This subtle shift in construal demonstrates how the selection of linkers can influence not just grammatical structure but also the interpretive nuance of a sentence. Even when the conceptual content remains constant, the way it is construed can significantly affect how meaning is understood and communicated.

11.4 Linguistic Aspects

Paired constructions highlight key elements of syntactic structure, such as parallelism, concord, and word order. **Syntactic structure** involves arranging words and phrases in a sentence according to grammatical rules, which plays a crucial role in effective communication. It aligns with our natural inclination for logical organization. These elements shape the way we understand and interpret language, making it easier to grasp the overall message. They serve as linguistic reflections of our thought processes. For instance, **parallelism** helps us by presenting information in a balanced way, which our brains find easier to process since we naturally look for symmetry. **Concord**, on the other hand, satisfies our need for consistency and coherence in language, which lightens our cognitive load and allows us to quickly understand a sentence when the subjects and verbs agree. Lastly, **word order** caters to our preference for structured information, making it simpler to follow and comprehend. When word order is correct, it maintains a logical flow and emphasis, guiding us in interpreting the meaning of the sentence.

11.4.1 *Parallelism*

Parallelism involves repeating the same grammatical form in different parts of a sentence, indicating that two or more ideas are of equal importance. Cognitive Grammar does not view parallelism as a formal syntactic constraint like traditional grammars do. Instead, it interprets parallelism through the lens of conceptual structure and symbolic representation. Parallelism occurs when similar symbolic structures are activated or aligned across clauses or phrases. It is not solely about syntax; it also involves conceptual resonance. Parallel structures are easier for the brain to process because they reduce the mental effort required for parsing and interpretation. This aligns with the idea that parallel structures often reflect parallel mental operations. When using paired constructions, it is essential to maintain parallel structure to ensure smooth flow and coherence. This means that elements linked should have a similar grammatical style, maintaining clear structure. For example, in *She not only enjoys painting but also loves sculpting*, parallel verb phrases are used: *enjoys painting* and *loves sculpting.* Parallel structure creates balance and improves clarity, making the sentence more coherent and easier to read.

Parallelism occurs in several distinct patterns, each reflecting a consistent grammatical structure that enhances clarity, rhythm, and readability. Here are the most common types of patterns:

Parallel words:

Neither cats nor dogs are allowed. (nouns)

She is both intelligent and hardworking. (adjectives)

He will either cook dinner or order takeout. (verbs)

She can either sing beautifully or dance gracefully. (adverbs)

Parallel phrases:

He is not only a great teacher but also a talented musician. (noun phrases)

She is not only full of energy but also rich in experience. (adjective phrases)

He will either be working on the presentation or preparing the data. (verb phrases)

She responded not only with great care but also with genuine concern. (adverb phrases)

Parallel clauses:

Not only does the teacher understand what the problem is, but she also knows what the solution might be. (noun clauses)

She hired both the candidate who was experienced and the one who was enthusiastic. (adjective clauses)

Either you will finish your work on time, or you will have to stay late. (verb clauses)

Whether you arrive early or you leave late, the door will be locked. (adverb clauses)

Parallel comparatives:

The -er, the -er

The harder you work, the stronger you become.

The earlier you start, the sooner you'll finish.

The more, the more

The more you practice, the better you get.

The more you read, the more you learn.

The more, the less

The more you worry, the less you enjoy life.

The more you talk, the less you listen.

The less, the more

The less you spend, the more you save.

The less I concentrate, the more I forget.

The examples of parallel structure demonstrate the dynamic nature of language and emphasizes the importance of recognizing patterns. This not only improves cognitive efficiency but also adds elegance to communication. They show that organizing words in a certain way can sharpen focus, enhance clarity, and capture attention. Cognitive Grammar views paired correlatives as tools for **conceptual symmetry**, rather than just grammatical symmetry. These structures promote structural harmony that goes beyond style; they play a vital role in how information is processed and understood. Paired correlatives do more than connect grammatical elements; they reflect mental operations that group, contrast, or equate ideas. In this way, they help shape thought as much as they shape language, guiding the listener or reader through a coherent conceptual landscape. In essence, parallelism is more than just a syntactic arrangement; it mirrors how the mind naturally organizes, aligns, and balances concepts to enhance clarity and coherence.

11.4.2 Concord

Concord refers to the grammatical agreement between different parts of a sentence, typically in terms of number, gender, or person. The most common form of concord is **subject-verb agreement**, where the verb aligns with its subject in both number and person, as in *She walks* versus *They walk*. It ensures that sentence elements match in form to reflect their relationship in meaning. Concord is simple, but essential for clarity and fluency in language. Unlike traditional grammar that sees concord as a mechanical rule in syntax, Cognitive Grammar treats it as a reflection of symbolic and conceptual coherence between linguistic elements. Cognitive Grammar sees concord not as a rigid rule but as a meaningful alignment between conceptual structures. It arises from how speakers mentally represent and relate ideas, not just how we follow grammatical formulas. If a speaker conceptualizes a collective noun as a unit, they may use singular agreement, as in *The team wins*. If they focus on individual members, plural agreement may emerge, as in *The team are arguing among themselves*. Concord patterns are not just mechanical or abstract rules; they are seen as symbolic pairings where the form, such as verb endings or plural markers, aligns with meaning, such as plurality, person, and conceptual focus.

Paired constructions can effectively demonstrate concord, contributing to grammatical accuracy, coherence, and impactful communication. When concord is properly maintained, these constructions highlight key elements with precision, allowing the intended message to resonate clearly with the reader or listener. Maintaining concord in correlative structures ensures that subjects and verbs agree in number and person, and that parallel elements remain balanced. This grammatical harmony helps convey the speaker's or writer's exact meaning, minimizing ambiguity and enhancing overall comprehensibility. As a result, paired constructions become more readable and engaging, strengthening the clarity and persuasiveness of the communication. Whether in writing or speech, concord plays a vital role in ensuring that ideas are delivered smoothly and understood effortlessly. Ultimately, concord in paired constructions fosters a smooth and logical flow, guiding the reader through the sentence with ease and reinforcing the coherence of the text as a whole. A language user's attention to agreement not only reflects linguistic competence but also enhances the clarity and impact of the message being conveyed.

The following examples show how concord in paired constructions improves precision and clarity.

Neither the students nor the teacher **is** coming.

Neither the teacher nor his students **are** coming.

Either the players or the captain **is** in the stadium.

Either the captain or the players **are** in the stadium.

Not only the players but also the captain **was** present.

Not only the captain but also the players **were** present.

The examples mentioned above emphasize the concept of subject-verb agreement, particularly within paired constructions. This is rooted in the principle of **proximity**, which dictates that the verb should match the closest noun, especially when dealing with compound subjects linked by paired correlatives. The proximity principle reflects how we associate verbs with the nearest noun, aiding clarity and meaning. By adhering to this principle, we can reduce cognitive load and enhance communication effectiveness, allowing readers to grasp the intended message more intuitively. In the first example, the verb *is* agrees with the singular noun *teacher*, the closest subject to the verb, making it clear that the teacher, along with the students, is not coming. In the second example, the verb *are* aligns with the plural noun *students*, the nearest subject, indicating that the students, along with the teacher, are also not coming. This pattern illustrates how proximity-based agreement can subtly shift the focus of a sentence, depending on which noun is emphasized. The principle of proximity ensures clarity and correctness by linking the verb to the nearest subject.

11.4.3 Word Order

Word order refers to how we arrange words in a sentence to make our meaning clear and precise. It shapes the structure and flow of what we say, ensuring that ideas unfold in a logical sequence. Each standard word order carries its own unique meaning, and even a small tweak can shift the entire message. Unlike Traditional Grammar, which treats word order as a rigid set of syntactic rules, Cognitive Grammar views it as a reflection of how speakers conceptualize and mentally structure information. In this framework, word order is not merely about syntax; it offers a window into how we think, perceive, and communicate meaning. Word order reflects how we mentally organize events or scenes. For example, placing the subject before the verb, as in English SVO (Subject-Verb-Object), mirrors how we often conceptualize agents acting upon objects. Cognitive Grammar emphasizes **profiling**, foregrounding the elements the speaker considers most salient. It also accounts for the speaker's **perspective** in discourse. Topical elements often appear earlier in a sentence because they are already activated in the listener's mind. Rather than being purely rule-driven, word order is shaped by **usage** patterns. Frequent constructions become entrenched in the speaker's cognition, influencing expectations and processing.

Dynamic word order in paired constructions aligns with Cognitive Grammar, reflecting how we structure meaning. Paired correlatives emphasize relationships, with placement subtly shifting conceptual focus.

For instance, placing *not only* before the subject rather than before the verb can highlight different parts of the sentence, depending on the speaker's emphasis. This is not merely a stylistic choice; it has cognitive implications. The speaker directs the listener's attention, influencing how the information is processed and retained. Additionally, paired constructions often aim to balance or contrast elements, with word order playing a vital role in maintaining that symmetry. By strategically selecting the sequence, speakers can improve clarity, rhythm, and rhetorical impact. This flexibility allows paired constructions to adjust to various discourse contexts, whether the aim is persuasion, storytelling, casual conversation, or detailed explanation. Paired constructions reveal grammar as a tool for shaping meaning, not a mechanical system.

The following examples demonstrate how variations in word order within paired constructions can shift meaning and emphasis:

> You can either stay here, or you can come with us.
>
> Either you can stay here, or you can come with us.

Both sentences are grammatically correct and convey the same basic proposition, yet the placement of *you* subtly shifts the conceptual focus. The first structure adheres to the typical subject-initial word order, foregrounding the agent *you* and lending the sentence a direct, conversational tone, akin to saying, *Hey, you have two options: stay here or come with us*. In contrast, the second structure begins with *either*, which reorients the listener's attention toward the existence of two distinct alternatives. This fronting of the paired correlative *either* profiles the binary nature of the choice itself, resulting in a slightly more formal or deliberate tone. In Cognitive Grammar, such variations in word order reflect differences in how speakers mentally structure and present information. Word order is not merely a syntactic constrain, it is a tool for conceptual organization, guiding the listener's attention and shaping the interpretation of meaning. By altering the sequence of elements, speakers can highlight different facets of a situation, emphasize contrast, or adjust the tone to suit the communicative context. This flexibility in word order enables nuanced expression, aligning grammatical form with cognitive intent and enhancing clarity.

> She not only won the race, but she also set a new record.
>
> Not only did she win the race, but she also set a new record.

Both sentences are grammatically correct and convey the same core message, yet the positioning of the subject subtly shifts the conceptual focus. The first structure presents the subject *she* at the outset, foregrounding her agency and actions, winning the race and setting a new record. This aligns with a more direct, narrative style that profiles the participant and her accomplishments.

In contrast, the second structure begins with *not only*, which introduces a more marked construction. This inversion places emphasis on the unexpected scope of her achievements, highlighting that she exceeded typical expectations. In Cognitive Grammar, this shift in word order reflects a change in **profiling**. The speaker chooses to spotlight the remarkable nature of the event rather than the agent herself. Such rearrangements are not merely stylistic; they represent different ways of conceptualizing and presenting information. By adjusting the sequence of elements, speakers can emphasize contrast, elevate tone, or draw attention to specific aspects of meaning. Flexible word order illustrates grammar's connection to mental representation and discourse context, where even small shifts enhance clarity, expressiveness, and impact.

Summary

In this chapter, I have explored **correspondence relations** and the use of **paired constructions**. The first is all about the connection between related elements. To create this connection, we rely on paired correlatives, those handy pairs of words that work together to link two equal parts of a sentence. Paired constructions showcase two main aspects: cognitive and linguistic. When discussing cognitive aspects, there are three cognitive processes at play: categorization, configuration, and conceptualization. **Categorization** involves grouping paired correlatives together and noting which examples are prototypical versus peripheral. This process helps establish a clear framework for understanding their usage. **Configuration** involves organizing paired correlatives into distinct domains, each serving a unique role within the language. This organization reveals the functions of paired correlatives, shaping structure and guiding interpretation. Lastly, **Conceptualization** involves distinguishing paired constructions that seem alike in meaning.

Shifting to the linguistic aspects, paired constructions display features such as parallelism, concord, and word order. **Parallelism** is the use of similar grammatical forms in related words, phrases, or clauses. Cognitively, it reduces processing effort by creating predictable patterns; when clauses or phrases align grammatically, the brain can more easily map meaning onto form. A parallel structure maintains balance and clarity. **Concord** refers to grammatical agreement between sentence elements, typically subject-verb or noun-pronoun. Cognitively, it reflects how language encodes conceptual harmony. Agreement in number, person, or gender ensures that the mental model of participants and actions remains coherent, thereby ensuring grammatical accuracy. **Word order** is the arrangement of words in a sentence to convey meaning clearly. It reflects how speakers conceptualize events, as different word orders reflect different perspectives. Cognitively, these features together reveal how grammar functions as a scaffold for thought, guiding comprehension by aligning linguistic form with mental representation.

Exercises

1. Combine the sentences into one, employing the paired correlative provided in brackets.

1. Their house is not big. Their house is not small. (neither ... nor)
2. He was famous at home. He was famous abroad. (both ... and)
3. She wrote the text. She selected the illustrations. (not only ... but also)
4. She is going to buy a camera. She is going to buy a DVD. (either ... or)
5. He seemed undecided to go. He seemed undecided to stay. (whether ... or)

2. Fill in the blanks with the most appropriate paired correlatives in the following sentences.

1. I can _______ fix the dryer _______ instruct on how to use it.
2. You can _______ call me _______ visit me in the office.
3. She _______ understood the topic _______ asked for help.
4. She couldn't decide _______ to watch TV _______ go out.
5. The man _______ washed the car, _______ he polished it.

3. Identify the cognitive dimension signaled by each paired correlative in the combination, noting its effect on meaning.

1. Our neighbor is both a teacher and a painter.
2. We can go either to the beach or the mountains.
3. I am unsure whether to buy a car or a motorcycle.
4. Scarcely had I finished reading when I fell asleep.
5. The pasta dish is as delicious as the rice dish.

4. The following sentences share the same content but use different paired correlatives. Explain how they differ.

1. He both lost his wallet and missed his train.
   He lost not only his wallet but he also missed the train.
2. The student is either energetic or ambitious.
   The student is neither energetic nor ambitious.
3. They haven't decided either to go out or stay in to watch TV.
   They haven't decided whether to go out or stay in to watch TV.
4. No sooner had she finished her homework than she started watching TV.
   Scarcely had she finished her homework when she started watching TV.

5. Hardly had she finished her homework when she started watching TV.
   Barely had she finished her homework when she started watching TV.

5. Explain why the following sentences are ungrammatical or awkward, and then write the correct version.

1. *She not only sings well but also dances.
2. *Either Arthur or Harry will say they can't go.
3. *The boys neither like to play soccer or basketball.
4. *Either Hazel or Lucy are appointed as the monitor.
5. *He not only likes to read books but he also likes to watch movies.

6. Create complex sentences using the paired correlatives, ensuring correct parallel structure and clarity of meaning.

1. Either ... or
2. Both ... and
3. Neither ... nor
4. Not only ... but also
5. Whether ... or

7. Choose the appropriate paired correlative to fill in the gap, ensuring it fits the meaning and structure.

1. I play ________ tennis ________ basketball, I am not good at sports.
   (a) either ... or (b) neither ... nor (c) both ... and (d) not only ... but also
2. Nora likes ________ badminton ________ tennis. She does not like both games.
   (a) either ... or (b) neither ... nor (c) not only ... but also (d) both ... and
3. ________ you study hard, ________ you will pass the exam.
   (a) If ... then (b) No sooner ... than (c) Scarcely ... when (d) Whether ... or

4 ________ had I put my umbrella away, ________ it started raining.
   (a) Rather ... than (b) If ... then (c) No sooner ... than (d) Neither ... nor

5. ________ had I reached the station when the train came.
   (a) Rather ... than (b) Hardly ... when (c) No sooner ... than (d) Neither ... nor

8. Each sentence below misuses a paired correlative. Identify the errors and give the correct versions.

1. She is not only talented but also hardworking.
2. Neither the movie nor the book was interesting to him.
3. You can either have tea and coffee with your breakfast.
4. They couldn't decide whether to go to the beach or stay home.
5. Both the teacher or the students were excited about the field trip.

9. Discuss how the paired correlatives contribute to the overall meanings of the following sentences.

1. She is not only talented but also hardworking.
2. You can either have tea or coffee with your breakfast.
3. Neither the movie nor the book was interesting to him.
4. They couldn't decide whether to go to the beach or to stay home.
5. Both the teacher and the students were excited about the field trip.

10. In Cognitive Grammar, why do paired correlatives appear as pairs, and what cognitive functions do they serve?

12

Complex Temporal Relations: Conceptual Asymmetry in Subordination

12.1 Introduction

In Chapter 11, I discussed **correspondence relations**, traditionally called **correlation**, which link elements so they align or map in meaning and structure. Now, in this chapter, I am going to dive into **conceptual asymmetry**, traditionally called **subordination**, which refers to a relation where one element is construed as primary and the other as secondary, creating an unequal dependency in meaning. It is the process of merging two clauses or units to form a subordinate construction. One is a **conceptually autonomous unit**, traditionally called the **main clause**, while the other is a **conceptually dependent unit**, traditionally called the **subordinate clause**. They create an unequal, hierarchical structure of meaning. The first is the main idea, while the second is the additional information. They are connected by a **marker of conceptual asymmetry**, traditionally called a **subordinating conjunction**, as in *She stays at home when it rains*. Subordinate constructions are shaped by prominence, profiling, and trajector-landmark relations. They link grammar with conceptualization to express intricate ideas.

12.2 Conceptual Asymmetry

In Cognitive Grammar, **conceptual asymmetry** refers to a relation in which two elements are not construed as equals. One element is foregrounded as dominant, while the other is backgrounded as dependent, creating a hierarchy, a layered organization of meaning where one governs interpretation and the other supports it. Traditionally, this relation corresponds to **subordination**, a grammatical structure in which a dependent clause attaches to an independent clause. The conceptually autonomous unit can stand alone, while the conceptually dependent unit cannot express a complete thought on its own. Instead, it elaborates, conditions, or specifies the conceptually autonomous unit, establishing a hierarchical relationship that highlights the conceptual importance of one idea over the other. These units are connected through a **marker of conceptual asymmetry**, traditionally known as a **subordinating conjunction**, forming a complex construction.

For example, consider *When the rain stopped, the children ran outside.* Traditionally, this sentence is categorized as a complex construction, with *the children ran outside* serving as the main clause and *when the rain stopped* as the subordinate clause. In Cognitive Grammar, this represents a case of conceptual asymmetry. The sentence features one autonomous unit (grounded process), *running*, and one dependent unit (integrated process), *stopping*. These are linked by the conceptual asymmetry marker *when*, indicating a temporal relationship between the units or processes. This construction showcases an unequal relationship where one element governs the meaning while the other supports it. The conceptually autonomous unit is foregrounded while the conceptually dependent unit is in the background. Rather than just calling the sentence complex, Cognitive Grammar emphasizes how the two conceptual units or processes are integrated into a unified conceptual structure. **Dependent units** are subordinate clauses that embed additional detail into a sentence while keeping the main clause the central focus.

Construal dimensions in subordinate constructions:In Cognitive Grammar, conceptual asymmetry goes beyond mere syntax; it reflects the deeper ways in which we think and organize our experiences. It is shaped by three key dimensions of construal: **prominence, profiling**, and **trajector-landmark organization**. A dimension of construal shapes how meaning is viewed, determining not only what is conceptualized but also how it is presented to the mind. Construal dimensions are not just technical notions; they are essential in guiding how we understand and convey information in our conversations, as they provide structure, coherence, and clarity to meaning-making. Moreover, they highlight the dynamic relationship between language and cognition, showing how linguistic choices mirror the mental processes through which we prioritize, frame, and interpret the world around us.

Prominence refers to the relative salience of an element within a conceptual structure, highlighting what stands out as most important in meaning-making. Conceptual asymmetry creates a layering between events: autonomous (main) and dependent (subordinate). The **conceptually autonomous unit**, the main clause, profiles a situation independently without requiring another clause for interpretation. The **conceptually dependent unit** (subordinate clause), by contrast, adds background information to the conceptually autonomous unit and requires it to complete its meaning. For example, in *He won't go out unless his friends join him*, the conceptually autonomous unit *He won't go out* stands alone as a complete conceptualization and carries the core meaning, while the conceptually dependent unit *unless his friends join him* provides the condition. It shows when or under what condition the action occurs, with prominence shifting between the two units. Emphasis on reluctance makes the autonomous unit prominent; emphasis on friends joining shifts prominence to the dependent unit.

Profiling refers to the process of selecting and highlighting a particular aspect of a conceptual structure as the focus of meaning, while the rest remains as background. It plays a crucial role in determining which parts of a concept are emphasized during communication, ultimately affecting how the message is interpreted by the listener or reader. For example, in *She went to the store because she needed groceries*, the conceptually autonomous unit is *She went to the store*, which captures the core action. The conceptually dependent unit, *because she needed groceries*, brings attention to specific elements: the cause and the necessity. It explains the reason for her trip to the store, emphasizing her need for groceries. This construction effectively conveys that her visit was motivated by her grocery needs. The conceptually dependent unit provides depth and context to the conceptually autonomous unit, helping us understand which part of the construction conveys the primary message and which part offers additional context or details. Profiling specific elements within a construction is essential for clear communication and comprehension.

Trajector-landmark organization refers to the relationship between two elements in a conceptual framework, where one element takes precedence over the other. The trajector is the focal point, while the landmark serves as the reference point. This setup is essential for understanding how meaning is constructed, as it emphasizes the interaction between the main element (the trajector) and its surrounding context (the landmark). It helps us make sense of spatial and temporal relationships in language. The trajector, as the more dynamic element, takes center stage, while the landmark, which provides context, typically plays a supporting role. The **path** is the line along which the trajector moves, whether in a literal or metaphorical sense. In complex sentences, the conceptually autonomous unit often functions as the trajector, while the dependent unit serves as the landmark. For example, in the sentence *Sarah was reading a book when the phone rang*, the conceptually autonomous unit *Sarah was reading a book* is the trajector, while the conceptually dependent unit *when the phone rang* is the landmark.

12.2.1 *Markers of Conceptual Asymmetry*

In Cognitive Grammar, **markers of conceptual asymmetry** signal the unequal relation between a conceptually autonomous (the main clause) unit and a conceptually dependent (the subordinate clause) unit. They establish a hierarchy in which the first profiles the primary, foregrounded concept, while the second profiles the secondary, backgrounded information. The markers link the two units into a coherent meaning structure. Traditionally, conceptual asymmetry markers are expressed through **subordinating conjunctions**. A subordinating conjunction is a word or phrase that links a dependent clause with an independent clause, resulting in a complex sentence. Common types of conceptual asymmetry markers in English are: (1) noun asymmetry markers, which include that-clauses, wh-clauses, and relative clauses; (2) adjective asymmetry markers, which include *who*, *whom*, *which*, *where*, *when*, *whose*, and *that*; and (3) adverb asymmetry markers, which convey different meanings: such as time (*when*, *as soon as*, *after*, *before*, *while*, *as*, *until*, *till*, and *since*), reason (*because*, *since*, *as*, and *now that*), contrast (*although*, *though*, *whereas*, *while*, and *however*), purpose (*so that*, *in order that*, *so as to*, *in order to*, and *lest*), condition (*if*, *even if*, *unless*, *whether or not*, *in case*, *in the event that*, *only if*, *otherwise*, and *or else*), and result (*so ... that* and *such ... that*).

12.2.2 Conceptually Dependent Units

In Cognitive Grammar, **conceptually dependent units** (integrated processes) are conceptually secondary and attach to conceptually autonomous units. They provide additional detail, context, or elaboration but cannot stand alone. They rely conceptually on the autonomous unit for interpretation and are linked to it by asymmetry markers such as *when* or *because*, enriching meaning without shifting the sentence's primary focus. Conceptually dependent units are backgrounded in interpretation, while conceptually autonomous units remain foregrounded. Traditionally, they are expressed through **subordinate clauses**, which cannot stand alone as complete sentences and depend on a main clause to express a full thought. Subordinate clauses provide specific information, such as time, reason, contrast, purpose, condition, or result, to the main clause, which carries the primary message. This interplay between the two clauses helps convey complex ideas more clearly, creating nuanced statements that express our thoughts more effectively. The act of linking the two clauses raises cognitive load during processing.

12.3 Cognitive Aspects

In Cognitive Grammar, we examine **conceptually dependent units** through the lenses of category, domain, and construal. These cognitive aspects are essential because they enhance our ability to process and interpret complex structures. The concept of **category** involves classifying dependent units (subordinate clauses) based on their function in relation to the autonomous units (main clauses). This classification helps us clearly understand their specific roles, which aids in linguistic analysis and communication. The concept of **domain** refers to the knowledge sphere in which a dependent unit operates. The spheres of knowledge (time, reason, contrast, condition, purpose, and result) help us identify the dependent units to which it belongs, contributing to our overall comprehension through mental organization. Lastly, the concept of **construal** allows us to conceptualize the meaning conveyed by both units together, enabling us to grasp the overall message more effectively and appreciate the perspective chosen by the speaker.

12.3.1 *Categorization*

Categorization is the mental act of grouping together the different meanings of a grammatical item into a specific category. Think of a category as a web of distinct yet related meanings tied to a particular item. At the center of this web is the **prototype**, which is the ideal example that represents the core properties of the category. This is the meaning that pops into your head first. Surrounding the prototype are the **peripheral** meanings, which are linked to it through various semantic extensions. These peripheral meanings are arranged based on how closely they relate to the prototype, determined by their similarities. This framework allows linguists to account for variation and flexibility in language use, recognizing that not all instances of a category must conform rigidly to the prototype. Instead, meanings can radiate outward, forming a gradient of typicality that reflects how language is actually processed and understood.

When it comes to conceptual asymmetry, there are three main types of conceptually dependent units: noun, adjective, and adverb. The nominal dependent unit is the prototype, functioning as core sentence elements, typically subjects or objects. For example, in the sentence *That things will improve is likely*, the nominal dependent unit carries the main grammatical role by serving as the subject. In contrast, adjectival and adverbial dependent units, while still important, are seen as peripheral because they function more like modifiers. These conceptually dependent units are less central to sentence structure and meaning, often providing optional or removable information without disrupting grammatical integrity. Adjectival dependent units modify nouns, as in *The man who won the lottery lives abroad*, while adverbial dependent unit modify verbs, as in *We weren't allowed in because we were late*. This distinction highlights how nominal dependent units embody the structural and functional essence of conceptual asymmetry, while adjectival and adverbial dependent units serve more supportive, descriptive roles.

The following sections provide detailed descriptions of each type of dependent units.

12.3.1.1 Nominal Dependent Units

Cognitive Grammar views **nominal dependent units**, traditionally referred to as **subordinate noun clauses**, as constructions that serve the role of nouns within a sentence. Unlike autonomous units, which can stand alone as complete thoughts, nominal dependent units require pairing with autonomous units to convey meaning. For example, in the sentence *I believe that honesty is essential*, the dependent unit *that honesty is essential* acts as a single noun, specifically as the direct object of the verb *believe*. Cognitive Grammar emphasizes the importance and versatility of nominal dependent units in sentence construction. These units can fulfill various roles, such as subjects, objects, or objects of prepositions. They can replace individual nouns regardless of their complexity and may contain additional verbs, adverbs, and prepositional phrases. For example, compare the simple sentence *My dog eats things* with the more detailed version *My dog eats whatever falls on the floor*. Cognitive Grammar regards nominal dependent units as crucial components of language, enriching overall meaning, providing depth, and serving as flexible participants within larger conceptual structures.

Common types of nominal dependent units include that-, wh-, if-, and relative dependent units. Understanding these types enables us to analyze language structure and meaning, facilitating the expression of complex ideas and relationships within sentences. In Cognitive Grammar, these units profile grounded instances of process types, as they are typically finite and anchored to the speech event through grammatical features such as tense and modality. Unlike gerundial, participial, and infinitival complement structures, which lack this anchoring, nominal dependent units offer a clearer temporal and epistemic connection to the speaker's perspective. They serve as cognitive building blocks, shaping our comprehension of language and its meaningful structures. These conceptually dependent units reflect how we mentally organize and interpret the world. Moreover, their unique ability to encapsulate entire propositions within a single syntactic unit allows speakers to package complex thoughts more efficiently, closely mirroring the way we mentally chunk information for processing and communication.

The subsequent sections offer detailed explanations of each type of nominal dependent units.

That-Dependent Units

A that-dependent unit is a type of finite nominal construction that usually begins with the word *that*. It is commonly used to convey a fact or an idea. In Cognitive Grammar, these units are seen as symbolic structures that connect conceptual content with linguistic form. They play a vital role in articulating complex ideas and relationships, often appearing after verbs that express saying, thinking, or feeling. We can think of them as falling between lexicon and grammar, underscoring their importance in conveying nuanced meanings and conceptualizations. Within Cognitive Grammar, that-dependent units are considered products of **construal**, which involves how speakers choose to shape and present their ideas. Specifically, that-dependent units involve **subjective** construal, where the speaker's viewpoint and mental state influence how the unit is expressed. For example, when someone says *I believe that she is right*, the that-dependent unit *that she is right* reflects the speaker's belief or mental stance. This construal lets the speaker frame the information from their own perspective. That-dependent units can serve as

Subject:	That he is coming is good news.
Direct object:	I knew that he was wrong.
Subject complement:	His hope is that he will succeed.
Appositive:	Your belief, that things will improve, is baseless.
Adjectival complement:	I am sure that things will improve.

Wh-Dependent Units

A wh-dependent unit is a type of finite noun construction that begins with a wh-word such as *what*, *who*, *which*, *when*, *where*, *why*, or *how*. These dependent units are essential for conveying specific information related to a noun or proposition. In Cognitive Grammar, wh-dependent units are viewed as symbolic structures that link conceptual content with linguistic form. They help both speakers and listeners organize and interpret information. Wh-dependent units are shaped by **construal**, which involves **focusing**, **perspective**, and **emphasis**. For example, in *I do not know what she said*, the wh-dependent unit highlights the unknown content, with *what* marking the informational gap. In *Tell me where they went*, the speaker adopts a perspective of inquiry, framing the clause from a position of incomplete knowledge. In *I wonder who broke the vase*, the agent is emphasized over the action or object. Through these and other examples, wh-dependent units reveal themselves as more than grammatical structures; they are cognitive tools that reflect how we construct and convey meaning, underscoring the deep connection between grammar and thought. Wh-dependent units can serve as

Subject:	Who will win the game is uncertain.
Direct object:	I do not know what he wants.
Subject complement:	Her question is why he did it.

Appositive:	My question, why he did it, was not answered.
Adjectival complement:	I wasn't certain whose house I was in.
Prepositional complement:	He was consulted on who should have the prize.

If-Dependent Units

An if-dependent unit sets a condition; the autonomous unit gives the outcome based on the condition introduced by it. We use conditional sentences to show that the action in the main clause can only happen if a specific condition in the dependent unit is met. If-dependent units let us imagine situations and their possible outcomes, real or hypothetical. Often, they show a dependency, meaning the autonomous unit occurs only if the condition is met, thereby emphasizing a cause-and-effect link between the condition and the result. For instance, in *If it rains, we will stay inside*, the if-dependent unit *If it rains* **foregrounds** the condition and highlights the dependency of the autonomous unit on that condition. The speaker chooses to present a non-actual or **potential** scenario *If it rains*. The speaker anchors the scenario to a possible future, shaping how the listener mentally situates the event. If-dependent units often imply a temporal relationship, the condition must occur before the result. This reflects **sequential construal**, where the speaker organizes events in a cause-effect timeline. If-dependent units can serve as

Subject:	If it rains, we'll stay indoors.
Direct object:	I wonder if she will come.
Subject complement:	His dream is if he wins the lottery.
Appositive:	The decision, if considered, will lead to success.
Adjectival complement:	She is uncertain if she takes that brisk.
Prepositional complement:	She is worried about if it will rain in the morning.

12.3.1.2 Adjectival Dependent Units

Cognitive Grammar views **adjectival dependent units**, traditionally referred to **relative clauses**, as constructions that modify or elaborate nominal expressions, functioning similarly to individual adjectives. They provide defining or non-defining information about the nouns, thereby enriching the conceptual content of the larger unit. They typically begin with relative pronouns such as *who*, *whom*, *whose*, *which*, and *that*. These pronouns connect the adjectival dependent unit to the noun it modifies, helping to create a cohesive sentence and convey a more complex idea. They play a crucial role in how we perceive and understand the relationships between different elements in a sentence. Adjectival dependent unit arise from the process of **construal**, particularly in terms of **specificity**, the level of detail and clarity with which a concept is expressed. They help pinpoint exactly which entity is being discussed. For example, in the sentence *The book that you lent me was fascinating*; the adjectival dependent unit (relative clause) *that you lent me* identifies which book is being referred to. Relative clauses can serve as

Subject:	The person who won the award is my friend.
Direct object:	The man whom you saw is my neighbor.
Subject complement:	The subject that I liked best was chemistry.
Appositive:	Linda, whose mother is a dancer, can dance well.

Defining and non-defining adjectival units:
Adjectival dependent units can be either **defining** or **non-defining**. In Cognitive Grammar, the two types serve distinct functions, distinguished by how speakers construe information. A **defining adjectival unit**, traditionally known as a **restrictive relative clause**, provides crucial details that help identify the noun. This information is essential for understanding exactly who or what is being referred to. Cognitively, the unit is tightly integrated with the noun it modifies, forming a single conceptual structure. In writing, defining units are not separated by commas and follow directly after the noun they describe. In contrast, a **non-defining adjectival unit**, traditionally known as a **nonrestrictive relative clause**, offers additional information about a noun that is already clearly identified. While this extra detail enriches comprehension, it is not necessary for identifying the referent. Cognitively, the unit is construed as parenthetical, a separate conceptual unit that adds supplementary meaning. In writing, non-defining adjectival units are set off by commas to reflect their detachment from the core noun phrase.

My sister who lives in London sent me a parcel.
My sister, who lives in London, sent me a parcel.

Both sentences convey the same idea, but differ in construal, that is, how speakers shape and present information to guide interpretation. In the first sentence, the adjectival dependent unit *who lives in London* is defining or restrictive. It identifies the referent, implying that the speaker has more than one sister and is referring specifically to the one residing in London. This unit is tightly integrated with *sister* as forming a single structure, requiring joint processing. This essential link is marked by the absence of commas in writing. In the second sentence, the adjectival dependent unit *who lives in London* is non-defining or nonrestrictive. It offers additional information about a referent that is already uniquely identified; presumably, the speaker has only one sister. This unit is construed as parenthetical, meaning it is conceptually separate from the noun it modifies. This looser link is marked by commas in writing. This indicates that the unit is supplementary, enriching the message without changing the core identification.

Ever-Words

In Cognitive Grammar, indefinite relative pronouns, commonly referred to as **ever-words,** convey the general meaning of "any." They reflect a **schematic construal**, evoking generalized, nonspecific content rather than pointing to particular entities. Ever-words introduce a sense of **generality**, indicating that the reference is not confined to a specific instance. For example, in *Whoever wins the race will receive a prize*, the identity of the winner is irrelevant; the sentence remains open-ended, allowing for flexible interpretation and accommodating uncertainty. In this way, ever-words collapse multiple possibilities into a single expression. By employing ever-words, speakers can express a wide range of meanings, adapting language to diverse contexts with nuance and flexibility. Cognitively, this highlights our ability to abstract away from specifics, thinking in terms of general categories rather than individual cases. Ever-words can serve as

Subject:	Whoever wants to come is welcome.
Direct object:	He says whatever comes into his mind.
Indirect object:	She told whoever would listen her sad story.
Subject complement:	His goal is to be whoever he wants to be.
Object complement:	You can tell me whatever names you like.
Adjectival complement:	He is happy whichever job offer he receives.
Prepositional complement:	Vote for whichever candidate you like.

12.3.1.3 Adverbial Dependent Units

Cognitive Grammar views **adverbial dependent units,** traditionally referred to as subordinate adverbial clauses, as constructions that elaborate on or provide additional details about the autonomous unit. They help us express complex relationships by modifying verbs, adjectives, or other adverbs. Adverbial dependent units begin with various asymmetry markers that convey different meanings, such as time, reason, contrast, condition, purpose, or result. These markers connect the dependent unit to the modified word. The use of adverbial dependent units is grounded in concept of **construal**, which highlights how language users perceive and interpret linguistic expressions. Construal is crucial for understanding how these units modify and provide context to the autonomous unit, thereby enriching the overall meaning of the sentence. For example, in *I walked before the sun went down*, the dependent unit *before the sun went down* modifies the verb *walked*. The asymmetry marker *before* connects the autonomous unit *I walked* with the adverbial dependent unit, showing the timing of the walking action.

Construal dimensions in adverbial dependent units:
In Cognitive Grammar, adverbial dependent units are shaped by three key dimensions of construal: **focusing**, **prominence**, and **perspective**. Together, they shape how adverbial dependent units are mentally structured and interpreted. A **dimension** refers to a basic parameter of **construal**, the cognitive lens through which speakers frame and describe a situation. Each dimension highlights a different aspect of how meaning is shaped in grammar.

Focusing highlights specific elements of a sentence, bringing them into salience. When applied to adverbial dependent units, it helps us understand which parts are being emphasized and how they relate to the autonomous unit. For example, in *She stayed at home because she was feeling unwell*, the autonomous unit *She stayed at home* serves as the focus, or trajector, while the dependent unit *because she was feeling unwell* provides supporting context as the landmark. This adverbial dependent unit explains the reason behind her action, highlighting the cause and enriching the conceptual structure of the sentence. The landmark offers background information that clarifies the circumstances under which the main event occurred. This dynamic between trajector and landmark demonstrates how speakers direct the listener's attention to the most conceptually prominent idea. Focusing, therefore, is not merely a grammatical function but a cognitive strategy for organizing meaning, shaping interpretation, and managing the flow of information in discourse.

Prominence highlights specific parts of a sentence, making them stand out as more important. When we examine adverbial dependent units, this aspect of construal helps us determine which elements are emphasized and how they relate to the autonomous unit. Typically, the autonomous unit takes center stage, while the adverbial dependent unit provides additional, less prominent information. For example, in *She started cooking dinner after she had finished her work*, the autonomous unit *She started cooking dinner* is the focal point as it conveys the main message. The adverbial dependent unit *after she had finished her work* adds some context but is less in the limelight. This adverbial dependent unit also emphasizes the timing, explaining when the autonomous unit takes place. Overall, this adds depth to the sentence by providing a temporal context. This distribution of prominence reflects how speakers guide the listener's attention, shaping interpretation by foregrounding certain ideas while backgrounding others.

Perspective involves looking at a situation from a specific angle or viewpoint. This angle influences how we present and understand information. When discussing adverbial dependent units, perspective plays a crucial role in how we perceive the connection between the autonomous unit and the adverbial dependent unit. These adverbial dependent units can alter the perspective by introducing reasons, conditions, or time frames that affect our interpretation of the autonomous unit. For example, in the sentence *We will go hiking if the weather is nice*, the autonomous unit establishes the primary action or event, while the adverbial dependent unit offers additional context from a particular perspective. The adverbial dependent unit *if the weather is nice* changes our perspective by introducing a condition that affects the autonomous unit of going hiking. It presents an alternative viewpoint, clarifying the condition that influences the autonomous unit. In this way, the reader perceives the situation and its conditions from the observer's perspective.

12.3.2 *Configuration*

In Cognitive Grammar, the meaning of an expression is derived from tapping into a wide range of cognitive domains. A **domain** is any configuration of knowledge that facilitates the understanding of a specific semantic unit. Each domain consists of various **facets** that correspond to particular experiences. These cognitive domains serve as the foundation for interpreting language, enhancing its depth and richness of meaning. By combining autonomous and dependent units, we can convey nuanced meanings and observe how different cognitive domains interact. Adverbial dependent units evoke six different domains: time, reason, contrast, purpose, condition, and result, each characterized by the information it conveys. These units play a vital role in crafting complex sentences, connecting ideas and providing crucial context. This interaction between domains allows speakers to construct meaning dynamically, drawing on experiential knowledge to shape how events, intentions, and relationships are conceptually framed.

In what follows is a characterization of the domains evoked by adverbial dependent units.

12.3.2.1 The Domain of Time

The domain of time refers to the conceptual space through which speakers understand and express temporal relationships between events. Within adverbial dependent units, this domain shapes how we mentally represent the sequencing, overlap, and duration of events. These units typically begin with temporal asymmetry markers such as *when*, *as soon as*, *after*, *before*, *while*, *as*, *until*, *till*, and *since*. Each marker activates a distinct facet of the temporal domain, reflecting specific experiential patterns: *when* corresponds to overlapping in time; *as soon as* signals immediacy; *while* aligns with simultaneity; *as* captures transitional overlap; *until/till* denote bounded temporal space; and *since* marks retrospective duration, anchoring an event or state to a point in the past. Adverbial dependent units of time function as symbolic structures that integrate form and meaning, allowing speakers to convey nuanced temporal relationships. Notably, modal verbs do not follow these markers directly; they typically appear in the autonomous unit rather than the dependent one. These units enrich discourse by providing temporal context, helping audiences interpret the timing, sequence, and prominence of events.

My mother smiled when she saw the surprise.
She left the room as soon as the meeting ended.
She will hand in her paper after she finishes it.
He checked his email before he left the office.
She listened to music while she was studying.
As I was walking home, I found a wallet.
The host will wait for him until he arrives.
I will wait here till you return.
He has been working as a teacher since he left college.

The adverbial dependent units begin with temporal markers, each highlighting a facet of an experiential pattern. *When* construes two events as occurring simultaneously or overlapping in time, highlighting their co-occurrence. *As soon as* emphasizes immediacy, construing the second event as following the first with minimal temporal distance. *After* profiles a sequential relationship, where one event follows another in time, foregrounding the order of actions. *Before* similarly emphasizes temporal precedence, but in reverse, focusing on what occurs prior to the main event. *While* invokes a parallel temporal frame, suggesting that two events are concurrently ongoing, often with equal prominence. *As* typically construes a brief or transitional overlap, often used to mark a moment of change or discovery. *Until* and *till* both construe a bounded temporal span, extending from a starting point up to a specific endpoint. While *until* is more formal, *till* carries a more colloquial tone. *Since* introduces a temporal anchor, marking the onset of a state or activity that continues into the present. This shows that grammar functions not merely as a structural scaffold but as a cognitive tool for expressing meaning.

12.3.2.2 The Domain of Reason

The domain of reason functions as a conceptual framework through which speakers interpret and articulate causal relationships between events. Adverbial dependent units symbolize the link between cause and effect, establishing a clear conceptual connection between the two. These units typically begin with asymmetry markers such as *because*, *since*, *as*, and *now that*. The domain comprises several distinct facets, each represented by a specific marker: *because* denotes direct causation; *as* indicates a resultant relationship; *since* conveys a conditional link; and *now that* expresses a newly activated condition. These units reflect the cognitive processes speakers engage in to clarify the rationale behind an event. By providing contextual detail, they enrich the meaning of the autonomous unit, offering deeper insight into the situation and supplying explanatory nuance. They reveal the underlying motivations of an action, making the sentence more informative and complete. These markers link the result expressed in the autonomous unit with the reason presented in the dependent unit. In doing so, adverbial units of reason foreground the reasoning process, emphasizing the cause as construed in the minds of listeners or readers.

She did not participate in the race because she had a sprained ankle.

As the articles are difficult to find, they are quite expensive.

Since the TV set was broken, we listened to the news on the radio.

Now that I have a car, I can travel more easily.

We now turn to each causal marker individually to investigate how it distinctively shapes the expression of causal relationships between events. *Because* introduces a direct and explicit causal link, **foregrounding** the reason and often implying a specific outcome. It allows for flexible construal, even leading a sentence to emphasize the cause more prominently. *As* and *since* convey a softer, more backgrounded sense of causality, typically used when the reason is assumed to be known or less central to the discourse. *As* tends to highlight the result, while *since* emphasizes the preexisting condition that justifies the action. *Now that* signals a recent change in circumstances, construing the dependent unit as a newly activated condition that enables or explains the main event. Each marker reflects a unique construal of causality, guiding the listener's attention to different aspects of the event structure. These subtle differences enrich meaning, enabling speakers to adapt expression to context and intended emphasis. This shows that these markers not only signal reason but reveal how speakers organize meaning.

12.3.2.3 The Domain of Contrast

The domain of contrast refers to the conceptual space in which contrasting elements are understood and interpreted. When applied to adverbial dependent units of contrast, this domain becomes particularly important for understanding how meaning is constructed. Adverbial dependent units of contrast typically begin with asymmetry markers such as *although*, *though*, *whereas*, *while*, and *however*. Each marker highlights a unique facet within the domain of contrast, reflecting specific patterns of human experience. *Although* signals a strong, emphatic, and clear contrast, preparing the listener for a direct contradiction. *Though* conveys a softer, more nuanced opposition, often reflecting a casual or subtle twist. *Whereas* conveys explicit and categorical contrast, clearly distinguishing between two opposing ideas. *While* suggests a gentler form of opposition, potentially implying simultaneity or simply a difference in approach or method. *However* functions as a turning point in discourse, offering an emphatic concession that leads the listener to reevaluate expectations; no matter the effort, the result does not change.

> Although she was tired, she continued working.
>
> Though it was expensive, I enjoyed the meal.
>
> Paul likes action films, whereas Lennie likes detective stories.
>
> Albert is traveling by plane, while Andrew is traveling by train.
>
> However hard she tried, she could not control her feelings.

The sentences above use asymmetry markers to demonstrate contrast, each with its own unique context and nuance. *Although* and *though* both prompt the listener to create a mental space where one proposition, for example, tiredness or expense, would typically hinder or reduce the other, but does not. *Although* signals a stronger, formal contrast, while *though* offers a softer, conversational opposition, often at sentence end. Adding *even* to *though*, but not to *although*, intensifies the concession, as in *She wore a coat, even though it was a very hot day*. *Whereas* and *while* both contrast ideas, but they structure the opposition differently. *Whereas* marks a categorical opposition, for example, Paul versus Lennie, *while* signals a gentler contrast. Cognitively, *while* blends actions or states, processing them in parallel rather than in opposition, for example, Albert's versus Andrew's travel methods. *However* signals a strong concession at the discourse level, prompting a reassessment of expectations and emphasizing that effort does not change the outcome. It acts as a pivot, redirecting the conceptual flow and highlighting the persistence of results despite opposing conditions.

12.3.2.4 The Domain of Purpose

The domain of purpose refers to the conceptual space in which an action or event is understood in relation to its intended outcome or goal. When applied to adverbial dependent units of purpose, this domain becomes a mental framework that connects means to ends, showing how one event is cognitively construed as serving or enabling another. These units are often introduced by asymmetry markers such as *so that*, *in order that*, *so as to*, *in order to*, and *lest* (meaning *so as not to*), leading into the purpose stated in the dependent unit. The domain is articulated through facets, each signaled by a marker. *So that* expresses purpose or intended result. *In order that* is more formal and emphasizes deliberate intention. *So as to* evokes a more abstract or stylistic connection between means and ends. *In order to* highlights a clear and deliberate link between action and intended outcome. *Lest* expresses purpose in terms of prevention. These units do not just describe events; they encode intentionality. The listener constructs a mental model where the first event is motivated by the second. Unlike causal dependent units that are back-looking, purpose dependent units are forward-looking, imagining a desired future state.

They trained hard so that they could win the match.

He saved money in order that he could buy a new laptop.

He exercised regularly so as to stay fit.

She woke up early in order to catch the first train.

He put on warm clothes lest he should catch a chill.

In the sentences above, the conceptual asymmetry markers activate the domain of purpose, each signaling a distinct nuance. *So that* introduces a goal-oriented mental space, linking the autonomous unit representing the cause to the dependent unit representing its expected result. This structure, typical of spoken language, highlights practical intent. *In order that* serves a similar purpose but with a more formal and intentional tone. It suggests a more structured and explicit connection between means and ends, often found in academic or written contexts. Cognitively, it emphasizes the deliberate planning behind the action. *So as to* introduces a slightly more abstract or stylistic connection, often used for rhetorical effect. *In order to* is more direct and formal, emphasizing a clear procedural link between action and goal. *Lest* introduces a negative purpose, aiming to prevent an undesirable outcome. It triggers a preventive conceptual space, where the action is driven by the avoidance of a potential threat. The use of *should* as the only compatible modal auxiliary reinforces the hypothetical and precautionary nature of the unit.

12.3.2.5 The Domain of Condition

The domain of condition is a conceptual space where one situation depends on another, forming a hypothetical link. Through adverbial dependent units, it lets speakers explore alternatives and interpret cause, possibility, and contingency. The dependent unit establishes the condition, while the autonomous unit reveals the outcome. The dependent units begin with asymmetry markers such as *if*, *even if*, *unless*, *whether or not*, *in case*, *in the event that*, *only if*, *otherwise*, and *or else*. The domain consists of several conceptual facets, each activated by a specific marker. *If* introduces a neutral, hypothetical condition. *Even if* adds concession, where the outcome holds regardless of the condition. *Unless* marks a negative condition, where the default outcome holds unless blocked. *Whether or not* makes the condition irrelevant, leaving the outcome unchanged. *In case* signals precaution, with the action anticipating a possible event. *In the event* is a formal version of *in case*, projecting a specific contingency. *Only if* restricts outcome to occur exclusively when condition is met. *Otherwise* presents the consequence if the condition is not met. *Or else* is similar to *otherwise*, but more emphatic or threatening.

If it rains, we will stay indoors.

We will go hiking even if it rains.

We will go to the park unless it rains.

Whether or not it rains, the event will be held outdoors.

Take an umbrella in case it rains.

In the event that it rains, the picnic will be moved indoors.

The picnic will be canceled only if it rains.

You'd better hurry up, otherwise you'll miss your flight.

We must be there by six, or else we will miss the beginning.

The asymmetry markers represent the domain of condition, each bringing its own unique sense of conditionality. *If* sets up a neutral condition, inviting the listener to envision a possible scenario where the outcome depends on whether the condition is met. *Even if* marks a concessive condition where the outcome holds despite the premise. *Unless* marks a negative condition; the outcome holds unless stopped. *Whether or not* signals irrelevance; the outcome remains the same regardless of external factors. *In case* signals precaution, prompting action for a possible event. *In the event that* presents a formal contingency, anticipating a clear, specific scenario. *In case* conveys informal precaution for possible events, while *in the event that* marks a formal contingency for a specific scenario. *Only if* marks a strict condition, limiting the outcome to that case alone. *Otherwise* often conveys a serious or cautionary tone. Finally, *or else* introduces a more emphatic or urgent consequence, sometimes with an implied threat or ultimatum.

12.3.2.6 The Domain of Result

The domain of result is a mental structure where outcomes are linked to their causes. It is like the backdrop that makes sense of an action by showing the effect it produces. In resultative constructions, the autonomous unit presents the cause, while the dependent unit gives its result, forming a causal sequence. In English, this domain is expressed through asymmetry markers like *so ... that* and *such ... that*, which emphasize the outcome and deepen its context. In Cognitive Grammar, the difference between these two markers lies in how each profiles intensity and structures mental imagery. *So ... that* shows how strong a quality or action is, drawing attention to an adjective or adverb. In the mind, it creates a sense of rising intensity that eventually passes a limit, which then brings about the result. *Such ... that* highlights the quality of a noun or event, drawing attention to a noun phrase. In the mind, it creates an image of categorization, placing the thing in a group of striking examples that naturally lead to a specific result.

I was so tired that I fell asleep immediately.

She is such a talented musician that she won several awards.

Both markers *so ... that* and *such ... that* evoke the domain of result, but differ in what is being intensified: one stresses degree, the other type. *So ... that* is typically paired with an adjective or adverb, foregrounding the scalar intensity of a state or action. For instance, in the sentence, the word *so* amplifies the adjective *tired*, and the dependent unit *that I fell asleep immediately* profiles the resulting event as a natural consequence of that heightened state. This sentence shows tiredness building until it passes a limit, making sleep unavoidable. In contrast, *such ... that* is paired with a noun phrase, emphasizing the type of an entity. In the sentence, the phrase *such a talented musician* places the subject in a group of people whose talent is strong enough to lead to notable outcomes. The dependent part *that she won several awards* then shows the result as evidence of that categorization. The mental picture here involves judging the person's abilities and imagining the effects those abilities can bring.

12.3.3 *Conceptualization*

Conceptualization is a mental skill that allows speakers to communicate in various ways and from different viewpoints. The way we interpret a linguistic expression is just as important as the actual meaning behind it. **Conceptual content** refers to the propositional meaning or the essential characteristics of a situation. On the other hand, **construal** is about how a speaker understands and conveys the meaning of that expression. The way a situation is construed directly impacts the choice of adverbial asymmetry markers. Even if two adverbial asymmetry markers convey the same content, their interpretations can differ, leading to variations in meaning. It turns out that even when these asymmetry markers appear to be synonyms, a closer examination reveals they are not exactly the same. The choice between them can subtly shift the meaning and tone of a complex sentence, influencing how the relationships within it are understood. This nuanced meaning arises from construal, where the speaker's perspective, shaped by their intentions or the context of the conversation, plays a crucial role.

To elucidate the semantic distinctions between competing adverbial markers, we will examine several illustrative examples.

Since I was late, I missed the lecture.

Because I was late, I missed the lecture.

Both expressions show the same basic idea: the speaker's lateness caused the missed lecture. Yet in Cognitive Grammar, the marker chosen slightly changes how that causal link is framed, shaping the way the listener mentally connects the two events. In the first sentence, *since* introduces a reason that is either assumed to be known or given as background. It opens a shared mental space, showing that the cause *lateness* is already part of the context or can be inferred from prior knowledge. The phrase works more as a contextual anchor than the main focus, helping the listener place the cause within a wider conceptual frame. In contrast, the second sentence uses *because*, which makes the causal link more explicit and specific. It leads the listener to build a clear path from the starting event *being late* to the result *missing the lecture*. Here, the cause is not taken for granted but directly stated, guiding the listener to picture the sequence with clarity and emphasis. In summary, *since* hints at a given cause, while *because* asserts it directly and clearly.

We must be there by six, otherwise we will miss the beginning.

We must be there by six, or else we will miss the beginning.

Both expressions communicate the same core proposition: arriving by six o'clock is necessary to avoid missing the start. Their difference lies in tone and construal. The marker *otherwise* conveys a softer, implied warning. It suggests that if the expected action is not taken, a negative outcome will naturally follow. In *arrive by six, otherwise you'll miss the start*, the missing is presented as the default negative result, something that happens unless the condition is met. In contrast, *or else* conveys a stronger, explicit warning. It does not merely imply the consequence; it asserts it directly, often with a sharper or even threatening emphasis. In *arrive by six, or else you'll miss the start*, the missing is stated outright, leaving no room for inference and pressing the urgency more forcefully. The key distinction between the markers is that *otherwise* carries a softer tone, implying a default consequence, while *or else* carries a stronger tone, asserting the consequence explicitly.

12.4 Linguistic Aspects

A linguistic aspect pertains to the structural elements and rules that govern the arrangement of words, phrases, and clauses in sentences. It delves into the details of sentence formation, encompassing aspects such as **punctuation**, **reduction**, and **parallelism**. These syntactic elements are crucial in ensuring that our sentences are clear, cohesive, and grammatically correct, thereby enhancing effective communication. **Punctuation** aids in clarifying meaning and delineating different parts of our writing. **Reduction** involves eliminating unnecessary elements to streamline our communication. **Parallelism** entails using similar grammatical structures for related ideas, fostering balance, rhythm, and clarity in both written and spoken language. Understanding these linguistic aspects is essential as they facilitate clear, coherent, and efficient communication, aligning seamlessly with the way our minds naturally process information.

12.4.1 *Punctuation*

Punctuation consists of signs that shape meaning in text, break up sentences and their parts, clarify our intent, and indicate where to pause or change tone. These punctuation signs serve as visual cues that help organize the information, breaking down the text into digestible pieces. This makes reading and understanding much smoother. In Cognitive Grammar, punctuation does more than just signal pauses or the end of a sentence; it is crucial for how we interpret and make sense of written language. It guides readers through the structure of the information, slicing the discourse into manageable chunks, which helps keep the flow of ideas clear. When used correctly, punctuation lightens the cognitive load by clearly showing how different parts of a sentence relate to one another, making it easier to process and remember what we read. It can also highlight specific parts of a sentence, giving the message more punch, and it is especially helpful in clarifying meaning in more complex sentences. At this point, there are two key guidelines to consider.

- When an adverbial dependent unit comes before the autonomous unit, it is usually followed by a comma.

  Although it was raining, we went for a walk.

  If you save money, you can buy a new home.

- When an adverbial dependent unit follows the autonomous unit, a comma is often unnecessary.

  We went for a walk although it was raining.

  You can buy a new home if you save money.

Both sentences convey the same basic idea, yet they differ in cognitive impact and processing dynamics. In Cognitive Grammar, meaning arises from how we mentally construe events. Placing the adverbial dependent unit at the beginning invites the listener or reader to process a contrast or condition before encountering the main action. This requires slightly more cognitive effort upfront, as the brain must retain the dependent unit and anticipate its connection to the autonomous unit. However, this structure aids comprehension by establishing context early, allowing the main event to be interpreted through a prepared conceptual lens. In contrast, placing the adverbial dependent unit at the end delivers the main action first, which is easier to process initially. The contrast or condition follow, reframing the action with added nuance or surprise. This structure is cognitively lighter at the outset but demands reinterpretation once the contrast or condition is introduced. In essence, the initial structure prioritizes context and logical framing, while the final structure emphasizes immediacy and narrative flow.

12.4.2 Reduction

Reduction involves trimming a unit by omitting certain words while preserving its core meaning. This technique is commonly used to make sentences more concise and improve their flow. In Cognitive Grammar, reduction is seen as a natural outcome of language use, reflecting how speakers conceptualize meaning, or how they speak and write in everyday life. It simplifies communication by eliminating elements that are implied by context, aligning with the way our brains process language efficiently and economically. By removing unnecessary components, reduction lowers cognitive load, making it easier to process and retain information. Reduced forms signal that the omitted content is already activated or easily inferred in the listener's mind. This shift in focus highlights what is most salient, allowing speakers to emphasize key concepts while trimming less relevant material. Over time, frequent reductions become entrenched in grammar through repeated exposure and cognitive habituation. In short, reduction is not a sign of laziness; it is a smart cognitive strategy for streamlining communication while preserving meaning. In the examples below, brackets indicate what is omitted but still understood.

Reduction in adjectival dependent units:
This involves omitting the relative pronoun (who, that, which) and the verb *to be* (is, was), as seen in the examples below:

Ann is the woman [who is] responsible for the error.

The two books [that are] on the shelf are his sister's.

The house [which was] built in 1900 is still standing.

In each case, the dependent unit is streamlined without losing its core meaning. This kind of reduction enhances sentence fluency and readability by eliminating implied elements. From a Cognitive Grammar standpoint, these reductions reflect how speakers mentally construe information, prioritizing salient features and omitting what is already activated or inferable in the listener's conceptual frame. By trimming redundant linguistic material, reduction lowers cognitive load, allowing the brain to process and retain key information more efficiently. It also shifts attention to the most relevant conceptual content such as the noun being modified, while backgrounding grammatical scaffolding. Over time, these reduced forms become entrenched in usage through repeated exposure and cognitive habituation, reinforcing their role in efficient communication.

Reduction in adverbial dependent units:
This involves omitting the subject and auxiliary verb, making the sentence more concise while retaining the essential meaning, as seen in the examples below.

While [I was] sitting in class, I fell asleep.

If [it is] possible, send me the file tonight.

When [he was] a youth, he did rock climbing.

Though [he was] tired, the runner finished the race.

Each example simplifies the dependent unit while maintaining its essential meaning. This kind of reduction is a natural tendency in language to streamline expression, especially when the omitted elements can be easily inferred from context. From a Cognitive Grammar standpoint, these reductions reflect how we mentally construe events: speakers emphasize the most important conceptual content while backgrounding information that is predictable or already known. By leaving out redundant elements, reduction lowers cognitive load, allowing listeners to process the sentence more efficiently. It also improves fluency and rhythm, especially in spoken discourse, where brevity and clarity are valued. Ultimately, reducing adverbial dependent units is not just a grammatical shortcut; it is a cognitive strategy that aligns with how we prioritize, interpret, and remember information during interpersonal communication.

Reduction in comparative structures:
This involves omitting the verb in the comparative structure, which is implied rather than explicitly stated, as seen in the examples below.

Nobody knows it better than I [do].	(unequal comparison)
She is taller than I [am].	(unequal comparison)
She is as smart as he [is].	(equal comparison)
I earn as much as you [do].	(equal comparison)
She sings as well as he [does].	(equal comparison)

Each structure is simplified while preserving its essential meaning. This kind of reduction reflects a natural cognitive strategy: when the meaning is clear and predictable, speakers omit redundant elements to streamline communication. From a Cognitive Grammar standpoint, this reduction aligns with how we mentally construe comparisons. The listener or reader automatically activates the missing verb based on context and prior knowledge, minimizing cognitive effort. By omitting what is already inferable, the speaker shifts focus to the comparative relationship itself, height, intelligence, earnings, or performance, rather than the grammatical scaffolding around it. This not only enhances fluency but also reinforces the salience of the comparison, making the sentence more efficient and easier to process. Over time, such reduced forms become entrenched in usage, reflecting the cognitive economy that underlies everyday language.

12.4.3 *Parallelism*

Parallelism involves using the same grammatical structure for similar elements, whether within a single sentence or across multiple sentences. When you include several dependent units, maintaining a parallel structure can significantly improve readability and coherence. It contributes to a balanced and harmonious flow in your writing. Cognitive Grammar views parallel structure as a crucial aspect of how we process and understand language. By establishing predictable patterns, parallel structures help our brains process information more efficiently, reducing cognitive load and improving both understanding and memory retention. Using similar structures not only highlights the connections between ideas but also reinforces one's message. They assist in organizing information logically, making it easier to comprehend. Additionally, the repetition of these structures enables quicker comprehension and better retention. These elements are essential for effective communication, aligning perfectly with the natural workings of our minds.

While he was running and she was walking, they enjoyed the fresh air.

Because she was tired and because he was hungry, they went home.

If you study hard and if you practice regularly, you will succeed.

In these examples, the adverbial dependent units have a similar grammatical structure. By using parallelism in these units, you can greatly boost the readability and flow of your writing. This not only makes it more engaging but also easier for readers to understand. From a Cognitive Grammar standpoint, parallelism reflects how our minds prefer symmetry and predictability in language. Repeating similar syntactic patterns helps the brain process information more efficiently by reducing the need to reanalyze each clause individually. It creates a rhythm that supports comprehension and retention, especially in spoken or narrative contexts. Parallel structures also evenly guide attention across ideas, allowing each clause to carry equal conceptual weight. This balance reinforces coherence and makes the relationships between actions or conditions more transparent. In short, parallelism is not just stylistic polish; it is a cognitively grounded strategy that enhances clarity, fluency, and impact, making ideas easier to process and more memorable.

Summary

In this chapter, I have explored **conceptual asymmetry**, the unequal prominence of elements in a cognitive structure. The structure is made up of two units. An autonomous unit, which provides the main conceptual content, and a dependent unit, which modifies, specifies, or relates to the autonomous unit. Autonomous units carry meaning independently, while dependent units rely on them to form complete expressions. They are connected by a marker of conceptual symmetry. Dependent units undergo three cognitive processes. In categorization, dependent units fall into three main types, each with its own role. Nominal dependent units can take the place of individual nouns in a sentence, no matter how long they are. Adjectival dependent units give us more details about a noun, while adverbial dependent units add depth and detail to the autonomous unit. In configuration, dependent units evoke six different domains: time, reason, contrast, purpose, condition, and result. In conceptualization, although two asymmetry markers may express the same content, their interpretations can vary, producing different meanings.

Looking at their structure, dependent units can be divided into six categories: time, reason, contrast, purpose, condition, and result, each defined by the specific information it provides. The choice to use an adverbial dependent unit often reflects how we perceive a situation. Additionally, dependent units can go through various syntactic processes. **Punctuation** helps ideas flow smoothly. It organizes sentences, signals breaks, and clarifies meaning, making writing smoother and more engaging. **Reduction** makes communication easier by leaving out elements that are understood from context. It avoids redundancy, keeps language concise, and allows readers to grasp the intended meaning without unnecessary clutter. **Parallelism** makes reading smoother. It adds rhythm and balance, helping ideas flow and making them easier to grasp. In Cognitive Grammar, these are not just surface features; they are strategies of conceptual organization that shape how language is processed, understood, and remembered.

Exercises

1. Identify the type of dependent unit used in the following sentences: nominal, adjectival, or adverbial.

1. I know the girl who won the prize.
2. Before I die, I want to see the Alps.
3. She can take whatever she wants.
4. I will not go until my friend arrives.
5. It all depends on whether or not she has the time.

2. Punctuation reflects a difference in meaning. This can be illustrated by analyzing the examples given below.

1. My neighbor who is a talented musician is helpful.
2. My neighbor, who is a talented musician, is helpful.

3. Fill in the blanks with an appropriate marker of conceptual asymmetry to highlight sentence meaning.

1. ___________ you should cheat me hurts me.
2. ___________ he came here is still unknown.
3. ___________ she said was completely wrong.
4. I often wonder ___________ he is getting on.
5. I wasn't certain ___________ house I was in.

4. Combine the following conceptually autonomous units using the asymmetry markers given in brackets.

1. She grew older. She gained in confidence. (as)
2. I waited at the bus stop. I saw him. (while)

3. She left a message. She went. (before)
4. I explained carefully. She didn't understand. (however)
5. He wore headphones. He didn't want to disturb anyone. (lest)
6. You won't be paid. You do not have leave of absence. (unless)
7. He did daily exercises. He wanted to lose weight. (in order)
8. I will see her. I will give her the letter. (as soon as)
9. He finished his training. He took a shower. (after)
10. I couldn't play the piano. I took lessons for years. (although)

5. The following sentences share the same content but use different asymmetry markers. How do they differ?

1. I was surprised when I opened the parcel.
   I was surprised as I opened the parcel.
2. As it was rare, it was expensive.
   Since it was rare, it was expensive.
3. It was so beautiful that we decided to go for a picnic.
   It was such a beautiful day that we decided to go for a picnic.
4. He likes classical music, whereas his sister likes rap music.
   He likes classical music, while his sister likes rap music.
5. As soon as the teacher entered the classroom, the students became quiet.
   When the teacher entered the classroom, the students became quiet.

6. The asymmetry marker *since* serves temporal, causal, and conditional functions. Identify each.

1. Since her graduation, she has been working here.
2. Since it was raining, they decided to stay indoors.
3. Since you have finished your work, you can leave.
4. Since the weather is nice, let's go for a short walk.
5. Since he is interested, he should attend the seminar?

7. The asymmetry marker *while* can function in temporal, causal, or conditional ways. Identify each use.

1. While the child played outside, the mother prepared lunch.
2. While he enjoys hiking, she prefers swimming.
3. While it was raining, they decided to go for a walk.
4. While he worked on his project, he listened to music.
5. While she was tired, she continued to work on her assignment.

8. The marker *as* serves temporal, causal, and comparative functions in dependent units. Identify each.

1. She smiled as she walked into the room.
2. He stayed home as he was feeling unwell.
3. She is as intelligent as her brother.
4. She sang as she cleaned the house.
5. He left early as he had an appointment.

9. Complete the sentences with the correct -ever word: *whatever, whenever, wherever, whoever, or whichever.*

1 _________ they are, they are not welcomed here.
2. You can choose _________ book you like from the library.
3. _________ you need assistance, just let me know.
4. _________ you go, I will definitely follow you.
5. She can wear _________ she wants to the party.

10. Select the correct option to complete each sentence, choosing the word or phrase that best fits the context.

1. _________ you finish your homework, you can watch TV.
   (a) Although (b) Before (c) Even if (d) After
2. He couldn't attend the meeting _________ he was feeling unwell.
   (a) although (b) because (c) whenever (d) so that
3. _________ spring arrives, we have to be prepared for more snow.
   (a) Because (b) Although (c) Until (d) Now that
4. _________ the alarm goes off, I hit the snooze button.
   (a) Now that (b) Because (c) Before (d) As soon as
5. You won't get better _________ you practice regularly.
   (a) unless (b) if (c) because (d) as

Conclusions

As we conclude our exploration of Cognitive Grammar, it is important to review the key principles that have guided our journey. Cognitive Grammar stands out with its unique features that differentiate it from other grammatical approaches, offering a fresh perspective on how language functions and how meaning is constructed. From our findings, we can draw both general and specific conclusions. General conclusions establish a strong knowledge base, emphasizing the fundamental assumptions that form the basis of cognitive analysis. These insights are applicable in various contexts, providing us with a broad understanding of language in use. Specific conclusions delve into detailed examinations of specific linguistic phenomena. These insights are more focused, illuminating the nuances of language. Together, these conclusions form a complex mosaic that demonstrates the deep connection between language and cognition. While general conclusions help us comprehend the overarching patterns of language usage, specific conclusions allow us to delve into the subtleties and intricacies of individual linguistic elements.

General Conclusions

Cognitive Grammar reshapes how we think about language by highlighting the inseparable link between form and meaning. It moves beyond traditional views that treat grammar as isolated rules, emphasizing instead the dynamic, meaningful nature of linguistic structure as rooted in human cognition. This perspective opens the door to several fundamental insights that deepen our understanding of how language functions as a symbolic system reflecting mental processes and experiences. The general conclusions of Cognitive Grammar encompass both grammatical and semantic insights, highlighting how these two aspects are deeply interconnected within the symbolic system of language.

Grammatical Insights

In Cognitive Grammar, grammar is not merely a set of abstract rules; rather, it is a meaningful, symbolic system deeply intertwined with human cognition. Grammar is not autonomous from meaning; it is inherently meaningful. It consists of symbolic units: pairings of semantic structures (meanings) with phonological structures (sounds or forms). These units range from morphemes and words to full sentences and texts; all regarded as symbolic constructions. Grammatical structure is seen as a reflection of semantic structure, with grammatical forms mirroring the mental organization of human experiences. The following conclusions highlight the essential grammatical insights.

- Symbolic categories, word classes in grammar, are defined based on their conceptual characteristics, highlighting the importance of meaning in this process. This cognitive approach contrasts with formal grammar models, which classify word classes based on their distribution, focusing instead on structural elements such as where words fit in sentences and which combinations are allowed.
- Grammar and language are deeply intertwined into our cognitive processes; they are not isolated functions in the brain. Instead, grammar is connected to other cognitive abilities, reflecting how we perceive, understand, and engage with the world around us. This challenges the idea of formal grammar models that suggest grammar can exist independently, treating it as a self-sufficient set of rules.
- Actual language use is fundamental to a usage-based perspective on grammar, where language structure and meaning emerge from cognitive processes and patterns of use, showing language's dynamic adaptability. This viewpoint sharply contrasts with formal grammar models, which often treat language as a separate system of abstract rules and structures, disconnected from context and practice.
- Grammar is adaptable and shaped by the context in which it is used. The fluid nature of language highlights how context plays a role in shaping both its structure and meaning. In this respect, Cognitive Grammar moves away from the strict, unyielding rules that formal grammar models impose on language structure, which often do not allow for much variation or context-driven interpretation.
- Grammar, semantics, and lexicon are all intertwined, making it impossible to fully grasp them in isolation. To truly understand

language, we need to appreciate the seamless interaction between these components. This stands in opposition to formal grammar models that treat these elements as separate processes, emphasizing the independence of syntactic rules from meaning and context.

- Symbolic structures combine into larger units when their conceptual content aligns in a coherent way. Integration is explained through a range of cognitive mechanisms, driven by meaning and processes of conceptual coherence. This stands in contrast to formal grammar models, which treat integration as governed by purely formal rules, detached from underlying cognitive mechanisms.
- Surface structure is the locus of meaning, where the form and conceptual content of linguistic units are directly linked. There is no hidden structure behind expressions; they are viewed as direct and transparent representations of meaning. This goes against formal grammar models, which usually consider grammatical structures as originating from deeper layers and shaped by transformational rules.
- Schemas function as mental templates that support language production and comprehension, drawing on patterns of usage, prior experience, and cognitive processes. These flexible schemas adapt to different contexts and communicative needs. This presents a challenge to formal grammar models, which rely on strict rules, prioritizing syntax while overlooking usage patterns and communicative context.

Semantic Insights

In Cognitive Grammar, meaning holds a central and foundational role; it is not an accessory to grammar but its very essence. Meaning is viewed as the mental representation or conceptualization that a speaker associates with a linguistic expression. It is not just about reference to external objects, but how we mentally construe and engage with experiences. Meaning is not fixed; it evolves through language use. Meaning is shaped by construal, which is not arbitrary but grounded in how speakers conceptualize their experiences. The following conclusions highlight the key semantic insights.

- Meaning is subjective. It relies on the way speakers conceptualize situations through diverse perspectives. This highlights how meaning in language depends on individual cognition, context, and interpretation. It challenges formal grammar models that focus solely on objective semantics tied to reference and truth conditions, treating meaning as fixed by how linguistic expressions match the world outside language.

- Meaning is encyclopedic. It draws from our extensive knowledge accessed through language. Meaning is actively created through our cognitive connections and the vast network of cultural, experiential, and world knowledge we bring to interpretation. This contrasts sharply with formal grammar models, which view meaning as fixed and unchanging, determined solely by the structure of sentences.
- Meaning is deeply rooted in embodied cognition. It is shaped by our interactions with the world, and grounded in lived experience that ties language to bodily and environmental engagement. This perspective highlights the fundamental connection between language and the lived realities that shape it. This viewpoint challenges formal grammar models that treat meaning as detached from real-life contexts.
- Meaning comes from cognition. It emerges from the workings of our brains. Meaning is not simply encoded in sentences; it is actively created by the mind through cognitive processes such as categorization, configuration, and conceptualization. This view is a departure from formal grammar models, which believe meaning comes from rules, treated as a fixed property of sentence structure.
- Meaning pervades all aspects of grammar. It is inherently present in every form of language. Each form carries its own meaning and even the smallest structures contribute to how ideas are conceptualized and understood. This stands in stark contrast to formal grammar models, which often treat certain forms as empty or meaningless, focusing solely on their structural roles, while neglecting their semantic dimensions.
- Lexical and grammatical elements are inherently polysemous. These elements often carry multiple related senses. These senses create categories that include both prototypes (the most typical examples) and peripheral elements (the less common ones). This diverges from formal grammar models, which strives for monosemy or fixed meaning, where each form is assumed to have a single, stable interpretation.
- Meaning resides in cognitive domains. These are conceptual structures in which language forms gather, each showcasing a unique facet. These forms both influence and are influenced by one another. This is different from formal grammar models, which treat forms in isolation, analyzing them as abstract units governed by syntactic rules rather than as meaningful elements connected to experience.
- Meaning arises from construal. It refers to how speakers construe or mentally frame a situation. It is not something set in stone; rather, it shifts depending on the perspectives of language users. This view departs radically from formal grammar models, which focus on

reference, entailment, and truth conditions. Each sentence has a fixed interpretation determined by rules of syntax and logical form.

Specific Conclusions

In Cognitive Grammar, **symbolic categories**, word classes in grammar, fall into two basic types: **things** and **relations**. Symbolic categories are distinguished by the conceptual content they symbolize rather than by rigid syntactic criteria, being defined more by the meanings they profile than by strict formal rules. **Things** are represented by nouns and noun phrases. **Relations** are divided into two types: atemporal and temporal. **Atemporal relations** comprise two subtypes. **Simple atemporal relations** are expressed by adjectives, adverbs, and prepositions, along with their phrases. **Complex atemporal relations** are expressed by gerunds, present participles, and infinitives. **Temporal relations** also comprise two subtypes. **Simple temporal relations** are expressed by verbs, verb phrases, and simple sentences. **Complex temporal relations** are expressed by compound sentences, correlative sentences, and subordinate sentences.

Below is a survey that provides detailed insights into each of the symbolic categories.

Things

Things are symbolic categories that profile entities, objects, or concepts. They refer to entities that can be conceived as objects or substances, whether they are concrete like a *tree* or a *house*, or abstract like *justice* or *freedom*. As independent conceptual entities, things retain their identity across space and time, regardless of the relationships they are involved in. They play the role of the building blocks of meaning, serving as the participants that relations connect. Their significance lies in how they anchor relations in a conceptual scene, helping us organize events and experiences and bring stability to our understanding of the world. Without nouns to profile things, relations lack substance to connect.

Things can be nouns or noun phrases, identifying participants in mental representations of the world.

Entity → noun

An entity is conceptualized as a thing, and a noun functions as the linguistic form that represents it. A noun is a symbolic structure that profiles a thing, a conceptual entity belonging to a specific category within a domain. For instance, the word *apple* represents a thing that belongs to the domain of fruits. Nouns do more than just label; they connect to our mental images of people, animals, objects, places, or ideas. Take the sentence *The sofa is new*. Here, the word *sofa* acts as a symbolic unit, representing not just a physical object but also a concept we hold in our minds.

Nominal expression → noun phrase

A nominal expression is understood as a conceptual thing, while a noun phrase serves as its linguistic representation. A noun phrase is a symbolic structure that signifies a specific instance of a thing in a given context. It consists of a noun along with any words that modify it. A noun phrase is more than just a collection of words; it provides additional information about the noun. For example, in *The careful driver avoided the accident*, the phrase *the careful driver* is a noun phrase where *driver* is the noun, modified by the determiner *the* and the adjective *careful*.

Relations

Unlike **things**, which are conceptualized as entities, relations focus on the connections and interactions between those entities. While things highlight isolated individuals, relations emphasize how these entities are conceptually interrelated. They do not exist independently; instead, they come to life through the connections they establish. Relations are not merely syntactic labels but cognitive structures that reflect how we mentally organize events: one entity (the trajector) is profiled against another (the landmark) through a relational process. For example, in *The boy kicked the ball*, *the boy* is the trajector (agent), *the ball* the landmark (patient), and the verb *kick* establishes the connection between them.

Relations can be either atemporal or temporal, with each category further divided into simple and complex relations.

Atemporal Relations

Atemporal relations are linguistic structures that express states, qualities, or abstract relations without reference to time. They are schematic characterizations of states, not processes. They capture how an entity is described and how one entity relates to another, without implying temporal progression. They show how language encodes nontemporal meaning. They illustrate the conceptual grounding of grammar: grammar reflects how humans conceptualize reality, not just how words are mechanically combined.

Atemporal relations can be either **simple** or **complex** depending on the number of elements involved.

Simple Atemporal Relations

Simple atemporal relations involve a single connection between entities that is not tied to any sense of time, making them static. This makes them essential for understanding how entities relate to each other in a fixed, unchanging way. They provide the cognitive basis for describing stable connections, distinct from relations that involve change or temporal progression. For example, in *The cup is on the table*, the *cup* is the trajector (the figure being profiled), while the *table* is the landmark (the background entity against which the cup is understood). The preposition *on* links them, describing a fixed spatial relation.

Representatives of simple atemporal relations are attributive predication (adjectives), peripheral predications (adverbs), and relational predications (prepositions).

Attributive predication → adjective

Conceptually, an attributive predication is a simple atemporal relation; linguistically, it is realized through an adjective. It functions as a symbolic unit that either highlights an inherent property of a noun or shapes the way a noun is conceptually construed. Structurally, adjectives modify nouns in two positions: **attributive**, as in *the beautiful sunset*, and **predicative**, as in *the sunset is beautiful*. In both cases, the adjective *beautiful* conveys the aesthetic property of the noun *sunset*, which serves as the trajectory, the main subject being characterized. Semantically, adjectives can be descriptive, as in *an honest dealer*; evaluative, as in *an impressive performance*; or relational, as in *a medical test*.

Adjectival expression → adjective phrase

An adjectival expression profiles a specific instance of a simple atemporal relation within a given context, with the adjective phrase functioning as the linguistic structure that represents it. As a symbolic unit, it elaborates or intensifies how a noun is conceptually construed by profiling a property or quality through a relational structure. For example, in *The party was too noisy*, the modifier *too* refines the adjective *noisy*, and the entire adjective phrase functions as a subject complement describing the head noun *party*. In *I found the party too noisy*, the same phrase operates as an object complement. Overall, an adjective phrase enriches a noun's description, adding nuance and clarifying its quality or property.

Peripheral predication → adverb

A peripheral predication designates a simple atemporal relation, and the adverb provides the linguistic form that represents it. In this structure, the adverb modifies the verb, which serves as the trajectory, the primary entity being affected. As a symbolic unit, the adverb highlights the specific quality of a verb, an adjective, or another adverb. For example, in *She sings beautifully*, the adverb *beautifully* modifies the verb *sings*, connecting the concept of beauty to the action of singing in our mental representation. Adverbs can express manner as in *She speaks slowly*, frequency as in *She always arrives late*, degree as in *The movie was slightly exciting*, time as in *We must leave now*, and place as in *They are playing outdoors in the garden*.

Adverbial expression → adverb phrase

An adverbial expression signifies a specific instance of a simple atemporal relation within a given context, with the adverb phrase serving as its linguistic realization. As a symbolic unit, the adverb phrase elaborates how a verb, adjective, or even another adverb is conceptually construed by ascribing a particular quality. For example, in the sentence *She whispered very quietly*, the intensifier *very* enhances the concept of *quietly* in our mental representation. Together, they form an adverb phrase that modifies *whisper* by specifying how the action was performed. Adverb phrases enrich our mental construal of events by either elaborating the action with extra detail or refining it with greater precision.

Relational predication → preposition

A relational predication profiles a simple atemporal relation, while the preposition functions as its formal linguistic representation. It is a symbolic unit that signifies a spatial and temporal relationship between two elements in a conceptual structure, helping to locate objects and events in space and time. A preposition profiles a trajector-landmark relation, where one entity, the trajector, is situated with respect to another entity, the landmark, in our mental representation. For example, in the sentence *The school is near the park*, the preposition *near* profiles a spatial relationship between the school (the trajector) and the park (the landmark), describing not the entities, but the school's proximity to the park.

Prepositional expression → prepositional phrase

A prepositional expression identifies a specific instance of a simple atemporal relation in context, and the prepositional phrase acts as the structure that encodes it in language. As a grammatical unit, it consists of a preposition and its complement, together indicating how one entity—the trajector—is situated relative to another—the landmark—within a broader cognitive framework. Such phrases enrich event conceptualization by specifying where, when, or under what conditions something occurs. For example, in the sentence *She sat on the chair*, the prepositional phrase *on the chair* locates the action of sitting. The preposition *on* profiles a spatial relation of support between the subject *she* and the object *chair*.

Complex Atemporal Relations

Unlike simple atemporal relations that are basic and involve a single connection between entities, complex atemporal relations are more intricate and involve multiple elements or connections wrapped up in a single expression. Both types are static in nature and do not involve any temporal progression. They detach actions from time and present them as concepts, qualities, or purposes. For example, in *Running is healthy*, *running* acts as a noun, representing an activity in general, not tied to time. It abstracts the activity into a timeless idea. It is treated as a concept, not as something happening now. This abstraction makes it a perfect representative of a complex atemporal relation in grammar.

Representatives of complex atemporal relations are nominalized processes (gerunds), attributive processual predications (participles), and ungrounded schematic processes (infinitives).

Nominalized processual predication→ gerund

A nominalized processual predication profiles a complex atemporal relation, with the gerund operating as its grammatical manifestation. In form, the gerund ends with the suffix *-ing* and functions as a noun, construing an activity as a noun-like entity. In meaning, it conveys two types of construal. In the sentence *She enjoys telling stories*, the gerund indicates immediate reality, depicting an action occurring in the present. In the sentence *She acknowledges making a mistake*, it refers to non-immediate reality, highlighting an event that has already occurred. In both cases, the gerund signifies a timeless concept rather than a specific instance of activity, showing how grammar encodes conceptualizations beyond mere formal rules.

Attributive processual predication → participle

An attributive processual predication profiles a complex atemporal relation and the participle embodies it in linguistic form. It occurs in two types. The present participle (*-ing* form) construes an activity as immediate, ongoing, or dynamic. In *the smiling child*, *smiling* denotes immediate reality, meaning the child is smiling now. It functions as a symbolic unit that conveys the mental conceptualization of the ongoing action. The past participle (*-ed/-en* form) construes an activity as non-immediate, completed, or stative. In *the injured player*, *injured* denotes non-immediate reality, meaning the player has already been injured. It functions as a symbolic unit that conveys the conceptualization of a past event.

Schematic processual predication → infinitive

Conceptually, a schematic processual predication represents a complex atemporal relation; linguistically, it is realized as an infinitive construction. Infinitives occur in three types. The bare infinitive, verb without to, construes an activity as immediate, neutral, or generic. It functions as a symbolic unit that conveys the conceptualization of an action in its abstract or unmarked form. The to-infinitive, verb with to, construes an activity as prospective, potential, or intentional. It serves as a symbolic unit that conveys the mental conceptualization of an action not yet realized. The for-to infinitive consists of a subject + for + to + verb. It highlights an action that is expected, intended, or desired by or for that subject.

Immediate activity → bare infinitive

Conceptually, an immediate activity represents a complex atemporal relation; linguistically, it is realized as a bare infinitive. The bare infinitive is the default stem form of the verb, used without the marker *to*. It presents the verb as a timeless, schematic process, stripped of tense or aspect. As a symbolic unit, it provides an abstract representation of the action, highlighting its immediacy and directness. For example, in *We watched them play*, the bare infinitive *play* indicates an action that is directly perceived, meaning the activity of playing was observed in real time. The sentence illustrates the immediate connection between the observed process and the act of watching, conveying direct and unmediated experience.

Prospective activity → to-infinitive

Conceptually, a prospective activity represents a complex atemporal relation; linguistically, it is realized as a to-infinitive. It acts as a symbolic pairing of form and meaning. Structurally, it begins with the marker *to* and functions as a noun. Semantically, it conveys two construals. In *She hopes to win*, the to-infinitive reflects potential reality, suggesting that the event is not guaranteed to happen. In *He managed to solve the puzzle*, the to-infinitive indicates projected reality, suggesting that the event is nearly certain to happen. In both cases, the to-infinitive signifies a prospective concept rather than a directly experienced process, showing how grammar encodes actions as abstract goals and intentions beyond mere formal rules.

Assigned activity → for-to infinitive

Conceptually, an assigned activity represents a complex atemporal relation; linguistically, it is realized as a for-to infinitive. The preposition *for* frames the subject as the agent of the to-infinitive, explicitly assigning the activity. This construction highlights a goal-oriented relationship in which the conceptually autonomous unit evaluates or sets conditions for the subject's action. The for-to structure conveys two key meanings: potentiality and indirectness. For example, *I am delighted for Sarah to get the award* signals a future event that is anticipated or intended, yet uncertain. In *The teacher arranged for Anna to lead the discussion* suggests indirectness, portraying the subject as somewhat detached and only mildly supportive.

Temporal Relations

Temporal relations are linguistic structures that express processes, events, or actions with explicit reference to time. They are schematic characterizations of dynamic occurrences rather than static states, capturing how an entity acts, changes, or interacts with another over time, always implying temporal progression. They show how language encodes the unfolding of meaning through time and illustrate the conceptual grounding of grammar. Grammar reflects how humans conceptualize reality as dynamic, not merely a mechanical combination of words. By situating events within temporal frames, grammar reveals the cognitive link between time and human experience.

Temporal relations can be either **simple** or **complex** depending on the number of entities and connections involved.

Simple Temporal Relations

Simple temporal relations involve one straightforward process occurring within a specific timeframe. It consists of a single event or action, with one verb and its participants. These relations focus on one process unfolding in time, making them easy to understand. In contrast, complex temporal relations profile more than one process and emphasize the interconnectedness between them. For example, the sentence *The child laughed* portrays a simple temporal relation, profiling a single process, laughing, as it happens over time.

Representatives of simple temporal relations are processes (verbs), verbal expression (verb phrases), and single-grounded processes (simple sentences).

Process → verb

In conceptual terms, a process denotes a simple temporal relation. In linguistic terms, it is structured as a verb. A verb is a symbolic structure that profiles a process, something that evolves through time rather than remaining static. More than a word denoting an action or state, a verb is a symbolic unit that highlights change, activity, and dynamic relations between entities. For example, in the sentence *The phone rang loudly*, the verb *rang* does more than name an action; it profiles a dynamic process, evoking the unfolding sound event in time.

Process → verb phrase

In conceptual terms, a process denotes a simple temporal relation. In linguistic terms, it is structured as a verb phrase, expressed by a verbal expression. A verb phrase is a grammatical unit that denotes an instance of a relation in a given context. It consists of a main verb, along with auxiliary verbs, modifiers, objects, or complements. A verb phrase is not merely a string of words; it constructs a conceptual image that profiles a relation and enriches the verb with added meaning. For example, in *She is walking to school*, the verb phrase *is walking* profiles an ongoing process, one we perceive as unfolding through time and grounded in personal experience.

Single-grounded process → simple sentence

In conceptual terms, a single-grounded process denotes a simple temporal relation. In linguistic terms, it is structured as a simple sentence. A simple sentence is a symbolic unit that typically involves one finite verb and its participants. As such, it offers a minimal conceptualization of a situation, construed either as a process occurring over time or as a stable relation. For example, *She jogs every day* is a simple one-verb sentence that communicates a full idea. It highlights the routine nature of jogging as part of daily life, illustrating the dynamic interaction between linguistic expression and mental representation.

Complex Temporal Relations

Complex temporal relations involve two or more processes, showing how they are connected in time. These relations usually consist of multiple verbs or conceptual units that are linked together. In contrast to simple temporal relations, which focus on just one process, complex temporal relations emphasize how several processes interact, often using markers of conceptual (a)symmetry like *but*, *therefore*, *because*, and so on. For example, *The child laughed because the clown entered* exemplifies a complex temporal relation, where the processes of laughing and entering are linked through the causal marker *because*.

Representatives of complex temporal relations are coordinate processes (coordinated sentences), discourse relations (transitional sentences), paired constructions (correlative sentences), subordinate constructions (subordinate sentences).

Conceptual symmetry → coordinated sentence

Conceptual symmetry conveys a complex temporal relation in thought and is articulated through a coordinated sentence in language. A coordinated sentence profiles a complex temporal relation by integrating two or more conceptually independent units into a single higher-level construction, typically indicated by markers of conceptual symmetry. For example, *He studied hard, but he failed* combines two distinct ideas, with the conceptual symmetry marker *but* highlighting the contrast between effort and outcome. Such coordination goes beyond mere linkage of words; it represents a cognitive integration of the ideas involved.

Conceptual shift → transitional sentence

A conceptual shift conveys a complex temporal relation in thought and is articulated through a transitional sentence in language. A transitional sentence integrates two or more conceptually independent units into a single higher-level construction, typically joined by a discourse connector. For example, *The evidence was weak, therefore the case was dismissed* combines two distinct ideas, with the discourse connector *therefore* highlighting the cause-effect relationship between the weakness of the evidence and the dismissal of the case. Such a transition goes beyond mere linkage of clauses, functioning instead as a meaningful integration of ideas.

Correspondence relation → correlative sentence

A correspondence relation denotes a complex temporal relation and is linguistically realized through a correlative sentence, signaling correlation and balance. A correlative sentence integrates pairs of equivalent elements through paired correlatives. For example, the sentence *Either we stay home, or we go out* consists of two balanced units linked by the correlative *either ... or*, which highlights a choice among alternatives.

This construction suggests that we are weighing different options and anticipating possible outcomes. Such correlation goes beyond simple pairing; it embodies a cognitive alignment of the ideas involved.

Conceptual asymmetry → subordinate sentence

Conceptual asymmetry profiles a complex temporal relation, and is linguistically realized through a subordinate sentence, highlighting dependence and hierarchy. It combines one autonomous unit with at least one dependent unit using a marker of conceptual asymmetry. For example, in *We decided to go for a walk although it was raining*, the dependent unit introduces a contrast: *although* signals the difference between the expected outcome, staying indoors, and the actual action, going for a walk. Such subordination goes beyond simply attaching clauses; it reflects a cognitive layering of ideas, where one is conceptually dependent on the other.

As we conclude our exploration of Cognitive Grammar, it is important to take a moment to appreciate the deep insights we have uncovered. This cognitive approach has really opened up new avenues for understanding language, showing us that it is not just a rigid set of rules but a vibrant, meaningful system that is closely linked to our thoughts and experiences. Grammar is not merely a structure for putting words together; it is a cognitive process that helps us express our ideas and feelings effectively. The way we communicate shapes how we perceive the world, and even influences our identities. This perspective connects language theory with practical use, enhancing our ability to communicate. In the end, Cognitive Grammar highlights the incredible power of language as a tool for thought, reflecting and influencing how we mentally represent our experiences. By adopting this viewpoint, we can discover new layers of understanding and appreciate the complex relationship between our minds and language, ultimately leading to richer and more effective communication in every aspect of our lives.

REFERENCES

Bennet, Phil. (2014). Langacker's cognitive grammar. In Jeannette Littlemore & John R. Taylor (Eds.), *The Bloomsbury companion to cognitive linguistics* (pp. 29–48). Bloomsbury Academic.

Biber, Douglas, Johansson, Stig, Leech, Geoffrey, Conrad, Susan, & Finegan, Edward. (1999). *Longman grammar of spoken and written English*. Longman.

Broccias, Cristiano. (2021). Cognitive grammar. *The Routledge handbook of cognitive linguistics*. Routledge.

Broccias, Cristiano. (2024). Cognitive grammar. *Oxford bibliographies in linguistics*. Oxford University Press.

Carter, Ronald & McCarthy, Michael. (2006). *Cambridge grammar of English: A comprehensive guide*. Cambridge University Press.

Croft, William. (2017). Cognitive grammar and syntax. *The Cambridge handbook of cognitive linguistics*. Cambridge University Press.

Croft, William, & Alan Cruse, D. (2004). *Cognitive linguistics*. Cambridge University Press.

Evans, Vyvyan, & Green, Melanie. (2006). *Cognitive linguistics: An introduction*. Edinburgh University Press.

Fauconnier, Gilles. (1994). *Mental spaces: Aspects of meaning construction in natural language*. Cambridge University Press.

Fauconnier, Gilles, & Turner, Mark. (2002). *The way we think: Conceptual blending and the mind's hidden complexities*. Basic Books.

Fillmore, Charles J. (1977). Scenes-and-frames. In Antonio Zampolli (Ed.) *Linguistic structures processing* (pp. 55–81). Springer.

Fillmore, Charles J. (1982). Frame semantics. In Linguistic Society of Korea (Ed.) *Linguistics in the morning calm* (pp. 111–138). Hanshin.

Geeraerts, Dirk. (2006). *Cognitive linguistics: Basic readings*. De Gruyter.

Giovanelli, Marcello. (2022). Cognitive grammar. In *The language of Siegfried Sassoon*. Palgrave Macmillan.

Hamawand, Zeki. (2002). *Atemporal complement clauses in English: A cognitive grammar analysis*. Lincom.

Hamawand, Zeki. (2003a). The construal of atemporalisation in complement clauses in English. *Review of Cognitive Linguistics*, *1*, 61–87.

Hamawand, Zeki. (2003b). For-to complement clauses in English: A cognitive grammar analysis. *Studia Linguistica*, *57*, 171–192.

Hamawand, Zeki. (2004). Determinants of complement clause variation in English. *English Studies*, *85*(5), 451–465.

Hamawand, Zeki. (2005). The construal of salience in atemporal complement clauses in English. *Language Sciences*, 27(2), 193–213.

Hamawand, Zeki. (2007). The construal of objectivity in atemporal complement clauses in English. *Word: Journal of International Linguistics Association*, *58*(3), 159–193.

Hamawand, Zeki. (2012a). Prepositional complement clauses in English: An exploration in cognitive grammar. *American International Journal of Contemporary Research*, 2(7), 146–156.

Hamawand, Zeki. (2012b). The pronoun *it*: A study in cognitive grammar. In Thomas Fuyin Li (Ed.), *Compendium of cognitive linguistics research*. Nova Publishers.

Hamawand, Zeki. (2014). Partitives: An exploration in cognitive grammar. *International Journal of English Linguistics*, *4*(1), 112–126.

Hamawand, Zeki. (2016). The notion of gradation in meaning: An Inquiry in cognitive grammar. *Cognitive Linguistic Studies*, *3*(2), 207–232.

Hamawand, Zeki. (2020). A cognitive grammar account of sentence types in English. *Linguistic Research*, *37*(3), 639–670.

Hamawand, Zeki. (2021). Construal. In Xu Wen & John Taylor (Eds.), *The Routledge handbook of cognitive linguistics* (pp. 242–254). Routledge.

Hamawand, Zeki. (2022). The construal of specificity in modification in English. *Cognitive Semantics*, *9*(2), 315–343.

Hamawand, Zeki. (2024a). Cognitive domains. In Thomas Fuyin Li (Ed.). *Handbook of cognitive semantics* (Vol. II). Brill.

Hamawand, Zeki. (2024b). The status of interjections in cognitive grammar. *Cognitive Linguistic Studies*, *11*(2), 74–295.

Hampe, Beate & Grady, Joseph E. (Eds.). (2005). *From perception to meaning: Image schemas in cognitive linguistics*. Mouton de Gruyter.

Huddleston, Rodney D., & Pullum, Geoffrey K. (2002). *The Cambridge grammar of the English language*. Cambridge University Press.

Lakoff, George, & Johnson, Mark. (1980). *Metaphors we live by*. University of Chicago Press.

Langacker, Ronald. (1986). An introduction to cognitive grammar. *Cognitive Science*, *10*, 1–40.

Langacker, Ronald. (1987). *Foundations of cognitive grammar, volume I: Theoretical prerequisites*. Stanford University Press.

Langacker, Ronald. (1988). An overview of cognitive grammar. In Brygida Rudzka-Ostyn (Ed.), *Topics in cognitive linguistics* (pp. 3–48). John Benjamins.

Langacker, Ronald. (1990). Cognitive grammar: The symbolic alternative. *Studies in the Linguistic Sciences*, *20*(2), 3–30. University of Illinois at the Urbana-Champaign.

Langacker, Ronald. (1991). *Foundations of cognitive grammar, volume II: descriptive application*. Stanford University Press.

Langacker, Ronald. (1994). Cognitive grammar. R. E. Asher & J. M. Y. Simpson (Eds.), *The encyclopedia of language and linguistics* (pp. 590–593). Pergamon Press.

Langacker, Ronald. (1995). Cognitive grammar. Jef Verschueren, Jan-Ola Östman, & Jan Blommaert (Eds.), *Handbook of pragmatics*, Manual (pp. 105–111). John Benjamins.

Langacker, Ronald. (2001). Discourse in cognitive grammar. *Cognitive Linguistics*, *12*, 143–188.

Langacker, Ronald. (2007). Cognitive grammar. In Dirk Geeraerts & Hubert Cuyckens (Eds.), *The Oxford handbook of cognitive linguistics* (pp. 421–462). Oxford University Press.

Langacker, Ronald. (2008). Cognitive grammar as a basis for language instruction. In Peter Robinson & Nick C. Ellis (Eds.), *Handbook of cognitive linguistics and second language acquisition* (pp. 66–88). Routledge.

Langacker, Ronald. (2008). *Cognitive grammar: A basic introduction.* Oxford University Press.

Langacker, Ronald. (2009). *Investigations in cognitive grammar.* De Gruyter.

Langacker, Ronald. (2013). *Essentials of cognitive grammar.* Oxford University Press.

Langacker, Ronald. (2015). Cognitive grammar. In Bernd Heine & Heiko Narrog (Eds.), *The Oxford handbook of linguistic analysis* (pp. 87–109). Oxford University Press.

Langacker, Ronald. (2015). Construal. In Ewa Dabrowska & Dagmar Divjak (Eds.), *Handbook of cognitive linguistics* (pp. 120–142). De Gruyter Mouton.

Langacker, Ronald. (2017). Cognitive grammar. In Barbara Dancygier (Ed.), *The Cambridge handbook of cognitive linguistics* (pp. 262–283). Cambridge University Press.

Langacker, Ronald. (2017). *Ten lectures on the basics of cognitive grammar.* Brill.

Langacker, Ronald. (2019). Construal. In Ewa Dąbrowska & Dagmar Divjak (Eds.), *Cognitive linguistics: Foundations of language* (pp. 140–164). Gruyter.

Lee, David. (2001). *Cognitive linguistics: An introduction.* Oxford University Press.

Manetta, Emily. (2021). Cognitive grammar. In James Stanlaw (Ed.), *International encyclopedia of linguistic anthropology.* John Wiley and Sons.

Panther, Klaus-Uve, & Radden, Günter (Eds.). (1999). *Metonymy in language and thought.* Benjamins.

Paradis, Carita. (2023). Cognitive grammar. *The Encyclopedia of Applied Linguistics*, 1–8.

Quirk, Randolph, Greenbaum, Sidney, Leech, Geoffrey, & Svartvik, Jan. (1985). *A comprehensive grammar of the English language.* Longman.

Radden, Günter & Dirven, René. (2007). *Cognitive English grammar.* Benjamins.

Talmy, Leonard. (2000). *Toward a cognitive semantics* (2 Vols.). MITPress.

Taylor, John. (1989). *Linguistic categorization. prototypes in linguistic theory.* Clarendon Press.

Taylor, John R. (2002). *Cognitive grammar.* Oxford University Press.

Ungerer, Friedrich & Schmid, Hans-Jorg. (2006). *An introduction to cognitive linguistics.* Pearson Longman.

INDEX